Rural Life
and Culture
in the Upper
Cumberland

Rural Life

and Culture

in the Upper

Cumberland

Edited by
Michael E. Birdwell and
W. Calvin Dickinson

The University Press of Kentucky

Publication of this volume was made possible in part by
a grant from the National Endowment for the Humanities.

The University Press of Kentucky
Scholarly publisher for the Commonwealth,
serving Bellarmine University, Berea College, Centre
College of Kentucky, Eastern Kentucky University,
The Filson Historical Society, Georgetown College,
Kentucky Historical Society, Kentucky State University,
Morehead State University, Murray State University,
Northern Kentucky University, Transylvania University,
University of Kentucky, University of Louisville,
and Western Kentucky University.

Editorial and Sales Offices: The University Press of Kentucky
663 South Limestone Street, Lexington, Kentucky 40508-4008
www.kentuckypress.com

Maps by Tom Nolan

Cataloging-in-Publication Data is available from
the Library of Congress.

ISBN 978-0-8131-9331-1 (pbk: acid-free paper)

This book is printed on acid-free recycled paper meeting
the requirements of the American National Standard
for Permanence in Paper for Printed Library Materials.

∞ ❀

Manufactured in the United States of America.

Member of the Association of
American University Presses

This book is dedicated to the memory of Jim Heard,

a gifted photographer and local history enthusiast.

CONTENTS

ACKNOWLEDGMENTS

No book project ever occurs in isolation. This volume is the result of hard work and the patience of a number of people who were generous with their time and energy, especially Jennifer Peckinpaugh of the University Press of Kentucky. Thank you for believing in this project. We would like to thank the following people for their help in making this project possible. Contributors, who often wondered if this work would ever be completed, willingly revised their chapters and listened to our suggestions.

Without the help of loved ones, work study students, and patient colleagues, the manuscript would never have been completed. Jodi McDonald proofread and typed several of the essays. Likewise, Laura Clemons read the entire manuscript for continuity and stylistic cohesion and tightened the work considerably. Todd Jarrell offered advice, reactions, and humor as the project went along. We would like to offer a special thanks to Mitch and Linda Hurst, who corrected mistakes in the articles with references to Billy Dean Anderson; likewise they were generous with images from their own collection.

Lucinda Barlow and Wes Burney provided invaluable assistance as student workers doing research, clerical work, and whatever else needed to be done. Candace Evitts and Amanda Posey retyped a number of the articles. Lois Clinton made all kinds of things happen as she used her formidable talents to acquire information and workers for us, while offering moral support as well. Thank you, Lois. Several people assisted in the acquisition and copying of images for this book, including Larry Slaboda of the Cookeville History Museum; Darla Brock, Susan Gordon, and Karina McDaniel of the Tennessee State Library and Archives; Paula Stover, Reda Bilbrey, Claudine Bilbrey, Margie Lewis, and Ronald Dishman of the Overton County Historical Society; and Bob Fulcher of Cumberland Trail State Park. Tom Nolan of Middle Tennessee State University provided the maps for this volume, Jim Heard graciously donated images from his own photography studio, and Roni Christian, whose grandfather performed with the group, donated an image of Flatt and Scruggs.

The Civil War remains a topic of currency in the Upper Cumberland and will for time to come. A number of people expressed interest in the Civil War article and made significant suggestions that proved worthwhile, including Larry Whiteaker, Janey Dudney, Kent Dollar, Jerry McFarland, and Linda Salts.

Several people provided information about the Tennessee Maneuvers. Nancy Jarrell, whose mother helped operate the USO in Cookeville, provided valuable insights. Many provided personal recollections of the maneuvers and how they affected the area, including Elmer Lee "Toots" Herd, Mark Harris, Sterling McCanless, Christine Jones, Eleanor Mitchell, and Savage Ragland, Jr. William and Marilyn Brinker were generous with their knowledge of the Cookeville USO, providing insights, research, and copies of the official maneuvers newspaper, *The Bounce*. Historian Mac Coffman added technical expertise to the article and clarified some nagging questions, while Kurt Piehler and Cynthia Tinker, at the Center for the Study of War and Society at the University of Tennessee at Knoxville, provided additional information. John Story shared recollections of his father, Osby, who served in the maneuvers with the 276 Combat Engineers. We would like to express our gratitude to Randall Clemons of the Granville History Museum, who provided images illustrating the maneuvers in the Upper Cumberland.

The article about Alvin York in popular culture would not have been possible without the help of George Edward York, Cletis York, Gerald York, David Lee, Mac Coffman, Buzz Davis, Rhee Ann Robinson, and the Sergeant York Patriotic Foundation.

We are indebted to a number of people who assisted in the article about the Upper Cumberland in film. We thank Jerry Williamson of Appalachian State University, Jim Crabtree of the Cumberland County Playhouse, Aimee Woods, Rick Woods, Mary Crabtree, Leon DeLozier, and Pat Ledford-Johnson, former commissioner of the Tennessee Music, Film and Entertainment Commission.

For assistance with the arts and crafts article, we thank Robie Cogswell of the Tennessee Arts Commission, Jane Morgan Dudney, Bob Coogan, and Ward Doubet of the Appalachian Center for Crafts, Bob Fulcher, Becky Magura of WCTE-TV, Claudine Smith, Walter Derryberry, Sally Crain, and Sam Bacon.

To the following people we owe a debt of gratitude for completion of the article concerning the Cumberland Homesteads: Emma Jean Vaden, Fannie Lue and Herman Burton, Orion Miller Sr., Foress Kidwell, Mike Smathers, Jim Crabtree, Alice and Gordon Patterson, and Vergie Denton.

Jim Jones provided significant information about the Socialist Party in Tennessee. We acknowledge John Nisbet, Bea and Glen Terry, Judy Roberson, and Barabara Westerbuhr for their help in making the Timberline article possible.

The following institutions supported this endeavor, and we could not have completed this volume without their cooperation: Cookeville History Museum, Tennessee Historical Commission, Tennessee State Library and Archives, Tennessee Technological University, Wilson County History Museum, Overton County Heritage Museum, Alvin C. York Patriotic Foundation, Cumberland County Homesteads Museum, the First Presbyterian Church of Cookeville, the Upper Cumberland Heritage Foundation, and the Granville History Museum.

A number of people deserve thanks for their interest in this project and their moral support, especially Randal Williams and Matthew Wilhelm. Other people to whom we are most grateful include Jeff Roberts, Judy Duke, Bob and Bertha Stoner, George Dickinson, Isaac Bohannon, Lindsey Pride and the *Herald-Citizen*, Homer Kemp, Denny Adcock of the County Music Hall of Fame, Susan Laningham, Liz Kassera, and others too numerous to mention. We thank you for your generous contributions that made this book possible.

Michael E. Birdwell
W. Calvin Dickinson

INTRODUCTION

Flagrantly violating King George III's proclamation of 1763 prohibiting expansion beyond the Appalachian mountains, long hunters entered Kentucky and Tennessee in 1769. Led by Daniel Boone, the party entered the Upper Cumberland region in search of game, furs, and land. Exploring what is now the Big South Fork River and Recreation Area, the long hunters crisscrossed between Kentucky and Tennessee in the rugged border region. A portion of the group continued south into current-day Fentress and Overton counties in Tennessee. As they were encamped near the headwaters of the Roaring River, a skirmish broke out between the long hunters and Nettle Carrier Indians. Long hunter Robert Crockett (no relation to the famed Davy Crockett) died in the battle, earning a dubious distinction. Crockett is purported to be the first white man of English extraction to die in middle Tennessee. Though an ignoble first in Upper Cumberland history, Crockett's death is only one of the little known regional events that were connected with the larger story of America. Boone went on to become the stuff of American legend, blazing the trail through the wilderness as an agent of Manifest Destiny, while Robert Crockett has largely been forgotten.

To call the Upper Cumberland the crossroads of American history would be a gross exaggeration, yet the region has been party to significant events in regional and national history. It has been home to a number of alleged firsts, some significant, others trivial. Marcus Huling and Andrew Zimmerman, while drilling a salt well on Martin Beatty's land in McCreary County, Kentucky, struck crude oil in 1818. Unsure of what to do with the thick black liquid, they attempted to market it as a patent medicine. This was, purportedly, the first commercial oil well in the United States. Alvin C. York of Fentress County, Tennessee, became America's most popular hero of World War I, achieving international fame. Graeme McGregor Smith of Cookeville, Tennessee, who opposed women's suffrage, was said to have been the first woman in Tennessee to register to vote when the Nineteenth Amendment was ratified. Author of the best-selling book of the 1920s, *The Man Nobody Knows,* Bruce Barton was born in Scott County, Tennessee. Kate Bradford Stockton, the first woman to run for governor in Tennessee, hailed from

Fentress County. The "Harmonica Wizard," DeFord Bailey of Smith County, Tennessee, was the first African American to break the color barrier on the *Grand Ole Opry*, long before Charlie Pride. Cordell Hull of Pickett County, Tennessee, became the first secretary of state in U.S. history to serve three terms, during Franklin Delano Roosevelt's administration.

Dreamers such as Moses Fisk set out, in 1797, to create the next great American metropolis. By his own estimation, Fisk calculated that the geographic center of the United States (when the Mississippi River was its western boundary) lay in the Tennessee Upper Cumberland. Fisk established the hamlet of Hillham, and one of the nation's first female academies, at what he hoped to be the nation's true crossroads. His calculations proved wrong, and today Hillham is still waiting for its great moment in history.[1]

Though southern in temperament and geography, the Upper Cumberland bears little resemblance to the deep South. Like many southerners, people of the Upper Cumberland are generally polite, move at a more leisurely pace, prefer to "visit" before getting down to business, and take pride in a sense of place. The hardscrabble lands of the plateau, Highland Rim, and escarpment were impediments to travel and settlement, and too poor to support a plantation economy. Cotton failed to flourish in a land with scant topsoil. Slaves, though they did exist in some parts of the Upper Cumberland, proved too costly for most people. The gang system associated with the plantation South, therefore, never existed in the region. The few slaves who existed were usually skilled or semi-skilled artisans, known as mechanics. A few free black communities in the Upper Cumberland in the pre–Civil War era added a layer of complexity to the issue of race and slavery in the region.

Religion, an important aspect of the region's history, proved divisive as the Civil War loomed nearer. People throughout the region disagreed over the issues of slavery and secession. Ministers and laity played key roles in the developing conflict. Pastors in Sparta, Tennessee, preached about slavery as a gift from God; whereas, circuit-riding Methodist minister Francis Asbury Wright denounced slavery as a sin and an abomination. Fault lines emerged based on family histories, geography, and religious affiliation. As a result, the Upper Cumberland region was bitterly divided over the war, and some people used it as a means of settling old scores.

This division is evident in another Upper Cumberland "first." On September 29, 1861, the initial skirmish of the Civil War in Tennessee

Map 1. Upper Cumberland region of Kentucky and Tennessee.

occurred at Travisville, in present-day Pickett County. This also marked the first time Federal troops set foot on the soil of the Volunteer State. Soldiers from the Twelfth Kentucky Cavalry, including James Ferguson, brother of the infamous Confederate guerrilla Champ Ferguson, pursued Confederate raiders into Tennessee. The personal nature of the conflict is evident in the inscription on a Travisville Cemetery tombstone. A simple stone decorated with a weeping willow flanked by two palm trees, it marks the grave of Rebel soldier James M. Saufley. Engraved on the stone is the date of that first skirmish, with the legend, "Killed by James M. Ferguson of the 1st [sic] Kentucky Cavalry." The stone not only identifies the man who killed James Saufley, but seems to issue the challenge: "Go get him!"

Though somewhat ambivalent toward African Americans before the Civil War, people of the region largely embraced the segregationist attitude of the Jim Crow South. Industrialization, with competition for various skilled and unskilled jobs, led to the demonization of blacks and a few instances of racial violence. As a result, the region's black population dwindled, and remains quite small throughout the entire Upper Cumberland.

Industrialization, better transportation, and the rise of mass media all played a role in opening up the region to the larger United States. As McDonald's and Wal-Marts fill the formerly rural landscape, the Upper Cumberland becomes more like any other place in America. People from Nashville and Knoxville have turned portions of the region into bedroom communities. Lake Cumberland in Kentucky and Dale Hollow Lake in Tennessee are jokingly referred to by locals as "Little Ohio," because of the number northern tourists. Not yet completely homogenized into the megalopolis America has become, the Upper Cumberland still remains a vast, largely untapped resource for local and national history.

Though relatively little scholarly investigation of the Upper Cumberland was done until the late twentieth century, Appalachian studies incorporate a vast body of material relevant to the region. The numerous scholars who have studied and continue to investigate Appalachia, have revealed not a monolithic area filled with mountain rustics, but a region with a rich history and cultural diversity. Though the plateau, Highland Rim, and the escarpment are a part of Appalachia, they have received less attention than the mountains and valleys to the east. The Upper Cumberland, similar in many ways to other Appalachian communities, is also different.

Appalachian studies grew out of a journalistic curiosity, as the region industrialized at the turn of the twentieth century. Stereotypes of violent, antisocial, superstitious, incestuous mountaineers emerged as a result of industrialization and such events as the Hatfield-McCoy feud. As Altina Waller explains in *Feud: Hatfields, McCoys and Social Change in Appalachia, 1860–1900*, most of the battles between Devil Anse Hatfield and his enemies took place in a courtroom, not at the end of a gun. The media blew the events out of proportion by playing on readers' prurient interests, fashioning a portrait of mountain southerners that, in large part, exists to this day. Cartoon stereotypes of Appalachians such as Barney Google and Snuffy Smith fueled American popular culture. More important, as Charles Wolfe points out in *A Good Natured Riot: The Birth of the Grand Ole Opry*, before audiences were allowed to watch the performances, Opry entertainers dressed in suits and ties. When the Opry was opened to the public, a conscious effort was made to make the performers fit the prevailing stereotype. Musicians dressed in faded overalls, with misshapen floppy hats and worn out brogans, because that is what the audience expected. Jerry Williamson examines the influence of the stereotype on the Hollywood film industry in *Hillbillyland: What the Movies Did to the Mountains and the Mountains Did to the Movies*. Tony Harkin's *Hillbilly: A Cultural History of an American Icon* traces the tumultuous, quixotic stereotype and why it continues to endure.

A number of books react to the stereotype. Bruce Wheeler and Michael McDonald's history of Knoxville, for example, tells the story of the rise of an important Appalachian city, reminding readers that Appalachia is not all rural and impoverished. Jim Goad railed against the stereotype in his controversial and blistering diatribe, *The Redneck Manifesto*.

Industrialization of the Appalachian South and the myriad problems that ensued spawned a host of scholarly works on the transition of the region from a subsistence agricultural/barter economy to an industrial-based consumer economy. In *Steamboating on the Cumberland*, Byrd Douglas chronicles the changes that improved transportation on the river systems. The river and its tributaries connected the region to the nation, opening up new worlds and possibilities to the inhabitants of the region. River towns reigned supreme as the locus of culture, commerce, and politics until the river was surpassed by the railroads and interstate highways. W. Calvin Dickinson, Michael E. Birdwell, and Homer Kemp further explore settlement patterns and the role of transportation in *Upper Cumberland Historic Architecture*.

Ronald Eller (*Miners, Millhands, and Mountaineers*), David Whisnant (*Modernizing the Mountaineer*), and Crandall Schiflett (*Coal Towns: Life, Work and Culture in Company Towns in Southern Appalachia, 1880–1960*) take issue with the prevailing stereotypes formed by journalists and Local Color writers who "discovered" the region. Rather than Bible-thumping, suspicious, intellectually challenged rubes who were easily cheated out of their birthrights, the first generation of industrial workers were eager to have more capital to better provide for their families. The logging industry, spurred by post–Civil War Reconstruction, was tied directly to the construction of railroads. Increased demand for lumber, coal, and steel directly affected the Upper Cumberland, and the era was an important transitional period in the region's history. Farmers felled trees in the winter and rafted the logs to markets in the months between planting and harvesting. Logging also put cash into the pockets of a number of mountaineers (such as Uncle Billy Hull, father of Cordell Hull) for the first time, spurring the desire for more hard currency.

Eller and Whisnant agree that financial security came at a high cost. For the first generation of industrial workers, the transition brought a sense of lost freedom and the death of an independent way of life. For the second generation, who grew up in company towns, working in mines and factories, subsistence agriculture gave way to creature comforts and the conveniences afforded by modernization. Although the concept of the company town generally evokes images of company stores taking advantage of families, brutal Baldwin-Felts agents terrorizing workers, and opposition to unions, Schiflett argues that not all company towns were hellish places where residents lived in fear of the company and its capricious managers. Some company towns, such as the Stearns Coal and Lumber Company in Kentucky,[2] though paternalistic, took pride in offering employees access to education, current entertainments, and a taste of the better life.

Two recent histories of the region provide an excellent framework for contextualizing the Upper Cumberland within Appalachian Studies—Richard B. Drake's *A History of Appalachia* and John Alexander Williams's *Appalachia: A History*. Additionally, Alan Batteau's *Invention of Appalachia* examines the different ways in which Appalachia has been defined, the different agendas that shaped those definitions, and the politicization and exploitation of the region. Just as Appalachia has been defined in a number of ways, so too, has the Upper Cumberland.

The Upper Cumberland region first emerged as a part of the Local

Color school in the stories of authors such as Mary Noilles Murfree of Tennessee and John Fox Jr. of Kentucky. Their stories played with the emerging stereotype, depicting the folk of the region as backward, benighted, and belligerent. Fox, known for such books as *Trail of the Lonesome Pine*, depicted outsiders as quasi-missionaries intent on bringing the fruits of industrialized civilization to the backwoods. Cumberland people, quaint throwbacks to a preindustrial era, needed to be saved from themselves.

The Local Color writers found an audience among the nation's urban readership, but local inhabitants took issue with their depiction in popular literature. The most important early chronicler of the Upper Cumberland, Harriet Simpson Arnow, was intent on telling a more balanced story of the region. A novelist with a keen sense of history, Arnow wrote two volumes about the region—*Seedtime on the Cumberland* and *The Flowering of the Cumberland*—marking the first serious attempts to tell the story of the area. Examining primary sources such as the Draper Papers, local newspapers, and archival material, Arnow's books are an essential starting point for understanding the Upper Cumberland.

Between the writing of Arnow's books and Lynwood Montell's *Saga of Coe Ridge: A Study in Oral History,* little about the Upper Cumberland reached an audience outside the region. Work was conducted mostly by enthusiastic—if not always reliable—local historians, genealogists, retired teachers, and amateurs. Dozens of pamphlets, informal documents, reports, church histories, and family trees fill the local history rooms of libraries throughout the region. Some are poorly written but contain important material; others are well written but lack adequate documentation, making it difficult for historians to them use with assurance. Public historians, such as James B. Jones Jr., of the Tennessee Historical Commission, compiled short narratives on the history of coal operations on the Cumberland Plateau, pre-TVA dam sites in the Upper Cumberland, and other important information. Professional historians, such as W. Calvin Dickinson and Mary Jean DeLozier, wrote county histories of Cumberland, Morgan, and Putnam counties. All three volumes had a limited run and are currently out of print.

The heir apparent to Harriet Simpson Arnow is Lynwood Montell, who has studied the region for over thirty years. Folklorist Montell collected an impressive body of oral histories, which put a host of human faces on the region. Interviewees recounted their experiences in light of the greater context of regional and national history. Montell's research has led him in a number of directions, from examining the heyday of the steamboat era (*Don't Go Up Kettle Creek : Verbal Legacy of the Upper Cumberland*), to the entertainment and daily life of the people (*Upper Cumberland Country*), to the proclivity for violence in the border region of Kentucky and Tennessee (*Killings*). Montell's work opened the door for a number of new scholars to examine and tell the stories of the region.

Jeanette Keith provides an important examination of modernization, progressivism, and local authority in *Country People in the New South: Tennessee's Upper Cumberland*. As cities such as Sparta, Gainesboro, and Cookeville emerged, along with a new local elite imbued with the desire to change the region, rural communities reacted. Leaders such as Rutledge Smith and his formidable wife Graeme McGregor Smith called for new roads, modern conveniences, and electrification, but people in the countryside envisioned the loss of political control to dandies living in the county seats. This culminated on a state and national level when John Washington Butler of Macon County, Tennessee, wrote a piece of legislation demanding a local voice in the recently enacted compulsory education bill of 1925. The Butler Act made it illegal to teach evolution in any state-supported school in Tennessee, leading to one of the most controversial court cases in American history—the Scopes Trial. Keith describes the transition of the local power base in the Upper Cumberland as agrarian life gave way to industrialization and the growth of metropolitan centers.

The Upper Cumberland region of Tennessee and Kentucky has been defined for this anthology as the drainage basin of the Cumberland River and its tributaries. Rising in Harlan County, Kentucky, the river flows 687 miles through the southern part of middle Kentucky and the northern part of middle Tennessee, emptying into the Ohio River in Livingston County, Kentucky. The section of the river north of Carthage, in Smith County, Tennessee, is the Upper Cumberland. The region includes Pulaski, Wayne, Russell, Cumberland, and Monroe counties in Kentucky, through which the river flows, and Clinton County, which is connected to the Cumberland by the Wolf River. Adair, Metcalfe, and Barren counties, though not part of the Cumberland River basin, are culturally related to the Upper Cumberland region. Lynwood Montell included all of these Kentucky counties in his definition of the Upper Cumberland.

Entering Tennessee in Clay County, the Cumberland River courses through Jackson, Trousdale, and Smith counties. The Caney Fork River adds DeKalb, White, Van Buren, and Cumberland counties to the drain-

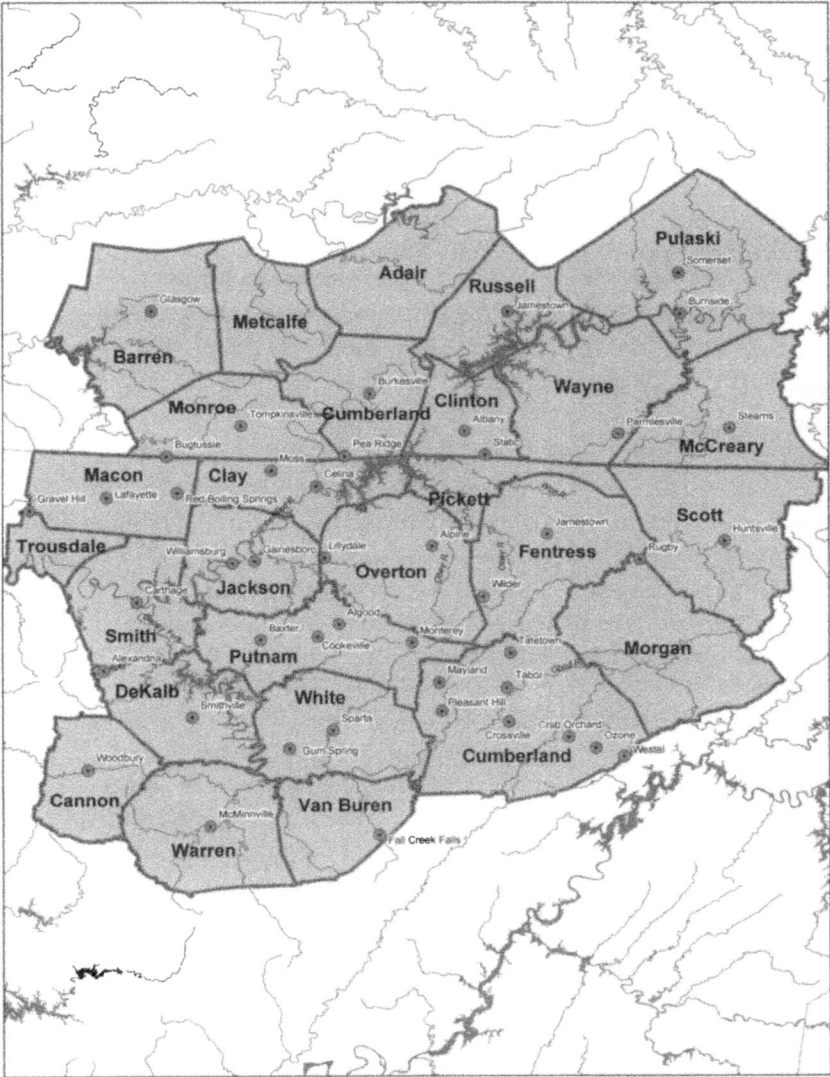

Map 2. Principal towns, counties, and rivers of the Upper Cumberland.

age area, and Putnam County is connected via the Calfkiller River and smaller arteries. Overton, Pickett, and Fentress counties are joined to the Cumberland River by the Big South Fork and the Roaring and Obey rivers. The Big South Fork and the Clear Fork drain Scott and Morgan counties into the Cumberland. Warren and Cannon counties join the Cumberland River basin via the Collins and Caney Fork rivers. Macon County is usually included in the Upper Cumberland region, even though it has no rivers; numerous creeks connect it to the water systems.

The Cumberland Plateau, extending from southern New York southwest to northern Alabama, forms the eastern side of the Upper Cumberland region. In Kentucky, parts of Pulaski, Wayne, and Clinton counties are on the plateau. In Tennessee, Scott, Morgan, Pickett, Fentress, Overton, Cumberland, Putnam, White, and Van Buren counties contain land on the plateau. The western sections of the Upper Cumberland include the Highland Rim of the plateau in Tennessee, and river/creek valleys in both Tennessee and Kentucky.

The first Europeans followed rivers or animal/Indian paths into the region. East-west Indian trails traversing the region included Tolonteeskee across northern Tennessee, and the Great East-West Trail through Fentress and Pickett counties in Tennessee, and through Clinton, Cumberland, Monroe, and Metcalfe counties in Kentucky. Settlers used the Chickamauga Path, a north-south Indian trail that ran out of northern Georgia and into the Upper Cumberland.

Because settlement of the area occurred east to west and west to east rather than north to south, the earliest improved roads ran east and west. In 1786, the North Carolina General Assembly commissioned a road through the region. Named Avery Trace after the surveyor of the route, Peter Avery, the wagon road was constructed by troops between Kingston, Tennessee, and Davidson County. It passed through Morgan, Putnam, Jackson, and Smith counties. Walton Road, named for William Walton of Carthage, was completed by 1801 between Kingston and Carthage. Built for some distance over the Avery Trace, Walton Road was fifteen feet wide, with bridges or causeways over the streams. Modern highway U.S. 70N closely follows the route of Walton Road. A Kentucky road from Williamsburg followed the Cumberland to Burkesville, then south and west through the Barrens until it connected with trails toward Nashville. Old Kentucky Road was a north-south trail that opened about 1830. It ran from Maysville, Kentucky, south through the Upper Cumberland toward Huntsville, Alabama. In the twentieth century, paved highways built by the states and the federal government, particularly Interstate 40 through Tennessee, opened the Upper Cumberland for economic development and increased population.

The earliest settlement community in the Upper Cumberland may have been Parmleysville, Kentucky, in 1780, now in Wayne County. The first white settlers moved into Clay County, Tennessee, that same year. Lilydale, in Clay County, and Fort Blount, in Jackson County, were both established in 1786. Fort Blount was a federal fortification, and the town of Williamsburg grew up adjacent to it. Jackson County was created by the Tennessee legislature in 1801, and Williamsburg became the county seat in 1806. Settlers founded Burkesville, Edmonton, and Tompkinsville, Kentucky, in 1789. Virginia created Pulaski and Cumberland counties in Kentucky a decade later. After the Third Treaty of Tellico with the Cherokees, in 1805, opened Tennessee's Upper Cumberland for settlement, several rural villages soon emerged. The Tennessee legislature created White County and Overton County in 1806, with Sparta and Monroe as the respective capitals.

In the twentieth century, Cookeville became the largest city in the entire region, and Somerset the largest in Kentucky. Cookeville had a population of 26,000 in 2000, and Putnam County's totaled 62,315. The population of Somerset was 12,924, and Pulaski County had 56,217. Pickett County had the smallest population, with 4,945 residents in 2000.

The population of the Upper Cumberland has been predominately Anglo-Saxon. During the Mississippian Period, few Indians lived in the region; it was a renowned hunting ground, but was considered an unfavorable living area. Indians lived only in the river valleys during this period. American settlers brought in some slaves during the nineteenth century, but as Wali Kharif's essay explains, the Upper Cumberland was not a major slaveholding region.

The economy of the Upper Cumberland in the early nineteenth century was based largely on subsistence agriculture, and farming was still the most important element during the twentieth century. Improved roads allowed agriculture to become commercial and eventually brought industry to the region. They also brought tourists and retirees, and during the second half of the twentieth century, tourism and retirement communities contributed significantly to the region's economy. Industry along Interstate 40, and particularly around Cookeville, Tennessee, improved the economy in the Tennessee region, and Somerset provided the same economic stimulus in Kentucky. Well known for the manufacture of luxury houseboats, Somerset's proximity to Lake Cumberland has made it an economic leader in the area.

This anthology is a study of the cultural history of the Upper Cumberland region, with "culture" defined in a broad sense. The largest number of essays are about "Popular Culture," which includes the lifestyles, activities, and entertainments of the inhabitants. "Material Culture" essays concern the tangible products residents produced in arts and crafts. The remaining essays deal with a necessary topic in any history of the South: the significance of war on the history and culture of the area.

In exploring Popular Culture, the editors include essays about folklore and religion by Lynwood Montell and Larry Whiteaker. Civil War stories are common in folklore, and stories about medical remedies are often repeated. Notable persons, both famous and infamous, are subjects of regional folklore. Religion includes all the denominations of Christianity that thrive in the area, the beliefs they espouse, and the rituals they practice.

Recreational activities are important in the Upper Cumberland, and they are sometimes unusual. Red Boiling Springs was the most famous vacation town in the area in the early twentieth century, and Jeanette Keith references the activities of this spa. Nudism found a home in the Upper Cumberland for natives and tourists in the late twentieth century, and Allison Barrell writes about the legal and practical problems of this recreational activity.

Wali Kharif recounts the contributions of African Americans in the region while underscoring their often distinct personal experiences. The civil rights movement of the 1960s generated very little violence in the region. Some racial integration resulted, and African Americans began to participate to a greater extent in politics, society, and the economy.

A study of Cumberland Popular Culture often reveals liberal leanings in this usually conservative region, most visible in the various socialist ideas and activities of the nineteenth and twentieth centuries. Calvin Dickinson's essay shows how Thomas Hughes, Elmer Wirt, Myles Horton, Abram Nightingale, and Kate Bradform Stockton represent this radical sentiment.

Popular literature has been surprisingly significant and important in the Upper Cumberland region. Allison Ensor details authors with national reputations who wrote about the region—Mark Twain, Mary Noailles Murfree, John Fox Jr., Charles Neville Buck, Harriet Arnow.

On the topic of entertainment, Charles Wolfe demonstrates that the region contributed significantly to modern country music, with Sidney
Robertson coming into the Upper Cumberland as early as 1936 to record
folk music for the Library of Congress. Michael Birdwell recounts the
surprising number of movies and theater productions that have taken
place in the area—*Inherit the Wind, Sergeant York, I Walk the Line, The
Specialist, The Jungle Book.*

The Material Culture section of this anthology includes arts and
crafts. Caves were important as living spaces, hiding places, and recreational locations, as Joe Douglas illustrates. Houses, particularly nineteenth-century structures, were also a product of material culture;
Dickinson details this activity. Nationally known artists such as Gilbert
Gaul and John Dodge lived and worked in the Upper Cumberland in
the nineteenth century, and lesser known artists painted here in the
twentieth. This anthology discusses only artists who have died, with
the exception of O.D. Abston, who turned ninety-nine in 2003. Fine
art—painting—has a long history in the Upper Cumberland, but crafts
have an even longer one because crafts were considered more useful.
Pottery, weaving, quilts, chairs, and baskets were all functional crafts.
Dolls and carvings provided children with pleasing toys.

The third theme, Warfare and Culture, involves the Upper Cumberland region in three of the four most important wars in American history—the Civil War, World War I, and World War II. The Upper
Cumberland experienced a bloody series of small engagements and guerrilla activities throughout the Civil War. These created much damage and
considerable hatred. James Jones's essay is the most detailed published
account of the Civil War in the Upper Cumberland. The region was also
the home of the World War I hero, Alvin Cullum York. York's story is
illustrative of life in the area, and his image and reputation represented
the region to the nation. World War II came directly into the Upper Cumberland when the U.S. Army used the region as a practice field for the
invasion of France in 1942, 1943, and 1944. The military maneuvers
altered some laws in the region, and even the face of the countryside.

Although the Upper Cumberland is one of the most beautiful parts
of Tennessee and Kentucky, with fast rivers, high mountains, deep coves,
and bountiful woodlands, fiction writers have used it as a setting for
their dramas, but historians have generally neglected the region until
recently. This anthology was prepared, in part, to "fill in the gap" of
knowledge concerning the Upper Cumberland. It is hoped that this book
will find a place in classrooms and libraries.

The editors express a deep debt of gratitude to the authors, many of whom conducted additional research for their essays in this volume. In many instances, their articles overlapped in interesting ways, and a number of characters or events appear in two or more stories. The authors were prompt with their submissions, and they were agreeable to suggestions about their writings. The essays have been heavily edited, and the editors assume all responsibility for any mistaken facts and analysis in the book. This anthology will surely not be the last publication concerning these subjects, but we hope this publication will spark additional interest, research, and writing about the Upper Cumberland region of Kentucky and Tennessee.

NOTES

1. Fisk graduated from Dartmouth and moved to Tennessee. He acted as part of the survey team that determined the boundary of Tennessee and Virginia.

During the antebellum period, Andrew Jackson raced horses in Smith and DeKalb counties. The Dauphin, Louis Philippe, slept at Dixona in Smith County while visiting America.

2. Stearns Coal and Lumber Company was founded by Justus Stearns of Michigan. Stearns started his career in the salt industry, moved on to lumber, and finally coal. Most of the company's holdings now belong to the National Parks Service and the National Forest Service.

Chapter 1

MINERALS, MOONSHINE, AND MISANTHROPES

The Historic Use of Caves in the Upper Cumberland

Joseph C. Douglas

Over the past two centuries, people in the Upper Cumberland used caves in several ways. One important early usage was for subsistence, as caves provided shelter from the elements and were sources of water for long hunters, travelers, and settlers. As permanent settlements increased throughout the nineteenth century, caves became somewhat less important as shelters but were thoroughly integrated into domestic household economies. Caves provided water for home use as well as cold storage, serving as both springhouses and root cellars. These interactions with the environment revealed a utilitarian emphasis in the culture of the Upper Cumberland, as the people were eminently practical in their approach to the natural world. Yet although these domestic and subsistence uses persisted well into the twentieth century, they represented only one theme in the complicated story of caves in the region. Caves were also potential sources of commodities, hidden and secretive spaces, natural curiosities, and social spaces.

Even before Virginians, North Carolinians, and others established permanent settlements, the Upper Cumberland was part of a larger commercial economy. Despite difficulties of transport, long hunters began to extract resources, mostly furs, skins, and to a lesser extent meat, for sale back east, while the land itself was sold as a commodity to speculators and hopeful migrants. Caves were entwined in commerce by the early 1800s, primarily as a source of saltpeter (potassium nitrate), one of the vital ingredients in gunpowder. Other substances were also mined from caves and sold, but a substantial trade in saltpeter developed along the Cumberland River. Between roughly 1800 and 1863, many dozens of caves across the region were mined for saltpeter. Emerging towns such as Carthage became collection areas, linking the Upper Cumberland to the gunpowder industries in Nashville, Lexington, and perhaps even DuPont's powder mills in Delaware. Long before the rise of substantial coal and timber industries, people in the region developed long-term extraction of cave minerals.

Yet subsistence and domestic use, coupled with commercialization, is not the whole picture of the environmental history of caves. Even if no substances were mined and a cave was unsuited for domestic use, caves were sublime manifestations of nature. As a result they were increasingly used as social spaces, where people met and engaged in a variety of noncommercial activities. People played music, danced, and even held church services underground. These activities bespeak a rich and complex relationship with the cave environment. It is clear that several patterns of conceiving of, and using, caves coexisted in the nineteenth and twentieth centuries. On the other hand, caves served as secret, hidden spaces, important for hermits, criminals, or ordinary folk seeking safe refuge during the disruptions of the Civil War. Later, moonshiners turned to caves as hidden production sites for their untaxed, illegal liquor.

Caves are not evenly distributed across the landscape of the Upper Cumberland. The top of the Cumberland Plateau contains relatively few extensive caves, though the sandstones of the upper sequence of Pennsylvanian-age rocks lend themselves to the formation of the shallow rock-shelters that are ubiquitous in the valley of the Big South Fork and common in the other plateau areas. Grassy Cove in Cumberland County is an exception to this generalization, as the limestones both on the mountain flanks and in the cove itself contain substantial caves.

In contrast to the short, shallow caves atop the plateau, numerous extensive limestone caves formed as river valleys cut deep into the Cumberland Plateau, exposing the Monteagle, Bangor, St. Louis, and Warsaw limestones below in the Mississippian sequence. In the tributary river valleys, such as the East and West Obey, the Caney Fork, the Calfkiller, and the Roaring, and along the dissected western edge of the plateau, hundreds of caves were formed by weak carbonic acid dissolving the limestone. Some passages continue to form, and function as active conduits for water flow; others, now dry and partially filled with sediment, represent former stream passages that were abandoned as the water table dropped. After the formation of a cave, secondary deposition creates interesting, and sometimes unique, minerals, commonly including calcite and gypsum. Eventually, breakdown of the host rock and erosion complete the cave's life cycle. Thus, caves of the Upper Cumberland are varied in their genesis, age, rock type, internal features, size, and stage of development. A variety of animals inhabit caves. Some are so well adapted they can live nowhere else, such as blind fish or crayfish. Other species, such as bats, use caves for critical parts of their life cycles, including hibernation and breeding.[1]

Concentration of caves in the western escarpment and valleys of the Cumberland Plateau means that some counties have tremendous numbers of them. More than 750 caves exist in White County, one of the highest concentrations in the United States, and Fentress County has more than 500. Putnam and Overton counties contain slightly fewer, between 350 and 400, and Cumberland and Pickett counties, with less exposed Mississippian limestone, have between 115 and 150 caves each. Areas primarily in Highland Rim uplands have fewer caves, though some significant ones exist in the St. Louis, Wasaw, and Fort Payne limestone formations. Thus, Clay, Macon, and Jackson counties each has only a few dozen caves. At lower altitudes, where the Highland Rim escarpment reaches the Central Basin, Ordovician rock units such as the Leipers-Catheys and Bigby-Cannon limestones are exposed. These areas contain many extensive caves; Smith County has some eighty caves, and DeKalb County has more than 100. With more than 2,500 caves, Upper Cumberland is among the great cave regions of the United States and, indeed, the world. They include many of the longest caves in the state, such as 30-mile-long Blue Spring Cave in White County. Cumberland Caverns, located just south of the Upper Cumberland in Warren County, has 28 miles of passages. Numerous caves extend a mile or more, with several more than 20 miles in length. Even typical small caves of the region were an important part of the regional environment, used by both cave-dwelling animals and the resident human population.[2]

While not determinative, specific characteristics of cave environments in the region were important factors in enabling particular uses by people, while making others less tenable. Size and shape of cave entrances and passages, temperature and humidity regimes, the presence or lack of water, and mineralogical and biological components all are important considerations. Although their morphologies vary widely, extensive caves usually have an entrance zone, where surface and subterranean environments meet; a transitional or twilight zone, where light levels drop and humidity, temperature, and energy flow fluctuations decline; and a dark zone, consisting of a relatively stable, low-energy environment. In the dark zone, the temperature is constant year round, approaching the yearly mean for the area. Most cave temperatures hover in the mid-50° F range, providing relative warmth in the winter and coolness in the summer. Humidity levels remain fairly constant in the dark zone, often approaching 90 percent. Some passages are much drier, though, because the streams that formed them are no longer present; as erosion occurred and the water table dropped, water abandoned the existing cave and began to form new ones farther below. Drier passages proved suitable for storing root and other crops such as potatoes, sweet potatoes, and apples, while damper passages served the same functions as springhouses. There, people stored milk, eggs, and other perishables not likely to suffer from exposure to moisture. Presence or lack of a running stream might affect a particular cave's usefulness as a domestic, municipal, or industrial water source, or as a source of water power. Finally, the presence in caves of minerals and other substances, such as chert, gypsum, alum, copperas, various salts, ice, guano, and especially cave saltpeter, made possible certain extractive activities. Other unusual mineralogical features, including those created by dripping water such as flowstone, stalactites, and stalagmites; erratic forms such as shields, helictites, and oulaphites (crystal flowers); and subaqueous forms such as rimstone dams and cave pearls, added to the allure and beauty of caves even when their commercial value was negligible.[3]

Long before settlement by Europeans, caves were important for Native Americans. They provided important elements for basic subsistence, such as shelter and water. Well over 4,000 years ago, one or two small groups of Native Americans entered a large cave in Fentress County and explored thousands of feet of its passages, although their reasons are unclear. Using tied bundles of dried river cane for torches, these early visitors left behind more than two hundred bare footprints, still preserved in a remote section of the cave. This represents the earliest known exploration of a deep cave in North America. Sometime afterward, between 2,700 and 3,400 years ago, Native Americans of the Archaic Period explored another large cave in Fentress County. In addition to examining thousands of feet of passage, they mined chert from the limestone walls and roughly processed it underground. They created art in the cave, engraving abstract and representational images into the limestone, including geometric designs and enigmatic figures. This tradition of making ceremonial art in caves, whether petroglyphs (engravings), pictographs (using pigments or charcoal), or mud glyphs (tool or finger tracing in thin mud veneers), persisted throughout prehistory all over the world. Scholars such as Dr. Jan Simek have identified dozens of these archaeological art sites, many of which are in Putnam, Cumber-land, White, and Fentress counties. Additionally, scholars suspect that Woodland Indians mined gypsum in Upper Cumberland caves; although no sites have yet been positively identified, the activity is known from Warren County, just to the south on the Cumberland Plateau.[4]

Woodland Indians also used caves for mortuary purposes. In some, the bodies of the dead were deposited in deep vertical pits. In White County's Chisum Chasm, several bodies were deposited in a pit 125 feet deep, remaining undiscovered until the early 1990s. In Overton County, Woodland Indians similarly used a 90-foot-deep pit for the same purpose. Other examples of this practice abound throughout the region.[5]

In other regions, the dead were either interred in sediments in the entrance areas of caves Native Americans inhabited or placed on ledges. Examples of these burials have been found throughout the plateau, and also in horizontal caves in Highland Rim counties. At one site in Jackson County, several caves, some with multiple entrances, are clustered along a waterway. Human burials were found deposited in almost every cave entrance and passage. At a cave in Clay County, prehistoric Native Americans explored the cavern and probably camped in the entrance room, where they buried the remains of several individuals in the floors of the rooms. They also left bodies on wall ledges above the passage floor. Thus, Native Americas used caves for a variety of purposes, which changed over time, revealing complex interactions with the natural environment.[6]

When long hunters entered the Upper Cumberland in the eighteenth century in search of pelts to sell, they carefully examined the natural features of the land, including caves, sinkholes, and cave springs. Much as Native Americans had done for centuries, these commercial hunters used dry, often shallow, caves for shelter. These offered comfort, as they were relatively warm in the winter hunting season and required little or no work before occupation, other than piling brush or cane across the entrance. In the 1790s, when North Carolinian Coonrod Pile entered the valley of the three forks of the Wolf River in Fentress County, he initially camped in a cave above the stream while he hunted in the valley.

When Americans established a permanent presence, settlers often temporarily lived in caves and shallow rock-shelters until they built cabins. This practice was so common that a term was coined for these subsistence spaces—rockhouses. Travelers and hunters on the Cumberland Plateau continued occasionally to camp in caves throughout the nineteenth and into the early twentieth century. Some early inhabitants sheltered livestock in caves; Adam Dale of DeKalb County stabled his horses in a large cave entrance on his land around 1800. This practice was remarkably persistent. Visiting Wash Lee Cave in Overton County in 1917, geologist Thomas Bailey noted that cattle were housed in the large entrance and interior chamber during cold weather.

Caves were also commonly used as preexisting shelters for various other activities. In the early 1900s, a cave on the Caney Fork River in DeKalb County occasionally functioned as a schoolhouse when the school building became unbearably hot. At about the same time, York Cave in Fentress County hosted church services, despite the difficulty of entering the cave via a 30-foot shaft. Use of caves as shelters took a different twist during the cold war, as many were designated fallout shelters and stocked with supplies in case of atomic war. In sum, the sheltering function of caves was well established in the culture of the Upper Cumberland, and people in the region adapted them to meet their needs for many years.[7]

Caves with active streams, or springs associated with caves, were also important for subsistence, providing water for hunters, travelers, and domestic household use. From the 1790s on, people migrating from eastern Tennessee to the Cumberland settlements often stopped at one particular cave spring in Crab Orchard, as several noted in their journals. Cave waters were such important resources that land grants and deeds often mentioned them, and the location of cave springs often affected decisions about exactly where to build a homestead. The large spring at Wolf River Cave was noted in a North Carolina land grant to Revolutionary War veteran Samuel Scott in 1800. In Jackson County, not far from the Cumberland River, a clear spring below an obvious cave proved important enough to attract the attention of a family of settlers, who built a home nearby and began to farm there. Cherry Cave, as it was later called, also served the family in other ways; it was used for cold storage of foodstuffs and making moonshine whiskey, and it was mined for saltpeter on a small scale. Many caves in the Upper Cumberland, like Cherry Cave, were used in a variety of ways to help support the domestic economies of families in the region.[8]

One of the most typical functions of Upper Cumberland caves was as a root cellar or springhouse; both functions were important and highly desirable in the long years before electricity and refrigeration. Soon after establishing residence, numerous families, and sometimes entire communities, turned to caves for cold storage of foodstuffs. Dozens of caves show physical evidence of this, and folklore, nomenclature, and occasional references in written sources suggest that many other caves also shared this usage. The common folk practice of preserving root crops—apples, dairy products, and even meat—in the cool, stable, underground environment was ubiquitous and persisted throughout the nineteenth and the first half of the twentieth centuries.

Comparatively dry caves were well suited for storing potatoes, sweet potatoes, apples, and perhaps others items. The names given to these sites often reflect their historic usage. Tater Caves exist in Macon, Putnam, and Fentress counties, and Potato Caves in Putnam and White counties. According to local folklore, Little Petty Cave in Smith County was used to store farm products, Trench Cave in Putnam County was used to store vegetables, and sweet potatoes were stored in Clay County's Sheals (or Fowler) Cave. Similarly, Flatt Cave in Jackson County was formerly used for winter storage of sweet potatoes, and Joshua Selby reportedly used his "Dark Cave" in White County to preserve potatoes and other food.[9]

Cave springs, better suited for preserving eggs, butter, milk, and other dairy products, were also quite common. The name of one Overton County cave, Springhouse Fissure, clearly suggests this historic use, as do the presence of a springhouse foundation at the cave's mouth or storage areas near pools or streams inside the cave.

Physical evidence inside caves often corroborates folkloric accounts and nomenclature. In other instances, artifacts suggest activities previously unsuspected. As late as the 1950s, Petty Cave in Putnam County still contained a low rock shelf used a hundred years earlier for storing vegetables, and Selby's "Dark Cave" still had wooden storage racks. Even today, Old Squires Cave in Smith County has wooden pallets, Cherry Cave has rock compartments, and Sheals Cave has the remnants of a wooden door, all used for protecting stored food. Flatt Cave also has a wooden door near the entrance, built for the same purpose. Other examples abound. These uses continued well into the twentieth century. At Leonard Cave in Clay County, the owners stored preserved fruits in Mason jars, probably after the cave was briefly converted into a nightclub in the mid-1930s. George Austin Cave in White County served as a water source and for the storage of milk, wine, and moonshine at about the same time. An old wooden container for bottles remains there today, confirming the practice.[10]

Sometimes the use of caves for water sources and cold storage was extended from domestic to the commercial or municipal sphere, as people in the Upper Cumberland built on established folk practices. They embraced entrepreneurial enterprises as towns in the region grew. W. J. Ward built a substantial dairy house at Ward Cave in White County around 1900, and managers of Seven Springs Hotel in DeKalb County stored food in a small cave on the banks of Sink Creek. Towns such as Livingston turned to substantial spring caves for their municipal and industrial water supplies, a practice that continued for many years. Moonshiners turned to caves as production sites for their illicit wares, in part because they were hidden spaces, but also because they were often the most reliable water sources in the limestone karst lands.[11]

The distinction between domestic economies and commercial activities was often blurred when it came to caves. People in the Upper Cumberland who used caves for domestic water sources and food storage increasingly extended these activities into the commercial sphere. The extractive industries, centered on caves, occasionally served domestic needs but were primarily commercial ventures. Mining for copperas, alum, Epsom salt, and especially saltpeter were common activities, characteristic of the fragmented process industries that began to appear in Tennessee in the late eighteenth and early nineteenth centuries. Little is known about mining of alum, a potassium aluminum sulfate used as an emetic and astringent, except that it was occasionally obtained from caves on the Cumberland Plateau by the early 1800s. According to one antebellum geologic report, the same was true of Epsom salt, a sulfate of magnesia. Copperas mining was more substantial. According to Francois Andre Michaux, a Frenchman who visited central Tennessee in 1802, local entrepreneurs mined caves along the Cumberland and Roaring rivers for the substance, a sulfate of iron used in black dye and ink, which was then exported to Kentucky. An 1812 account of a cave on the Caney Fork, appropriately called Copperas Cave, noted that two men had already extracted significant amounts of the substance (along with alum), but that large deposits remained. These ventures were modest in scope, oriented to local markets in Tennessee and Kentucky, and did not continue much beyond the initial pioneer period. Yet this was not the case for the most important extractive cave industry, saltpeter mining.[12]

Saltpeter, or potassium nitrate, was a crucial ingredient in making gunpowder, though it had several other minor uses as well. Saltpeter mining began in east Tennessee by the time of the American Revolution and spread into the Upper Cumberland by the 1790s. In 1794, a hunter named Joseph Bishop mined saltpeter from a cave, to produce gunpowder for his own use. Folklore suggests he obtained his saltpeter from Old Squires Cave in Smith County, and though it is impossible to verify this positively, the cave showed clear signs of sediment removal when it was rediscovered in 1997. Other small-scale saltpeter mines in the landscape's many caves and rock-shelters appeared soon afterwards. By the early 1800s, as international conflicts threatened foreign supplies and the price of saltpeter skyrocketed, many inhabitants of the Upper Cumberland entered the business.[13]

The saltpeter industry peaked just before and during the War of 1812, only to ebb after 1815, although some small-scale production continued in the following decades. Salt Petre (or Chitwood) Cave in Red Boiling Springs was well known as a source of nitrates by the 1810s and was extensively mined during the period, presumably to meet the needs of the American military forces in the War of 1812. In Jackson County, the Chaffin family purportedly mined saltpeter, for more than a hundred years, from a cave on Flynn's Creek. By the 1820s they worked Rains Roberts's Old Salt Peter Cave on Blackburn's Fork, where they processed the saltpeter in a powder mill. This gunpowder reportedly went to Andrew Jackson's troops in the Battle of New Orleans, a tale told about many of the early saltpeter operations in Tennessee. John Haywood's 1823 history of Tennessee noted many saltpeter caves that had been mined in the previous decade, especially on the Cumberland and Caney Fork rivers. So ubiquitous was the industry that storekeeper Joel Harper of Carthage advertised in an 1811 issue of the *Carthage Gazette* that he accepted payment for his goods in cash or saltpeter. Like other commodities from the region, much of the saltpeter went down river to Carthage and eventually to Nashville.[14]

Although the slump in prices after the war led to a decline in saltpeter production, some caves remained active in the following decades, such as the one Tobias Mordock worked in Fentress County in 1824. Reports exist of caves in White County and elsewhere producing saltpeter in the 1820s, 1830s, and 1840s, though mostly for household use or local markets. By the 1850s, when foreign supplies were again interrupted and prices rose, large-scale mining resumed all across the region. This second peak lasted into the Civil War, when the state of Tennessee, and later the Confederate States of America, contracted with numerous small producers for the commodity. England's Cave on the Calfkiller River was extensively mined, beginning in the mid-1850s. So promising was the lure of great profits from saltpeter that a speculative frenzy developed, as its value increased 1,000 percent, only to collapse in the latter stages of the Civil War. Dozens of other caves in the Upper Cumberland were also mined between 1860 and 1863, marking the climax of saltpeter mining in the region, the state, and the entire South.[15]

Saltpeter was mined in more than seventy-five Upper Cumberland caves between the 1790s and 1860s, resulting in significant, localized environmental degradation. Mining disrupted cave ecosystems, led to loss of biological habitats, and destroyed important archaeological sites. Above ground, the industry stimulated timber cutting for firewood and the production of charcoal and potash, all of which were required to process saltpeter and make black powder, a combination of saltpeter, charcoal, and sulfur.

Saltpeter works and powder mills were hazardous to livestock and human alike. Livestock fell ill from water polluted by leachate from the extraction process. Miners faced the hazards of rock-fall and dust- and smoke-related lung diseases. Grinding and mixing gunpowder was a delicate business, prone to explosions. Around 1854, John Roberts was badly injured when the powder mill at Waterloo in Overton County exploded. Dickey Matthews was not so lucky; he died in 1859 in an explosion at his father's powder mill in Grassy Cove. For the miner and mill worker alike, the saltpeter business was hard, dirty, and dangerous work. Generally, local men comprised the workforce, but slaves and conscripts also worked in some mines and mills. Other powder mills, such as the ones in White and DeKalb counties, were more fortunate, but these, too, went out of business when the price of saltpeter and gunpowder plunged after the Civil War. Still, old ways persisted for a long time, and some small-scale production for domestic or local use continued in the following decades. The last recorded saltpeter mining operation in the state, and one of the last known anywhere in the United States, was in Pratt Cave in Pickett County around 1890.[16]

After the demise of saltpeter mining, people in the Upper Cumberland continued to use caves for small-scale industrial production and power. It is likely that people extracted guano, a potent fertilizer, from dry caves with large bat populations. Commercial guano mining is well documented slightly further south on the Cumberland Plateau, in Warren and Van Buren counties.

William York, father of World War I hero Alvin York, housed his blacksmith shop in a shallow cave on his property in Fentress County. Numerous cave springs provided water and hydro power for a variety of industrial activities. In DeKalb County, the stream issuing from Gin Bluff Cave powered a cotton mill, while nearby Cripps Mill Cave turned the grinding stones of a gristmill for many decades. Big Springs Cave, also in DeKalb County, served as the water source for a commercial trout farm in the mid-twentieth century. Mill Cave in Grassy Cove provided power for several grist mills, as did several caves on the Caney Fork River.[17]

Caves are, by definition, hidden spaces, not generally visible from the surface. As such, they have been used for a variety of secretive purposes since the earliest days of American settlement. Caves were appropriate refuges for hermits and persons fleeing peril. They served as lairs for individual fugitives, criminal gangs, and illegal enterprises. People also temporarily hid property or disposed of incriminating evidence underground. These adaptive uses shifted over time, revealing both the strength and flexibility of the cultural conception of caves as hidden spaces.

Hermits seeking to escape society have used remote, hidden caves since the early days of the American colonies. While most famous hermits in America lived in New England, New York, or Pennsylvania, the Upper Cumberland certainly had them. In Scott's Gulf of the Caney Fork, a hermit lived in a small cave, now called Amber's Den, near the bank of the river. As was often the case, once his presence was revealed, local inhabitants considered it unacceptable. Deemed insane, the hermit was removed from his refuge and bundled off to an asylum. Fentress County had a well-known hermit, John Smith, who lived in a shallow cave within the confines of Pickett State Park, not far from the Wolf River.[18]

More common was the use of caves by criminals. In the early nineteenth century, highwayman John Murrell's gang purportedly hid in Blue Spring Cave in White County, where they also disposed of the corpses of murder victims. In one celebrated case from the 1830s, Archibald Kirby murdered Peter Elrod and threw his body into a White County sinkhole called Hell Hole. In one Overton County cave, a skeleton was discovered in 1936, seventy years after the man, probably Sye McDonald, was reportedly killed by the Ku Klux Klan. Later in the nineteenth century, Pedigo Cave and Jim Cave, both in DeKalb County, were used by solitary fugitives from justice. In the late 1970s, Billy

Flowstone formation in a cave near Cookeville, Tennessee. Photo by the author.

Dean Anderson hid and lived in a small cave near his mother's house in Fentress County, before he was killed in a shootout with the Federal Bureau of Investigation. In the mid-1990s, a murder victim was found in a cave in DeKalb County, and in October 1999, a corpse discovered in a cave in White County led to the arrests of four persons for first-degree murder.[19]

When bushwhacking and guerrilla warfare wracked the Upper Cumberland during and after the Civil War, caves proved useful hiding places. A history of White County notes an argument between two men during the war, leading to one of them, Bud Carter, kidnapping the other and holding him for ransom in a cave. The Copeland family of Overton County hid their meat in a cave on hearing of the approach of Union partisan Tinker Dave Beatty. Keeton Windle of Putnam County hid his horses from Union troops in a large nearby cave. Other stories tell of people hiding even more valuable property in caves, such as gold or silver, but they remain uncorroborated.[20]

Many people hid in caves during the war. In a twist on the usual story, Bill Young of Upper Gum Springs hid from the depredations of the Webb gang by staying in a cave at night. Abe Smith, a supporter of the Confederacy, hid in a cave during the war, but Union troops captured him by following his footprints in the snow. Unionist Sam Sells hid from Confederates in a cave, though he was later captured while fighting for the United States. Some men from both sides hid in caves, including a man who hid near Alpine and another who hid on the Obey River. As the war destroyed legitimate civil authority and led to a breakdown of the social order, ordinary people hid property or even themselves in caves.[21]

The most prevalent industrial use of caves after the Civil War was for an illegal endeavor, moonshine production. For this illicit industry, caves were important not just by providing a sheltered work space or important sources of water in karst lands, but also because caves were hidden spaces. Beginning in the late nineteenth century and continuing throughout the first half of the twentieth century, moonshiners turned to dozens of caves and rock-shelters in the Upper Cumberland to produce their wares. At first, moonshiners simply sought to avoid taxes on their product following the Civil War, but after Tennessee went "bone-dry" in 1909, whiskey production became illegal. This soon led to an increase in underground distilling, which peaked between 1920 and 1940. Moonshine ventures were cottage industries, requiring a workforce of just a few men in seasonal operations, usually during the fall, to make a product sold to both local and distant markets. Illegal stills became a common feature of the Upper Cumberland landscape, especially in its caves, and even today artifacts from these operations bear silent witness to the extent of the industry.[22]

Caves offered whiskey producers a reasonable chance of remaining undetected. This was vital and meant the difference between making a profit or spending time in jail. Because of the illegal nature of the activity, little written documentation exists beyond an occasional newspaper account when a site was discovered. One such account of an 1879 raid by revenuers on a cave moonshine operation in Clay County reported that the authorities captured several men and destroyed a 60-gallon-capacity copper still, along with 500 gallons of mash and miscellaneous equipment and supplies. Reports of raids on cave sites are relatively rare, suggesting that the strategy of going underground proved fairly effective.[23]

Local folklore, nomenclature, and the presence of artifacts often provide the only clues as to which caves moonshiners used. For instance, Bunkum Cave in Pickett County received its name from the production of moonshine whiskey in the entrance room, presumably in the late nineteenth century. Thomas Bailey, a young geologist working for the state of Tennessee, visited caves in the region in 1917, recording folklore and physical evidence that linked numerous caves to the moonshine industry, including Bilbrey Cave and Saltpeter Cave, both in Putnam County, and Harrison Cave in Pickett County. Almost forty years later, in the mid-1950s, noted cave biologist Thomas C. Barr examined numerous caves in the area and reported several additional underground moonshine sites, based on oral histories and artifacts. Although most sites were long abandoned, he observed that a few moonshine caves remained active. In general, the moonshine industry began to decline following World War II, as transportation systems improved and bootlegging gradually supplanted local production. By the 1960s, moonshine production in caves had virtually disappeared.[24]

Most stills were placed in cave entrance rooms that the moonshiners deemed suitable for the activity, based on the cave's morphology, the presence of water, and location. Occasionally, some operators ventured deeper into the cave environment. This involved much more work, because the distilling equipment, supplies, and some sort of lighting system had to be transported through rough, narrow passages. High humidity levels and the problem of smoke from the operation created a more difficult work environment, yet some judged the trade-off between additional work and reduced risk of discovery worthwhile. At Cherry Cave, evidence proves that a moonshine still was once erected in the cave's main entrance room, where a skylight entrance just above functioned as a chimney. Around 1930, moonshiners erected a still deep inside the cave, in a stream passage several hundred feet from the entrances, solely to reduce the risk of discovery. For moonshiners, as for hermits, bandits, fugitives, and ordinary inhabitants, caves were valued as hidden spaces, revealing a third important form of environmental interaction in the Upper Cumberland.[25]

Juxtaposed with the widespread use of caves for subsistence and domestic necessities, for extractive industries and power, and as hidden spaces, caves in the Upper Cumberland were also viewed as natural curiosities and potential social spaces. Throughout the nineteenth and twentieth centuries, property owners, neighbors, and many others visited hundreds of caves simply to see the unusual environment, marvel at the natural wonders found there, and enjoy the social experience of seeing these places with people. Almost all of the large caves, and many lesser ones, became well known locally as interesting places to see, and many generations of families in the region visited them. People in the Upper Cumberland, as in other parts of the country, found beauty in caves, which they often regarded as sublime manifestations of God's handiwork. As noted previously, York Cave in Fentress County was used for church services partly because it offered shelter, but also because of the cultural conception of caves as part of sublime nature. Many caves were seen as appropriate places for social outings, picnics, dances, or simple sightseeing. The entrance of Rainbow Cave in Overton County featured a spectacular waterfall more than 100 feet high that, at times, created a magnificent rainbow in the sinkhole that generations of local folk came to view and enjoy. These outings were in no way related to commercial or domestic use; they reflected a different impulse in the culture of the region.[26]

These nonutilitarian and noncommercial connections with the natural environment were strong, as attested to by the presence of dozens or, in cases such as Buffalo Cave in Fentress County, hundreds of names written on the cave walls from social and recreational outings. Although these trips began long before the Civil War, the pattern of use persisted. During the war, local folks continued to make outings to caves. The curious nature of caves also appealed to Union soldiers serving in the state; John C. Reed of the Eleventh Ohio Infantry explored South Carthage Cave as a diversion while his regiment was posted nearby.

Social and recreational visits greatly increased in the decades after 1865. These visits were informal and spontaneous, but organized outings to particularly well-known caves also became common by the end of the nineteenth century, such as the yearly school outings by students from Grandview Normal Institute to Grassy Cove Saltpeter Cave.[27]

So popular were the conception and usage of caves as natural curiosities and social spaces that several entrepreneurs attempted to open caves as profitable businesses featuring underground tours or even dances. That one could commercialize caves for tourists had long been known, as many people from Tennessee and Kentucky visited Mammoth Cave of Kentucky, which had been a successful tourist site since the 1820s. Development of Upper Cumberland caves lagged in the nineteenth century, partly because of the established dominance of Mammoth Cave, transportation difficulties, and the ubiquity of caves in the area. By the twentieth century, conditions began to change and a commercial cave industry emerged.[28]

Neil Fisher Cave, discovered in 1916 on the banks of the Caney Fork River in Smith County, was soon opened as a commercial venture called Rip Van Winkle Cave. Operators hoped to attract visitors from neighboring counties as well as rail travelers from outside the region. Leonard Cave in Clay County had been known for perhaps a hundred years or more, having been mined for saltpeter; it was used for informal recreational outings in the nineteenth century. In 1935, local entrepreneurs opened the cave to the paying public as Cavern Dance Hall, featuring string bands, dancing, food, and tours. Delightfully cool in the summer, it offered sheltered space for dancing, but the main attraction was the unusual nature of the cave environment. Although a shooting at the site ended the business venture, it attracted local residents as well as tourists from the nearby resort town of Red Boiling Springs. Even after the demise of the Cavern Dance Hall, Leonard Cave continued to attract informal visits. As late as the 1980s, two voluntary organizations, seeking to raise funds, used the cave as a "haunted house" during the Halloween season. Indeed, as at Leonard Cave, the social and recreational use of caves has generally outlasted many of the other uses in the past.

Caves are no longer the focus of extractive industries, underground moonshine operations have largely been abandoned, and caves are no longer much used for food storage; yet, many people in the region still enjoy a social and recreational outing to a nearby cave, primarily to experience the wonders of the subterranean environment. In the mid-1950s, Cumberland Caverns in Warren County opened to the paying public. On the edge of the Upper Cumberland, this tourist cave proved profitable and has introduced many visitors to the underground environment in a safe, pleasant manner. The attraction of caves remains strong today.[29]

Although this essay has only sketched the environmental history of caves in the Upper Cumberland, and several important topics such as the arrival of cave science and cave conservation in the region have been neglected, we can reach some conclusions about the relationships between culture and environment. First, people of the Upper Cumberland, both before and after American settlement, saw caves as an integral part of the landscape, using them in a variety of ways that shifted over time. Native Americans used caves as ceremonial spaces, for shelter and water, and as sources of important cultural materials such as chert. Long hunters and early travelers mostly used caves for subsistence, as they provided shelter, water, and saltpeter, an important ingredient for gunpowder. Once more permanent settlements were established, caves became adjuncts to domestic economies, providing water for household use and cold storage for foodstuffs. These uses continued throughout the nineteenth and the first half of the twentieth centuries. At the same time, the commercial use of caves began in earnest, as a widespread but fragmented saltpeter mining industry grew up in the region. Although this industry ebbed and flowed in response to market demand and prices, saltpeter mining characterized the history of many caves in the region and resulted in significant degradation of the underground environment and adjacent surface areas.

Even after the collapse of saltpeter mining, the commercial use of caves persisted, as they continued to provide water, power, and industrial work spaces. The most widespread use of caves for industrial production after the Civil War, for manufacturing moonshine, was driven by the hidden nature of caves as much as any other single factor. In a few cases, the cave was commercialized, even though no substances were extracted and no products were manufactured, as a few caves in the region were developed as tourist sites in the twentieth century.

Caves were conceived of and used as hidden spaces from the early days of settlement through the contemporary period, as a variety of people, properties, and activities went underground to remain secret. Normally, people using caves in this manner were attempting to hide from the reach of civil authorities, but when order broke down in the region, such as during the Civil War, the use of caves as hidden spaces became more widespread. The most prevalent of these activities, moonshining, disappeared only as larger social and economic changes made the usage unprofitable. Although these activities led to some physical modifications within the cave, they generally did not result in large-scale degradation of the environment.

People of the Upper Cumberland regarded caves as natural curiosities and important social spaces. They visited caves for recreation, to enjoy the company of their fellows, and to see the wonders of the natural world. Though important for making a living, caves were also places where people related to the sublime and to each other. This emphasis on the noncommercial and nonutilitarian value of caves, and by extension of nature, lent depth, complexity, and even ambiguity to the relationship of the Upper Cumberland people with their culture and the environment.

NOTES

1. Edward T. Luther, *Our Restless Earth: The Geologic Regions of Tennessee* (Knoxville: University of Tennessee Press, 1977): 43–62; Thomas C. Barr, "Caves of Tennessee" *Tennessee Division of Geology Bulletin* 64 (1961): 3–54; George W. Moore and Nicholas Sullivan, *Speleology: Caves and the Cave Environment* (St. Louis: Cave Books, 1997): 171.

2. *TCS Caves List* (Nashville: Tennessee Cave Survey, 2001); Larry E. Matthews, *Cumberland Caverns* (Huntsville, Ala.: National Speleological Society, 1989): 317.

3. Moore and Sullivan, 33–78.

4. Jan F. Simek, "The Sacred Darkness: Prehistoric Cave Art in Tennessee," *Tennessee Conservationist* (March-April, 1997): 27–32; Jay D. Franklin, "Excavating and Analyzing Prehistoric Lithic Quarries: An Example from the 3rd Unnamed Cave, Tennessee," *Midcontinental Journal of Archaeology* 26:2, 199–218; George M. Crothers, Charles H. Faulkner, Jan F. Simek, Patty Jo Watson, and Robert C. Mainfort, eds. *The Woodland Southeast* (Tuscaloosa: University of Alabama Press, 2002): 502–24; Erin Elizabeth Pritchard, "The Prehistoric Use of Hubbards Cave, Tennessee" (Knoxville: University of Tennessee, Master's Thesis, 2001): 118.

5. Ibid.; Larry E. Matthews, "Descriptions of Tennessee Caves," *Tennessee Division of Geology Bulletin* 69 (1971): 75; personal correspondence with Alan Cressler, 1993.

6. Author's notes on Jackson County caves April 20, May 22, and May 25, 2002; author's notes on a Clay County cave, December 1 and 8, 2001, January 20 and 22, 2002.

7. Fentress County Historical Association, *History of Fentress County, Tennessee* (Dallas: Curtis Media, 1987): 8, 50–51; Thomas G. Webb, *DeKalb County* (Memphis: Memphis State University Press, 1986): 10; Thomas L. Bailey, "Report on the Caves of the Eastern Highland Rim and Cumberland Mountains,"

The Resources of Tennessee (Nashville: State Geological Survey, April 1918): 108. York Cave has been known since at least 1813. See Albert Ross Hogue, *One Hundred Years in the Cumberland Mountains: Along the Continental Line* (McMinnville, Tenn.: Standard Printing Co., 1933): 59; Marjorie C. Douglas, "Shelter from the Atomic Storm: The National Speleological Society and the Use of Caves as Fallout Shelters, 1940–1965," *Journal of Spelean History* 30:4, 91–106.

8. Samuel Cole Williams, ed., *Early Travels in the Tennessee Country, 1540–1800* (Johnson City, Tenn.: Watauga Press, 1928): 426, 504; Hogue, 71; Bailey, 106; author's notes on Cherry Cave January 13 and 20, 2002.

9. *TCS Cave List;* Bailey, 87, 123; Barr, 274, 516; Matthews, "Descriptions of Tennessee Caves," 79.

10. Barr, 274, 516; personal observations of Squires Cave (July and September, 1997); Sheals Cave (January 13, 2002); Rogers Cave (January 20, 2002); notes on Leonard Cave (December 1, 2001); Joseph C. Douglas, "Water, Milk, Whiskey and Wine: Historic Use of a Small Tennessee Cave in the First Half of the Twentieth Century," *Journal of Spelean History* 27:3 (2000): 39–41.

11. Barr, 517–18; "The Seven Springs Hotel," *The Eagle* (McMinnville, Tenn.: n.p., 1981): 60; See also Joseph C. Douglas, "An Environmental History of American Caves, 1660–1900" (Houston: University of Houston, Doctoral Dissertation, 2001).

12. Thomas Wray, "Minerals from Tennessee," *The American Mineralogical Journal* 1:4: 265; J. M. Safford, *A Geological Reconnaissance of Tennessee* (Nashville: State of Tennessee, 1856): 117; Timothy J. Barlow, *The Life and Writings of Moses Fisk* (Collegedale, Tenn.: College Press, 1980); 40; [Charlestown, Virginia] *Farmer's Repository* October 27, 1809.

13. Marion O. Smith, *Saltpeter Mining in East Tennessee* (Maryville, Tenn.: Byron's Graphic Arts, 1990): 32; John W. Gray, *The Life of Joseph Bishop*, Reprint (Spartanburg, SC: The Reprint Company, 1974): 81; Sue W. Maggart and Nina Sutton, eds., *The History of Smith County Tennessee* (Dallas: Curtis Media, 1987): 43; personal observation of Squires Cave, July and September 1997.

14. Vernon Roddy, *Thousands to Cure: On the Early History of Red Boiling Springs, Tennessee with Selected Supporting Materials* (Hartsville, Tenn.: Upper Country People Probe, 1991): 11, 21–22, 148, 223–24, 235; Eliza G. Rogers, *Memorable Historical Accounts of White County and Area* (Collegedale, Tenn.: College Press, 1972): 64; Works Progress Administration (WPA), *Records of Putnam County: Richard F. Cooke's Survey of Plat Book 1825–1839* (Nashville: Historical Records Survey, 1939): 97; John Haywood, *The Natural and Aboriginal History of Tennessee,* Reprint (Kingsport, Tenn.: Kingsport Press, 1973); Maggart and Sutton, 43.

15. Wanda Sewell Hatfield, compiler, *Entry Books of Fentress County, Tennessee, 1824–1901* (Signal Mountain, Tenn.: Signal Mountain Press, 1990); Reverend Monroe Seals, *History of White County* (n.p., 1935): 82; Marion O. Smith, "England Cave (Cave Hill Saltpeter Pits) in the Late 1850s," *Tennessee Caver* 3: 1–3.

16. Douglas W. Plemons, "The Nitre Gardener's Guide and Home Companion: The Saltpeter Survey, 1994," *Journal of Spelean History* 29:1, 31–36; Walter S. McClain, *A History of Putnam County, Tennessee* (Cookeville, Tenn.: Quimby Dyer & Co., 1925): 122; Cora and Nettie Stratton, compilers, *And This Is Grassy*

Cove (Crossville, Tenn.: Crossville Chronicle Publishing Co., 1938): 11; Arthur Weir Crouch, *The Caney Fork of the Cumberland* (Nashville: n.p., 1973): 46, 48, 50; Webb, 330; Bailey, 114.

17. Bailey, 131–34; William J. Crocker, "Alvin York," in *Heroes of Tennessee,* Billy M. Jones, ed. (Memphis: Memphis State University Press, 1979): 124; Will T. Hale, *History of DeKalb County, Tennessee* (McMinnville, Tenn.: Ben Lomand Press, 1969): 115–16, Barr, 159–61; Matthews, "Descriptions of Tennessee Caves," 111, 122; Stratton and Stratton, 11; Crouch, 46, 48; Joseph C. Douglas, "Miners and Moonshiners: Historic Industrial Uses of Tennessee Caves," *Midcontinental Journal of Archaelogy* 26:2 (2000): 251–67 (hereafter "Miners and Moonshiners").

18. Monroe Seals, *History of White County* (Spartansburg, SC, 1974): 92; Ross Cardwell, "History of Scotts Gulf," Unpublished mss, 15 pp.; personal correspondence with Ross Cardwell, November 29, 2002.

19. Hale, 102–3; Bailey, 90; Barr, 169; Seals, 24, 82; Webb, 363; Lonnie Carr, "Bone Cave or Murrells Cave," *Tag-Net Digest* (October 14, 1999); Darlene Anthony, "Billy Dean Anderson's Hideout Cave," *N.S.S. News* (November 1979): 262, 271; "Human Bones Found in Overton Identified," *Putnam County Herald* (August 27, 1936): 8; Knight Stivender, "Police, Mom, Pals Beat Disabled Son to Death," Nashville *Tennessean* (October 2, 1999): 1.

20. Rogers, 50; *Echoes from the Foothills* (Nashville, Tenn.: Asher Young, 1977): 69–70, 80, 87.

21. Rogers, 52; *Echoes from the Foothills*, 94–95, 98.

22. Joseph C. Douglas, "Caves and Moonshine: A New Area for Historical Inquiry," *Journal of Spelean History* 26:4, 79–81; Douglas, "Miners and Moonshiners," 259–61.

23. "Tracked to Their Lair: Illicit Distillers Captured in Clay County Cave," *The Nashville Daily American* (February 4, 1879): 4.

24. Bailey, 114, 117–18, 122–23; Barr, 230, 350.

25. Barr, 273; author's notes on Cherry Cave.

26. Federal Writers Project of the WPA, *Tennessee: A Guide to the State* (New York: Hastings House, 1939): 507, 509; Douglas, "An Environmental History of American Caves," 183–220.

27. Will C. Peavyhouse and Merle (Tipton) Peavyhouse, *A History of Buffalo Cove, Tennessee* (n.p., 1969): 5; author's notes on Buffalo Cave, May 20, 2000; Joseph C. Douglas, Marion O. Smith, and Jan F. Simek, "Identification and Analysis of a Civil War Soldier's Name in South Carthage Cave, Tennessee," *Tennessee Caver* 2:1(2002): 4–15; Bryan Stanley, *The Way It Was, Crossville, Cumberland County* (Nashville: Parthenon Press, 1983): 202.

28. William R. Halliday, *Depths of the Earth: Caves and Cavers of the United States*, 2nd ed. (New York: Harper and Row, 1976): 3–49; Douglas, "An Environmental History of American Caves."

29. "A Wonderful Cave Near Lancaster, Tennessee," *Carthage Courier* (August 24, 1916); Bailey, 128–29; interview with Don Braswell, December 26, 1998; interview with Darryl Braswell, November 39, 2001; Roddy, 278–79; *WPA Guide*, 367; *Red Boiling Springs News* (August 17, 1935): 3; Matthews, *Cumberland Caverns*, 143–48.

Chapter 2

SHELTERING THE PEOPLE

Folk Architecture in the Upper Cumberland Region

W. Calvin Dickinson

The first American settlers in the Upper Cumberland region before 1800 built temporary dwellings, one-room structures constructed of round logs and crude notches, with a door and a few windows. Many had dirt floors, and many probably had stick and mud chimneys; some may have had no chimney.

Second homes for these early settlers may also have been log, but they were built more carefully for permanent occupancy. Now the logs were hewn with broadax and adze, usually only on two sides. Yellow poplar, chestnut, and the various varieties of oak were the woods most commonly used.

Notches were cut into the ends of the logs as substitutes for nails. Of the eight or ten notches used in America, pioneers in the Upper Cumberland region used the square notch, the V notch, and the half-dovetail notch. The half-dovetail was by far the most popular because of its beauty and practicality. The slopes of the notch pulled each log toward the inside of the house, securing it against kicking out and eliminating the necessity for pins or nails.

Though some of the earliest log houses were built near rivers or navigable creeks, which were the easiest mode of transportation, the majority were built on hills rather than in valleys because "the river bottoms were quite unhealthy when the country was new."[1] They usually faced south, southeast, or southwest, with the second largest number facing north; thus the south-north axis was most common.[2]

Growing families necessitated expansion of the houses in all directions. Original cabins may have been single-pen—one room—structures,

Elderly men examine half-dovetail notches near Cookeville, Tennessee, 1930s. The man on the far right is Potter Greenwood. Courtesy of the Tennessee State Library and Archives.

either square or rectangular, almost always with even measurements—twelve by twelve, sixteen by sixteen, fourteen by sixteen, sixteen by eighteen, and so on. Most were also story-and-a-half structures, with the half-story being about four feet high. The upper level was useful for storage and for children. A full second story might be added later, an open porch added to the front, and a shed addition to the rear.[3]

One of the earliest log houses still standing is the Greenberry Wilson house in the Burke Community of Cumberland County. Built in 1797 by Wilson, the original house was a story-and-a-half single-pen structure constructed of cedar logs, twenty-four by fourteen feet. A similar structure was the John Wheeler house on Dry Fork Creek in Jackson County. This single-pen house, with one and a half stories, was built of chestnut logs with V notches.

An easy method to double living space was to build a second cabin beside the first, with about ten feet of space between them. The two were connected with a breezeway, or dogtrot. It was easier to build two cabins than to join logs at the ends.[4] The dogtrot could be used in the summer as a cool room or hall, and in the winter it served as a dry

Dixona, early log house in Smith County, Tennessee. Photo by the author.

storage area. Dixona at Dixon Springs in Smith County, built about 1788, may be the oldest dogtrot still standing. The Frank Gilliland house at Oak Hill in Overton County was an early dogtrot structure, built by Adam Gardenhire about 1800. It was story and a half with two twenty-four-by-eighteen pens. A poplar log kitchen was located in a separate building behind the house. Log barns and slave houses completed the estate. Another early dogtrot house was the Southard-Floyd home at Baker's Crossroads in White County, built about 1796 of oak logs with square notches. This structure was a full two stories in height, with a dogtrot on each level. The Fancher house in White County, built about 1850, was another two-story dogtrot with square notched logs.[5]

After sawmills were established in the Upper Cumberland region, cheap milled lumber became more readily available. Many people covered log houses with weatherboard, and many constructed new houses of milled lumber. The Fanchers sheathed their log house with weatherboard, and the Matthew Cowen house in Putnam County's Buffalo Valley, built about 1800 of logs, was expanded with a second story and three dormers. These additions were built with milled lumber, and the logs were covered with milled weatherboard.

Double-pen houses built with milled lumber were common in the Upper Cumberland region. Two styles were the saddlebag and the tenant designs. The saddlebag positioned the two pens back to back against a central chimney with two fireplaces. Each pen had a front door. The Harlan/Miller saddlebag in Monroe County, Kentucky, was built about

1820. The tenant design was a late-nineteenth-century adaptation of the saddlebag; it had two pens with front doors and a central flue serving stoves in each pen.[6]

An early house built of lumber was the Samuel Caplinger home at Temperance Hall in DeKalb County. Constructed about 1821, it was built in a method rarely used in Tennessee. Carpenters used the old "post and beam," or braced-frame technique, with the wooden frame consisting of hewn walnut timbers joined by mortise and tenon joints penned together with wooden pegs. Brick and mortar "nogging" filled spaces between the timbers. Exterior walls were hand-planed weatherboard, and the interior was plastered.

About 1820, larger and more stylish houses began to appear in the Upper Cumberland. Some homes were weatherboard, but many were brick. Stone buildings were rare in the early history of the region, although native building stone, both limestone and sandstone, are plentiful in the area. The Rock House east of Sparta in White County, built in the 1830s, was one of the few examples of rock structures. A scarcity of skilled stonemasons may explain the absence of stone buildings.

Bonded brick, rather than brick veneer, was a construction technique used in the early nineteenth century. Ordinary bond, with six stretcher rows and one header row, was most common, although numerous examples of Flemish bond can be found. Flemish bond used alternating stretcher and header bricks in the same row. Three early brick homes in White County used Flemish bond—the Moses Sims house, the Simpson house, and the Clark-Brock house.

Federal and Greek Revival architectural styles are the earliest found in the Upper Cumberland because of the relatively late date of the region's settlement. Both styles were rectangular block structures with symmetrical facades. Federal style usually had no portico, but featured a highly decorated front entrance with a fanlight window above the door. Greek Revival style is characterized by a gabled portico with round or square columns. The interior floor plan of both styles was usually the central hall design, with one or two rooms on either side of the hall.

McMinnville, south of the Upper Cumberland in Warren County, has the best remaining examples of Federal-style structures. The Black home of 1825 and the Ridley-Heneger house of 1829 are still well maintained, but the Miller house on U.S. 70 north of McMinnville is in shambles. The Simpson house, south of Sparta in White County, was built in the Federal style, with a beautiful front door; a Greek Revival

Beechwood, a Federal-style house in Smith County, Tennessee. Photo by the author.

portico was added later. The Bradley house and David Burford's "Beechwood," near Dixon Springs, are other Federal-style homes.

Numerous examples of Greek Revival style can be found in the Upper Cumberland. The Clark-Brock house north of Sparta is a beautiful illustration. Built by Daniel Clark about 1820, the two-story brick structure was square. Brick pilasters strengthened the front and side

The Clark-Brock Greek Revival house in Sparta, Tennessee. Photo by the author.

walls, and round wooden columns supported the full-length portico. "Carthage Heights" in Smith County was a later example, constructed by William Cullom about 1848. The three-bay facade has a central bay portico with four pairs of square Doric columns and pilasters. The floor plan is central-hall design, with a beautiful curved, cantilevered staircase in the hall. The interior trim is walnut, painted in a feathering pattern. An elaborate basement is divided into five rooms. Several one-story houses imitating the Greek Revival style can be found in the region.[7]

After the destructive period of the Civil War, the Upper Cumberland adopted the eclectic styles of architecture that had appeared in the North before the war. The balloon frame construction technique, manufactured decorative materials, and railroad transportation allowed builders in the region to participate in the modern styles. Gothic Revival, Italianate, Second Empire, Queen Anne, and "I" styles all appeared in simplistic forms and as decorative characteristics on plain houses. The first four were highly decorative styles, and the use of manufactured materials brought in by railroad made them popular.

Gothic Revival was the style for large mansions in New England, Ireland, and Great Britain. In the Upper Cumberland, Gothic Revival decoration was common under the gable overhangs and the eaves. No expensive homes were constructed in Gothic Revival. Churches represent the best examples of this late-nineteenth-century style. The First Methodist Church in Carthage may be the best example. Built in 1889 of brick, the church has a steep pitched roof, a graceful tower, standing buttresses, brick dentils, and beautiful pointed-arch stained glass windows. Other extant examples are Broad Street Church of Christ in Cookeville and the First Presbyterian Church in Sparta. Some Carpenter Gothic churches, made of wood, are Chestnut Mound Methodist Church, Wolf River Methodist Church, the Presbyterian Church at Allardt, and First Methodist Church in Algood. The First Methodist and Cumberland Presbyterian churches in Cookeville were other illustrations, now demolished.

Italianate style was not common in the South, and houses built in this design were rare in the Upper Cumberland. A tower was the most distinguishing characteristic of this style, and shallow-pitch roofs, rounded arch windows with decorative lintels, and heavy decorative brackets under the eaves were other characters. The Sperry house in Sparta, which had its tower removed, and the James Williams house in Gainesboro, which has a tower, are examples of this style in the region. The Clay County Courthouse in Celina, built in 1872, copied this design

The James Williams Italianate-style house in Gainesboro, Tennessee. Photo by the author.

with its square cupola or tower, and with its rounded arch windows and doors. Some decorative brackets were also used. Most examples of Italianate decoration can be found on the facades of late nineteenth-century business buildings in the small Upper Cumberland towns. Cookeville, Sparta, Livingston, Carthage, and other towns all exhibit the style on their business squares and streets.

Second Empire style was even more rare in the Upper Cumberland, but one of the most beautiful buildings in the region was constructed in this design. The Smith County Courthouse in Carthage, built in 1875, used the mansard roof, the distinguishing characteristic of the style. Rounded arch windows and doors, oval dormers, decorative brackets, and a compound cupola decorate and distinguish the building. Pioneer Hall at Pleasant Hill Academy in Cumberland County is the only other public structure built in the Second Empire style.

The Queen Anne design, in both two-story and one-story versions, was copied many times in the region around 1900. With hipped roofs, wraparound porches, bay windows, and Palladian windows, the style used an asymmetrical facade. Constructed of brick or wood, decorative materials included fish-scale shingles, stick work, and spindle work. Floor plans generally did not include central halls, and the rooms tended to be small. Upper Cumberland examples are the Jere Whitson house and the Samuel B. Yeargin houses in Cookeville, the Smith houses on Main Street in Smithville, the Taylor and Arney houses in Livingston, the Dr. Jackson houses in Liberty, and the Cummings house in Sparta.

More examples of the I-House style are found in the Upper Cumberland than of the other designs discussed here. The unusual name comes from the fact that the style was first identified in the states of Illinois, Iowa, and Indiana. Also, the design uses an "I," or rectangular, shape. I-Houses were two stories high, two rooms wide, and one room deep, usually with central hall; they often had three bays. They might have L or T additions on the rear, and they might or might not have porches on front and/or on the rear. Chimneys might be gable-end, saddlebag, or single central. Typically, I-Houses were constructed of wood, and decoration varied from plain to ornate. They can still be found in abundance, both inside and outside of towns, in the Upper Cumberland region. Lynwood Montell discovered the I-House in several subtypes in southern Kentucky.[8] Many now stand abandoned and neglected, but many are occupied.

In the twentieth century, several new styles were introduced into the Upper Cumberland region. With the faster transportation and communication of the new century, the local region was concurrent with the remainder of the country in introducing the new styles. Classical Revival (Colonial Revival and Neo-Classical), Tudor Revival, and Bungalow (Craftsman) designs were all built in the Upper Cumberland in the first half of the twentieth century.

The Classical Revival styles, Colonial Revival and Neo-Classical, were similar, both finding inspirations in the designs of the first half of the nineteenth century. Colonial Revival copied the Georgian and Federal styles, and Neo-Classical used the columned porticos of Greek Revival style. Colonial Revival homes were either brick or weatherboard, and they usually had symmetrical facades. The gabled or hipped roofs were often decorated with dormers. Sometimes they had columned porches of one or more bays, and the centered front doors might be decorated with crowns and/or pilasters. Many attractive examples of this style were built by the newly moneyed businessmen of the region. The Wilson house on Main Street in Gainesboro, the William Bradley Ray house in Monterey, the Hugo Gernt house with a gambrel roof in Allardt, and several fine residences on Dixie Avenue in Cookeville, are illustrative of the design.

Two public buildings in the Classical Revival style were Farr Hall and Henderson Hall on the Tennessee Tech campus. The Science Build-

The William Bradley Ray Colonial Revival house in Monterey, Tennessee. Photo by the author.

ing (Farr Hall) was designed in the Colonial Revival style by Hart, Freeland and Roberts of Nashville; it was built in 1929. A brick structure with fourteen-inch walls, the three-story building had four panels of brick laid in Flemish bond, and a brick course between the second and third floors was also Flemish bond. A hipped roof covered the structure. Quoins denoted the recessed entrance, and twenty-three-foot unfluted columns with Ionic capitals guarded the door.

The Engineering Building (Henderson Hall), completed in 1931, was designed in the Colonial Revival style by R. H. Hunt and Company of Chattanooga. A brick structure, it consisted of three stories and a basement, topped by a slate hip roof. Quoins delineated the corners of the building on the upper two stories. Smooth stone blocks covered the pedimented main entry of the first story. Above this was a semicircular arched opening embellished with a stone cartouche surrounded by foliated scrolls. The interior of the Engineering Building had plastered walls, terrazzo floors, hardwood doors and trim, and brass door hardware. The hardware on the windows—chains, handles, and locks—was also brass. Each floor had a central hall extending north and south, with classrooms and offices on either side of the halls.[9]

Neo-Classical homes were numerous in the Upper Cumberland, and churches also adopted the style. Classical columns supporting porches are the most obvious characteristic of the style on both houses and churches, and dormers and highly decorated central doorways were common. In Cookeville, several examples of the Neo-Classical style can be found on North Dixie and North Washington avenues. The W. B. Carlen home on Dixie, constructed in 1921, and the Jared-Lowe home on North Washington, constructed in 1903, are both notable examples. The Joe L. Evins home in Smithville adopted the Neo-Classical style when it was remodeled.

Several churches in the region feature the Neo-Classical style. The First Presbyterian Church in Cookeville is a typical example. Constructed of red brick in 1910–1911, the building was fronted by a wooden gable supported by four fluted wooden columns. A decorated front door and arched stained glass windows on the sides completed the attractive structure. The First Methodist Church in Monterey, built about 1900, was similar, with wooden gabled portico and arched stained glass windows. Salem Baptist Church in Liberty was also built in the Neo-Classical style in 1927. Its unusual feature was a cloister vault, a dome consisting of four curved surfaces separated by groins, which rose to a point from a square base. It also had a four-columned portico and arched windows.

The most popular style for homes in the Upper Cumberland region in the first half of the twentieth century was the Craftsman or Bungalow style. Relatively inexpensive and easily built, several interpretations of this design could be bought as a kit of parts from Sears, Roebuck, and Co. Most designs used in the Upper Cumberland were one- or one-and-a-half-story structures. Characterized by low-pitched gable roofs with wide eaves and heavy decorative eave brackets, and by gabled porches with massive square columns of varied materials, the structures used stucco, brick, stone, wooden shingles, or clapboard wall materials. Overton County residents may have constructed the largest number of Bungalow homes, but the oldest sections of Cookeville— Eighth Street, Tenth Street, Maple Avenue, and Dixie Avenue—have numerous examples. The Sam Agee house on Highland Street in Sparta, built in 1907, is one of the most unusual examples. The curved returns of the eave brackets gave the structure an Oriental appearance.

The Tudor Revival style of the early twentieth century was very different from the Bungalow style, but it was relatively inexpensive and quite popular. Livingston residents built a number of houses in this design, and several were constructed on Cherry Street, Freeze Street, and Eighth Street in Cookeville. Service stations in Gainesboro and Cookeville were also constructed in this style. Characteristics of Tudor

The Sam Agee Craftsman-style house in Sparta, Tennessee. Photo by the author.

Revival are steeply pitched gable roofs, half-timbering on the walls, pointed or roundtop windows and doors, and massive chimneys on the front or gable ends of the building. One historically important example of this design is the Pelot house, constructed in the 1920s on U.S. 70 east of Crossville. This may have been the first home constructed of

The Pelot Tudor Revival house near Crossville, Tennessee, made from Crab Orchard stone. Photo by the author.

Crab Orchard stone. The Rankin house in Carthage, built of stone in 1929, is another interesting example of Tudor Revival. In Gainesboro, Ward Draper, a wealthy merchant, built a large Tudor Revival home on Main Street. It was a brick structure with red ceramic tile roof. In Cookeville, the Walter Greenwood house on Dixie Avenue was also brick. It was built in 1929–1931.

The Depression of the 1930s and World War II in the 1940s slowed home construction in the United States. The government constructed some buildings during the 1930s and 1940s, but privately financed homes, churches, and other structures were not constructed in great numbers, because of the lack of materials, manpower, and finances.

The Public Works Administration (PWA) and the Works Progress Administration (WPA)—agencies of the U.S. government's New Deal program of the 1930s—constructed public buildings such as schools, post offices, and office buildings. The Civilian Conservation Corps (CCC) and WPA constructed lakes and parks. Capshaw School and the Tennessee Tech Campus School were WPA projects in Cookeville, Gentry School in Putnam County was built with New Deal monies, Liberty Elementary School in DeKalb County was constructed by the WPA in 1939, the two buildings of Alpine Institute in Overton County were built of Crab Orchard stone by the WPA, and the Oak Grove School in Overton County was constructed of Crab Orchard stone by the New Deal Agency. Federal monies financed the Art Deco-style Smith County High School in Carthage in 1940, and New Deal money and laborers even built a new football stadium for Tennessee Tech in 1933–1935.

Only Overton and Putnam counties received public office buildings through the New Deal. The Overton County Courthouse was remodeled in 1933 and 1934, and the Bohannon Building was constructed across the street in 1936, for additional county offices. The two-story Bohannon Building was constructed of Crab Orchard stone in the Art Deco style.

WPA labor constructed post offices in Crossville, Livingston, and Sparta. The Livingston and Sparta buildings were red brick, and the Crossville structure was constructed with Crab Orchard stone. All were Colonial Revival style. Marion Greenwood painted a mural in the Crossville building entitled "The Partnership of Man and Nature." It depicted an agricultural scene on one side and a Tennessee Valley Authority (TVA) dam on the other. The Livingston Post Office mural, "The Newcomers," painted by Margaret Covey, depicted a new family welcomed to the Cumberland region by earlier settlers.[10]

The CCC and WPA programs constructed all the state parks in the Upper Cumberland region. Most counties had army-operated CCC camps, where young men lived and worked. Typically, CCC workers began the park project, then WPA workers completed it years later. Pickett Park in Fentress County was first, but Standing Stone (Overton County), Cumberland Mountain (Cumberland County), Fall Creek Falls (Van Buren County), and Rock Island (White and Warren counties) quickly followed. The stone and log work in these parks—cabins, walls, and dams—is still a reminder of this work in the 1930s. Standing Stone and Pickett parks still maintain the original log cabins that first tourists rented. Standing Stone even has remnants of the CCC work camp. Smaller local parks were also built by these New Deal agencies. Quinland Lake north of Cookeville, Meadow Park Lake west of Crossville, and Zollicoffer Park southwest of Livingston were all examples of these smaller projects.[11]

After World War II, building resumed at a furious pace, and new styles developed. Modern designs dominated in the 1950s and 1960s, but in the 1970s, 1980s, and 1990s the styles reflected some characteristics of nineteenth- and early twentieth-century designs.

The history of architecture in the Upper Cumberland regions of Tennessee and Kentucky reveals no styles or designs unique to the area. Fred Kniffen and Henry Glassie thought the dogtrot design originated in Tennessee, but later historians have not agreed.[12] This region has generally copied styles from the East and the North, usually following each style at a later time. However, one can find excellent examples of all the national designs in the Upper Cumberland, mostly built in a more modest size and decor than in other parts of the country. Materials native to the region were used, creating variations in the recognized styles. Wood was so plentiful that the Gothic style was usually rendered in this cheaper version, resulting in the "vernacular Gothic" variation. Building stone, although plentiful in the Tennessee Upper Cumberland, was used sparingly. Only Crab Orchard stone, a beautiful sandstone, was plentiful, and that was used only in a restricted area of the region. Thus, the Upper Cumberland region reflects American national building styles in modest designs.

NOTES

1. A. V. and W. H. Goodpasture, *Life of Jefferson Dillard Goodpasture* (Nashville: Cumberland Presbyterian, 1897): 12.

2. W. Calvin Dickinson, Michael E. Birdwell, and Homer Kemp, *Upper Cumberland Historic Architecture* (Franklin, Tenn.: Hillsboro Press, 2002): 19–20.

3. Lynwood Montell found several examples of "one-level cabins" in southeastern and south central Kentucky in the 1970s, but in the Upper Cumberland section of Tennessee these most basic structures were very rare by that time. Most in Tennessee were story-and-a-half structures. William Lynwood Montell and Michael L. Morse, *Kentucky Folk Architecture* (Lexington: The University Press of Kentucky, 1976): 11.

4. Ibid., 21. Montell found that both pens in most dogtrot houses in southern Kentucky were constructed at the same time. One of the few exceptions to this was the Thompson home in Green County. Thompson built the first square pen in 1829, and later added a rectangular pen.

5. Dickinson et al., *Upper Cumberland Historic Architecture*, 16–17, 24, 27.

6. Montell and Morse, 22–27.

7. W. Calvin Dickinson, "Smith County Historical Homes," *Tennessee Anthropologist*, XVII:1(spring 1992): 82.

8. Montell and Morse, 32–40.

9. Dickinson et al., *Upper Cumberland Historic Architecture*, 106–8.

10. Carroll Van West, *Tennessee's New Deal Landscape* (Knoxville: University of Tennessee Press, 2001): 54, 70.

11. Ibid., 165, 183, 185, 208.

12. Fred Kniffen, "Folk Housing: Key to Diffusion," *Annals of the Association of American Geographers*, LV (December 1965): 561; Henry Glassie, *Patterns in the Material Folk Culture of the Eastern United States* (Philadelphia: University of Pennsylvania, 1966): 88–89.

Chapter 3

SAINTS, SINNERS, AND DINNERS
ON THE GROUNDS

The Religious Legacy of the Upper Cumberland

LARRY WHITEAKER

In frontier days, Tennessee's Upper Cumberland was, by all accounts, a rugged area of rivers and creeks, wooded plateaus, hills, and hollows. A raw-boned land, it attracted raw-boned people who, in turn, produced rugged preachers determined to "chase out Satan" and bring salvation's message to the area. Bud Robinson, a traveling preacher said to have preached more than 33,000 times, captured this "grab 'em by the throat" approach in his famous prayer: "Lord, give me a backbone as big as a saw log, and ribs like the sleepers under the church floor; put iron shoes on me, and galvanized breeches. And give me a rhinoceros' hide for a skin, and hang a wagon load of determination up in the gable end of my soul, and help me to sign the contract to fight the devil as long as I've got a fist, and bite him as long as I've got a tooth, and then gum him 'til I die. All this I ask for Christ's sake. Amen!"[1]

This forceful, even belligerent, approach to religion characterized much of the early efforts to establish churches in the region, and traces of it can still be found in parts of the area today.

Bands of Native American hunters no doubt conducted the first religious ceremonies in the Upper Cumberland, but the historical record is silent on these activities; even the archeological evidence of religious practices is sparse. According to one tantalizing legend, the "standing stone" monolith near the present city of Monterey in Putnam County had religious significance for Indians, but no proof of this has ever been found.

49

The religious history of the region really begins in the 1790s, when settlers from the scattered Kentucky and Tennessee communities and new migrants from east of the Appalachians moved to the upper reaches of the Cumberland River. By 1805, when the Treaty of Hopewell ended Cherokee claims to the region, hunters, farmers, and others were already living in the area that became Smith, Jackson, Overton, and White counties, and some of the people were already participating in efforts to bring organized religion to their new communities.

There is no agreement among historians on when settlers established the first church in the region, but virtually all contemporary records and historical commentaries agree that the frontier regions of Kentucky and Tennessee needed the civilizing influence religion offered. Threats from Indian raiding parties, outlaw bands, and the like were real and continued to be a menace into the nineteenth century. Dangers and hardships coarsened the men and women and gave them a reputation of being barbarians. One shocked visitor to the frontier described these people as rough-hewn types who lived in crude cabins built much like Indian wigwams and who depended more on hunting than on agriculture. For entertainment they "have frequent meetings for the purposes of gambling, fighting, and drinking. . . . They fight for the most trifling provocations, or even sometimes without any. . . . Their hands, teeth, head and feet are their weapons, not only boxing with their fists, . . . but also tearing, kicking, scratching, biting, gouging each others eyes out, . . . and doing their utmost to kill each other."[2]

Fortunately for the settlers trying to bring religion to the Upper Cumberland, their arrival coincided with the spread throughout Kentucky and Tennessee of a religious revival called the Second Awakening. Characterized by camp meetings—where people numbering in the thousands gathered to hear preaching for several days and nights—the revival was also noted for fervent sermons depicting the horrors of hell and the joys of heaven and "exercises"—emotional outbursts on the part of the listeners that took the form of jerking, dancing, running, holy laughing, and "treeing the devil." This Awakening began in Kentucky in the late 1790s and quickly spread into Sumner and Davidson counties in Tennessee and points eastward. This, in turn, led several religious bodies to start intense evangelizing in the area to bring the revival converts into their particular denomination.[3]

One of the earliest denominations to make its way into the Upper Cumberland was the Methodist Church. In the early nineteenth century, they were still relative newcomers to the American religious scene.

Arising in England in the 1730s, Methodism—so called because of their intense study of the Scriptures and their devotion to biblical rules or methods—was a reform movement, led by John and Charles Wesley, within the Anglican Church. The Methodists formed discussion groups that met in homes and attempted to get the church to return to the simplicity of the New Testament model. In personal matters, they stressed not only conversion but the striving for a higher level of sanctification that approached personal perfection. Soon banned from Anglican pulpits and churches, they fostered a mission to the colonies that produced American Methodists by the 1760s. With tensions between British and American Methodists high at the conclusion of the American Revolution, John Wesley assisted American Methodists in becoming a separate group in 1784.[4]

Under the vigorous leadership of Bishop Francis Asbury, Methodists established a system of circuit-riding preachers to bring their message to the isolated farmsteads and communities in Tennessee and Kentucky. The typical circuit rider was a young unmarried male, literate enough to read the Bible, who could put his worldly goods into his saddlebags, mount his horse, and ride hundreds of miles on his circuit through all types of weather, braving threats from brigands, unfriendly settlers, Indians, and wild beasts. He preached wherever he could find an audience—a house, a barn, a crossroads, or in the open air. Present at the first camp meetings, Methodists soon became a fixture at the annual revivals, and by the 1810s, they had turned the spontaneous camp meeting into the organized camp meeting that became the main means of Methodist recruitment for the next half century. After the Civil War, the church gradually turned the camp meeting into a "protracted meeting" (or revival), in which people no longer camped at the site but came to hear preaching for several nights in a row. This kind of revival became the model for membership drives used by Methodists, Baptists, Presbyterians, and other denominations in the region from then until the present.[5]

The Methodist circuit riders' sermons found a receptive audience among Upper Cumberland people. Rejecting John Calvin's and other Reformation leaders' contention that salvation was reserved for the few people whom God had chosen, the preachers told their listeners that salvation was available for anyone if the person would only repent of his sinful state, believe in Jesus Christ, and ask for God's forgiveness. Vivid descriptions of hell's torments bolstered the preachers' message of a loving, forgiving God who longed to be reunited with His children.

Temperance Hall Methodist Church in DeKalb County, Tennessee. Photo by the editors.

This emphasis on personal unworthiness and saving grace ignited spiritual fires in thousands of Methodist converts.[6]

As for their influence on social life, the Methodists' greatest efforts were attempts to eliminate alcohol consumption and activities such as gambling, dancing, and cursing. In 1844, the Northern Methodists' attacks on slaveholding split the denomination into Northern and Southern branches—a schism that would not be eliminated until the twentieth century.

Among noted Methodist ministers who visited the Upper Cumberland were Peter Cartwright and Lorenzo Dow. Later in the nineteenth century, Isaac Woodard in White County gained fame for debating preachers from other denominations, and in Fentress and Cumberland counties the circuit-riding F. A. Wright became legendary in the Methodist community. A Methodist church may have existed at Paron in Overton County as early as 1800. The Grassy Cove Methodist Church in present-day Cumberland County began in 1803. Around 1810, the Pleasant Grove Methodist Church organized in what later became Putnam County and was joined by the Salem Methodist Church in 1820. The formation of the Roaring River circuit in 1803 in Overton County attests to additional energies being exerted to bring the Upper Cumberland into the Methodist camp.[7]

Also reaping the benefits of the Second Awakening and making an early appearance in the Upper Cumberland were the Baptists. Despite later claims by Baptist leaders that they could trace their church all the way back to John the Baptist, this denomination arose in England in the early 1600s as an offshoot of the Puritan movement. The Puritans, attempting to purify the Church of England, had absorbed the teachings of the French theologian John Calvin, especially his contentions that the Christian church should be reformed on the New Testament model and that only the people elected by God for salvation would be saved. Influenced as well by the contemporary Anabaptists in the Netherlands, the English Baptists rejected infant baptism, embraced adult baptism, but retained most of the other Puritan doctrines. One division among them, however, was over Christ's atonement. General Baptists argued that Christ had died for everyone, and thus salvation was open to all. Particular Baptists—influenced by Calvin—contended that Christ had died only for those predestined by God for salvation. From the start, Baptists revealed a proclivity for division.[8]

After emerging in Rhode Island in the 1640s, American Baptist groups spread slowly into the other colonies, where they seldom found a warm welcome and often found hostility and even persecution. Aided somewhat in the South by the Great Awakening of the 1740s, they were still an insignificant group until the opening of Kentucky and Tennessee toward the end of the century. The new territories provided the Baptists an area where they were not in conflict with an established church, such as the Anglicans or the Congregationalists, and where no government would harass them, as had been the case in Virginia and other colonies. Congregational in governance and with no hierarchy to answer to, Baptists could establish new churches whenever and wherever they pleased. Ministers, moreover, were easy to find because the Baptists did not require their preachers to be educated or even literate. The ministers were men from their church who became convinced that they had a "calling" to preach, and who had convinced their fellow Baptists to license them to preach now and then ordain them when they had proved themselves. Unpaid, these preachers worked as farmers, merchants, and in other occupations during the week and brought the Lord's message to their neighbors on Sundays.[9]

Being uneducated, these men preached a simple message of hell and damnation versus heaven and eternal happiness. Hampered at first by their Puritan background and its stress on predestination, by the early 1800s preacher after preacher and congregation after congregation were edging toward a more inclusive salvation message that offered the hope of salvation for everyone who would believe, repent, and be baptized.

One of the earliest Baptist churches in the Upper Cumberland was Salem Baptist Church at Liberty in DeKalb County. Cantrell Bethel served as its pastor from its founding in 1809 until 1837. Another early church was Caney Fork Baptist in what later became Putnam County. In 1821 Baptists organized a church in White County and in the same year founded the Wolf River United Baptist Church in Overton County (now Pickett).[10]

The denomination's tendency to split brought new churches with different stands on doctrinal issues. By the end of the nineteenth century the region included Hardshell Baptists and Softshell Baptists, Freewill, Primitive, Missionary, and separate churches for the African American population. By the late twentieth century, in White County alone there was the Missionary Baptist Church, the Baptist Church of Christ, the Baptist Church of Christ Based on the Scriptures, the Free Will Christian Baptist Church, and the Two-Seed-in-the-Spirit Baptist Church.

Like the Methodists, with whom they were often at "war" for each other's adherents, the Baptists attempted to bring social order to the Upper Cumberland. In general, they opposed drinking alcohol, cursing, fighting, dancing, partying in any manner, gambling with cards and dice, horseracing, and cockfighting. Within each congregation, the leaders disciplined the members, sometimes to the point of excluding them from the church. The few extant church records list reasons for exclusion such as "communing with other denominations," "failure to attend church services," "taking part in shooting matches," "not paying debts," "producing an illegitimate child," and, on several occasions, "committing adultery." Dancing and drinking could also get a member kicked out.[11]

Presbyterians, who actually started the camp meetings in Kentucky and Tennessee, made a discernable but less obvious impact on the Upper Cumberland than did the Methodists and the Baptists. Originating in Scotland and England during the sixteenth-century Reformation, the Presbyterians attempted to restore the church to the biblical model, in which church government was in the hands of elders (presbyters). Under the leadership of John Knox, they became Scotland's dominant Christian body and constituted one of the main lines of the Puritan movement in England. They largely embraced John Calvin's Reformed doctrines, especially those emphasizing predestination in salvation matters. Some Presbyterians arrived in the American colonies during Puritan times, but the vast majority came with the Scots-Irish immigration during the early 1700s. Settling in the back country of Pennsylvania, Virginia, and the Carolinas, they began to send and support ministers in Kentucky and Tennessee, establishing some of the earliest churches in the region and also founding some of the earliest schools.[12]

Closely supervised by their hierarchy of sessions, presbyteries, and synods, Presbyterian ministers had to be not only pure in doctrine, but college-educated. The latter requirement made the men intellectually vigorous but did not prepare them to reach the largely uneducated frontier people. Almost by accident—or by the will of the Holy Spirit, according to the ministers—they found access to the frontier mind by way of the camp meeting revivals, where, often joined by Methodist and Baptist ministers, they put aside their knowledge of Hebrew and Greek and appealed to their audience by means of emotion-filled sermons concerning hell and heaven. James McCready, Barton Stone, and other Presbyterian preachers enjoyed enormous success at Cane Ridge, Kentucky, and other camp meetings, but the ministers' tendency to ignore predestination and other traditional doctrines and to embrace the "exercises" produced great unease among the more staid Presbyterians east of the mountains. Ordination by frontier presbyteries of men who failed to meet the denomination's educational requirements caused further problems. Within a few years of his great success at Cane Ridge, Barton Stone renounced his Presbyterian ties and began his own Christian movement to end denominations and restore religion to its earliest simplicity. In 1810, denominational issues of doctrine and education remained unresolved to the point that the Presbyterians split, with several of the Tennessee and Kentucky presbyteries withdrawing to form the Cumberland Presbyterian Church. Another schism came when Presbyterians split over the slavery issue, producing the northern-based Presbyterian Church, USA, and the southern-based Presbyterian Church, U.S.[13]

Although the earliest church in White County was a Presbyterian one established at Cherry Creek in 1800, the denomination developed slowly in the Upper Cumberland. Fewer than a dozen churches had been founded before the Civil War, and these were largely churches set up by the Cumberland Presbyterians. A growth spurt came after the war, however, with the Cookeville Cumberland Presbyterians forming their church in 1867 and enjoying steady membership growth. Rural communities such as Dry Valley and Mount Herman in Putnam County established Cumberland churches, and by the 1890s Cookeville had Rolling Chapel, a black Cumberland Presbyterian congregation.

In the midst of this expansion, a crisis arose for local Presbyterians in 1906 when the Cumberland Presbyterian general assembly voted to unite with the Presbyterian Church, USA—the northern branch. Several Upper Cumberland congregations refused to give up their Cumberland Presbyterian identity, especially since union meant having fellowship with Yankees! Pro-union and anti-union factions sprang up in the Cookeville Cumberland Presbyterian congregation, causing a split that led the pro-union group to establish its own church as a member of the Presbyterian Church, USA.[14]

Having a major influence on the region throughout most of the nineteenth century and even greater influence in the twentieth was the group called, at various times, Christians, Disciples of Christ, Churches of Christ, and Christian Churches (Independent). What all members had in common was the Restoration movement that began in Kentucky, Tennessee, Ohio, and western Pennsylvania in the early 1800s. Led by Barton Stone, the former Presbyterian minister, and father and son Thomas and Alexander Campbell, the Restorationists attempted to get beyond the rampant denominationalism of the era and restore the fellowship of the earliest Christians and recreate the primitive Christian church. Stone, in his "Christian only" movement in Kentucky and Tennessee, strove to eliminate denominations, church hierarchies, and creeds and to establish fellowship with anyone who professed to be a Christian. The Campbells, particularly Alexander, put more stress on restoring the primitive church, believing that the New Testament contained the blueprint for the kind of church that God wanted Christians to have.[15]

The Restoration movement was, in part, a rejection of the emotional excesses found at the camp meetings and in many frontier congregations. Alexander Campbell, indeed, endorsed the inductive reasoning associated with Francis Bacon and John Locke as a tool to discover God's directions for His church in the New Testament. In the 1820s, while still loosely associated with Baptists in western Pennsylvania and western Virginia, Campbell began publishing the *Christian Baptist*, a journal that became the major outlet for Restoration views, and, after breaking with the Baptists in 1831, continued defining the Restoration stance in his journal *Millennial Harbinger*.[16]

Assisted by the Restoration evangelist Walter Scott, Alexander Campbell touted a simple Christianity based on the Bible and the Bible only, as summed up in the phrase, "Where the Scriptures speak we speak, where the Scriptures are silent we are silent." This meant that the Restoration church was to have no name except the church of Christ or church of God, was to be governed by a plurality of male elders assisted by male and female deacons, was to celebrate the Lord's Supper each Sunday, and was to have preaching done by the elders or other male members.[17] Membership was by means of a baptism that fully immersed the adult believer under water. Walter Scott's contribution was his "five finger" exercise that laid out the path to salvation: belief that Jesus is the Christ, repentance, and baptism for the remission of sins on the part of the individual, and then forgiveness by God and the gift of the Holy Spirit and eternal life by God. (Noting that people usually do not have six fingers, Scott combined the last two into one "finger" of his exercise.)[18]

The Restoration movement gained more momentum in 1832 when the Stoneites joined with the Campbell group to form the Disciples of Christ. Here was a vigorous alternative to people troubled by the doctrinal disputes that continually beset the Baptists, Presbyterians, and other denominations, and its simple, down-to-earth approach to Christianity had wide appeal, particularly in Kentucky and Tennessee.[19]

River baptism in Cumberland County, Tennessee. Courtesy of the Tennessee State Library and Archives.

The earliest Restoration church in the Upper Cumberland was the Rock Springs Church of the Barton Stone "Christians only" variety and was established in what became Clay County in 1805. Smyrna Church of Christ in Putnam County dates back to 1815. The first black congregation was formed at Free Hill in Clay County in 1816. In the 1820s, converts set up additional churches in White and Jackson counties.

As years passed, though, the movement found neither the unity among Christians that Barton Stone sought nor the primitive church for which Alexander Campbell strove. Instead of unity came division. By the 1850s and 1860s, congregations were splitting over matters such as support for missionary societies and instrumental music as an aid for worship services. Whether or not to have Sunday schools, to have salaried preachers, or to drink from one cup or many smaller cups at the Lord's Supper were other issues that divided the group. By the early twentieth century, the Restoration movement had splintered into the more liberal organ-playing and missionary-society-supporting Disciples of Christ and the more conservative noninstrument and antimissionary-society Churches of Christ. By and large, the Upper Cumberland churches were of the latter group. Adding further irony to the unity goal, the

Disciples of Christ split again in the 1940s and 1950s, leaving a remnant of the Disciples group and creating the separate Christian Churches (Independent). By the 1960s, all three fellowships arising from the Restoration movement had a footing in the Upper Cumberland.[20]

Concerning membership, the gravest threat to Upper Cumberland churches in the nineteenth century was the Civil War. The war not only suspended civil government in the region and forced schools to close, but it greatly disrupted religious activities. Attendance fell as young men went off to fight and as ministers either joined them on the battlefields or became military chaplains. On the home front, politics sometimes split congregations, either forcing the minority out of the church building or causing the congregation to stop services altogether. The lawlessness in the Upper Cumberland, furthermore, did not spare the churches. Outlaw and guerrilla bands did not hesitate to waylay people on their way to and from church, and on occasion disrupted services while in progress. After the war, bitter memories of wartime incidents prevented some congregations from reuniting or having fellowship with one another.[21]

After the war and for a period that lasted at least into the second half of the twentieth century, the four major groups—Methodists, Baptists, Presbyterians, and the Church of Christ membership—almost totally dominated spiritual matters in the region and played major roles in shaping the Upper Cumberland's social and cultural life. During this time, the Methodists split nationally with the rise of the Holiness movement, but when groups such as the Nazarene Church arose from the Holiness movement, they endorsed rather than challenged the moral code associated with the major groups. Likewise, when the Pentecostal movement created the various churches of God, in the early 1900s, and later introduced several churches into the area, the social and cultural impact of the Pentecostal Church differed little from that of the earlier denominations.

The most significant impact that organized religion had on the Upper Cumberland, other than a spiritual one, was its imposition of a code of conduct for "respectable" people. This code was not unique to the region and, indeed, was in evidence throughout the nation in the late nineteenth century. Sometimes called the Victorian code or Victorian morality, it had been shaped and refined for decades by Congregationalists, Presbyterians, Baptists, Methodists, and other major denominations to provide guidelines for the American people, who sought to live moral and respectable lives. With rare exception, the Upper Cumberland churches of all persuasions endorsed these guidelines and, at times, made them even more rigorous.

In addition to obeying the Ten Commandments, area residents who wished to retain their respectability (or gain it) did the following: joined a church, attended services regularly, supported the preacher, refrained from drinking alcohol, stopped making alcohol, opposed individuals and businesses that manufactured or sold alcohol, stopped gambling on horse races, cockfighting, and the like, condemned fornication, and ceased cursing (at least in public). Some of the stricter groups banned makeup and short hair for women, forbade dancing and other "frivolous" activities, and in the twentieth century, frowned on movie-going.[22]

This is not to imply that the religious groups promoting this code were always successful. Parts of the region—such as Putnam County's "bloody eighth" district, where feuding and murder seemed almost recreational activities—remained immune to the code's influence. At times in the late nineteenth and early twentieth centuries, moonshiners flourished, bootleggers provided liquor, gamblers plied their trade, and even a few prostitutes provided their services. Area residents danced and attended movies, and women wore makeup and, in the Roaring Twenties especially, cropped their hair and raised the hemlines on their skirts and dresses. Rebellion against the code was found in virtually every community. And even the church services occasionally came under attack. In rural areas, especially, many of the adult men and teenage boys stayed outside the church building when services were under way. They gossiped, told jokes, chewed tobacco, smoked, whittled wood, and, occasionally, drank alcohol. The young men often disturbed the young women inside by standing outside the building windows and calling the women by name or nickname, throwing things at them, and, in general, trying to get their attention. More violent incidents sometimes occurred when the young blades on the outside attacked a man sitting too close to a woman claimed by one of the outsiders. "Disturbing religious services" was one of the more frequent charges sheriffs brought against those they arrested.[23]

But the church groups promoting the code of conduct fought the "rebels" tirelessly, even to the point of becoming involved in politics to get laws passed to ban alcohol, close down gambling dens, and stop businesses from opening on Sundays. Not until the 1960s would the moral code begin to fray at the edges and a more liberal code of conduct develop in the region.

Dinner on the grounds at a White County, Tennessee, church. Courtesy of the Tennessee State Library and Archives.

The other major impact of organized religion was to help create a sense of community and at the same time to hold the community together. Elementary schools, which dotted the countryside, held fundraising pie suppers, cakewalks, carnivals, and such, bringing the community people together and creating bonds. The churches forged a similar community bond by not only providing the socializing attached to church services but holding picnics, dinners on the grounds (where each family brought a prepared dish), revivals, and "decoration" days at the church cemeteries (where people gathered once a year to clean the graves and put flowers on them). People, regardless of religious affiliation, attended these activities and events, where they renewed friendships, welcomed newcomers, visited with neighbors and relatives, and, if they were single, found and courted potential mates.

By the 1950s and 1960s this sense of community was eroding throughout the Upper Cumberland. Counties consolidated their schools, closing of most of the rural institutions. New economic opportunities away from the Upper Cumberland lured young people especially and, sometimes, entire families out of the region. Church membership suffered, occasionally to the point that the congregation ceased to hold services.

In Cookeville, where new factories arrived in the 1950s and 1960s and where Tennessee Polytechnic Institute evolved into a university, the new factory jobs and administrative positions and the increased student enrollments and new professors brought other religious groups into the Upper Cumberland, further eroding the dominance of the major groups. The Roman Catholic Church had enough adherents that, in 1949, Catholics began holding regular services. Three years later, they had a sanctuary on Washington Avenue. The Episcopalians arrived in Cookeville in 1949 as well and, by 1958, had built a church a few blocks from the Catholic structure. By 1954, the city's centennial, Cookeville not only had thriving Methodist, Baptist, Presbyterian, and Church of Christ congregations, but had an Assemblies of God Church, a Church of God of Prophecy, a Church of God (Anderson, Indiana), and a Church of God (Cleveland, Tennessee). All three varieties of Presbyterians were represented. The Catholic Church, the Episcopal Church, the Church of the Nazarene, and one small Pilgrim Holiness Church also had a presence.[24]

During the 1970s and until the end of the century, the outward flow of people from the region's rural communities continued, but the populations of Cookeville and several other communities increased. The completion of Interstate 40 in Putnam and Cumberland counties, particularly, caused a growth spurt, and the building of resort communities such as Fairfield Glade and Lake Tansi in Cumberland county brought not only more people to the region, but religiously diverse people. By the 1980s, for example, Mennonite groups had arrived in Fentress and Overton counties, and several regional communities had facilities for the Church of Jesus Christ of Latter Day Saints—the Mormons. Jehovah's Witnesses, the Seventh-Day Adventists, and the Unity Church had built churches as well. Several Pentecostal churches, including the rapidly expanding Trinity Assembly in Algood, found fertile missionary ground in the region. In Fairfield Glade, the United Church of Christ (the remnant of the old Puritan Congregationalist Church) had a new congregation. Christian Scientists, followers of Mary Baker Eddy, had a reading room and meeting place in Cookeville. As the new millennium approached, Jews for the first time in people's memories gathered in Putnam County to hold services. On the Tennessee Technological University campus, Muslims met each Friday to conduct their services as well.

From a wilderness to a sparsely settled frontier area, from a rural community region to one increasingly dominated by Cookeville, the largest city, the Upper Cumberland has endured significant changes over the past two hundred years, and this is certainly true in its reli-

Putnam County, Tennessee, sign demonstrates the diversity of belief today. Photo by the editors.

gious practices. At first dominated by the Methodist, Baptist, Presbyterian, and Church of Christ versions of Christianity to the point that these groups could—and did—set the moral and social tone for the Upper Cumberland, the region had developed much more religious diversity by the 1960s and 1970s. When this happened, new challenges to the established religious groups arose and began to make inroads into their dominance over social habits. While the churches had once united to keep liquor establishments out of the region, for example, by the 1990s, Jackson County and Clay County had liquor stores and Cookeville and Crossville sold liquor by the drink. A growing number of nonreligious people voted for these changes, but so did a vastly increased number of people who belonged to religious organizations that embraced liquor drinking in moderation. Another example of change is in Sunday-closing laws. They were once ubiquitous and vigorously endorsed by the churches, but they had disappeared by the new millennium. Churches in the region still prohibit their members from engaging in various practices such as dancing, but their control—if not their influence—over nonmembers' behavior has virtually vanished.

By the last quarter of the twentieth century, many of the regional churches had to deal with a paradox: their membership was steady or in some instances even growing, but their influence over their communities was waning. To meet this challenge to their moral hegemony, some congregations assumed a "circle the wagons" stance, in which they increasingly looked only to the needs of their own members and withdrew from community activities. But others, in recent years, have launched vigorous efforts to reach out to the unchurched—not by mounting more revivals and knocking on more doors, but by taking meals to the elderly, providing clothing to those in need, caring for the sick, and doing other kinds of social service. What changes this new emphasis will have on the region's religious development only the future can reveal.

NOTES

1. Quoted in William Lynwood Montell, *Upper Cumberland Country* (Jackson: University Press of Mississippi, 1993): 90.
2. Fortescue Cuming, in Arthur K. Moore, *The Frontier Mind: A Cultural Analysis of the Kentucky Frontiersman* (Lexington: The University of Kentucky Press, 1957): 54.
3. Sydney E. Ahlstrom, *A Religious History of the American People* (New Haven and London: Yale University Press, 1972): 429–55.
4. Ibid., 324–26.
5. Ibid., 436–39.
6. Ibid., 438.
7. Robert L. and Mary Eldridge, *Bicentennial Echoes of the History of Overton County Tennessee, 1776–1976* (Livingston, Tenn.: Enterprise Printing Co., 1976): 112; Stephen Mansfield and George Grant, *Faithful Volunteers: The History of Religion in Tennessee* (Nashville: Cumberland House, 1997): 66, 73; Peter Cartwright, *Autobiography of Peter Cartwright, Backwoods Preacher*, W. P. Strickland, ed. (Cincinnati: Cranston and Curtis, n.d.): 91–126.
8. Ahlstrom, 171–73.
9. Ibid., 442–43.
10. For church establishments, see Mary Jean DeLozier, *Putnam County, Tennessee, 1850–1970* (Nashville: McQuiddy Publishing, 1979): 80.
11. Montell, 96.
12. Ahlstrom, 265–67.
13. Cartwright, 29–56; Paul Conkin, *Cane Ridge: America's Pentecost* (Madison: University of Wisconsin Press, 1989): 164–78; Richard T. Hughes, *Reviving the Ancient Faith: The Story of Churches of Christ in America* (Grand Rapids, Mich.: William B. Eerdman's Publishing Co., 1996): 92–116.
14. For more details concerning this, see DeLozier, 186–87.
15. Hughes, 47–63.
16. Ibid., 21.
17. Both Stone and Campbell believed that the New Testament authorized female deacons, but very few of the early Restoration churches had women

serving in this capacity. By post–Civil War times, the deacons were invariably male. For Campbell's view on church equality, see Robert Richardson, *Memoirs of Alexander Campbell* (Germantown, Tenn.: Religious Book Service, n.d.), vol. II: 126.

18. Ibid., 52.

19. Ahlstrom, 447–52.

20. Ibid., 822–23.

21. F. A. Wright, *Autobiography of F. A. Wright of the Holston Conference, M.E. Church*, J. C. Wright, ed. (Cincinnati: Cranston and Curtis, 1896): 41–51.

22. For the moral code in national context, see Larry Whiteaker, *Seduction, Prostitution, and Moral Reform in New York, 1830–1860* (New York & London: Garland Publishing, Inc., 1997): 159.

23. DeLozier, 199; Montell, 95–96.

24. DeLozier, 276–77.

Chapter 4

ASHES TO ASHES

Burial Upper Cumberland Style

RICHARD C. FINCH

"Tomb rocks"—a folk expression that can still be heard among old timers in the Upper Cumberland region—can be very telling of a region's people and their social development. New England is well known for its piously erudite slate gravestones somewhat grimly decorated with skulls, soul-effigies, hourglasses, and other symbols of mortality. Such stones accurately reflect eighteenth-century Calvinist attitudes. The tombstones found along the foothills of the Cumberland Plateau are very different, but no less interesting, and just as revealing of the character and social evolution of the Cumberland people. The following observations result from visiting nearly 2,000 graveyards in a swath along the western Cumberland Plateau and adjacent Highland Rim from southernmost Kentucky to northern Alabama.

The earliest graves to be found in organized burying grounds in the Cumberland region are generally marked with nothing more than rude fieldstones as headstones, commonly paired with smaller rocks as footstones. These tomb rocks bear no inscriptions, and serve only to indicate the grave locations. The rocks selected may be any shape, depending on what was conveniently at hand, but slab-shaped rocks were preferred. Chattanooga Shale—an extremely fissile black shale—was widely used in graveyards along the Highland Rim where it crops out. Because of the ease with which it splits into flagstones, it is locally known as slate rock. This same characteristic that made it a natural choice for grave markers renders it highly susceptible to deterioration by weathering, and thus a poor choice for markers in the long run.

As the region became more heavily settled, gravestones were more formalized. Inscribed stones dated as early as 1817 have been observed in the Rocky River Valley. By the 1830s, shaped and engraved markers had become the rule for all but, apparently, the poorest families. These cut stones were not all professionally engraved. Some roughly shaped and crudely lettered headstones are the works of amateurs—perhaps friends or family members of the deceased. Others are clearly the work of practiced stonecutters, local artisans such as Lee Moles of Overton County, whose distinctive lettering styles, original spellings, and unusual decorative devices can often be found in several cemeteries within a particular area. Some of these men cut stones only as a sideline or public service, but by the mid-1800s there were several full-time professional stonecutters in the Cumberland region of Tennessee. Paramount among these was a stonecutter who served the Sparta-Quebeck area. This artist was highly skilled and prolific. Over a period of several decades he turned out hundreds—perhaps several thousand—of finely shaped and neatly engraved sandstone markers. He employed a wide variety of classic upright tombstone shapes and a number of decorative motifs. Among the latter are asterisks, palm trees, and simple geometric marks.[1]

The materials carved by these Tennessee stonecutters were, with rare exception, locally quarried, and therefore were limestone or sandstone. Where it was available, sandstone appears to have been preferred. This may be attributable to superior resistance to weathering and, perhaps, because at certain outcrops sandstone could be found deposited in thin, smooth-surfaced beds. Limestone markers are generally thicker stones, thin-bedded limestone being uncommon in this region. Furthermore, limestone bedding planes are rarely very flat, so limestone markers would have required more dressing before being engraved.

The overall favorite source of tomb rocks was the widespread sandstone now known to geologists as the Hartselle Formation. Indeed, as shall be seen, the outcrop limits of the Hartselle exerted a geologic control of the development of the region's most characteristic grave style, the "comb grave."

Graveyards of the Cumberland region are noteworthy for the variety of covered graves that have been found here. Even before the profession of stonecutting became well established in the Highland Rim–Cumberland Plateau region, a distinctive style of grave covering had made its appearance. In Overton County's Roaring River Cemetery, a rough-hewn squarish block of sandstone dated 1822 stands at the head of two long slabs of the same rock. These slabs lean together like

Comb graves in the Okalona Cemetery in Overton County, Tennessee. Photo by the editors.

the sides of a puptent or comb of a roof, covering the grave of J.H. Bilbrey. This is the earliest noted example of what the old timers call a "comb grave." A comb grave at picturesque Mt. Pisgah Methodist Church near Quebeck is dated 1817, but the style of the headstone suggests that the marker and cover were erected some decades later.

Comb graves are clearly the most outstanding style of folk grave to develop in the region. A typical tomb consists of two flat sandstone slabs leaned together to form a protective roof above the full length of the grave. Comb graves in the Rock Island–McMinnville area (White and Warren counties) employ triangular end stones underneath the comb to support the side slabs. Combs here are rarely accompanied by head-stones, and, in fact, are generally devoid of any inscription. The grave-yard visitor is left to speculate on the who and when of these interments. A few of these combs are constructed with limestone slabs, especially in the southernmost part of the area.

From Rock Island north, most combs are accompanied by an en-graved headstone, but in the Sparta area a number of cemeteries feature combs with the inscription cut on one of the side slabs. Davis Cemetery in Scotts Gulf seems to be unique in featuring side-scribed combs en-graved in cursive writing. (This small graveyard is also the site of a unique mushroom-shaped marker at the head of a comb grave.) The side-scribed combs seem to be a transitional form between the unmarked combs to the south and the fully monumented combs to the north. The reader interested in seeing both side-scribed and normally marked combs should visit Mt. Pisgah Cemetery, one of the largest and finest assemblages of comb graves extant.

Farther to the north, in Overton County, the comb-grave tradition reached it apogee. Although the updated combs of the McMinnville area somehow impart a feeling of greater age, the comb style may have begun in Overton County with the 1822 burial in Roaring River Cemetery. Here the custom seems to have been almost universally accepted by the late nineteenth century. Certainly the custom survived the longest here, the most recent combs being erected in 1968 in a small cemetery east of Jamestown. It was in Overton County, around Allred, that the most original variation of the comb style evolved, the truncated triangle style.

The "truncated triangle style"—for want of a better name—features both head- and footstones, tied together by a long iron rod. This tie rod eliminates the need for the triangular end stones used in other combs, directly supporting one of the side slabs, with the remaining slab (generally the left-hand slab) leaning on the first. Both the head- and footstones are shaped like tall isosceles triangles with the uppermost corners cut off. The only differences between the two stones are

Comb graves in the France Cemetery in White County, Tennessee. Photo by the editors.

Box graves, Falling Springs Cemetery, Overton County, Tennessee. Photo by the editors.

the greater height of the headstone and, of course, the fact that it is lettered. Viewed in the dusky light of the setting sun, the stark, harsh geometry of the comb graves en masse creates a haunting, moody scene, a sort of Tennessee Stonehenge.

Who cut the first of these simple but effectively shaped stones, and when, and why, are unknown to me. Much of the credit for popularizing this style must go to the Vaughn family, who, for three generations, cut and engraved stones from their quarry in the Hartselle bench above Allred. Bill Vaughn, who resided in Livingston, cut his last stone around 1935; before that he, his father, and his grandfather supplied markers for many hundreds of persons in Overton and surrounding counties. Most, if not all, were of the truncated triangle style, and all were skillfully lettered in a handsome block print chiseled by hand, without benefit of stencil. The Vaughns had perfected their style and stuck by it. A "comb set" sold for $30, according to Vaughn.

Not many combs were erected after Bill Vaughn quit the business, but a few combs in the Allred area bear dates in the 1940s. These stones have the appearance of work by the Vaughn family, perhaps indicating that the family's work was carried on by apprentices, or was simply copied because it was admired. The last combs were erected in 1948, 1956, and 1958 at cemeteries in western Overton County, and in 1969 at Stockton Cemetery in Fentress County.

Some 257 graveyards with combs were plotted for this study. Of the many hundreds of comb graves observed, most were constructed of sandstone from the Hartselle Formation. Although the combs are not as widespread as the Hartselle itself, one can see that their distribution is related to the presence of this formation. The comb graves at Riverside Cemetery in McMinnville, at Viola, and at Pelham are made of limestone slabs, reflecting a southward decrease in the content of the Hartselle and a corresponding increase in shale and limestone content. This decline in the utility of the Hartselle as a quarry stone may well be a factor in the failure of the comb style to propagate farther southward.

Other materials have also been used to construct combs. At Eureka Church of Christ on Highway 30, east of McMinnville, is the "ritz" of combs, made of striped marble. Quite a few instances of metal combs are known, generally made of corrugated "tin" roofing—probably used as a cheaper alternative to cut stones, or possibly erected in the waning phases of the custom when local stonecutters no longer worked with Hartselle. One notable exception to these speculations is a row of neat metal comb graves in Cunningham Cemetery south of Cookeville. Here, the combs were fashioned of galvanized sheet metal, with seams meticulously riveted and caulked with tar. These carefully wrought combs were not cheap substitutes.

Coffin-shaped stones in an Overton County, Tennessee, cemetery. Photo by the editors.

There are also two known instances of concrete combs. One is found at Okolona Cemetery in Overton County—a cemetery notable for its great variety of grave types. It was erected in 1958, a time when Hartselle sandstone slabs were no longer being cut. The other is found near the community of Curlee, in Cannon County, south of Readyville. It was erected in 1911, but the cemetery is one of the few comb sites well removed from the Hartselle outcrop, which probably accounts for its use of concrete.

Three questions are inescapable: how did the comb tradition arise, what purpose do the combs serve, and do comb graves exist anywhere else outside this region? Only the last question can be answered with certainty: a single comb grave exists near Denton, Texas, and at least one graveyard with combs at the Witt Springs community, Arkansas; and an area of comb graves has been found in northern Alabama. Comb graves are also known from at least three graveyards in the area of the Cumberland River just west and northwest of Williamsburg, Kentucky. The Cumberland region of Tennessee, however, has no significant competition for the comb grave championship.

NOTE

1. For more information about comb graves, see Brent Cantrell, "Traditional Grave Structures on the Eastern Highland Rim," *Tennessee Folklore Society Bulletin* LXVII:3 (October 1981): 93–103.

Chapter 5

"FEVERS RAN HIGH"

The Civil War in the Cumberland

JAMES B. JONES JR.

Enthusiasm ran high in the Upper Cumberland in 1861, leading to public brawls over secession. In June, Judge Guild of Overton County called for immediate hanging of Union sympathizers. In July, four men in Jamestown assaulted a well-known Unionist.[1] When Overton County Judge Horace Maynard attempted to speak against secession at the Livingston courthouse, a mob threatened his life, forcing him to flee. As he left, Maynard promised he would denounce secession the next day in Monroe. Pro-Confederates said that if he tried to speak, the audience would be forcibly dispersed. Maynard spent the next day rounding up Union sympathizers, and by the appointed time, roughly three hundred armed partisans showed up displaying the Stars and Stripes. Speaking against secession with no interruption, Maynard promised to continue the cause for the Union throughout the region.[2] Fifty-four Gordonsville women indicated their pro-Union feelings in a postsecession petition to Military Governor Andrew Johnson in November 1862: "We . . . offer our services for the purpose of aiding to put down the rebellion and will be very much obliged if you will supply us with arms and if you will please send them immediately[;] if not we will arm ourselves and bushwhack it."[3] Amanda McDowell of the Cherry Creek Community in White County made a more thoughtful commentary. On May 4, 1861, she confided in her diary that there would be "many a divided family in this once happy Union. There will be father against son, and brother against brother. O, God! . . . That men should in their blindness rush so rashly to ruin, and . . . drag with them so many thousands of innocent and ignorant victims! . . . [I]n my feeble opinion they will have cause to repent their rashness."[4]

Fighting in the Upper Cumberland has largely been overlooked by historians, who prefer to study larger battles such as Shiloh, Chickamauga, and Franklin. Yet the war experienced in the region was just as intense, and many wounds inflicted by the conflict fester even today. Though no large-scale battles occurred, many small actions were conducted by local guerrilla forces. Often, it did not matter for whom they fought, because they sought nothing more than plunder. Murders, lacking the sanction of military necessity, were a common occurrence. Civilians suffered a host of privations at the hands of Federal and Confederate troops. As Amanda Meredith Hill of Sparta later remembered, "[S]oldiers both Confederate and Yankee would take anything they wanted without paying for it."[5] War ravaged the landscape, destroying some of the region's finest homes and businesses. Rebels razed the Bon Air spa in White County because its owner had opposed secession. In the Upper Cumberland, the war literally pitted brothers against brothers, as in the case of Confederate guerrilla Champ Ferguson and his brother James, who fought for the Federal army.

In August 1861, the Confederate congress passed The Alien Enemies Act with the intention of quelling internal rebellion. Anyone refusing to recognize the Confederacy and retaining allegiance to the Union was an enemy alien. "Tories" were given forty days to join the South or leave. If they remained but refused to support the Confederacy, they could be deported and their property confiscated.[6] J. D. Hale of Overton County condemned secession; his life was threatened as a result. He first sought refuge in the Wolf River Valley near Pall Mall, but eventually moved into loyalist Kentucky. His sixteen-year-old son, however, was taken prisoner by Confederates and Hale's property, including a slave, was confiscated.[7]

Union sympathizers crossed the line into Kentucky, enlisting in the Federal army at Camp Dick Robinson. "Many of them had squirrel rifles and shotguns; many others were unarmed. Their clothes were in tatters, and their feet bleeding from cuts received on rocks in the mountains." In September, Brigadier General George H. Thomas took over training and organizing troops there.[8]

Confederate partisans faced similar difficulties. In October 1861, twenty-one citizens from Livingston wrote Governor Isham G. Harris to express their fear regarding Federal guerrillas, who were so brutal they were "taking scalps and plunder as trophies":

> [W]e are left at the mercy of our foes, a portion of whom are still about Albany, Ky., daily scouting along our border, and this, too, after these recent visits to Burkesville and Albany, which have so stirred up our enemy as to cause him to seek the very first opportunity for retaliation. Notwithstanding we have sent out nearly 1,000 fighting men, embracing nearly every man capable of bearing arms who could be spared from home under any ordinary state of the warfare, we are thus driven to the necessity of raising more men to save our homes and property.[9]

Men and women from all walks of life found themselves caught up in the conflict. Impartiality proved impossible. Gainesboro lawyer John P. Murray eagerly supported the Confederacy, recruiting a regiment that trained at Camp Zollicoffer three miles south of Livingston.[10] Governor Isham G. Harris commissioned Stokely Huddleston of Livingston at the rank of colonel, ordering him to raise and train troops at Camp Myers near Monroe. Fentress County, which had voted against secession, soon had a Confederate training facility, Camp McGinnis, established in the Wolf River Valley to suppress Union activity. Fentress County was crucial to the Confederates because it marked the point of a possible Union invasion via Albany, Kentucky.[11]

Brigadier General Felix K. Zollicoffer advised Adjutant General Sam Jones about the strategic importance of the Upper Cumberland. He noted that the principal gaps in the Cumberland Mountains led directly into the vicinity of Camp McGinnis, while the plateau offered thirty to forty miles of broad, flat land. "There are innumerable bridle-paths intervening between Cumberland Gap and Camp McGinnis. My purpose is to form a chain of infantry posts at Cumberland Gap, Big Creek Gap, Camp McGinnis and Livingston, for which I have 33 infantry companies, all but one regiment very raw troops."[12]

With fortified defensive positions lacking, Zollicoffer's concern that Union forces would attack was underscored by Tennessee's first military engagement of the Civil War. On September 29, 1861, Confederates encamped in what was then Fentress County. Just days before, they had raided the saltpeter works in Celina, Kentucky, retreating to Tennessee with their loot. Resting near the Methodist Church at Travisville, the Rebels believed they had evaded Federal forces. Colonel William

Hoskins of the Twelfth Kentucky Cavalry sent Captain John A. Morrison on a reconnaissance mission to determine the location and strength of the Confederate marauders. Once their numbers were known, Captain Morrison, Lieutenant Silas Adams, and men from the Hustonville Home Guards rode off for Travisville. Morrison surprised the force of roughly one hundred Rebels and ordered them to surrender. A skirmish ensued, resulting in four dead Confederates. One of Morrison's men, Private Thomas Huddleston, captured two prisoners and two horses, "after accomplishing which, to use his own expression, 'He looked for more, but they had all fled.'" Rattled Confederates broke ranks and retreated into the hills, abandoning the gunpowder they had stolen.[13]

There are interesting aspects of this first military engagement in Tennessee. The two men captured by Private Huddleston were treated with a leniency uncommon later in the war. "The prisoners were brought this side of the line, when, after taking a solemn obligation to prove faithful to the United States Government, they were released."[14] More important, Captain Morrison's infantry literally represented the first Union troops on Tennessee soil after secession. This occurred before Forts Henry and Donelson fell. Perhaps most significant, the scale of the affair was typical of the Upper Cumberland theater of war.[15]

Federals probed Confederate defenses. An intelligence report on November 11, 1861, noted the number of Rebel camps and unit strength: "[F]orces consisted of two regiments infantry and about 650 to 700 cavalry, the same that had heretofore been stationed at Camp McGinnis, in Fentress County (the cavalry), and at Camp Myers, in Overton County, near the old town of Monroe, two regiments infantry, under Cols. Stanton and Murray."[16] Confederates "armed with stolen Home Guard muskets, with pistols, shot-guns, common rifles, &c., just what they can lay their hands upon," grew alarmed when they heard about Federal reconnaissance "moving upon them with a large force, and the infantry regiments fled precipitately" until they reached Camp Zollicoffer. Rebels "talked boldly" until they realized the Union force was nearby. Cavalry units retreated to Camp McGinnis, building obstacles on the Jamestown road, but no combat resulted from the reconnaissance.[17] Not all Federal intelligence was genuine, however, and rumors ran rampant. Throughout Camp Dick Robinson, it was said that troops at Camp McGinnis, referred to as the "Bull Pups," were actually convicts released from the Tennessee State Penitentiary to fight for the Rebel cause.[18]

As Rebels drilled in Overton and Fentress counties, they learned to improvise because the Confederate governments in Nashville and Richmond could not provide necessary supplies. Spencer Bowen Talley, who was stationed at both "Camp Jollicopper [sic]" and Camp Myers, remembered "we had no arms save a few old squirrel rifles and an occasional pistol, though most all the boys had huge butcher knives. . . . We spent only about two hours in the forenoon and two hours in the afternoon drilling. So the rest of our time was spent in reading and writing

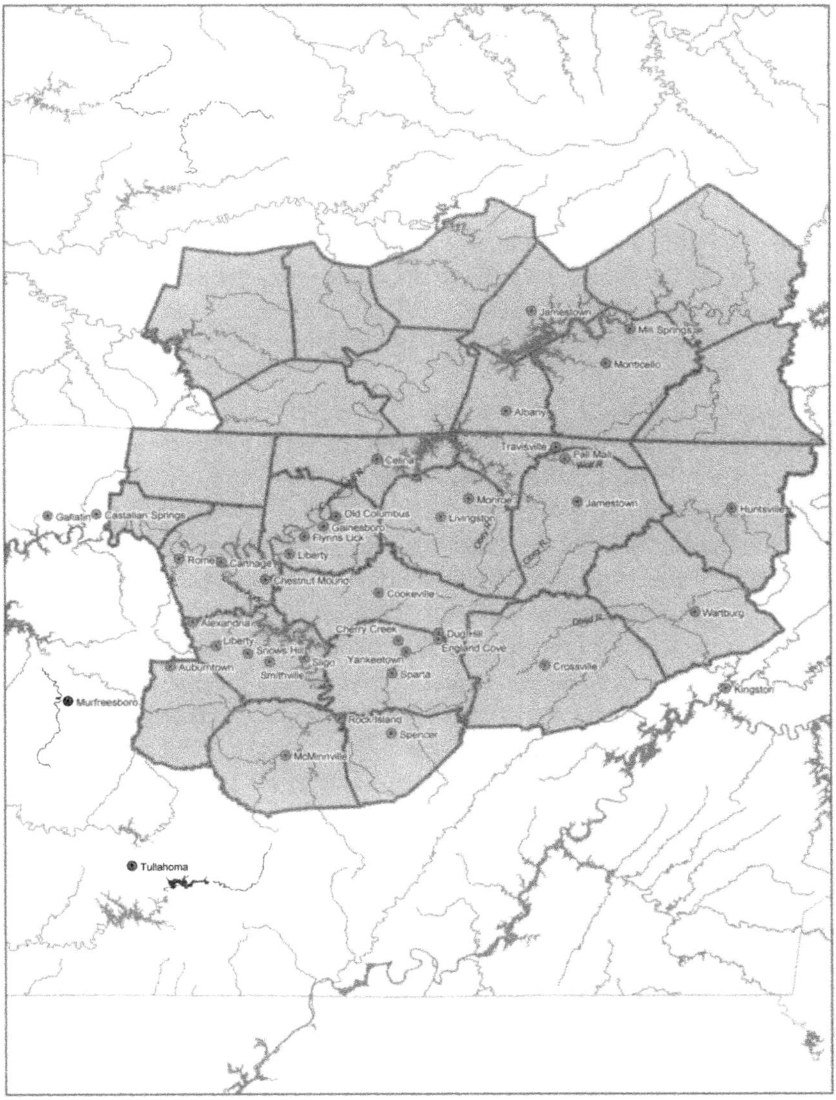

Map 3. The Civil War in the Upper Cumberland.

to our home people and taking lessons in cooking."[19] Because of the scarcity of proper firearms, soldiers fashioned homemade pikes or depended on antique weapons of Mexican War vintage.

Colonel John P. Murray, the ranking officer at Camp Zollicoffer, complained bitterly to General Albert Sidney Johnston. "Supplies could not be had near Jamestown, which place is situated on the summit of [the] Cumberland Mountains, and is almost as sterile as the great African desert." His force included ten companies with 915 privates, yet there were only 665 guns among them. Discouraged by the terrain, lack of provisions, and Tory sentiment in the border country between Overton, Fentress, Scott, Morgan, and Campbell counties, Colonel Murray found the task daunting in the extreme. Securing transportation routes to General Zollicoffer's forces at Cumberland Gap to protect against Federal encroachment proved frustrating. "I desire to leave this section of the State because I think there is no prospect of active service here, nor do I think this border needs protection. . . . I implore you to remove me from this point to some place where I can better serve my country."[20]

A curious attitude, indeed, for the border was vital for troops on either side. As they drilled, Rebel soldiers at Camps Zollicoffer and Myers prepared for an invasion of Kentucky. Many later fought in the Battle of Mill Springs, which resulted in General Zollicoffer's death.[21]

As preparations for the battle of Fort Donelson ensued, Confederate Major General George B. Crittenden reported to General Albert Sidney Johnston about the difficulties he faced in fortifying the Upper Cumberland. Crittenden claimed Gainesboro was indefensible. Even worse, he could not occupy Livingston or establish defenses at any point on the road connecting it to Walton Road "for want of transportation to carry supplies to the camp from the river." Thus, he urged occupying the superior position at Chestnut Mound in Smith County, where supplies could be hauled from river landings. Even more important, Chestnut Mound was already connected with Carthage by the Walton Road.[22]

With the fall of Fort Donelson and later Nashville to Union forces in February 1862, Federal commanders made concerted efforts to halt Rebel activity in the Upper Cumberland. Colonel Frank Wolford, affectionately called "Old Wolf" by his troops, commanded a regiment composed of mountaineers from both sides of the Kentucky-Tennessee border. He led two unsuccessful expeditions against the Confederate guerrilla leader Captain Oliver P. Hamilton, who operated throughout Jackson and Overton counties in Tennessee and Monroe and Cumberland counties in Kentucky. In late April, Wolford received orders to "proceed to Nashville via Livingston and Cookesville [sic], and capture or disperse all the guerrilla and rebel companies" en route. It was a dangerous mission, as participant Major John A. Brents observed: "The officer who issued this order certainly did not understand the nature of the country and the strength of rebel forces on the route. If he had, it seems to me that he would not have sent so small a force into a hostile country without any support to rely upon and no way to retreat." Guerrillas could depend on the citizenry to "assist the rebel troops in every way possible."[23]

In April, four companies of "Old Wolf's" force invaded Celina, Tennessee. They found the town practically devoid of males, leaving the women to fend for themselves. One defiant woman proclaimed, "Colonel, I am not afraid of you or any of your soldiers and I don't suppose that any of these ladies are; if so, they are not genuine southern ladies."[24] Reactions of women sympathetic to the South amazed and confused Major Brents. "The women are wholly enlisted in the southern cause. They cannot be too kind to their soldiers; nor will they permit the men at home to see any peace till they join the army."[25]

Wolford's men moved on to Livingston, engaging in small skirmishes along the way. Federals surprised Confederate pickets who sought shelter and warmth from heavy spring rains. They captured eight Rebels. News spread that Union soldiers had laid siege to the town; many people fled their homes in fear of rapine and murder. Women pleaded for their houses to be spared from the torch and for the lives of their husbands and sons. That evening, April 24, Wolford's men bivouacked in the Overton County Courthouse and houses near the square.[26]

Wolford's troops traveled to Cookeville and Gainesboro in the following days. En route, they encountered guerrilla leader Champ Ferguson disguised as a Federal soldier. Ferguson fled in the direction of Cookeville, screaming, "For God's sake, don't let the Rebels kill me!" Confused Federals let him pass, believing his ruse:

His pursuers . . . dashed on after him. . . . Sergeant Floyd and Dr. J. C. Riffe . . . concluded to take a tilt at Ferguson. . . . They came close behind him, and fired. He took the bridle between his teeth . . . firing over his shoulder with a pistol in each hand. He never looked back, but kept his head down. Floyd's horse was shot, and he was compelled to stop. Dr. Riffe . . . received a slight wound in his shoulder, but still pressed forward until he reached Ferguson's side . . .

then fired deliberately . . . his pistol against Ferguson's body. The latter abandoned his horse, and made his escape in the heavy timber by the road-side. He was once more saved by his coat of mail.[27]

They captured thirty of Ferguson's men. After bivouacking in Cookeville, Old Wolf pressed on for Gainesboro, capturing more Rebels along the way. Foraging proved difficult. Citizens of Overton, Putnam, and Jackson counties had little to offer in the way of food, clothing, or other provisions, and they were hostile to sharing with their avowed enemy.[28] Upon arriving at Gainesboro, the Federals discovered that Captain Oliver P. Hamilton's company had "skedaddled" when they learned of Wolford's approach. Major Brents regarded Gainesboro as "the worst hole in Tennessee or anywhere else. *The people are actually mean.* . . . I never want to see the place again. I met with only two or three clever people in the town."[29]

In May 1862, Confederates captured Union sympathizer Alexander Huff. His captors tortured and later "cruelly murdered [him] near the Three Forks of the Wolf River."[30] John Duncan and John Rich, both Unionist members of the Home Guard, were killed in Fentress County by Rebels from Camp McGinnis at the same time.[31]

After the Corinth, Mississippi, campaign in 1862, Confederate forces under General Braxton Bragg recouped their losses, renewing their strength in the Chattanooga environs. Here Bragg planned his next move—the invasion of Kentucky. By late August, it became increasingly apparent that the Confederate army would invade Kentucky, using the Cumberland Plateau as the thoroughfare to reach the Bluegrass State.

On August 24, 1862, four days before Bragg's army initiated its advance, a brief Federal occupation of Sparta occurred. Its location on the Nashville-Knoxville Post Road and its proximity to the Caney Fork River made Sparta strategically important. It was also an excellent source for forage. A letter written by a Confederate soldier mentioned that "Yankees are occupying Sparta at present, having moved up last night." Six days later, however, Federal Brigadier General J. T. Boyle wrote Major General Horatio G. Wright: "One of my scouts reports rebel force at Sparta, Tenn., of considerable strength." Consequently, the first Federal occupation of Sparta lasted a week or less. Yankees withdrew to avoid the certain danger presented by the approaching Army of Tennessee. Although the town would be occupied again, sentiments of Spartans were strongly pro-Confederate.[32]

Although historians have focused attention on the fighting associated with the Kentucky campaign of August 27–October 12, 1862, they have neglected a smaller struggle that took place in the Upper Cumberland at the same time. Writing from Kentucky on October 28, Colonel William Clift, commanding the Seventh Tennessee Infantry (U.S.), reported his activities in Fentress, Scott, Monroe, Morgan, Anderson, and Roane counties for the period of July–October 1862. Assigned to break up guerrilla bands, Champ Ferguson's among them, harass Bragg's army, and recruit members for the Seventh Infantry, his missions proved nominally successful, except perhaps in Anderson County.

In those intervals when not scouting, Clift kept his men busy "fortifying an eminence near Huntsville, Scott County, Tenn." This defensive position attracted the attention of Confederate commanders, who attacked the earthworks on August 13. The outcome was a forgone conclusion, as the Federals were outnumbered 250 to 2,000. Raw recruits of the Seventh Tennessee Infantry panicked and left the "breastworks in wild confusion." More seasoned soldiers remained at their posts, resisting the greater force for "an hour and forty minutes," until their numbers had dropped from fifty to twenty. Colonel Clift then ordered a retreat, "which was conducted in good order, carrying with them our guns without any loss." Bravery and cowardice matching any recounted in the famous battles was apparent in Huntsville that day.[33]

Clift continued his antiguerrilla forays, even though his command had diminished. Incorporating guerrilla tactics, he took to the surrounding forest and kept his troops in the most obscure parts of the Upper Cumberland, posting his pickets twenty to twenty-five miles from the camps of the Seventh and within a short distance of the enemy's lines. This allowed him to evade detection until "Gen. Bragg's army retreated out of Kentucky." Clift sent out a patrol during the last two weeks of October 1862. This counterguerrilla squad "passed over Scott, Morgan, and Fentress Counties, Tennessee, and had a skirmish with Ferguson's guerrillas, killing four of them, and among the number was the cruel murderer Capt. Miliken." At the end of October, patrols went out, aimed at breaking up insurgent groups that wandered "in the mountains between the line of Kentucky and Tennessee and the Tennessee River and sometimes in the counties of Clinton and Wayne, Kentucky."[34]

In November 1862, both sides carried out a number of raids in Smith County. Because of its location on the Cumberland River and the Walton Road, Smith County had strategic importance to both sides. John Hunt Morgan's cavalry proved a constant irritation to Union troops between

Rome and Hartsville. Federals depended on wagon caravans for distribution of supplies from river landings. Once wagons were on the road, they often fell prey to Morgan's cavalry. Small, concentrated affairs, skirmishes resulted in few deaths and theft of property.

Colonel John Marshall Harlan (later a U.S. Supreme Court justice) encamped at Castallian Springs in the fall and winter of 1862–1863. His correspondence provides insight into warfare in Smith County. In frustration, he lamented: "On the morning of the 28th, a forage train consisting of 10 wagons was sent from the Second Indiana Cavalry, under an armed escort of 40 men . . . an escort which would seem sufficient, and *which if properly handled*, would have proven itself efficient. When the train reached a point about 2 miles east of Hartsville on the Carthage road, it was attacked both in the front and rear by Rebel cavalry. *The train was surrendered without any resistance whatever on the part of the escort.*"[35]

Harlan was incensed at Lieutenant Brush surrendering the wagons without a fight. Major Samuel Hill immediately sent a detachment of ninety men to try to retrieve the lost material. His troops met no resistance until they reached Rome, where fighting ensued with Colonel Bennett. Hill successfully recaptured seven wagons and eight men, then chased the Confederate raiders to a point twelve miles south of Rome, where they gathered reinforcements. Hill withdrew, and the Rebels chose not to pursue him.[36]

Though Confederates had the support of the civilian population, problems were evident by November 1862. The southern army was plagued by desertions, and increased efforts to refill the ranks did more damage than good. Between November 1 and November 30, the Confederate army based in Sparta conducted conscript sweeps up and down the Cumberland River between Gainesboro and Celina. Sporadic sweeps were later conducted in Carthage, Jamestown, Liberty, Gainesboro, Sparta, and Celina until the war's end.

After 1863, the war exacted more pain and suffering on average citizens. Personal water craft were plundered and destroyed, and forage expeditions became the routine means of supply for both armies. Union and Confederate armies confiscated corn, pigs, horses, mules, and just about anything else useful. Skirmishing increased with greater frequency as forage grew scarcer in those months before crops were planted.[37]

Adversities suffered by local inhabitants are evident in a raid ordered by Union Major General George Thomas in February 1863. Colonel John T. Wilder and Captain Eli Lilly spearheaded the excursion to

Liberty, Alexandria, Auburntown, and Carthage.[38] Wilder's men routed Confederates encamped at Liberty, seized stores of flour and bacon, and destroyed a gristmill near Carthage. They razed the mill because "it was used for the grinding of the grain of the loyal people to make food for the Rebels." Wilder's troops confiscated ninety-one horses and nineteen mules.[39] Greeted warmly by the inhabitants of Alexandria, General Thomas's troops were "treated to the sight of our glorious old flag, which a lady had successfully hidden during the reign of terror under the rebel Gen. Bragg."[40]

Major General Joseph J. Reynolds's section of the same successful search and destroy expedition is worthy of note. Reynolds discovered that, among the lower classes—those whose property and sons had been taken by the Confederate army—the degree of Union loyalty was highest, making them paupers at the hands of their neighbors. Reynolds wrote: "If the present state of things is permitted to exist much longer, the Union people will be without subsistence, and will be compelled to leave the country or live off the rebels, the latter they will not be permitted to do, and the former many of them cannot do." Since the men who held political power in such areas exhibited no Union sentiment, "the only effectual mode of suppressing the rebellion must be such a one as will conquer rebellious individuals at home as well as defeat their Armies in the field. . . . The remedy for this state of affairs appears very simple: despoil the rebels as the rebel army has despoiled the Union men. Send the rebels out of the country, and make safe room for the return of loyal men."[41] Reynolds believed that, with sufficient military backing, those poor farmers would make formidable allies in the ongoing struggle. If a farmer held Union sympathies and Federal forces came to take supplies, he received a voucher to be reimbursed after the war. Should a pro-Confederate farm be visited by Yankees, needed supplies were simply taken.

When General George Crook established headquarters at Carthage in March, he planned the construction of earthworks on the south side of the river opposite town, intending to equip it with artillery. He sent regular forage parties to secure supplies, ordering the arrest of Confederate sympathizers. Crook's troops reported that "all the suitable [stock] has been taken out of this country."[42] As Crook scrounged for supplies, Confederates conducted their own forage raids and conscript sweeps in three counties between Carthage and Celina. Combined efforts of Yankees and Rebels heaped more suffering on the Upper Cumberland's citizenry.[43]

General Crook made infrequent reports to his superiors. When prodded by the Chief of Staff in Nashville, future President James A. Garfield, he grumbled, "I cannot establish a courier line unless I have cavalry to keep the enemy from coming on this side of the river. The Rebels have taken all the horses from this section of the country except for old brood-mares and fillies. Were my men mounted on these, in any movement requiring expedition, I would have to dismount and go on foot." Crook confessed about Rebel resistance, "I was never completely beat out before, but I have to acknowledge that I can do nothing against this cavalry with my infantry. I cannot entrap them in any possible way, for they have spies and scouts all over this country."[44] He reported that U.S. gunboats conducting forage missions along the Cumberland between Carthage and Celina were often attacked by Confederate cavalry.

Federal wagon trains remained vulnerable to Confederate raiders. A forage train of eighteen wagons guarded by two companies of infantry, numbering seventy-three men, was captured on March 8, 1863. When it neared its destination, 140 Confederate cavalry attacked. Crook claimed the affair represented another example of his "utter failure to accomplish any result here without cavalry." Moreover, he could not acquire horses because all the "suitable [stock] has been taken out of this country, so it is impossible to mount my men." Confederate guerrillas continued to attack Federal boats on the Cumberland in March, adding to Crook's frustration.[45]

Union guerrillas/bushwhackers were equally intimidating in the Upper Cumberland. On March 9, 1863, a brief skirmish occurred at Smoky Creek in Scott County. According to the diary of Confederate William A. Sloan, who led a counterinsurgency force from Brimstone to Smoky Creek, they had not gone far when they were fired on by Captain Rheagan's Union bushwhackers. Sloan wrote that

> [s]everal rounds were exchanged before the enemy was repulsed,
> which was unusual stubbornness for bushwhackers, as they
> usually fire one round and then run. Rheagan's party numbered
> 23 men. . . . [A]ll of Scot [sic] County and a great deal of contiguous territory, both in Tennessee and Kentucky, is a solid bed of
> rugged and precipitous mountains, cut and gashed in all directions with deep ravines, and all having rushing streams of water
> in them. Most . . . inhabitants live along these streams, though
> some live high up on the mountains. . . . [R]oads along these

streams are often mere trails, and the mountains bordering the streams are often so steep and craggy that bushwhackers can conceal themselves in good rifle range of a road and fire into a column of cavalry with perfect impunity, as it would often require one hour of hard climbing on foot to reach them, and by that time they are as fleet-footed as a deer. If they had the courage and discipline of soldiers they would be hard to conquer, but that is where they are lacking. The crack of a gun seems to inspire them with an irresistible inclination to run.[46]

One of the better-known fights in the Upper Cumberland region occurred at Snow's Hill in DeKalb County, on April 7, 1863. It developed from the movements of a 3,600-man Federal foraging expedition from Murfreesboro to DeKalb County that lasted from April 2 to April 8, 1863. After learning Confederate cavalrymen were in Smithville, Colonel John T. Wilder's "Lightning Brigade" chased the Rebels out of town. Wilder reported his day's work:

All escaped us but one company of 39 men, commanded by a lieutenant, who were taken. . . . I had communicated with Col. Monroe, at Alexandria, directing him to move up to Liberty . . . which he did with alacrity, skirmishing occasionally with small parties of the enemy, and driving them in so that they fell into our hands. We pursued the enemy over and beyond Snow [sic] Hill, but failed to overtake him. We again went into camp. While foraging in the evening, Maj. Carr, Seventy-second Indiana, surprised and captured a party of 10 rebels, and brought them into camp.[47]

General J. A. Wharton's Confederate brigade fled Smithville, while Wilder's men captured his rear guard and destroyed Rebel supplies, including 5,000 bushels of wheat and large quantities of bacon. They also captured roughly 80 prisoners, 350 horses, and a number of slaves.[48]

By April 15, 1863, General Crook reported to Garfield about a recent expedition, sending three regiments to Rome "to protect the boats at that point." While returning by way of Middleton, they encountered a large Confederate force. Skirmishing occurred "without much result on either side." Crook revealed his desire to initiate a "secret plan" along the Cumberland River between Carthage and Gallatin, asking when supplies and gunboats might arrive from Nashville. "We need them," he concluded, because Confederate bushwhackers were "on the rampage" on the Winchester side of Caney Fork River.[49]

While Crook waited for supplies and saddles, he reported on the expedition being conducted between Liberty and Alexandria in DeKalb County. He suggested that a pincers movement—one prong from Carthage, the other from Murfreesboro—would solve his chronic problems. Many of his soldiers were "at Nashville and some have got themselves detailed, &c., producing a very demoralizing effect on this command." He pleaded: "Will you please give me an order so I can get these men whenever I find them?"[50]

In the meantime, a Federal assault took place at Celina, Tennessee, on April 19; Union troops shelled and burned the town. Local citizens were outraged at the wanton destruction, especially since churches were razed as well. Union troops numbering 1,200–1,500 crossed the river into Celina without "even giving the citizens any warning of their intention." Celina's citizenry were regarded as combatants because of their partiality for the Confederacy, and Union troops felt no compassion for them. Orders demanded: "arrest all Federal deserters and kill all Rebels found armed and belonging to the commands of Col.'s Hamilton, Ferguson, & c." The entire town, save only four houses, was demolished.[51]

Another serious event was the skirmish between Union and Confederate forces near Sparta on August 9, 1863. Major General Nathan Bedford Forrest sent Colonel George Dibrell on a mission to gather as much beef as possible. Dibrell was also ordered to keep track of General Rosecrans's movements. While in White County, Dibrell's troops camped at his farm two miles south of Sparta. Federal forces of the Fourth Michigan Cavalry under Charles H. Minty, though slightly outnumbered, attacked, hoping surprise would be on their side. Minty sent the Seventh Pennsylvania and the Fourth Michigan up the east side of the Calfkiller Valley to Sperry's Mill, driving Dibrell's men across Wild Cat Creek. While in pursuit of Dibrell's cavalry, one Federal drowned and fifteen fell wounded. Because of their familiarity with the terrain, the Rebels withdrew into the wooded hills and regrouped.[52] Fighting continued; Champ Ferguson's irregulars and enthusiastic Sparta citizens joined the fray at Wild Cat Creek. Dibrell reported that "by the time the fight was over, the ladies in the neighborhood had cooked and sent to us a breakfast for the entire regiment."[53]

Ten days later, Confederate forces were chased, ironically, out of Yankeetown in White County. That fight began as part of Dibrell's cavalry encountered a scout from the Fourth Michigan, near the Eleven

Gen. George Dibrell of White County, Tennessee. Courtesy of the Tennessee State Library and Archives.

Mile House on the road between Rock Island and McMinnville. A running skirmish followed, resulting in the defeat of Dibrell's forces after a hard fight. Yankees chased them all the way to Kingston, while wounded Confederates and Federals were left in citizens' houses along the way.

After the battle, Colonel Minty filed a report, boasting: "Of course I whipped Dibrell. His men were scattered about the country like blackberries. . . . I think it doubtful if they return to Sparta."[54] Overly self-satisfied, Minty reduced the size of the Federal army at Sparta. He chose to garrison at Rock Island instead, because his horses were exhausted and Sparta's immediate environs represented exceedingly hostile territory. Meanwhile, Dibrell's cavalry, who had not given up the fight, scoured the countryside for provisions, while keeping an eye on Minty's movements.[55]

Amanda Meredith Hill recalled numerous skirmishes in and around Sparta. During the Federal occupation, "the country was overrun with Union troops."[56] To entertain themselves, a group of Confederate soldiers held a dance at the Old Bailey place east of Sparta. The noise attracted attention and "a bunch of Yankee soldiers raided the dance. The Confederates had to hide under beds, jump out the windows and such to escape. They were greatly outnumbered, and were surprised."[57] Lieutenant Jim Revis took refuge under a high four-poster bed, and was later ridiculed for his lack of grace. To save face, Revis swore that he would receive satisfaction from the Yankees who had humiliated him. Lieutenant Revis and his men engaged the enemy a few days later. Outnumbered, the fight went badly for the Rebels. Private Jonathan Hill's horse bolted "and ran right into the Yankee ranks with Uncle Jonathan aboard, and of course he was killed. After he fired all the shots from his pistol he used it for a club."[58]

Civilian suffering rarely appeared in official reports of military officers. Two letters from Jackson County residents to Lieutenant Andrew J. Lacy illustrate the devastating impact of the war on Confederate sympathizers. John Matheney wrote Lacy apologizing for his "murmuring and complaining . . . lamenting too much the sorrows that have . . . almost over whelmed me. . . . Our beloved state is in a desolate condition. . . . Many have become disheartened and are almost ready to give over the struggle." Confederate losses on the battlefield and constant harassment of civilians by ubiquitous forage expeditions caused Matheney to conclude that their reverses were "brought on us for our sins for the great dissipation, prodigality and wickedness that is amongst us." He wrote that Federals on the north side of the Cumberland River exacted considerable damage on the people there. A neighbor named

McKinley lost all of his horses and mules, eleven slaves, and household furniture to Yankee raiders. Federals captured and imprisoned James W. Draper and his son, and they burned F. W. Price's home to the ground.[59]

Matheney's claims were corroborated by William Lacy in a letter to

Lt. Andrew Jackson Lacy of Jackson County, Tennessee. Courtesy of the Cookeville History Museum.

his son on May 24, 1863. Federal troops took personal property at will, while destroying mills and houses wherever they went. Out of fear, William wrote A. J. that he had sold his oxen, steers, and a young horse, keeping them out of the grip of the Union army for the time being.[60]

Farmers tended crops uneasily, knowing their harvest was likely to be confiscated. Union and Confederate bushwhackers, who owed no true allegiance to either side, ransacked farms, harassed citizens, and stole anything they considered potentially valuable. In Fentress County, marauders who claimed to be under Union orders looked for "Secesh" sympathizers near the Kentucky border. Rumors informed them that William "Billy" Hull and Alec Smith were trafficking with the Rebels between Camp McGinnis and Livingston. The gang, led by Jim Stepp and Riley Piles, found Hull and Smith at the home of Cindy Lovelace. Without hesitation, they drew weapons and fired, shooting Smith through the head, immediately killing him. A second shot hit Hull in the face, shattering the bridge of his nose, blinding his right eye, and passing through the back of his neck. He fell to the ground unconscious, a bloody mess. Lovelace covered him with her apron, pleading with Stepp and Piles not to shoot him again.

Miraculously, Hull lived with a scarred face and missing eye. After recuperating, he pursued his would-be murderer into Kentucky. He found Stepp, who, surprised to see Hull alive, begged for mercy. Realizing no quarter would be given, Stepp ran. Hull shot him in the back, then walked up to the body and fired more shots into the prostrate guerrilla to ensure his death. Hull's brother Bud said that "he felt no more worry over that than if he had killed a rabbit."[61]

One Confederate regular who organized guerrillas into an effective fighting force was Colonel John M. Hughs, Twenty-fifth Tennessee [C.S.A.] Infantry. Hughs, once a hotelkeeper in Livingston, Tennessee, was familiar with the Upper Cumberland area.[62] By late August intelligence made it evident that Federal forces en route to Knoxville "were passing through both Overton and White Counties." Hughs sent scouts, who found the report to be true. "They were passing in considerable force, both via Sparta and Livingston, and had completely cut off my communication with the army both by Crossville and Kingston and by Jamestown, Tenn." Hughs reported to General Bragg that the sizable Federal presence upset his abilities to raise more men, but his soldiers "could employ ourselves . . . operating against the enemy, whose presence had greatly emboldened the Union tories, and they were becoming very troublesome, going in bands, robbing and murdering citizens and soldiers. To punish these villains a little fighting was necessary."[63]

From early September 1863 to April 18, 1864, Hughs had many "encounters with the enemy." Although a regular army officer, he operated as a Confederate partisan and retaliated against Union guerrillas in the Upper Cumberland, causing Federal forces to send in cavalry and infantry in an effort to subdue his attacks.[64]

Antiguerrilla operations in Middle Tennessee from the last of October to the first of November 1863 were a priority for General Thomas and the Army of the Cumberland. Fighting took place between November 14 and 26, 1863, when General Ambrose Burnside sent the entire First Tennessee Cavalry and a contingent of the Ninth Pennsylvania Cavalry to Sparta to reestablish Federal control of the town. Native Tennessean Colonel John Brownlow, son of the disputatious "Parson" William G. Brownlow, replaced Colonel Minty and took up residence in Sparta, establishing fortifications at strategic parts of the town.

The colonel reported that on November 24 his men skirmished with guerrillas, who had entered Sparta on three roads. Brownlow boasted he had "whipped Col. Murray's force, killing one, wounding 2, and capturing 10 men," of whom one was a lieutenant of Champ Ferguson. The First Tennessee Cavalry also captured several horses and arms and destroyed some ammunition. Brownlow understood that Colonel Murray had sent for reinforcements from the guerrilla bands of Hughs, Hamilton, Daugherty, and Ferguson. Brownlow gloated, "I will give them hell if they come."[65]

On November 26, Brownlow's scouts fired on irregulars two miles from Sparta, killing or wounding several, while destroying the Rebels' extensive salt works. This was accomplished with the trifling loss of two slightly wounded men. Although Rebels had threatened to burn a number of mills nearby, the colonel reported they could prevent such action.

The final battle occurred on November 30 near Yankeetown. Guerrillas ambushed Lieutenant Bowman. A running skirmish ensued, with guerrillas driving Bowman across the Calfkiller River, killing four Federals, wounding one, and capturing five U.S. troopers in the pursuit. Brownlow went directly to Bowman's aid, "and drove the enemy (numbering 500) 8 miles, killing 9 and wounding between 15 and 20." Brownlow exaggerated his victory, saying he had squelched Rebel activity in Sparta. The next day, Confederates attacked a supply train, killing eight guards from the Ninth Pennsylvania and seizing the cargo.

Soon after, Colonel William B. Stokes of the Fifth Tennessee Cavalry, also a native Tennessean, on orders from Thomas, replaced Brownlow in Sparta.[66]

Sending Stokes to Sparta was "not in the best interest of law and order," for Stokes had an awkward status. Earlier a Union captain had shot Stokes. During the assailant's court-martial, General Rosecrans intervened on his behalf because "experience and observation warrant distrust of Col. Stokes carefulness and fidelity to truth and justice in dealing with his officers and men." The sentence was commuted from death to a dishonorable discharge. Ironically Stokes, who was pro-Union and commanded a Federal regiment, was known as a "Yankee hater."[67] Spartans hated Stokes with good reason. During his occupation of the town, he ordered that the floors of the Methodist church be ripped up so that it could serve as a stable.[68]

In a December 1863 raid, Colonel H. LaGrange descended on Yankeetown to "clear out a force of guerrillas there, estimated at about 400 or 500 in number." LaGrange's force stopped six miles outside of Yankeetown and sent scouting parties in on all roads. They found no enemy; "all citizens reported that but 3 [guerrillas] had been seen" in town on that day. Scouts soon learned that all of Hughs's force had gone north and were at Spring Creek or Sinking Cave, about six miles east of Livingston.[69]

General Crook, meanwhile, struggled to maintain Federal control near Carthage. Reinforcements arrived in October, including three companies of mounted infantry and one company of black troops. Armed blacks did little to assuage fears among locals. Union soldiers continued to destroy gristmills, granaries, and salt works in the area, while Rebel guerrillas burned what few bridges remained over the Cumberland River's tributaries. Lack of bridges endangered soldier and civilian alike, and in December 1863, eight soldiers and horses of the Second Indiana Cavalry drowned trying to cross the Caney Fork in DeKalb County.[70] Many people who were not active guerrilla fighters, but who refused to swear an oath of allegiance to the Union, endured constant abuse. Crook merrily reported that "we took all the serviceable stock we could find and made prisoners of the men wherever practicable."[71]

During the winter of 1864, Colonel Stokes's Fifth Tennessee Cavalry encountered a contingent of Champ Ferguson's men near Yankeetown. Fighting ensued, resulting in the capture of twelve prisoners and about twenty mules and horses. Union forces confiscated everything that could be scavenged. They killed Captain Conley, Jack Koger, Bill Allcorn, Milt

Hawkins, and others. Most of these men were known to have been engaged in "murder, robbery and rape; in fact, all were accessory to the outrages committed through this country." His colleague, Colonel McConnell, conducted similar operations at Cookeville and Livingston, killing twenty-three and capturing forty guerrillas. Stokes estimated the declining Confederate strength to be only five hundred or six hundred men, "finely mounted but poorly armed."[72]

On February 18, 1864, Stokes "occupied all the deserted houses in town, barricaded all the streets, and fortified around my artillery." Though comfortably quartered in the abandoned homes of Sparta, Stokes was ill at ease, for local resistance led him "to fight for every ear of corn and blade of fodder I get." Uncomfortable with reports that deserters from the Confederate army continued to join Colonel Hughs, he felt no better with the knowledge that "[t]he people are thoroughly and decidedly disloyal, but a great many are taking the oath. The oath of allegiance has been found on the persons of several soldiers we have killed. The country is rocky and mountainous, and very hard for cavalry to operate in. I have to fight rebel soldiers and citizens, the former carrying the arms and doing the open fighting; the latter, carrying news and ambushing."[73] Stokes held a grudging admiration for Hughs, believing him a "brave, vigilant, and energetic officer." He particularly liked Hughs's ability to keep his men reigned in, for "there is little or no robbing done by the guerrillas." On February 22, 1864, three hundred irregulars on the Calfkiller River attacked two companies of the Fifth Tennessee Cavalry, who were returning from a scout. Confederates "under the command of Hughs, Ferguson, Carter and Bledsoe" soon overwhelmed them. On February 23, guerrillas under the command of Captain Carter attacked one of the Federal pickets near Sparta, using a *ruse de guerre,* clothing six Confederates in Federal uniforms. According to Stokes, "[A]s those dressed in our uniform approached the vedettes they told them not to shoot, that the rebels were after them. . . those in gray appeared a few yards in the rear of those in blue hallooing to them to surrender[;] the story appeared very plausible. And the ones in blue immediately rushed upon the reserve pickets." Four Union soldiers died as a result of the charade, three after surrendering. Stokes claimed that "a great many" Rebels were dressed in Federal uniform when his two companies were attacked. Disgusted by the affair, he praised Hughs while damning Carter, for Hughs did "not allow this barbarity, but his subordinate officers practice it."[74]

Fighting on and near rivers was intense because they were the primary supply line for both armies. In February 1863, reports reached Major General William S. Rosecrans that Confederates were building flatboats on the Caney Fork near Sligo in DeKalb County. Federal intelligence assumed it to be the work of John Hunt Morgan, speculating that he intended to use the boats to ferry men and supplies along or across the river below Carthage and drive north into Kentucky. This led to joint army-navy patrols along the Caney Fork between Carthage, Sparta, and Liberty. The expedition destroyed twelve Confederate boats of varying description. In light of the Rebel activity, General Rosecrans sent twenty-six transport ships and four tinclads from Nashville up the Cumberland River to Carthage under the direction of General George Crook. Rebels attacked the fleet from the shore as the flotilla steamed upriver, but exacted little damage. Reports indicate that Crook received orders to carry out a combined naval-cavalry expedition from Celina through Livingston, Fentress County, and into Kentucky up to Norman's Landing near Monticello.[75]

General Ulysses S. Grant, in Nashville, ordered a Federal riverine expedition up the Cumberland River. It began just before Christmas 1863, and ended a few days after New Year's. U.S.N. Lieutenant Commander LeRoy Fitch led the mission, which had three objectives: to convoy some steamers up river from Nashville to Carthage; to ascertain if any coal was to be found "upon the river in condition for shipment" to Nashville; and to explore the river as far up as Big South Fork for the viability of steamboat navigation.[76]

The task force, consisting of 140 sharpshooters under Lieutenant Colonel Andrew J. Cropsey of the 129th Illinois Volunteer Infantry, rode in the transports and the army gunboat. Early on the morning of December 29, Fitch led the tinclad gunboat *Silver Lake No. 2*, the steamboats, and barges up river. Jackson County, he had been warned, was the seat of operations for several guerrilla bands. Fitch reported: "it fully merits its reputation, for we had scarcely touched the county line before guerrillas were discovered on the lookout for us."[77] At every one of the numerous bends of the upper reaches of the Cumberland River, Confederates harassed the convoy. Rebels attacked the tinclad at five places along the serpentine river. The flotilla met resistance at Ray's Ferry, Flynn's Lick, Gainesboro, Ferris Woodyard, and two miles below Celina at Bennett's Ferry. Guerrillas of varying numbers hid among the thick brush high on the bluffs above the river, peppering fire toward the boats. "Though they manifested much zeal and skill," in each case gunboats and sharpshooters returned fire, "dispersing the Confederates" along the banks and hills. Cropsey opined that the only county still under Rebel control was "Jackson, or that part of it south of the Cumberland, and Overton, as far east as Obey's River." Otherwise, citizens of the Upper Cumberland were "reported loyal, and the people from the banks greeted us with unmistakable demonstrations of joy."[78]

Along the river to Creelsboro, Kentucky, Fitch encountered no more armed Rebels. Fitch found coal at the mouth of the Obey River, a supply that had been partially destroyed by Confederates. Falling water levels compelled him to turn downstream or be trapped on a sandbar in hostile territory; he did not reach the Big South Fork. The

Union colonel Shelah Waters of Warren County, Tennessee. Courtesy of Joseph C. Douglas.

expedition ended on January 4, destroying several Confederate flatboats on its return trip. Fitch remarked that they "would have destroyed Gainesboro, a notorious rendezvous for guerrillas, but Military Governor Andrew Johnson objected on the grounds that the buildings were needed to establish a military post there."[79]

The importance, even the occurrence, of riverine warfare is little appreciated in most studies of the Civil War in the Upper Cumberland. River battles often produced the greatest amount of damage, as illustrated by the total destruction of the town of Old Columbus. Between January 28 and February 8, 1864, a joint army-navy campaign pushed into Jackson County intent on ending Union resistance in the region. Sailors under the command of Major Garret steamed up river to Flynn's Lick, while the Seventy-first Ohio Volunteer Infantry trudged overland via Chestnut Mound. The area between the road and the river was swept, and the Federals intended to move on toward Livingston after clearing resistance in Jackson County.[80]

Colonel H. K. McConnell of the Seventy-first Ohio Infantry, with Tennessee troops under the command of Major Garret, marched from Chestnut Mound to Jackson County. They pursued Hamilton's guerrillas, fighting them in running skirmishes all the way to Flynn's Lick.

About twenty Confederates died in these hit-and-run incidents. Colonel Stokes's Fifth Tennessee Cavalry joined the effort, rooting out Rebels in the country from Sparta to Cookeville.[81]

Old Columbus, which no longer exists, was situated approximately three miles north of Gainesboro, between the Cumberland and Roaring rivers. Colonel McConnell reported, "Finding Old Columbus . . . to be the veriest [sic] den of thieves and murderers, I removed the women and children and burned it. I have no means of knowing the number of mules and horses taken."[82] Old Columbus lay in total ruin. Everything that could be scavenged was confiscated by Union troops and the town totally destroyed.

McConnell commented on destruction in the region: "I have the *honor* to respectfully suggest that the country between Carthage and the Cumberland Mountains through which we passed is bordering on famine. Families without regard to politics are eaten out and plundered by those common enemies of mankind . . . until even those formerly wealthy are utterly reduced, and many of the poorer are now actually starving." His remarks make clear how the war harmed nonbelligerents, but he added, coldly, that *"they brought it upon themselves."* Rebels in Jackson, Fentress, and Overton counties went to Glasgow and other towns in Kentucky to "purchase goods, contraband and otherwise, using little restraint," McConnell observed, but he believed that "for the time being" guerrilla activity had been subdued.[83] His use of the qualifying term indicated McConnell's belief that the guerrilla threat would endure as long as the war lasted.[84]

Colonel T. J. Harrison, Thirty-ninth Indiana Mounted Infantry, reported on January 21, 1864, that he sent an expedition of two hundred men to Sparta to kill guerrillas in that vicinity. Divided into five parties, Harrison's force remained in the area five days. During that time he killed four, wounded five or six, and captured fifteen, including a captain and lieutenant, thirty horses, and twenty stands of arms.[85]

As Federals sought guerrillas, Confederate partisans under the command of Colonel Hughs attacked "Tinker" Dave Beatty's forces, killing seventeen, capturing two, and "effectually dispersing the whole gang."[86] Stokes's Fifth Tennessee Cavalry, which rivaled any guerrilla's bloodthirstiness, suffered the wrath of livid Confederates on February 22, 1864, at the Battle of Dug Hill, perhaps the bloodiest episode in White County history. Hughs ambushed a party of "picked men" of the Fifth Tennessee Cavalry under Captain Exum on the Calfkiller River. Earlier, Exum's command, men from Smith and DeKalb counties, had "refused to treat us as prisoners of war, and murdered several of our men whom they had caught straggling from their command." Although outnumbered 110 to 60, Hughs attacked the Yankees, leading an assault that has been enlarged by folklore. Fighting was "severe in the extreme; men never fought with more desperation or gallantry. Forty-seven of the [Federal] enemy were killed, 13 wounded, and 4 captured; our loss was 2 wounded." Some say Rebels not only shot at troops from the Fifth Tennessee, but also stoned them. When the melee ended, Hughs's men supposedly slit the throats of their fellow Tennesseans. Other stories say the Federals tried to surrender, but Hughs chose to execute them.[87]

A Federal account of the blood-drenched warfare at Dug Hill purported that, in addition to the three or four soldiers killed in combat, "nineteen others were taken prisoner and deliberately murdered after they had surrendered and given up their arms." Heads of some prisoners were "riddled with balls, one man receiving seven bullets." The carnage enraged Colonel Stokes, who blamed Champ Ferguson and issued an order to "take no prisoners. A desperate contest commenced in which our loss was seven or eight killed and but a few wounded and that of the guerrillas not less than a hundred killed and a large number wounded." The Calfkiller River ran red with the blood of the fallen

Champ Ferguson historical marker in White County, Tennessee. Photo by the author.

from both sides. Captain Blackburn claimed victory over the Confederates, claiming that Champ Ferguson was among the wounded.[88]

A few miles away in the Cherry Creek community, Amanda McDowell heard the fighting and worried that the outcome might bring retribution. "[T]here was a dreadful fight up the river yesterday," she wrote. Rumors reported "35 to 40 enemy" had been killed while only two Rebels suffered wounds. The lopsided victory made her wonder if "they lay in wait for them and . . . killed them after they surrendered. . . . What a dreadful pass the country has come to! It is awful to think of men slaughtered in such a style." Before the battle, many of her neighbors considered going into Sparta to take the oath of allegiance to the Union, but news of a Confederate victory renewed their faith in the southern cause. Appalled to hear that some neighbors celebrated the slaughter, she wrote: "I can't rejoice. I cannot be glad at any death, at any murder, and what is it but murder."[89]

On March 12, 1864, Federals ambushed Rebels at William Alexander Officer's house in Overton County. Two hundred Union soldiers from Colonel Stokes's Fifth Tennessee Cavalry surrounded the house. They fired into the house through the windows, interrupting the breakfast prepared by Mrs. Officer. Six unarmed Rebels were brutally murdered, each person's body riddled by the hail of bullets. Stokes's men dragged a seventh man, Texas Ranger Lieutenant R. B. Davis, outside. They tied Davis to a gatepost, where they subsequently executed him.[90]

Officer's son, Confederate Private J. H. Officer, scrambled into the second-story loft, eluding Stokes's onslaught. He survived the attack and stayed hidden until the Federals went on their way. In the course of the melee, Mrs. Officer was accidentally shot. William Officer pled with Stokes to spare his house from the torch. Stokes ordered his men not to set fire to the house and allowed Officer to tend to his wife's wound.[91]

Conditions were dreadful in the Upper Cumberland, even for Union guerrilla leader "Tinker" Dave Beatty. A rare letter from the Fentress County guerrilla chief, dated April 10, 1864, to Military Governor Andrew Johnson claimed that he had held Fentress County for the Union for three years without assistance. Now he needed government relief. The Upper Cumberland had been so ruthlessly and thoroughly plundered that even this resourceful brigand faced hard times. Beatty let it be known that if something was not done soon, "starvation will appear among us—families are today suffering for want of bread." Everyone's livestock was gone or suffering from lack of fodder. He implored the governor to send food for the sake of the women and children.[92]

While Beatty sought assistance, it appeared that the intense efforts of the Fifth Tennessee and Thirteenth Kentucky cavalry had finally subdued Colonel John Hughs. By mid-April he was rumored to be once again near Sparta and anxious to take the oath of allegiance to the Union. The rumor did not impress Amanda McDowell: "Col. Hughs sent [word] into Sparta that he was coming in to take the oath and bring his whole command, but he did it just to fool the Yankees. I say (I think) he acted the fool; the Yankees stayed several days longer than they would have done. Of course they will never put any confidence in what he says again. He thinks he is so smart. It will take hard knocking to knock the conceit out of him. I do not think the people are faring any better in some instances since the Yanks left than they did before, but it won't do to say."[93]

Meanwhile, many continued to support Champ Ferguson, sometimes to their own peril. In mid-July 1864, Ferguson's guerrillas successfully raided Federal cattle reserves near Kingston, Tennessee. The Fourth Tennessee Infantry (U.S.) made a pursuit to England Cove, but there discovered that the stock had been divided and driven into different parts of White County. Citizens offered no help to the pursuing Yankees, denying any knowledge of Ferguson's raid. Incensed, the Federal commanding officer, Major T. H. Reeves, impatiently decided to take action against them. He considered all citizens in the area to be "aiders and abettors to the thieving band" and ordered everything in the area to be seized. Reeves's men "plundered every house from here to Sparta . . . for distance of fifteen miles down the valley every house where good stock, arms or goods of a contraband nature could be found, the most unparalleled plunder was committed." Reeves's men then charged into Sparta with orders to "take no quarter."[94]

On July 15, 1864, Reeves declared martial law in Sparta. He had every man in town arrested. The women and children "all expected the town to be burnt up and all the citizens killed." Reeves allowed his troops to sack the town, though he spared it the torch. After terrorizing the populace, he released most of the prisoners and moved out the next day, leaving the citizenry destitute and demoralized.[95]

Reeves reported on the location of Confederate guerrillas. Captain Clark's gang operated above Spencer, Van Buren County. Camp Kearsey was the base of operations for some thirty guerrillas who raided near Smithville. Another guerrilla leader, Dunbar, led some seventy-five men in Overton County, mostly stragglers from Morgan's command. White County was the province of Champ Ferguson. "These are all the organized bodies now in those mountain ranges," added Reeves, "they are all regular desperadoes, taking no prisoners at all."[96]

By the latter part of 1864, Federals gradually regained control of the Upper Cumberland. In September 1864, two scouts—one to Cookeville, Sligo, and Smithville, the other to McMinnville, Sparta, and Tullahoma—rode out. The first, led by Colonel Thomas J. Jordan, found no Rebels, only "vague reports" of their activity. Marching on the Cookeville road from Sparta, a few Confederates were seen; Jordan surmised they were trying to reach east Tennessee via the Obey River. He continued south into the Sequatchie Valley without incident. The second scout reported that Captain Williams was rumored to be camped twenty-three miles north of Sparta at "Sinking Cane." The Confederate presence in the Upper Cumberland was dwindling.

The Federal presence was winding down in the Upper Cumberland by March 1865. Major General R. H. Milroy had "about 200 men of the Twenty-ninth Michigan and Forty-second Missouri at McMinnville under a very efficient officer, who are actively engaged in scouting and sending guerrillas and their friends to hell." He knew of no Confederate forces operating or assembling in the vicinity of the Calfkiller River. Scouts made their way down the Collins and Calfkiller rivers with no difficulty. The mission of a U.S. Navy patrol on the Cumberland from Nashville to Big South Fork in March 1865 was to pacify people along the river. H. A. Glassford, Acting Volunteer Lieutenant, reported to General Thomas, that he made "landings at all important points and at many farm-houses and impressed the people with your desires and intentions in regard to themselves as forcibly as possible." For the most part, the message was welcome. Yet there was some apprehension; on March 12, a report indicated one hundred guerrillas remained active, having crossed the Cumberland from Celina at the mouth of the Obey River. These may have been the forces that skirmished with Federal troops after the war's end at Livingston and Celina, May 18, 19, and 22, 1865.[97]

Law and order returned after the arrest of Champ Ferguson. According to a brief story in the *Chattanooga Daily Gazette*, Ferguson was captured by a force led by Major Blackburn: "Champ has a very possessing appearance, and does not look like a bad man. He is fully six feet high, dark hair and complexion, and has an eye like an eagle. He is a strong, athletic man. He was taken at some point in East-Tennessee and expected to be pardoned as a prisoner of war, but the authorities could not 'see it in that light' and Champ will have to answer for his 'unvalorous deeds.'"[98]

Amanda McDowell wrote hopefully in her diary on May 31: "It

seems like a new world to have peace. Everything is so quiet and calm, the civil law will be established in this country." Except for a number of revenge killings and other murders, relative peace descended on the Upper Cumberland with the end of spilled blood, fear, and hatred. The war was over, yet many a memory sustained the detestation, causing hatred to burst forth sporadically, manifesting itself in a variety of killings into the next century.[99]

Reunion of veterans of the Eighth Cavalry (ca. 1900). Courtesy of the Cookeville History Museum.

Notes

1. Thurman Sensing, *Champ Ferguson: Confederate Guerrilla* (Nashville: Vanderbilt University Press, 1942): 231; Noel C. Fisher, *War at Every Door: Partisan and Guerrilla Violence in East Tennessee, 1860–1869* (Chapel Hill: University of North Carolina Press, 1997): 43.

2. Major John A. Brents, *The Patriots and Guerrillas of East Tennessee and Kentucky: The Sufferings of the Patriots, Also the Experiences of the Author as an Officer in the Union Army, Including Sketches of Noted Guerrillas and Distinguished Patriots* (New York: Henry Dexter Publishers, 1863): 23–24.

3. LeRoy P. Graf and Ralph Haskins, eds., *The Papers of Andrew Johnson, Vol. 6, 1862–1864* (Knoxville: University of Tennessee Press, 19): 45 (Hereafter cited as *PAJ*). Ages ranged from nine to sixty; most were single and many were related. The petition indicates pro-Union attitudes of some women in Smith County who were not innocent bystanders.

4. Amanda McDowell, *Fiddles along the Cumberland*, Lela McDowell Blankenship, ed. (Utica, Ky.: McDowell Publications, 1988): 46–47.

5. Amanda Meredith Hill, "My First 85 Years: The Memoirs of Amanda Meredith Hill, Sparta, Tennessee" (Sparta, Tenn.: partial typescript, n.p., 1941): 15; Sensing, 91; Betty Jane Dudney, "Civil War in White County, Tennessee, 1861–1865" (Cookeville: Master's Thesis, Tennessee Technological University, n.p., 1985): 11.

6. Fisher, 50.

7. Brents, 20, 24.

8. Brents, 10–11, 75; Fisher, 52. Camp Dick Robinson was located in Garrard County, Kentucky, between Lancaster and Danville and was organized in August 1861.

9. *Official Records of the Union and Confederate Armies of the War of the Rebellion* (Washington, D.C.: U.S. Government Printing Office, 1880–1901): Ser. I, vol. 4: 381–83. (Hereafter *OR*.)

10. Spencer Bowen Talley, "Memoirs of Spencer Bowen Talley, First Lieutenant of the Tennessean Twenty-eighth Regiment Company F" (Lebanon, Tenn.: typescript in the possession of Jerry McFarland, n.p., n.d.): 5.

11. Brents, 26, 90; Thomas Lawrence Connelly, *Army of the Heartland: The Army of Tennessee, 1861–1862* (Baton Rouge: Louisiana State University Press, 1967): 14.

12. *OR*, ser. I, vol. 4: 381–83.

13. *OR*, ser. I, vol. 4: 284–85; J. C. Wright, ed., *Autobiography of A. B. Wright, of the Holston Conference M.E. Church* (Cincinnati: Cranston and Curtis, 1896): 42–43; Sergeant E. Tarrant, *The Wild Riders of the First Kentucky Cavalry: A History of the Regiment in the Great War of the Rebellion, 1861–1865*. Reprint (Lexington, Ky.: Henry Clay Press, 1969): 39; Brents, 29, 63, 101–3, 162.

14. Brents, 63; *OR*. ser. I, vol. 4: 205.

15. Brents, 103.

16. *OR*, ser. I, vol. 4: 286–87

17. Ibid., 352; Fisher, 51.

18. Tarrant, 38–39.

19. Talley, 7.

20. *OR*, ser. I, vol. 52, pt. II: 192; Brents, 117.

21. The Battle of Mill Springs is also known as the Battle of Fishing Creek. For more, see Jerry McFarland, William Newkirk, and David Gilbert, eds., *The Battle of Mill Springs, KY, January 19, 1862* (Somerset, Ky.: Mill Springs Battlefield Association, 1999).

22. *OR*, ser. I, vol. 4: 345–46; vol. 7: 855.

23. Brents, 121–22.

24. Ibid., 79–88.

25. Ibid., 166.

26. Ibid., 127.

27. Ibid., 51–52.

28. Ibid., 128–29.

29. Ibid., 132.

30. Wright, 44.

31. Ibid.

32. *OR*, ser. I, vol. 16, pt. II: 433–34, 456.

33. Ibid., 858–59.

34. Ibid.

35. *OR*, ser. I, vol. 20: 24–26. Emphasis added.

36. Ibid.

37. *OR*, vol. 20, pt. I: 14–15; pt. II: 308. Stones River took place December 31, 1862–January 1, 1863.

38. Eli Lilly later earned fame and fortune as a pharmaceutical magnate.

39. *OR*, ser. I, vol. 23: 42–46.

40. Ibid., 46.

41. *OR*, ser. I, vol. 23: 42–46

42. Ibid., 157–58.

43. Ibid., 668.

44. Ibid., 170–71.

45. *OR*, ser. I, vol. 23, pt. I: 130, 140–41, 161–62, 169, 172.

46. Confederate Collection, Diary of William E. Sloan, mfm 154 (Nashville: Tennessee State Library Archives [TSLA], March 9, 1863).

47. Ibid., 200–203.

48. Ibid., 200.

49. Ibid., 240; vol. 30, pt. III: 53.

50. *OR*, ser. I, vol. 23, pt. II: 243.

51. *OR*, ser. I, vol. 31: 248–49; *OR*, ser. I, vol. 23, pt. II: 785; vol. I: 149. The town was rebuilt a few miles west of its original location.

52. *OR*, ser. I, vol. 30: 921.

53. *OR*, ser. I, vol. 23: 846–48.

54. *OR*, ser. I, vol. 52: 438.

55. *OR*, ser. I, vol. 30, pt. III: 79; Dudney, 20–26.

56. Hill, 14.

57. Ibid.

58. Ibid., 14–15.

59. Confederate Collection, Letters—Lacy, Andrew Jackson, 1862–1863, box C-28, folder 17 (Nashville: TSLA). (Hereafter, Lacy Letters.)

60. Ibid.

61. Untitled photocopy of an article in the collection of the Cordell Hull State Historic Site, n.d. Billy Hull was the father of Cordell Hull, secretary of state under Franklin D. Roosevelt.

62. *PAJ*, vol. 6, fn 2, 539.

63. *OR*, ser. I, vol. 30, pt. II: 646–47.

64. Ibid.

65. *OR*, ser. I, vol. 31, pt. I: 437, 573–74.

66. Ibid., 591; Fisher, 81–82.

67. Quoted in Dudney, 33.

68. Ibid., 38.

69. *OR*, ser. I, vol. 31, pt. III: 332.

70. *OR*, ser. I, vol. 31, pt. III: 320.

71. *OR,* ser. I, vol. 30: 802.

72. Ibid., 162; ser. I, vol. 32, pt. I: 8.

73. Ibid., 416–17.

74. Ibid., 416.

75. Ibid., 71–81; *OR,* ser. I, vol. 23, pt. II: 32–33, 71–72, 82, 85, 96.

76. *OR,* ser. I, vol. 31: 644–45.

77. *OR.,* ser. I, vol. 25: 644–45; see also, *Naval OR,* ser. I, vol. 25: 647–50.

78. Ibid.

79. Ibid., 645.

80. *OR,* ser. I, vol. 32, pt. I: 155–56.

81. Ibid.

82. Ibid., 155. Federals captured 102 prisoners, wounded eight and killed thirty-three.

83. Ibid., 156. Emphasis added.

84. Among the destruction occurring during the war included razing courthouses in Fentress, Overton, and Putnam counties. Deeds, marriage certificates, and other documents lost to the fires complicated business transactions in the region for more than a generation.

85. Ibid., 7.

86. Fisher, 79. David Crockett "Tinker" Beatty, a Union guerrilla leader on the Cumberland Plateau, was as notorious as Champ Ferguson, the infamous Confederate leader. There are few references to him in the *OR.* One source indicated the whereabouts of "Tinker" Dave's hideout: in an extensive cave system near the town of Montgomery about a mile northwest of Wartburg called Beatty's Cave. Beatty, "the leader of those mountain patriots," was entrenched and fortified with thousands of acres cultivated in corn and other grain for subsistence.

87. Ibid., 55–57; Dudney, 35–38.

88. *Report of the Adjutant General of the State of Tennessee of the Military Forces of the State, from 1861–1866* (Nashville: 1866): 442.

89. McDowell, 230–31.

90. Five soldiers were from the Eighth Texas and the other from the Third Alabama Infantry.

91. National Register of Historic Places Nomination Form, "Officer Farmstead Historic District Overton County, Tennessee" (Nashville: Tennessee Historical Commission, 2000); *OR,* ser. I, vol. 32, pt. I: 494–95.

92. *PAJ,* vol. 6, 666–67. Beatty requested payment for defending the region.

93. McDowell, 234–35.

94. *OR,* vol. 39: 351–54; Fisher, 91.

95. *OR,* vol. 39: 351.

96. Ibid., 354.

97. *OR,* ser. I, vol. 49, pt. II: 1, 3, 10.

98. *Chattanooga Daily Gazette,* June 1, 1865.

99. McDowell, 280–81; William Lynwood Montell, *Diary of Amanda McDowell* (Lexington: University Press of Kentucky, 1986): 9–12, 156–59, 164–65.

Chapter 6

SLAVERY, FREEDOM, AND CITIZENSHIP

African American Contributions to the Upper Cumberland

WALI R. KHARIF

African Americans appeared in the Upper Cumberland in the late eighteenth century. Some came before statehood, and several accompanied the first settlers brought into the Tennessee wilderness by John Sevier and James Robertson.[1] On the eve of America's Civil War, they made up 12.4 percent of the total Upper Cumberland population. They comprised 10 percent or more of the populations of only eight counties—four each in Kentucky and Tennessee. The overwhelming majority were enslaved and lived in the rural countryside. Only nine hundred free African Americans lived in the entire region.[2] Free Africans and slaves were not uniformly distributed in the Upper Cumberland. Some counties, such as Clinton County, Kentucky, and Cumberland and Fentress counties, Tennessee, had black populations of less than 4 percent of the total populations. Smith County, Tennessee, on the other hand, had almost a quarter of the entire region's African American population.

In the antebellum period, slaves were considered chattels. They could be purchased, sold, traded, willed, hired out, used as collateral, and for the most part, treated just like livestock. Slaves could be sold as intact families or separately.[3]

Enslaved blacks found solace and strength in the family. There was no stereotypical slave family. Many slaves lived in extended families. Some included the father, mother, children, grandparents, uncles, and aunts. Others were broken homes with only one parent, usually the mother, and the children. Family members lived in constant fear that at any time the selling of a family member could shatter the unit. In some instances, even mothers were separated from their young children.

Nevertheless, the family was resilient, and older members taught younger ones how to cope with enslavement.

They also found comfort in religious worship; most worshipers were Christians, embracing the denominational practices of their masters. Though they attended church services with their masters, they sat in separate pews. Some churches allowed slaves and free blacks to become members of the congregation. Larger church buildings had second-floor galleries to accommodate slaves. Smaller churches partitioned the blacks from the whites.

A handful of slaves passed as infidels, a euphemism used by Christians to identify non-Christian worshipers, some of the Islamic faith.[4] In spite of the risk involved, some slaves met secretly for services separate from whites. Such gatherings were illegal and, if discovered, resulted in the punishment of slaves and any freedmen involved.

Church services offered an opportunity to socialize with other blacks from adjoining areas. Slaves met and amused themselves in other ways as well, especially through music. They entertained with banjos and guitars, dancing, and songfests. On special occasions, such as fall harvest, holidays, and weddings, slaves from surrounding farms engaged in the festivities. Slave women further amused themselves with quilting bees while slave men hunted and fished.[5]

Slaves worked in a wide variety of occupations, though most were employed as agricultural workers and domestics. They prepared, planted, cultivated, and harvested fields of tobacco, cotton, and various grains; tended the livestock; handled the essential chores of the big house, such as gardening, cooking, cleaning, laundering, nursing children, and so on. Some worked in mines, the lumber industry, or were hired out as laborers. Others worked on docks and rivers. Farmers who needed artisans hired skilled slaves. Among the most sought were blacksmiths and iron workers. Slave employment was limited only by the restrictions imposed by whites. For example, Tennessee slaves were prohibited from practicing medicine, and those who did could be punished with up to twenty-five lashes on the bare back.[6]

Disorderly slaves and those not meeting work quotas were subject to corporal punishment, most commonly whipping. Female slaves also endured humiliating and painful whippings. In fact, corporal punishment of women of color marked one distinction between the treatment of black women and white women, even white indentured servants.

Though a minority, free African Americans lived in the region. Most were manumitted. Some, such as George Githrow of Warren County,

Former slave with ancestor's portrait. Courtesy of the Tennessee State Library and Archives.

Tennessee, a drummer in the Continental army at Yorktown, gained freedom for military participation.[7] A few earned their freedom for meritorious service, whereas a small number were freed by their natural fathers. There were also industrious individuals, skilled craftsmen, who purchased their freedom.

A handful of free African Americans in the Upper Cumberland owned slaves, usually family members. Since slaveholding states placed heavy capitation taxes on each free African American, it was, ironically, in the best financial interest of a free black head of family to retain family members in slavery rather than give them their freedom. In 1830, three free black heads of families in the Upper Cumberland owned a total of four slaves: two in Adair County, Kentucky, and one each in Overton County and White County, Tennessee.[8]

Although free African Americans represented a class above slaves, they endured constant reminders that they were not whites' social or political equals. They suffered discrimination, denigration, insults, and were restricted in what they could do. Miscegenation laws forbade intermarriage with whites. Furthermore, laws prohibited free African Americans from striking white persons, even in self-defense. In Kentucky, hitting a white person was punishable by a whipping of thirty lashes on the bare back, "well laid on."[9]

These people shouldered the burden for proving their status, and were required to carry an annually renewable certificate of freedom at all times. A copy had to be filed with the county court where they resided. Renewal could be denied if the individual's behavior warranted. Rebecca Budman, a Smith County resident, was known as a free woman. She had no papers, however, to document her freedom. Working to establish her freedom legally so that her children would not be considered slaves, Budman took her case to court because free or slave status legally passed from mother to child, not from the father. Smith County justices decided in her favor, declaring her free. Thus, Budman protected her children from the cruelties of slavery.[10]

Whites in the Upper Cumberland imposed curfews on free African Americans who had to exercise restraint and discretion to remain free. Restrictions limited what they could buy or sell and to whom. Except in isolated areas where there was pressing danger, laws forbade them from owning firearms.[11]

Required by law to be gainfully employed, some freedmen worked as paid laborers alongside slaves. Others farmed, peddled goods, performed skilled labor, and made up a sizable proportion of the tradesmen and mechanics in the Upper Cumberland. Enterprising free black women ironed clothes, prepared and cooked food, and tended the ill to raise money.[12]

Free blacks and slaves reacted against the institution of slavery. Runaway slaves offer a gauge of restlessness, and the Upper Cumberland had its share of them. Although the overwhelming majority were young males in their teens and twenties, young enslaved females also took flight. Between 1790 and 1816, women comprised 21 percent of Tennessee's runaways. This number dropped to 12 percent between 1838 and 1860. Still, more than one of every ten runaways in Tennessee was a woman.[13] They ranged from mulattoes, passing as whites, to recent arrivals. Most were illiterate. Some bore scars from physical abuse, while others carried tribal markings.

After the Civil War, substantial political and social tension affected the Upper Cumberland. Former Confederates and sympathizers tried to continue running the affairs of their communities. Outrages against African Americans occurred in Overton County, Tennessee, in 1868. Guerrilla activity was so dominant in Fentress County, Tennessee, that Governor William G. "Parson" Brownlow sent the militia to restore order. Actual armed confrontations often occurred between freedmen and whites. Newspapers openly referred to blacks in derogatory and demeaning language, routinely calling them darkies, niggers, and coons. Their skin color was further ridiculed as jet black, pitch black, blue black, charcoal black, tolerably black, and obnoxiously black.[14] Such derision in the media created and buttressed negative stereotypes, often resulting in violence against blacks and a further deterioration of their Thirteenth, Fourteenth, and Fifteenth Amendment rights.

Lynching represented an extreme and deadly means of social control. A group acting outside the legal-judicial system executed summary judgment against an individual, resulting in death. Lynchers made the accusation, passed sentence (which was always death), and carried out the execution. There was no limit to how victims were executed; some were hanged, others were shot, dragged to death, or burned at the stake. The National Association for the Advancement of Colored People (NAACP) compiled a record of lynchings in the United States from 1889 to 1918. In that period, 357 lynchings occurred in Tennessee and Kentucky. Of 190 victims in Tennessee, 155 were freedmen. In Kentucky, 120 of 167 victims were African Americans. According to NAACP records, only seven lynchings occurred in the Upper Cumberland. Four were in Tennessee: one each in DeKalb County (Charles Davis, white man, for rape), Macon County (John Winston, black man, for murder), Putnam County (Charles Washington, black man, accused of rape), and Smith County (Ballie Crutchfield, black woman, for theft). The other three lynchings occurred in Kentucky: Metcalfe County (John Wilcoxson, black man, for murder), Wayne County (Fomit Martin, black man, for barn burning), and Monroe County (Arch Bauer, black man, for murderous assault).[15]

Total, White, Free Black, and Slave Populations in the Upper Cumberland in 1860

Kentucky Counties	Total Population	Whites	Percent White	Free Blacks	Enslaved
Adair	9,509	7,847	82.5	60	1,602
Clinton	5,781	5,503	95.2	20	258
Cumberland	7,340	5,874	80.0	53	1,413
Metcalfe	6,745	5,914	87.7	50	781
Monroe	8,551	7,612	89.0	17	922
Pulaski	17,201	15,819	92.0	52	1,330
Russell	6,024	5,453	90.5	12	559
Wayne	10,259	9,244	90.1	28	987
subtotals	71,410	63,266	88.6	292	7,852

Tennessee Counties	Total Population	Whites	Percent White	Free Blacks	Enslaved
Cumberland	3,460	3,321	96.0	18	121
DeKalb	10,573	9,533	90.2	15	1,025
Fentress	5,054	4,865	96.3	2	187
Jackson	11,725	10,467	89.3	46	1,212
Macon	7,290	6,244	85.6	117	929
Overton	12,637	11,452	90.6	98	1,087
Putnam	8,558	7,840	91.6	36	682
Smith	16,357	12,015	73.5	114	4,228
White	9,381	8,074	86.1	162	1,145
subtotals	85,035	73,811	86.8	608	10,616
TOTALS	156,445	137,077	87.6	900	18,468

Sources: Eleventh Census of the United States, Population, 1890; *Negro Population in the United States: 1790–1915* (New York: Arno Press and New York Times, 1968); *A Century of Population Growth: From the First Census of the United States to the Twelfth, 1790–1900* (Baltimore: Genealogical Publishing Company, 1970).

Even the threat of lynching had a tremendous impact on freedmen in the Upper Cumberland. A case in point is an incident that occurred in the city of Lafayette, located in Macon County. Following the Civil War, many southern sympathizers in Macon County exhibited harsh feelings toward former slaves and their white Republican allies in the area. This bigotry and racism made life difficult for blacks there. However, it was not until after the turn of the century that whites in Lafayette conspired to get rid of all black residents. As late as 1910, 13.4 percent of the Lafayette population was black. The town's blacks were run out of Lafayette after Dave Winston allegedly killed a Civil War pensioner for his money. Authorities arrested Winston and placed him in jail, but he was released after making bond. As he left town, a white mob shot him to death. Unsatisfied with Winston's death, whites used the incident to justify running out the town's remaining black population. Lafayette citizens issued an ultimatum for blacks to leave town or face Winston's fate. To show that they meant business, they detonated half a stick of dynamite in the yard of each black resident. An exodus followed, with blacks leaving their property behind. Some dispossessed blacks relocated in nearby Gravel Hill; others left the county entirely, some moving to Hartsville in neighboring Trousdale County.[16]

Unwanted in some towns and communities dominated by whites, many African Americans found solace and security in concentrated black settlements that blossomed after the Civil War. Where feasible, blacks living in the Upper Cumberland formed enclaves in small, isolated neighborhoods in rural and mountainous parts of counties, or separate quarters in segregated towns.

Black settlements, regardless of size, afforded some degree of community organization. They generally contained schools, churches, burial sites, and self-help societies. Festive occasions were observed with community picnics, excursions, patriotic or religious programs, sporting events, and decorations.[17]

In his 1968 autobiography, renowned African American historian and political scientist W. E. B. DuBois alluded to the importance of black communities when he discussed his experience with public education in rural Tennessee during the summers of 1886 and 1887. DuBois completed teacher training in Lebanon, Tennessee, east of Nashville. He then walked from community to community in search of a school for blacks in need of a teacher. DuBois also described the African American communities he encountered. He observed in Alexandria that "cuddled on the hill to the north [of where the whites lived] was the village of the colored folks, who lived in three- or four-room unpainted cottages, some neat and homelike, and some dirty." DuBois further noted that though the dwellings were scattered about, they were located in close proximity to what he called "the twin temples of the hamlet," the Methodist and Baptist churches. DuBois stated that when he crossed the stream at Watertown he came across a small settlement in DeKalb County that contained such a school. Named for former Confederate Captain J. D. Wheeler, who donated the building, Wheeler school was located in a rural area bordering Wilson and DeKalb counties, and was in need of a teacher. Unused since the Civil War, the school, unlike many others, was not a church structure. The presence of a schoolhouse led DuBois to believe that the small settlement was more than an aimless collection of dwellings and had some social structure.[18]

No incorporated black towns existed in the Upper Cumberland; however, the region contained three significantly distinct black communities located at Tate Town (Cumberland County), Free Hill (Clay County), and Gravel Hill (Macon County), Tennessee. Though none ever exceeded 350 residents at their peaks, each contained public schools, small businesses, and community entertainment centers.

Tate Town was located near the confluence of the Coal and Black Drowning Creek on the Jamestown Road in Cumberland County, Tennessee. The town was named for Methodist preacher John Tate, one of the first forty blacks to locate there after the Civil War. These first residents were former slaves of a Morristown man named Childs, who allowed the freedmen to use this land. Blacks quickly built a school that doubled as the church. There was also a community cemetery in which several early residents were interred. Initially financed by black residents, it later received county funding. Most residents belonged to the Methodist denomination. Residents farmed for a living, with many renting from nearby white landowners. The community declined by 1900, and by 1912 no longer existed; former residents moved to nearby Harriman.[19]

Free Hill community was established before the Civil War on hilly and isolated land northeast of Celina, Tennessee. It became a refuge for free blacks and a hideout for runaway slaves in the Upper Cumberland. After the Civil War, blacks continued to move into the community. During its heyday in the 1920s, Free Hill was home to hundreds of residents. Once there were as many as two grocery stores, three clubs, two eateries, two churches (African Methodist Episcopal and Church of

Christ), and a school. Free Hill residents raised their own food and were highly independent of outside assistance. The community declined with the advent of the Civil Rights era. Most residents left the area in pursuit of better employment and living conditions outside of the region. Still, as late as 1990, the community contained 110 residents and four establishments.[20]

Free black Tennesseans founded another distinguishable community at Gravel Hill. Established in the antebellum period, it was located in the area where Macon, Trousdale, and Sumner counties converge. After the Civil War, the population peaked at 247 in 1870, but a slow decline began thereafter. During the late nineteenth and early twentieth centuries, the community had its own post office and contained one Baptist and two Methodist churches, a self-help organization, a public school, and two short-lived institutions of higher learning. Many blacks left the region during the Depression and World War II years, traveling north in search of better jobs and working conditions.[21]

African Americans in the Upper Cumberland proved successful in establishing schools, churches, and societies. Oftentimes, churches sponsored events to raise money for educational as well as religious purposes. This was a common practice because, in many instances, the church structure also served as the educational facility.

In the postbellum era, religious worship continued to be important, and African Americans in the Upper Cumberland belonged to various Christian denominations. Most numerous were Colored Methodists Episcopal (CME), African Methodist Episcopal (AME), African Methodist Episcopal Zion (AMEZ), Methodist, Baptist, and Church of Christ, though a few affiliated with the Presbyterian and Catholic churches. Where no structure existed, residents met in homes, businesses, and lodges. Black churches not only catered to spiritual needs, but helped educate the next generation of black civic leaders. Considering the general state of race relations before the *Brown vs. the Board of Education of Topeka, Kansas (Brown Decision)* of 1954, churches served as community centers and common meeting places for fraternizing. With few public accommodations available to rural African Americans, churches filled that communal void. Churches proved significant because, in most cases, they were the only institution wholly under black control.

Enthusiastic singing punctuated church services. Many small congregations lacked the funds to purchase songbooks, so hymns were "lined out" during the services. An individual who knew the particu-

lar songs pronounced the words of each line in advance. Then the rest
of the congregation sang that line.

Every community made arrangements for burial of the dead. It was
incumbent that the church and family ensure timely and orderly inter-
ment. Black burial and funeral practices after the Civil War carried over
from those of the slavery era. The deceased's family kept the body in
the home, where it was washed with soda water or some emollient,
groomed, and dressed. Family members, friends, and persons wishing
to show their last respects sat all night with the body, which was usually buried the next day.[22]

In most black communities, rudimentary medical care was available. Commonly, community matrons or midwives assisted in childbirth
in individual's homes.[23] Though some pregnancies and other illnesses
required the services of trained physicians, in the late nineteenth and
early twentieth centuries African Americans in the Upper Cumberland
often resorted to home remedies. In many instances, even when medical
services were available, families preferred home cures and remedies.
Cold and flu were commonly treated with peppermint leaves and "black
oil." Matrons administered castor oil for "purging" the body, or as a
preventive measure against illnesses. Other home remedies included
"croup grease," asafetida balls, chewing tobacco to ease bee stings, sheep
nanny tea for measles, and sheep sorrel and various other herbs for
general health.[24] In addition, it was not uncommon in the Upper Cumberland to seek out the services of faith healers and fortune-tellers.

Black Americans entertained themselves with secular singing. They
engaged in guitar, fiddle, and banjo playing. Some musicians made their
own instruments and played lovely music using washboards, spoons,
and jugs. A popular Upper Cumberland black musician of the post-
World War II era was Robert "Bud" Garrett. Featured occasionally as
blues soloist at folksong festivals in such places as Memphis, Nashville,
Knoxville, and Baltimore, Garrett earned fame for "I Got a Place in Free
Hill," his own talking blues composition.[25]

Generally, African Americans in the Upper Cumberland lived in
segregated communities, or were relegated to distinct sections and areas apart from where whites lived. Each village had its "Bush Town," as
the black section in Cookeville was designated, or the more derisive
"Niggertown," as the Carthage community was called. The black section of Alexandria, Tennessee, was simply called "the Hill."[26] Before the
Brown Decision, segregation and discrimination were common. Blacks
and whites were separated at local recreation parks, at social events, on

Black musicians, Hud Roberts, Darton Roberts, and Calvin Roberts, from Overton County, Tennessee. Courtesy of Overton County Heritage Museum.

common carriers, at political events, in schools, and at various entertainments. In theaters, African Americans sat in the balcony. In some areas, such as public pools, African Americans were forbidden to participate at all. Public restrooms and other accommodations were segregated by race. Segregation persisted into the 1960s. Race relations followed a recognized pattern, with African Americans subservient, and whites in positions of authority. Limited interracial interaction impeded socialization. As a result, African Americans belonged to separate Masonic lodges, American Legion posts, fraternal organizations, and clubs. Additionally, the few independent black businesses that existed in the Upper Cumberland depended mostly on black clientele.

Segregation and discrimination pervaded the world of the black traveler and consumer. Hardship of travel was exacerbated because few eateries deigned to serve African Americans. At some restaurants— though they paid the same price for food and drinks as whites—blacks were forced to pick up their purchases from the rear, carry their items out in a bag, or eat on a makeshift table in the kitchen outside of public view. Oftentimes, restaurants provided black patrons with paper plates, plastic utensils, and paper cups, while white customers ate from china plates, drank from glasses, and used flatware. Blacks desiring refreshments at drugstores or other shops received service only if paper cups

were available. Shoppers were not allowed the courtesy of trying on
clothing or jewelry before purchasing them. Racial discrimination affected health care and legal dealings, for black patients and clients had
to enter professional offices from a rear door. Even treatment of medical
emergencies could evoke white hostility. Often denied emergency medical care because of the color of their skin, many blacks found hospitals
unwilling to admit them.

In the last quarter of the nineteenth century, the black population
decreased in the region as some left for greener pastures. Further decline occurred in the twentieth century, with substantial losses coming
in the Depression era (1930–1942). Many left because of the lack of
employment opportunities. Some left because of the social dynamics of
the Jim Crow system.

The year 1954 proved pivotal in the quest for African American
civil rights. On May 17, the United States Supreme Court, by unani-
mous vote, declared segregation in public schools of the nation unconstitutional. This decision compelled African Americans and whites in
the Upper Cumberland to acknowledge that there was no place for separate accommodations. Over the next several years, this legal precedent
would be applied to other areas. Despite the *Brown Decision*, civil rights,
and voting rights legislation, change was slow in coming to much of the
South.

Students at the Darwin School. Courtesy of Cookeville History Museum.

Not until the mid- to late-1960s were Tennessee's Upper Cumberland schools desegregated. Putnam County schools were the first to integrate, following a fire that destroyed the all-black Darwin School in January 1963. Darwin School, much like Jackman High School in Adair County, Kentucky, was the only black high school in the region, and surrounding counties arranged for their students to attend school there. When Darwin School burned, authorities in White, Overton, Clay, and Jackson counties had to accommodate their black high school students. Jackson County schools integrated in the fall of 1963. In that same year, DeKalb County desegregated its schools. Black and white students in Smith and Macon counties, however, did not attend integrated schools until 1965.[27] Although only 28.9 percent of African Americans throughout Tennessee attended integrated schools in 1966, Upper Cumberland blacks were attending desegregated schools.[28]

Incidents of bad race relations occurred during the early days of integration. In some instances, white students and teachers manifested varying degrees of racism. A young African American female in DeKalb County claimed that one teacher made no effort to conceal his racism. In her own words, "[He] would not let me go to the bathroom, but would let all the other [white] students go. I was the only black in class, so I felt that he was prejudiced. I kept raising my hand but he still would ignore me."[29]

A black educator, who, as a student, rode a Trailways bus to Lebanon during her first two years of high school, remembered that the county sheriff caused an incident on the first day that DeKalb County High School integrated in 1963. The sheriff attempted to intimidate the four young African Americans. The teacher recalled that, "Just as we were about to get started, in walks the sheriff . . . with his gun on his hip. He followed us around saying, 'Get out of here,' and 'You don't have any business here.'" The students were spared when Thomas G. Webb, the school's librarian, led the students away from the sheriff, staying with them until the authority left.[30]

Civil rights marches and protests were rare in the Upper Cumberland. Voter registration drives did not occur because black voters typically had access to the ballot. This is not to imply that African Americans were content with segregation, and therefore did nothing to eliminate the practice where it existed. In Cookeville, blacks took subtle actions to end segregation. They desegregated the Princess Theater in 1963. Some local blacks, believed to be affiliated with the NAACP, approached the owner, Leon DeLozier, suggesting it was time to integrate Cookeville's movie theater. DeLozier removed the "White" and "Colored" signs, and the African Americans entered the theater and sat in the ground floor once reserved for whites. All went well except for a single white complaint. Almost immediately thereafter, the Putnam Drive-in, also owned by DeLozier, integrated.[31] In 1965, the Cookeville Holiday Inn desegregated. This occurred after black debaters from Fisk University at a college debate sponsored by Tennessee Technological University refused to participate if their contestants were not lodged in the same hotel with other visiting white schools.[32]

Isaac Bohannon, principal of the Darwin School. Courtesy of Cookeville History Museum.

Because of their small numbers, black voters generally made a minor impact on election results. In some areas, African Americans voted well before the franchise was mandated by the Civil Rights Act of 1964 and the Voting Rights Act of 1965. John Dowell, an Alexandria resident, first voted in 1941. Aline Garrett of DeKalb County cast her first vote in the 1950s. On the other hand, Dixie Ann Thompson of Silver Point did not register to vote until 1964. In the 1960s, African Americans became more politically active. Robert Evans, longtime resident of Smith County, served on the County Court, and along with Roy Carter, served on the District Court there. Described as affluent, Smith County resident Jim McKinley served twenty-six years on the Carthage City Council. He also served as vice-mayor for six years. McKinley credited white mayor James Clay for encouraging him to run for the City Council.[33]

In the early 1970s Cookeville businessman John McClellan Sr., was the first African American to hold elected office in Putnam County. Sitting on the Quarterly Court in 1972, forerunner to the County Commission, he served as Justice of the Peace for the 10th District. The Putnam County *Light* described McClellan as "an intelligent man who helped bridge the gap between the black and white citizens of Putnam."[34] In 1995, Ms. Johnnie Wheeler of Cookeville became the second African

American, and first black woman, elected to the County Commission in Putnam County.[35]

The transition from enslavement to freedom was as much psychological as it was legal. Slavery created a caste and value system ingrained in and sustained by laws. The institution was as varied in the Upper Cumberland as it was elsewhere. In some areas, whites and African Americans held mutual respect for each other, or at least shared their skills simply to survive.

After emancipation, African Americans in the Upper Cumberland struggled for acceptance as equal citizens. They constantly found themselves victims of the miscarriage of justice, racially motivated violence, and stereotyping. Still, they managed to establish communities. Blacks established institutions; provided community entertainment and social events; promoted education and learning; provided medical care and spiritual support; and performed last rites for the dead.

Though race relations were generally better in the Upper Cumberland than in other parts of the South, there are no easy explanations of why this was so. In some communities, unlike much of the South in general, African Americans and whites lived next door to each other, forging friendships well before the *Brown Decision*. Positive relations existed in some locations because African Americans had been raised by white families, and vice versa. Such associations likely eliminated some misgivings as individuals came to know each other and care for each other within the constraints of law.[36]

The number of African Americans was so small, especially in high school enrollment, that the fears of white parents abated. In addition, the local media, politicians, and school officials did not sensationalize the race issue. This certainly was a significant factor. Finally, the lack of a concerted, direct confrontation of segregated institutions by African Americans cannot be discounted.

NOTES

1. Robert E. Corlew, *Tennessee: A Short History* (Knoxville: University of Tennessee Press, 1987): 209.

2. *Eleventh Census of the United States, 1890,* part I, Population; *Negro Population in the United States: 1790–1915* (New York: Arno Press, 1968).

3. Marion Brunson Lucas, *A History of Blacks in Kentucky* (Frankfort: Kentucky Historical Society, 1992): 17, 20.

4. An unidentified correspondent out of the state of Tennessee, cited in

Will T. Hale, *History of DeKalb County* (McMinnville, Tenn.: The Ben Lemond Press, 1969): 100.

5. Lowell H. Harrison, "Memories of Slavery Days," *The Filson Club Historical Quarterly* 47:3 (July 1973): 248–50.

6. Lucas, 8; Corlew, 212; Acts of Tennessee, 1835–1836, 167; 1831, 122–23; 1851–1852, 252. Also refer to John C. Inscoe, *Appalachians and Race: The Mountain South, from Slavery to Segregation* (Lexington: The University Press of Kentucky, 2001).

7. Will T. Hale, *History of Warren County* (McMinnville, Tenn.: Standard Printing Company, 1930): 42.

8. Carter G. Woodson (ed. & comp.), *Free Negro Owners of Slaves in the United States in 1830* (New York: Negro Universities Press, 1924 copyright, 1968 reprint): 4, 32; and *Fifth Census of the United States, 1830*, Population.

9. *Digest of Statute Laws of Kentucky*, vol. II (1834): 1474. This provision was challenged and declared unconstitutional since it conflicted with Article X, sections 10 and 15, of the Kentucky Constitution of 1799. Punishment for striking a white person was reduced to a fine and imprisonment.

10. Carole Stanford Bucy, *Tennessee Women: A Guide for Teachers* (Nashville: League of Women Voters of Tennessee, 1993): 36.

11. Ibid.

12. Lucas, 56, 112; Hale, *History of DeKalb County*, 100. Also refer to Jeanne Cannella Schmitzer, "The Black Experience at Mammoth Cave, Edmonson County, Kentucky, 1838–1942" (University of Central Florida, Master's Thesis, 1996): 38.

13. John Hope Franklin and Loren Schweninger, *Runaway Slaves: Rebels on the Plantation* (New York: Oxford University Press, 1999): 210–13.

14. Allen Trelease, *White Terror: Ku Klux Klan Conspiracy and Southern Reconstruction* (New York: Harper and Row, 1971): 177–78.

15. NAACP, *Thirty Years of Lynchings* (Washington, D.C.: NAACP, 1919): 65–68.

16. Harold Blankenship, *History of Macon County, Tennessee* (Tompkinsville, Ky.: Monroe County Press, 1986), 167, 169–70.

17. Cookeville *Press*, July 26, 1894; Cookeville *Press*, June 14, 1894; Thomas G. Webb, *A Bicentennial History of DeKalb County, Tennessee* (Smithville, Tenn.: Bradley Print Co., 1995), 156; interview of Ezra Jones, October 25, 1978, Russell Spring, Kentucky; interview of Laura Grider, March 18, 1997, Somerset, Kentucky.

18. W. E. B. DuBois, *Autobiography of W. E. B. DuBois* (New York: International Publishers, 1968): 115–16, 119. For more about the Wheeler School, see *Atlantic Monthly*, LXXXIII (January 1899): 100.

19. Helen Bullard and Joseph Marshall Krechniak, *Cumberland County's First Hundred Years* (Crossville, Tenn.: Centennial Committee, 1956): 144–45.

20. Elizabeth Peterson and Tom Rankin, "Free Hill: An Introduction," *Tennessee Folklore Society Bulletin* L:1 (1985): 5, 6, fn 9–10; see also, Clay County Homecoming '86 Historical Book Committee, *Clay County Tennessee* (Paducah, Ky.: Turner Publishing Co., 1986): 55.

21. Blankenship, 106, 168–69.

22. James Corbet Shirley, Metcalfe County, Kentucky; tape-recorded interview, March 7, 1994.

23. Interview of Emma Crabtree, May 19, 1976, Jackson County, Tennessee; interview of Dixie Galbraith White, April 16, 1976, Gainesboro, Tennessee. Dixie Ann Thompson, Silver Point, Tennessee; tape-recorded interview by Melissa Spear, March 4, 1995. Emma Crabtree, Jackson County, Tennessee; tape-recorded interview, May 19, 1976. Margaret Grady, Columbia, Kentucky; tape-recorded interview, September 1994. "[Dunbar] delivered babies all over the country. They'd come after Aunt Lindy. [But] these was [sic] white babies! She was a funny woman. She never would have very much to do with people our shade [black people]."

24. Dixie Ann Thompson, Silver Point, Tennessee; tape-recorded interview, March 4, 1995. Elizabeth Denton Allen, Burkesville, Kentucky; tape-recorded interview by Elizabeth Reed, March 2, 1992. Walter Maxey, Burkesville, Kentucky; tape-recorded interview, December 29, 1975.

25. Ann Romaine, "In Memoriam: Robert 'Bud' Garrett (1916–1987)," *Tennessee Folklore Society Bulletin* LIII:1 (1988): 27–28.

26. DuBois, 119.

27. Southern Education Reporting Service, *A Statistical Summary, State by Sate, of Segregation-Desegregation Activity Affecting Southern Schools from 1954 to Present, Together with Pertinent Data Enrollment, Teachers, Colleges, Litigation and Legislation,* 6 Vols. (Nashville, Tenn., n.p., 1957–1964): 9.

28. Tennessee State Department of Education, Equal Educational Opportunities Program, "Desegregation Report on Tennessee's Public Elementary and Secondary Schools, Fall 1966," 2, 4, 5, 7.

29. Carroll Ellen Gaines, DeKalb County, Tennessee: tape-recorded interview, April 26, 1995.

30. Jackie Smith, Smithville, Tennessee: tape-recorded interview by Tiffany Hatcher, 1995. The four black students were Jackie Smith, Linda Stokes, William Tubbs Jr., and Robbie J. Lee.

31. Leon DeLozier, Cookeville, Tennessee: tape-recorded interview by Matthew Wilhelm, March 4, 1998; tape and transcript in possession of the author.

32. Mary Jean DeLozier, *Putnam County, Tennessee, 1850–1970* (Nashville: McQuiddy Publishing, 1979): 300, 304–5, 324.

33. Robert Evans, Carthage, Tennessee: tape-recorded interview, Lafayette, Tennessee, July 13, 1994. James E. McKinley Sr., Carthage, Tennessee: tape-recorded interview, June 9, 1994.

34. Putnam County *Light* (November 2, 1995); DeLozier, *Putnam County,* 324.

35. Putnam County *Light* (November 2, 1995).

36. Ella and J. C. Moss, Smith County, Tennessee: tape-recorded interview, September 1994; Annie Lee Hayne Black, Riddleton, Tennessee: tape-recorded interview, June 9, 1995.

Chapter 7
_____

"THAT'S NOT THE WAY I HEARD IT"

Traditional Life and Folk Legends of the Upper Cumberland

WILLIAM LYNWOOD MONTELL

As a folklorist and oral historian, I am committed to the study of traditional life and culture of people whose names, actions, attitudes, and behaviors are seldom, if ever, included in history books. The thrust of my academic endeavors for more than forty years has been to write about local people as they perceive themselves.

Some historians and folklorists might disagree with me, but I deem stories (or narratives) to be the strongest force in creating and maintaining a strong sense of identification with state, region, community, and home place that most of us know, appreciate, and understand. Thus, because social and economic change is inevitable, one must not neglect to preserve a record of the average person's role in a region's cultural heritage. The Upper Cumberland is a subregion of Appalachia that is physically characterized by lush rivers and creek valleys, secluded coves, and upland areas of beautifully sculptured rolling hills and the plateau. Most people of the area now work in the county-seat towns in factories, schools, banks, hospitals, hardware and department stores, and farm produce houses. Yet, many of them continue to live in rural areas on the ancestral lands once occupied by their parents and grandparents. Such dependence on the land provides pleasant memories and a vicarious sense of generational continuity.

Much of the folklore and folklife found in the Upper Cumberland springs from the frontier period that began in the last quarter of the eighteenth century, and continued across the years because of generational occupation of the same soil, decades of shared experiences, and a strong desire to maintain cultural stability and historic continuity. People here are wedded to the land, and the land holds precious memories.

Pioneer settlers in the Upper Cumberland brought along certain items, including iron kettles, feather beds, quilts, seed for the first year's planting, and the necessary farming implements and tools. Included, too, were their traditional ideas about farming, tending livestock, hunting and fishing, preparing food, schooling of the young, socializing, and worshiping God. Many of these traditions were to undergo change, however, in the demanding new environment. If the early settlers had previously been accustomed to frequent and formal worship, they soon became accustomed to visits by circuit-riding preachers, brush-arbor meetings (services held within the shade of large trees), accompanied by bountiful dinners on the ground.[1]

Early agriculture of pioneer settlers was subsistence in nature. Clearing the land of trees to make room for agricultural pursuits was a task faced by pioneers and subsequent generations alike, until the early years of the twentieth century. Residents approached this major hurdle communally, as men united efforts in cutting trees, trimming away tree tops

Children on the porch of a typical home early in the twentieth century. Courtesy of the Tennessee State Library and Archives.

and limbs and stacking the brush into piles, rolling huge logs together, and burning them once adequate drying had taken place.

Making things by hand has been an integral part of the area folklife activity since pioneer times. Scholars point out that folk crafts often combine both functional and decorative elements, and that the utilitarian aspect of traditional crafts (i.e., making objects for practical use) ties them most clearly to historical times. In *Seedtime on the Cumberland* and *Flowering of the Cumberland*, Harriet Arnow, a native of the Kentucky Upper Cumberland, chronicled certain facets of the early history of practical skills in everyday life. She observed that the first settlers used skills they had learned traditionally, along with intuitive knowledge, to fill basic needs with materials near at hand. The pioneer era encouraged widespread proficiency in many kinds of handwork.[2]

Self-sufficiency on the Upper Cumberland frontier made the acquisition of traditional skills commonplace well into the twentieth century in remote parts of the area, where rugged terrain and relative isolation kept many families reliant on subsistence farming, hunting, fishing, musseling (for buttons and pearls), whiskey making, and forest-related livelihoods. Similar economic conditions created trends toward specialization in some crafts among families and individuals during the early years of the nineteenth century—a trend that remains unabated at the beginning of the twenty-first century.

Folk architecture in this part of the Upper South exhibits the skills of local builders, who were craftsmen in their own right and often employed the same tools as those who made baskets, chairs, tool handles, and other handmade objects. During frontier times and subsequent years, homes served as food storage areas as well as living quarters. Hanging from nails protruding from the upstairs ceiling beams were dried beans, corn, pumpkins, and numerous other home-produced items preserved for consumption during winter months. Onions and potatoes were stored in the loft area. During cold weather, it was common practice to add a layer of cover to these stored food items every time a quilt was added to the beds occupied by the people. In early spring, as occupants discarded each quilt or blanket from their beds, a corresponding coverlet was removed from the onions and potatoes.

Small children of the same gender usually slept in a bed located in the same room as their parents. At other times, the father and a small son slept in one bed while the mother and a small daughter slept in another bed in the same room. Husband and wife had to wait until the children were asleep before they could enjoy intimacy together. Three elderly women told of times when their parents thought the kids were asleep but were not. I asked one woman who had numerous siblings how her parents ever found enough privacy to have that many children. "Hump-h-h," she jokingly retorted, "the other kids had to go to school, didn't they!"

Early log homes, along with clapboard and brick houses built years later, were the setting for family and community groups who gathered around the fireplace in the evenings, especially during the winter months. Generally, one member of the family assumed the role of storyteller, while others sang old songs and ballads that had been brought along from the Carolinas, east Tennessee, Pennsylvania, and Virginia. These were often the same songs, with but minor variations, as those brought across the ocean by the first European immigrants. These items of traditional lore, along with innumerable folk beliefs, customs, and practices, provided mental ties with previous generations.

To ensure health and longevity across the years, Upper Cumberland residents depended on the land to provide medicinal cures for illnesses and bodily injuries. Some remedies had been prepared and brought onto the frontier from the seaboard colonies, or from the Old World. Others were developed as the people became familiar with the flora and fauna.

The subject of folk healing includes all ideas about health and diseases and the means of controlling them. Until the 1950s, scientific validity was not important to the groups of people who used folk healing practices. To them, folk medicine solved problems of disease and illness in a way that was acceptable to the group. Folk medicine frequently worked because members of the group believed that it worked. The placebo effect proved strong. If people thought they would be cured, often they were.

Older generations did not have access to scientific medical technology. There were few trained physicians scattered across the area, usually located in community, town, and trade centers. People who lived away from these areas had an especially hard time obtaining the services of a licensed physician. Thus, because of the lack of medical services, people in these rural areas developed their own beliefs and practices related to prevention and cure of diseases.

Back then, most medical doctors operated surgically with knives, often at home on the kitchen table; thus, most preferred a home cure to being cut open. Because hypodermic needles were used by early physi-

Pickett countian Ira Scott cut and snaked logs in the same manner as his forebears.
Photo by David Sutherland.

cians only to relieve pain in the final hours of life, hypodermic shots to
the common folk became symbolic of the end of life.

There was a strong belief that God, through nature, provided a
cure for all ailments. Specifically, the herbs and plants that grow wild
were used for various remedies. And it did not cost anything to go into
a field, a thicket, or wooded area to search for a medicinal root or plant.

A member of the black Sadler family who lived on Martin's Creek east of Carthage was Uncle Med Sadler, who is still remembered for three things that he kept under his bed at all times: a wash pan full of water to drown his troubles, an axe with the blade turned upward to cut body pain, and a shotgun to keep away evil spirits. Additionally, Uncle Med served as a weather prophet. It is said that in the event of a drought, he would kill a snake and tie it to a tree to predict rain. If its body turned in a certain direction, rain would soon come.[3]

Local folk culture is typically dominated by families who have occupied their ancestral home for three or more generations. When dealing with generational family folklore, one must look at the family as a reflection of its strong ties to the old homes, to known recollections of past generations. This is what I choose to call generational bonding through family traditions.[4]

The Upper Cumberland has historically been identified with the process of folk legendry. That was true of the area in its early years, and it is equally true today. These historical legends concern family, community, and region. And they deal with topics of all varieties, from ghosts to local character anecdotes, and from the Civil War to recent local killings.

The Civil War served to crystallize the history and culture of the Upper Cumberland. Families were torn apart by divided loyalties, as guerrilla bands on both sides of the conflict daily raided some part of the area, taking items they could carry away on horseback, and killing or torturing those persons who resisted them. A limited number of official battles were fought in the Upper Cumberland, but this was perhaps the nation's leading area for guerrilla activities. These bands consisted of outlaws and renegades. Though devoted to either the Northern or Southern cause, they were chiefly interested in what they could amass for themselves. All too numerous are oral stories that tell of fathers and sons brutally murdered and of traumatized wives and daughters left behind to bury the mutilated bodies of their men. Cordell Hull, secretary of state under President Roosevelt, described his Fentress (now Pickett) County homeland during the Civil War as a "living hell."

Not only did the Civil War produce a large body of legends, the war also changed the psyche of the Upper Cumberland for years to come. An air of defeatism and pessimism gripped the entire area, and this was reflected in song and local balladry for decades following the Civil War.

All persons interested in tracing their family roots know that even when they acquire the names of ancestors from formal records, they do not learn anything about their ancestors' daily lives, social activities, and economic livelihood. For example, what do formal records tell them about how their great-grandparents or great-great-grandparents felt about brother fighting brother during the Civil War? Or perhaps the time one of a grandparent's siblings was caught and jailed for making and selling a batch of moonshine whiskey?

Formal records are truly important and significant in genealogical research efforts, but they seldom provide the personal information and descriptions found in stories. People's oral historical accounts, which have typically not been written down, reveal a rich repository of what local life and times were like one hundred fifty years ago, or even just twenty years ago.

Until 1950, or thereabout, families and neighbors who remained in the Upper Cumberland sat around on the weekends and engaged in storytelling sessions, both to ward off boredom, and perhaps to teach the kids who were present something about their local heritage and family history. Personal stories and family legends that describe real people serve to sustain and reinforce family ties and generational continuity.

The people of the Upper Cumberland use four types of oral narratives in recalling personal and generational social and economic activi-

Rogers family in the Calfkiller River Valley of White County, Tennessee. Photo courtesy of Ken Thomson.

ties, some that represent pleasant memories; some that do not. These are personal, family, community, and regionwide stories.

Personal stories represent oral history based on a testimony that says, "I was there; I saw or took part in the action; and this is what happened." By way of illustration, many first-person accounts describe the days when steamboats ran the Cumberland River. Back then, in addition to the major landings that lined the river, virtually every farmer who owned property bordering the river had a private landing. If a farmer had a quantity of corn or other farm produce he wished to sell, he would flag down a passing steamboat by waving his hands and yelling so that the captain or deckhands could hear him. The boat would then dock and pick up his agricultural products. In like fashion, if the farmer or his wife had ordered goods from a distant merchant, the boat would stop to deliver these items. A wonderful first-person account of what childhood times were like when steamboats were still plying the Cumberland was told by Lena Howell Martin of Jackson County:

> When my second daughter was four or five years old, she and a friend were out playing. My daughter said to her friend, "There's a steamboat coming. Let's flag it down!!" Well, she went to waving and flagging down, and the captain went to blowing his whistle for the landing. That like to have scared my little daughter to death. She ran to the back of the house where it wasn't underpinned, and she crawled back under the floor of the house. Well, my little girl didn't know it, but I had ordered a bed for her, and the boat was stopping to put the bed off here at the landing. But she thought she's the one that flagged the boat down. That scared her to death.[5]

Another personal account provided by Willie Frogge of Pickett County tells how and why he, as a young boy, ran away from home:

> When I was seven years old, I was boring some holes with an auger, and my step-daddy threatened to whip me up there in Wayne County. So I just ran off and went to the house to ask my mother how to get over into Tennessee. She said, "What do you want to know that for?" I told her that I might want to go over there sometime. So she told me, said, "You'll go across that mountain to get to Travisville. And there's a pipeline across the

road. You turn there to go over to Uncle John Jennings's house over there on Shellot Creek." I said, "Well, I think that I'll just step over there." So I just lit out. Well, I could hear wagons all the way behind me going across that mountain. I walked until I got tired and hungry. There was three old Dishman women who lived beside the road. So I stopped and bummed me something to eat. They gave me a piece of ham and a piece of cornbread. They wanted me to set down and eat. I told them no, that I didn't have time. Well, I eat on that ham and bread for four or five miles. I'd eat some, then run some more. Eat another bite, then run some more. Years later, I went back to thank them.

I went on across Bald Rock Mountain after passing across Turkey Mountain, then through Slickford, then up Dry Hollow, and on to Chestnut Grove. When I finally got to Travisville, I went in to find out where the pipeline was at. Well, you could have tracked me because of the flow of blood from my feet. I had to walk on them sharp limestone rocks; just cut my feet something awful, and the blood was coming out. I told this fellow that I was trying to get to Rob Upchurch's place. That's right close to Sgt. York's birthplace. Just on the hill above his old birthplace. Well, Old Man Manuel Anderson was there. I never will forget that he was riding his big yaller horse. He said, "I'm going across from here to Shellot. I'll carry you on behind me here on this horse." He carried me on up there, then said, "I'll just take you on up to Rob and Nanny Upchurch's place."

Well, Nanny wrote a letter that night and mailed it the next morning telling my mother that I was there. She got answer back in a few days from my mother who said that she couldn't believe that I'd made it that far. That was about forty-six miles, but I made it. It wasn't much of a road. Just an old dirt road.

When I got there, Rob was up in the field working. When he come to the house, he went up to a store and bought me my first pair of shoes. That was the first shoes I ever had, and I was seven years old.

I began working on this pole road, but was still under age. I was fourteen at that time. Nanny Upchurch tried to get me to quit, but I wouldn't quit, so she wrote my mother, and my mother wrote them a letter telling them that I was under age and not to work me. This boss man brought the letter to me, read it to me, then said, "I hate to see you quit as bad as you hate to quit. But take your mules

and put them in the barn and unharness them, then come back
and I'll give you the money, but I'm not firing you."[6]

The second category of historical legends consists of stories told by
persons who are one or more generations removed from what they are
describing. They know of an event or topic, not because they were
there personally, but because they talked with someone. The information thus obtained by the interviewer is secondhand. It may not be as
trustworthy as a firsthand account, but is historically valuable when
used appropriately and in proper context. Whether or not the historic-
ity of such oral accounts can be proven, all of them are worthy of being
recorded. Living generations may learn much about their ancestors from
narratives told over and over in family and community circles. This
form of folk history is often a family's only meaningful link with its
past.

An example of a humorous family story was told by Edd Moody of
Moodyville, Tennessee, about his father, who had passed along the account to family members: "One night my dad came home late. There
was a big bench there in the house where the water buckets were set.
On this particular night, somebody had set a slop bucket up there. The
room was sort of dark. Well, Dad picked up a water dipper and stuck it
over in this bucket that he assumed had water in it. He put his lips to
the dipper, stuck his tongue out a few times, said, 'Humm, this tastes
kinda salty.' Come to find out, he'd drunk a dipper full of hog slop, and
he just about died when he found out what he had done."[7]

Community and regionwide stories or legends comprise the third
and fourth categories of stories told by local people. These may be first-
person accounts describing events that occurred within the storyteller's
lifetime, then picked up and retold by community members, or they
can be descriptions of something that happened two hundred years
ago. Community or regional legends exist because many people in the
area know them and recount them at every opportunity as part and
parcel of shared history. Many of these stories are based on fact; others
are unverifiable hearsay. But whether true or simply believed to be true,
such stories provide people with a strong sense of belonging to a particular community or to a specific group within the larger area.

There are countless eccentric character stories that describe, for
example, the ugliest man or woman of all time in the community; the
stingiest person who ever lived there; the meanest person who ever
walked on two legs; or the sweetest little old lady who ever lived.

An epitome of country doctors was Dr. McDonald of Alpine in Overton County, Tennessee. Courtesy of the Tennessee State Library and Archives.

Of all the various types of community and regional legends, those about the Civil War are most common. This is no wonder, as numerous accounts tell of father fighting against son, brother against brother, and neighbor against neighbor. One such regionwide legend claims that Champ Ferguson (Rebel renegade from Clinton County, Kentucky, who had moved to White County, Tennessee) killed his Unionist brother James. The legend asserts that, on learning James had been wounded in battle and was in a hospital in Virginia, Champ rode on horseback to the hospital and went to James's bedside, pulled a gun, and aimed it at the brother's head:

"'My God, Champ, don't shoot me,' James begged, 'Can't you see that I'm dying?'

"'Then I'll just help the process along,' Champ responded, as he twice pulled the trigger and killed him."[8]

Pall Mall resident Luther M. York provided the following account about one of Champ Ferguson's attempts to kill Union guerrilla Tinker Dave Beatty. Ferguson and Beatty were continual opponents during the war, and Beatty was as notorious in his own way as Ferguson. Beatty's home was in Fentress County, but his hideout was in an extensive cave system in Morgan County near Montgomery. If Confederate soldiers entered the area, Beatty sounded a horn and his irregulars gathered at the cave. His men once repulsed 1,500 Confederate cavalry men. As the war progressed the hostility between Beatty and Ferguson grew more violent.[9] Luther York recounted:

> The story goes that they met one day in Jamestown, Tennessee. They got up within shooting distance before they recognized each other and then Ferguson shot Tinker Dave. In order to escape, Tinker Dave swung down by the side of his horse hanging onto his horse's neck, the horse shielding him from further shots by Champ Ferguson. He escaped over into the head of Rock Castle Creek, one of the canyons that heads up near Jamestown. Well, he spent quite a few months over there recuperating from the wound inflicted by Champ Ferguson there on the streets of Jamestown.[10]

Another Tinker Dave Beatty legend, filled with much family information, was provided by Sara Jane Koger, Jamestown, as initially told by her grandmother:

Loafers and Storytellers on the courthouse lawn, Celina, Tennessee, 1991. Photo by the author.

Oh, I've heard my grandmother Mary Choate, who married John Franklin, talk about many different things, like back in the Civil War when she was trying to raise her family and about them almost starving to death; they couldn't get nothing to eat back through the Civil War. And she had one son, George Franklin, that joined the army when he was sixteen. He went in as a water boy, or something like that. I've got a letter here that I got from him when he was a hundred years old. And he wrote a real good plain letter. Told when he joined the army and all about it. Grandmother had ten children and her husband died when my mother was two years old. And Grandma, of course, had a rough time a-raising the kids back at that time. This boy was sixteen and he was the oldest one. So he just joined the army. She didn't want him to join, she said, but Tinker Dave Beatty had a bunch of guerrillas and my grandparents were living on Tinker Dave's place. He [her son] told her that he'd rather join the regular army, that if he stayed at home, Tinker would want him to go with the guerrilla bunch and he didn't want to do it. So he just joined the army.

Grandmother Franklin said that she raised a little colt. Said she raised it from a baby colt, and said it was an awful pretty little thing. She said it was as gentle as it could be. And a bunch of soldiers come one time and was going to take her mare. . . . She said she went out to try to keep them from catching it. Said she knowed if they ever got a bridle on it, said they had one of them big old cavalry bridles so heavy, said it looked like it weighted him down. And, of course, she got mad. She got out and got her a switch. It'd run off and they'd follow it around. And said there was a fence up above their house and a big long bottom. She said she guessed [it was] a mile long. And said she hit the little mare with the switch and it went over that fence and took off up that bottom. Said that soldier—there was two of them trying to catch it. Said he started up after it. She said to this soldier, "I wish you would go up there. I seen a bunch of Tinker's men go around the bluff this morning." She said he turned around and went back, left them alone.

She also had a heifer. And they come and got the heifer. They'd up them a halter on it and started to take it off. And her and one of her boys started after them, begging them to leave it and not to take it. And she said these soldiers were two boys that she had known for a long time. They began begging, too, for them to leave it. So they turned her calf loose and she took it back.

She'd set and tell things like that all the time. She would just set and talk, and us kids would just set down and listen because we had nothing else to turn our attention to. We had no television, no radio, or nothing like that to get our mind off on something else. We'd set and listen to her tell things that happened, and I always remembered.[11]

Another community/regionwide story involving violence is the twentieth-century saga of Billy Dean Anderson. Regarded by the people of Pall Mall in Fentress County as a good, God-fearing person who would never cause harm, Anderson was brutally shot and killed by the FBI on July 7, 1978. In the intervening years, Anderson rose to the level of folk hero in the guise of a Robin Hood who was forced to break the law because of corrupt officials.

Born in the Wolf River Valley on July 12, 1934, near the home of World War I hero Sergeant Alvin C. York, Anderson grew up in his maternal grandparents' house. As he matured, inhabitants of the valley were convinced that Anderson would become a Holiness minister. Ironically, his first brush with the law involved firing shots into the Methodist Church at Pall Mall.

Between 1959 and 1962 Anderson was arrested numerous times for a variety of offenses. According to legend, he committed armed robbery in California, Indiana, Ohio, and Kentucky. Anderson also gained a reputation for escaping from his captors. Stories about his exploits, and his boasts that no jail could hold him, began making the rounds with law enforcement officials.

A shootout in 1962 added to Anderson's growing notoriety. Billy Dean Anderson and George Long were pursued by highway patrolmen in Jamestown. The car they were driving was pulled over in front of the local funeral home. One trooper, Steve Webb, reportedly ordered Anderson out of the car, hitting him in the face and cursing him. Anderson responded by shooting the policeman. George Long exited the vehicle and had his hands on the roof of the car when Trooper J. T. Elmore shot back. Long received bullet wounds that left him totally paralyzed from the waist down. Webb and Elmore shot Anderson three times, leaving him partially paralyzed. He wore braces on both his legs. After his parole from prison in 1966, Anderson moved for a time to Indiana. When he returned to Fentress County in 1967, Anderson was harassed by the sheriff and a deputy and coaxed into another gun battle, resulting in two consecutive seven-year sentences for attempted murder. After only two years in jail, Anderson was paroled and told to leave the Volunteer State. He returned to Indiana and worked at a gas station. In 1970, Anderson was accused of pulling a gun on a customer, who reported the incident to authorities. Tried and convicted, he received a sentence of twenty-five years in the Indiana State Penitentiary. Friends and relatives in Pall Mall remain convinced that Anderson was framed.

Paroled in 1973, Anderson returned to Tennessee only to be involved in another gun battle in Fentress County. The shootout occurred as a result of a botched robbery attempt of a local beer joint by Anderson and Mitch Fitzgerald. Deputy Junior Hatfield arrested Anderson and Fitzgerald.[12] During his brief incarceration in the Fentress County jail, authorities reputedly abused Anderson, hiding his crutches and physically torturing him. The sheriff, Buster Stockton, feared retaliation from Anderson and had him transferred to the Morgan County jail. While in a holding cell in Wartburg, Anderson and another inmate escaped. Anderson's name was placed on the FBI's "most wanted" list in January 1975. Anderson fled to Fentress County, taking up residence in a cave on his grandfather's farm. With the aid of local Pall Mall citizens, Anderson made the cave habitable to hide from the authorities.

During the period of his evading the law, Anderson continued to develop his skills as a painter. Gifted with a strong visual style, the fugitive painted biblical images, especially pictures of a strong, muscular Christ. Many of Anderson's paintings were given to friends and family in the valley in exchange for food, provisions, and their silence.

In the meantime, law officials and the FBI began staking out Anderson's mother's home. Tipped off that he would visit his mother on July 4, dozens of federal and state policemen surrounded the farm. Because of local sympathies, Sheriff Tommy Williams and Fentress County law officers played no significant part in the tragedy that unfolded. Federal agents staked out around the Anderson homestead and attacked Billy Dean Anderson just after he climbed over his mother's fence on July 7, 1978. Anderson made it about twenty feet beyond her property when FBI agents opened up with 12-gauge shotguns. Two blasts ripped through Anderson's body and he fell in a heap on the ground. Although Anderson was still alive and in great pain, FBI agents waited for nearly one-half hour before they called for medical assistance. When it arrived it was too late, and Billy Dean Anderson lay dead on the blood-soaked ground. The slaying of Anderson enraged the Pall Mall community.

Country stores, such as this one in southeastern Overton County, Tennessee, in 1979 were community necessities and social gathering places. Photo by the author.

Locals argued that Billy Dean had not done enough to be gunned down in the name of the law. They believed that state and federal officials played into the hands of a corrupt former Fentress County sheriff who harbored a vendetta. Stories abound of Buster Stockton's mistreatment of Anderson, from hiding his crutches to physical abuse. In the eyes of locals, Billy Dean Anderson continues to be regarded as a good Christian man who loved his mother.[13]

Stories told within the families and communities across the Upper Cumberland help residents retain identity with family and community members who have moved away from home, or have died. Sometimes these wonderful narratives, whether about agricultural pursuits, architectural matters, community arts and crafts, folk medicinal practices, the Civil War, or natural disasters, deal with persons three, four, or five generations back in time. Thus, stories and legends serve as bonding agents. They provide people with a sense of generational continuity— ties with their ancestors who might otherwise be unknown to contemporary family members and the generations yet to come: "Overall, there is a feeling of warmth and togetherness in these stories, and they provide an overwhelming sense of community. Families were large and, at times, life was hard. But ingenuity, self-sufficiency, hard work, love, and a good sense of humor were all that was needed to survive."[14]

As illustrated here, folk history is a body of oral narratives told by people about themselves and other locals. These stories articulate the feelings and attitudes of individuals and groups about the events and persons described. Folk history is people's history—history from a very personal point of view. It is intricately tied with the subjectivity of those who talk about it, and it is often history from the bottom up— history in which the people themselves become their own chroniclers.

NOTES

1. Lewis Wirth, "The Limitations of Regionalism," in Merrill Jensen, ed., *Regionalism in America* (Madison: University of Wisconsin Press, 1951): 391.

2. Harriet Simpson Arnow: *Seedtime on the Cumberland* (New York: Macmillan, 1960); *Flowering of the Cumberland* (New York: Macmillan, 1963).

3. Katherine Anderson, Gainesboro, October 2, 1991.

4. Local folklore may be divided into two basic categories: Historical Folklore and Cyclical Folklore. Historical Folklore deals with the contemporary facets of everyday life—events often based on family traditions. Family Folklore includes heirlooms, souvenirs, hand tools, dishes, and other products of

material culture, but the family stories comprise the most significant category of family lore.

Three categories of family stories are Family Origins (e.g., courtship stories, how the family name originated), Historical Episodes (e.g., migration stories, ties to state or national events), and Family Characters/Personalities (e.g., heroes, eccentric characters, bravery and blunders).

Cyclical Family Folklore includes customs and rituals that are adhered to regularly. Three basic story types fit these cycles: Everyday customs and rituals (e.g., eating habits, bedtime stories), Special Annual Occasions (e.g., birthdays, holidays), and Occasional Special Days (e.g., weddings, graduations, baptisms, retirements).

As to the function of family folklore, it provides family members with a sense of knowing and identification with past generations; it places the family in a broader perspective; it helps maintain family bonds; and it creates identity for individual family members.

5. Quoted in William Lynwood Montell, *Don't Go Up Kettle Creek: Verbal Legacy of the Upper Cumberland* (Knoxville: University of Tennessee Press, 1983): 142–43.

6. Told by Willie Frogge, Pickett County, circa. April 1978 tape.

7. Told by Edd Moody, Moodyville, Pickett County, January 5, 1978.

8. Though Champ Ferguson's brother James did indeed die during the war, he was not murdered by Champ. After the Battle of Saltville, Champ entered a Union hospital tent and murdered his former friend, Lieutenant Eliza C. Smith, who fought with the Federals in the Thirteenth Kentucky Cavalry. Ferguson intended to kill Colonel Charles Hanson as well, but his plans were thwarted. The Saltville murder led to a Federal indictment, resulting in Ferguson's hanging as a war criminal on October 20, 1865. See Thomas D. Mays, *The Saltville Massacre* (Abilene, Tex.: McWhiney Foundation Press, 1998): 59, 63, 71; Major John A. Brents, *The Patriots and Guerillas of East Tennessee and Kentucky: The Sufferings of the Patriots, Also the Experiences of the Author as an Officer in the Union Army* (New York: Henry Dexter Publishers, 1863): 36–60; Larry H. Whiteaker, "Champ Ferguson's Civil War," *Tennessee: State of the Nation*, 2nd ed., Larry H. Whiteaker and W. Calvin Dickinson, eds. (New York: American Heritage Publishing, 1998): 99–104.

9. Frank Moore, ed. *Anecdotes, Poetry, and Incidents of the War: North and South, 1860–1865* (New York: Bible House, 1867): 383; Basil Duke, *History of Morgan's Cavalry* (Cincinnati: Miami Printing and Publishing Company, 1867): 416–18.

10. Told by Luther M. York, Pall Mall, July 1, 1972, to Linda White.

11. Sara Jane Koger, Jamestown, August 3, 1979, tape.

12. Purportedly, Anderson never fired a shot. According to local testimony, Fitzgerald took credit for firing a 30.06 rifle in the direction of the authorities during the gun battle, saying that Anderson did not participate in the shooting.

13. William Lynwood Montell, "When the FBI Wants You, . . . They Want You Dead," unpublished conference paper presented at the American Oral History Association, 1986.

14. Jana Pickering, class research paper, Western Kentucky University, November 1992.

Chapter 8

"NOW, THERE'S A STORY"

The Literature of the Upper Cumberland

ALLISON ENSOR

At one time it was common for teachers and scholars to dismiss the whole of American literature as insignificant compared with British and continental literature. Once American literature came to be appreciated, there was still little regard for Southern literature. And when Southern literature came into its own, there was little concern for the literature of Appalachia. In most studies of Appalachian literature, the higher mountains to the east have received the greatest attention from scholars. Yet it should be evident from all that has been said that the Upper Cumberland has made its appearance in poetry, fiction, and non-fiction. This would surely have been news to me during the sixteen years that I was a student in Cookeville, for it seemed that almost everything important in American literature happened in New England, New York, or Chicago or perhaps the Mississippi River Valley or the far West. I saw little evidence that anyone had ever written about my place. The rivers, lakes, mountains, and most of all, the people of this area have their place and will continue to figure in the literature of Appalachia, the South, and the United States.

In one sense, the literature of the Upper Cumberland begins with the various nonfiction accounts of travelers as they passed through "the wilderness," land that was controlled by the Native Americans as late as 1805. The eighty-mile road traversing the region was familiar to such travelers as Andre Michaux, French botanist (1795 and 1796); Reverend Green Hill (1796); Francis Bailey, an Englishman (1797); Abraham Steiner and Frederick Schweinitz, Moravian missionaries (1799); Francis Asbury, bishop of the Methodist Episcopal Church (1800 and 1802);

and botanist Francois Andre Michaux (1801). All left a record of their journeys, though few are more eloquent than Francis Bailey: "I saw the base of the mountains ranged in majestic orders before me, bidding defiance to my approach, and indicating the difficulties I should have to encounter." Again and again accounts mention the landmarks of that hazardous journey: Fort Southwest Point (Kingston), Spencer's Hill (Crab Orchard), Daddy's Creek, Drowning Creek, the Flat Rock (Monterey), Blackburn's (Baxter), Flynn's Creek, Fort Blount. Interestingly, none of those authors mentioned the famous Standing Stone, a remnant of which has stood for years in Whittaker Park in Monterey.

There may have been a number of nineteenth-century diary keepers in the Upper Cumberland, but I am aware of only one whose work has been published. At a men's boarding school called Cumberland Institute in White County, about eight miles from Sparta (and the same distance from Cookeville), Amanda McDowell kept a diary throughout the Civil War era. Her father, Curtis McDowell, built and operated the school where they lived at the time. Her diary, edited by her direct descendant, Lela McDowell Blankenship, was published as *Fiddles in the Cumberlands* (1943). The book contains portions of Amanda's diary and a number of letters and documents.[1] Entries began May 4, 1861, less than a month after Fort Sumter was fired on, and ended July 11, 1866, over a year after the conclusion of the war. Her very first entry demonstrates her horror at the outbreak of hostilities:

> Little thought have I had that I should ever live to see civil war like this, our goodly land, but so it is! The Southerners are so hot they can stand it no longer, and have already made the break. There will be many a divided family in this once happy Union. There will be father against son and brother against brother, O, God! that such things should be in a Christian land. That men in their blindness should rush so rashly to ruin. . . . They are taking on considerably at Sparta. Have raised a secession flag and are organizing companies at a great rate. . . . God grant that it may not prove so serious a matter as we are all fearing![2]

It was Easter Monday, April 17, 1865, before Amanda and her family learned that the Confederacy had been defeated. Lee's surrender at Appomattox had occurred more than a week earlier, on Palm Sunday, and Lincoln was assassinated on Good Friday, though Amanda was unaware of it. The text of the diary was seriously damaged when Amanda decided to eliminate from it every mention of the man she had formerly loved, Larkin Craig, a man who joined lawless bushwhackers and compounded his guilt by marrying another woman.

Amanda and her diary also appear in Lela McDowell Blankenship's *When Yesterday Was Today* (1966), a book that is part fiction, part family history. A central focus is Blankenship's father, Jackson McDowell, at one time the antisecessionist editor of the *Cookeville Times*. Since most of the immediate area was pro-Confederate, his sympathies quickly got him into trouble, and he was jailed in Cookeville for a time before heading north. In a long passage of recollection, Jackson McDowell mentions a startling "fact"; in Nashville in the 1850s, while working in a print shop, he had a brief acquaintance with a friendly, amusing teller of tales named Sam Clemens. If the future Mark Twain was indeed working in Nashville in the 1850s—or was ever in the city at all—no Twain scholar has ever found evidence to support the claim.[3]

A third book by Lela McDowell Blankenship, *The Uneven Yoke* (1962), again a blend of history and fiction, looks back to the early nineteenth century when the Rascoe, Swindell, and Knowles families journeyed westward from North Carolina across the mountains. They settled in White County near the intersection of the Caney Fork River and the Old Kentucky Road. One is surprised to hear Cookeville mentioned several decades before its founding, but for the most part the book is convincing in its incidents and dialogue.

One of its central characters, Patsy Rascoe, certainly would strike any modern reader as an early feminist. "I just want to see the day when women are made equal—if they are equal intellectually," she declares at one point, a radical view indeed for that time and place. On the subject of her daughter's distrust of marriage she says, "Mahala is sensible. . . . She knows that a man would make her give up her freedom. A man sets a trap that closes on a woman, leaving her without any of the pleasures of youth, and places her instead in work and trouble throughout the years."[4]

A strong and resourceful woman, Patsy saved the day more than once by acting quickly and decisively. She proved willing to challenge male authority figures—even a Methodist bishop who proposed to turn her out of the church for her heresies—but really because she rejected him and supported her daughter's rejection of him. As the novel proceeds, years pass, the Civil War is fought, Reconstruction comes and goes, and in the last pages, the family celebrates the fiftieth anniversary of its arrival at the Upper Cumberland.

Much more poetry has probably been written in the Upper Cumberland than has ever been published. One whose work found its way into print early was Robert P. Hudson, author of *Roving Footsteps* (1880), *Songs of the Cumberlands* (1887), identified on its title page as "a series of poems descriptive of scenes and incidents among the Cumberlands and throughout the South," and *Southern Lyrics: A Series of Original Poems on Love, Home, and the Southland* (Nashville, 1907). Hudson, a native of White County, grew up in Walling, at the Horseshoe Bend of the Caney Fork River. The river is prominent in a number of his poems, such as "By Caney Fork's Stream" (1877) and "Ode to the Caney Fork" (1884). Part of the latter addresses the river itself:

Robert Hudson. Frontispiece for *Southern Lyrics: A Series of Original Poems on Love, Home, and the Southland* (Southern Lyrics Publishing, 1907).

Crystal river, circling, seething,
Foaming river, babbling, moaning,
Pearly river, bright, reflecting,
Playful river, ever laughing,
Pleading river, always calling,
Rushing river, now unwieldy,
Wild, deep river, oft defiant,
O my river of all rivers![5]

Not all of Hudson's poems deal with the Upper Cumberland scenery; many are addressed to Kitty Lou, Josephine, Lula, Marietta, Ellen, Nannie, Rachel, a whole gallery of women with whom he was romantically involved. Other poems wander far afield, to "Our Nation's Centennial, 1876," the "World's Exposition (New Orleans, February, 1885)," Georgia, Florida, Mexico, and "Los Angeles" (1905).

A later Upper Cumberland poet was Clara Cox Epperson, a Gainesboro native whose name the Cookeville public library bore for many years. Through her leadership, members of the Cookeville Book Lovers Club donated the books that launched the library. Epperson held a number of state offices, including poet laureate, and for years wrote columns for the *Putnam County Herald*. She acted as editor of the poetry page in the *Tennessee Club Woman*. Though Epperson failed to publish a collection of her poetry, in 1973, thirty-six years after her death, a Tennessee Tech English professor, Lottie Farr, collected a number of her poems in a small book called *Scraps of Verse and Prose from Heartsease*. ("Heartsease" was the name of Epperson's home in Algood.) The book, published by Tech's English Department, did not receive wide distribution. Many of the poems concerned the family, religion, nature, and the special days of the year. Although the Blue Ridge Mountains and the French Broad River figure in her poems, no Upper Cumberland landmarks appear; the poem most obviously connected with the area is "My Muffin Cakes." This humorous poem—something of a rarity in the book—expresses the author's feelings at having some of her poems rejected at the same time her muffin cakes took first prize at the Putnam County Fair:

> My poems may not rank so high,
> Perhaps rarely one an honor takes,
> But at our Agricultural Fair
> I win cash on muffin cakes.
>
> My verses may not win your heart,
> And over this my heart aches,
> But I shall win you when you taste
> My old-fashioned muffin cakes.
>
> And some day if you come to me
> When earth is luring color takes,
> I shall not read my poems to you
> But feed you on my muffin cakes.[6]

The recipe for the prize-winning muffin cakes was included in the book, following the poem, which Farr says was given to her in the 1930s.

Another poet whose roots lie in the Upper Cumberland is Jim Clark, a native of Byrdstown who grew up in Cookeville. Now a professor and writer-in-residence at Barton College in Wilson, North Carolina, Clark published two collections of his poetry, *Dancing on Canaan's Ruins* (1983) and *Handiwork* (1998). His stories and poems have appeared in the *Georgia Review, Prairie Schooner, Southern Poetry Review,* and elsewhere; his poem "At Dusk" was read on Garrison Keillor's "Writer's Almanac" in 1999. Titles of some of his poems clearly reflect the Upper Cumberland, for example, "Dawn Below Cordell Hull Lake" and "Moonrise at Dale Hollow Lake." A series of poems called "Songs from the Lost Map's Legend" includes sections headed "Granville," "Window Cliffs," "Bee Rock," and "Cookeville." Some of these are quite brief and do not contain nearly as much description or local color as the title might lead one to expect. The poem on Cookeville has only two lines: "Nowhere/ to get lost." I would say that the poem is open to more than one interpretation; perhaps it means that everyone is so friendly here that one cannot be lost for long. Or does it mean that if one is going to get lost, Cookeville is definitely not the place to do it? Or that Cookeville is such a small place that there is no place in it that one *can* get lost? Somewhat longer is Clark's "The Land under the Lake," written for his parents' fiftieth wedding anniversary. Though it begins with a familiar Bible story, it soon moves to the flooding of much of the land and many buildings when Dale Hollow Lake was created:

> I think of Noah, his family spared,
> Riding that bark of gopher wood above,
> The good lands of home, now submarine paired
> Beasts below waiting for news of the dove.
>
> Less sublime than God's wondrous instruction
> The voice of the Washington bureaucrat
> Told of the Dale Hollow Dam's construction--
> Good farms, long held, flooded in nothing flat.

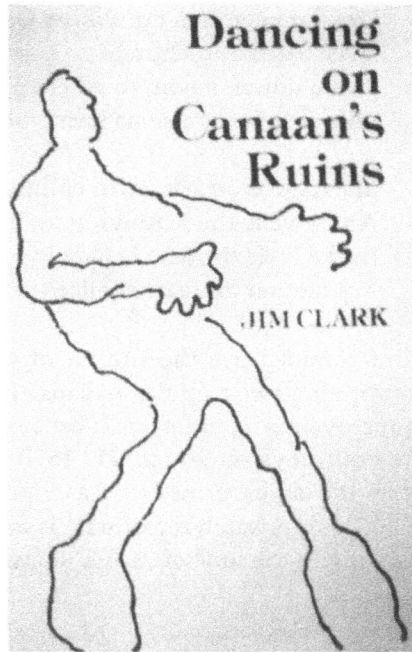

Frontispiece from Jim Clark's *Dancing on Canaan's Ruins.*

One summer on a houseboat we drifted
Over barns and churches, cornfields, and cribs,
Swam down, down, to where gauzy light sifted
Like silt through some barn's or house's ribs.

Marriage is an ark, with children safe below,
And love is the land lying under the lake.
In the little drowned chapel years ago
My mother and father slice their wedding cake.

I cannot leave the subject of Upper Cumberland poetry without
mentioning two popular ballads. The first details one of the most famous events of nineteenth-century Cookeville, the hanging of the
Braswell boys on March 27, 1878, witnessed by what was for many
years the largest crowd ever assembled in the county. Parker Glenn, or
D. P. Glenn, a watch repairman, is said to have written the words, which
are sung to the tune of "Life's Railway to Heaven," omitting the chorus.
It begins:

Come, my friends, and near relations,
Come, and listen to my song;
I will sing about the Braswells,
About the men who were hung.

Through stanza after stanza the hanging is detailed—Joe's confession,
Teke's denial—with a strong moral at the end, warning one and all against
the evils of liquor.

Death under quite different circumstances is described in "The Ballad of Barney Graham," by Della Mae Graham, the young daughter of
the leader of the United Mineworkers' strike at Wilder, in Fentress
County, in 1933. According to most accounts, Graham was shot in the
back by mining company thugs:

On April the thirtieth,
In 1933,
Upon the streets of Wilder
They shot him, brave and free.

Graham's death is referred to in another song from that time and place,
"My Children Are Seven in Number":

They shot Barney Graham our leader,
His spirit abides with us still;
The spirit of strength for justice,
No bullets have power to kill.

Another protest song, written by one of the striking miners, Uncle Ed Davis, "The Wilder Blues," was first sung at a mass meeting in the community, addressed by Socialist leader Norman Thomas, on March 5, 1933. Apparently Davis's song was a bigger hit than Thomas's speech. Its refrain ran as follows:

I've got the blues,
I've shore-God got 'em bad.
I've got the blues
The worst I've ever had!
It must be the blues
Of the Davidson-Wilder scabs.[7]

The first fictional journey between Nashville and Knoxville occurs in Anne Newport Royall's *The Tennessean: A Novel Founded on Facts* (1827), perhaps the earliest fictional treatment of the Upper Cumberland in 1873. Mark Twain and his Hartford neighbor Charles Dudley Warner published *The Gilded Age: A Tale of To-day;* its opening chapter is set in "Obedstown," based on Jamestown, the Fentress County seat, in what Twain calls the "Knobs of East Tennessee."

Mark Twain never visited the area, though his older brother Orion was in Jamestown several times during the nineteenth century. I presume that Twain's unflattering description of the land and its people came entirely from his family's experience as residents in Fentress County in the 1820s and 1830s. The narrator said that the area "had a reputation like Nazareth, as far as turning out any good thing was concerned." To some extent Twain's picture of mountain ignorance, laziness, eccentricities of speech, and general worthlessness was to be repeated again and again by later writers of Appalachian fiction, especially during the time when it was written largely by outsiders. The naturalist John Muir, traveling through the area in September 1867, confirms as a firsthand observer the picture painted by Twain: "Passed the poor, rickety, thrice-dead village of Jamestown," he recorded in his journal, "an incredibly dreary place."[8]

In *The Gilded Age* father Si Hawkins buys 75,000 acres of Tennessee land, believing it will make his children fabulously rich at some future date. "*We'll* never see the day . . . but *they'll* ride in coaches, Nancy!" he tells his wife. "They'll live like princes of the earth; they'll be courted and worshiped; their names will be known from ocean to ocean!" With his dying breath, Hawkins tries to utter once more the magical phrase "the Tennessee land." In the 1830s, Twain's father John Marshall Clemens purchased 75,000 acres in Fentress County (100,000 acres according to a footnote in Twain's autobiography) under a similar illusion. But the land's brightest promise was not fulfilled, either in the novel or in real life. There was, of course, no factual basis for the novel's scheme of having Congress pay the Hawkins family $3 million for the Tennessee land as a site for the Knobs Industrial University, "a vast school of modern science and practice" that was to make "intelligent, trained workmen" of recently freed African Americans. In fact, the bill provided that the school would be open "to all persons without distinction of sex, color, or religion," rather unusual at a time when even the state university was open only to white males! The great experiment in racial and gender integration goes untried, however, since the bill passed the House but lost in the Senate. Such troublesome matters as the difficulty of transportation and the scarcity of African Americans in the area were not considered.[9]

Less than ten years after publication of *The Gilded Age*, a Mississippi woman, Sherwood Bonner, traveled northward to Tennessee. Though she seems to have planned to visit Rugby and Rogersville, there is no evidence that she got farther east than Putnam County, where she apparently stayed at Bloomington Springs, west of Cookeville. That onetime resort is mentioned several times in the four stories Bonner published in *Harper's Weekly* in 1881: "Jack and the Mountain Pink," "The Case of Eliza Blaylock," "Lame Jerry," and "The Barn Dance at the Apple Settlement." Bonner collected these in her *Dialect Tales* two years later.

The first story printed, "Jack and the Mountain Pink," takes place in the summer of 1878. A young man named Selden leaves friends gathered in a Nashville hotel and heads off to "Cumberland Mountain." After arriving at Bloomington Springs, he visits the Window Cliffs in southern Putnam County near Burgess Falls, in company with Sincerity Hicks, a mountain girl who has agreed to show him the way. Not the "mountain pink" his friends had urged him to find, Sincerity, as he notes in the final line, was "a Cumberland bean stalk." Moonshining, that staple of early Appalachian fiction, has its place here, too, and several stories involve the activities of Capt. James Peters, a government agent famous for his raids on mountain stills.[10]

Sherwood Bonner may have come here first, but it was not long before the Upper Cumberland received attention from a second woman writer, Mary Noailles Murfree of Murfreesboro. In fact, it may have been Murfree's earlier success that inspired Bonner's visit to Tennessee. Under her male pseudonym, "Charles Egbert Craddock," Murfree published in the *Atlantic Monthly* of March and April 1884 "Drifting Down Lost Creek," set in

Mary Noailles Murfree. Courtesy of the Tennessee State Library and Archives.

Sparta and the eastern part of White County. Apparently, Murfree liked the story quite well, since it stands first in her collection *In the Tennessee Mountains* (1884). The devotion, courage, and endurance of its heroine, Cynthia Ware, are memorable indeed, as she so daringly comes down the mountain to Sparta on a day when the governor of Tennessee is there as a part of his campaign for reelection. Cynthia's petition of clemency for her lover finds favor with the governor, though not with members of either her family or his; they cannot approve what they call "wild junketing after gov'nors an' sech through all the valley country, whar she war n't knowed from a gate-post, nor her dad nuther." Sadly, the ungrateful Evander Price forgets Cynthia and rejects the mountains, eagerly embracing the industrialism of the outside world. It is significant that he married a telegraph operator, a symbol of new technology.[11]

If Bonner and Murfree found the Upper Cumberland attractive, Will Allen Dromgoole could not be far behind. In 1886 Dromgoole, who did not have to invent a masculine pseudonym since her parents named her William, published *The Sunny Side of the Cumberland* in Philadelphia. A sentimental love story, it contained an account of an 1880 trip beginning at Sparta, proceeding eastward through Bon Air, Clarktown, and so on, eventually turning southward and ending in the area of Beersheba Springs and Monteagle. Another Dromgoole story set in the Upper Cumberland was "The Leper of the Cumberlands." First published in the Boston *Arena* in 1893, its focus was the Milksick Mountain (now Gum

Spring Mountain) in White County, southwest of Sparta. In *The Sunny Side of the Cumberland*, she had written ominously of "Milksick Mountain, whose summit rises skyward with all of the grandeur and boldness of the surrounding peaks; as if no curse rested upon it to forbid habitation, and poison the hardy and vigorous vegetation which thrusts its root into the accursed boundary." ("Milksick Mountain" is also referred to in Murfree's "Drifting Down Lost Creek," though without the sinister connotations Dromgoole gives it.) In addition, Dromgoole's story "The Light of Liberty" takes place somewhere along the Caney Fork, and her book *A Moonshiner's Son* (1898) must have a White County setting, since one reads about Calfkiller River and the stage stand at the Old Rock House east of Sparta. This famous landmark, built in the 1830s, is said to have numbered among its patrons Andrew Jackson, James K. Polk, and Sam Houston.[12]

Early in the twentieth century, the well-known short story writer and author of *The Devil's Dictionary*, Ambrose Bierce, published a story called "Three and One are One," in *Cosmopolitan* (October 1908). Ostensibly set "near Carthage, Tennessee," at the time of the Civil War, it has little to do with Smith County. Barr Lassiter, a young Unionist, leaves home in 1861 to join the Federal army, much to the disgust of his pro-Confederate father, mother, and sister. Two years later, when his unit is active in the area, Lassiter seizes the opportunity to come home for a visit. His secessionist father, mother, and sister will not speak to him, a silence he attributes to their political differences.

The Kentucky Upper Cumberland is rich in literary voices since the turn of the twentieth century. John Fox Jr., a native of the Bluegrass region, began his fiction-writing career with "A Mountain Europa," which ran in two installments in the *Century* in 1894 and was published separately in 1899. Set near Jellico, on the Kentucky-Tennessee border, it is the story of a romance between a mining engineer from New York and a mountain girl who is the daughter of a moonshiner. Fox followed this with "A Cumberland Vendetta," which also appeared in *Century* and then served as the title story for his 1895 story collection. Set in the mountains along the Cumberland River in southeast Kentucky, it focuses on a feud between two families, the Lewallens and the Stetsons, and on the love relationship between Martha Lewallen and Rome Stetson, whose name invites the reader to make comparisons with a more famous feud between the houses of Montague and Capulet. Fox's first notable novel was *The Little Shepherd of Kingdom Come* (1903), a historical romance set before and during the Civil

War; the central character, Chad Buford, comes to the Cumberland
Mountain settlement of Kingdom Come, where Melissa Turner, a mountain girl, falls in love with him. Complications arise when he is taken
to Lexington, where he falls in love with a beautiful and aristocratic
young woman, Margaret Dean. Their relationship has its high and
low points, accentuated by her support of the Confederacy while he
joins the Union army. With *The Trail of the Lonesome Pine* (1908), Fox
achieved perhaps his greatest success, as it was a best-selling novel,
the subject of several film treatments, and a popular outdoor drama.
Again there are feuding families, the Tollivers and Falins, and a romance between outsider John Hale, a Kentucky native educated at
Harvard, and mountain girl June Tolliver, in which all ends well.

   Following John Fox Jr., though never as widely read, was Charles
Neville Buck, whose most popular novel was *The Call of the Cumberlands*
(1913). In it, Samson South leaves the Kentucky hills to become a painter
but later gives up his career, returning home to lead family and friends
in their feud with the Hallman family. Buck tells a story of the female
outsider in *Battle Cry* (1914), in which Juanita Holland comes to the
Kentucky hills to establish a school and falls in love with a local man,
Anse Harvey. Buck's final novel, *Mountain Justice* (1935), is a mystery
involving a Louisville surgeon accused of murder who flees to the moun-

Miners at Wilder, Tennessee, in the 1930s. Courtesy of the Tennessee Technological
University Archives, Harding Collection.

tains. Buck includes a good deal about the agitation and violence associated with coal mining at the time.

Coal mining is also prominent in James Still's novel *River of Earth* (1940), in which the fortunes of the Baldridge family are seen from the perspective of the narrator, who recalls the time when he was a child and the family constantly moved from one coal camp to another. The father always sought work, while the mother always wanted to settle down. The novel carries the family through several years of births, deaths, hardships, and occasional happiness. Finally, the family leaves Kentucky, but with little assurance that their lives will be better elsewhere.

Harriet Arnow, a native of Wayne County who lived for several years on the Big South Fork of the Cumberland River, wrote nonfiction books containing much information about the area in which she grew up: *Seedtime on the Cumberland* (1960), *Flowering of the Cumberland* (1963), and *Old Burnside* (1977). The first two focus on the Upper Cumberland during the late eighteenth and early nineteenth centuries, covering many aspects of pioneer life. The last is a kind of memoir for the town to which Arnow's family moved in 1913, part of which now lies beneath Lake Cumberland. Readers generally may be more familiar with her fiction, beginning with *Mountain Path* (1936) and *Hunter's Horn* (1949). In the latter, Nunn Ballew is obsessed with killing King Devil, a fox larger than life, to such an extent that he neglects his farm and his family. *The Dollmaker* (1954), surely Arnow's best-known novel, concerns Gertie Nevels, whose family moves during World War II to Detroit, where her husband gets a factory job and the family lives in a housing project—a far cry from their life in the mountains of Kentucky.

By the twentieth century, the Upper Cumberland region was far more accessible, thanks to the building of the N. C. & St. L railroad to Sparta and also to the completion of what became the Tennessee Central Railroad across the area. Additional access was provided in the 1920s by the highway so grandly called "the Broadway of America," or "Memphis-to-Bristol Highway," or Tennessee 1. The highway is designated U.S. 70 N and U.S. 70 S in this area.

Caroline Gordon, though more associated with Clarksville, Monteagle, and Sewanee than with the Upper Cumberland, included in her second novel, *Aleck Maury, Sportsman* (1934), a section called "Caney Fork." Her male narrator, based on Gordon's father, is seventy years old when he travels into the hills of middle Tennessee, looking for a place to settle and fish. He encounters a man sitting on a cracker barrel who informs him about the place between Sparta and McMinnville where the Caney Fork and Collins rivers meet. "The Tennessee Power Company," he explains, "had bored a tunnel through the base of the next mountain and turned the two streams together. They had put up a seventy-foot dam, too, and three miles above the dam another beautiful stream came in, Rocky River."[13] The place is Rock Island, and the precise description of the area comes from the fact that Gordon worked on parts of the novel while she and her husband, Fugitive poet Allen Tate, visited her father at the Hillside Inn (mentioned in the novel) near Walling.

The Caney Fork runs north from Rock Island to the point where it enters the Cumberland River, a little east of Carthage and near a significant part of the setting of Gordon's novel *The Women on the Porch* (1944), is a place called Swan Quarter. At the beginning of the book a young woman arrives in the area, having driven her green convertible roadster down from New York. "Before her," says the narrator, "the road rose steeply. Pigeon Hill. If you kept on over the hill you would come to Carthage. Carthage was where everybody walked the streets you knew. But you would not stay in Carthage. You would drive on."[14]

Ed Bell's *Fish on the Steeple* (1935) takes its name from the fish on the weathervane of the Church of Christ in Smithville. Although the town is never named in the novel, its characters and events are said to have been so thinly disguised that local residents resented the book. To some, Bell's novel was in the Faulkner-Caldwell school of Southern degradation, with its scenes of sex and violence and of troubled relations between whites and blacks. The KKK administers a beating to a black woman known to be the mistress of a prominent white man. A good deal of the plot involves a love triangle as two young men pursue Pete Hopper, the beauty of the town. She goes to bed with one of them, and then when the other dies in a fire, regrets not having slept with him also, since he was just as deserving. In the mid-1930s this story was not what respectable citizens wanted written about their town.

Although Bowen Ingram's *Light as Morning* (1954) begins and ends in Nashville, the narrator, Cornelius "Les" McCoin, and his father travel east out of the city to attend a family reunion at the old home place, now threatened with flooding by the lake created behind Center Hill Dam, southwest of Cookeville on the Caney Fork River. The time is 1949, which is right for the formation of Center Hill Lake, though in the novel the dam appears to be on the Cumberland and is constructed by TVA rather than the Army Corps of Engineers. Kitty, an attractive young woman of the McCoin family, falls in love with Bill Katona, a northerner of Hungarian descent involved in the construction of the dam—a match strongly opposed by those who see him as a foreigner and a Communist.

In a later novel, *Milbry* (1972), Ingram goes back to an earlier time, beginning in 1910. Again her central character is a young person, Milbry Prewett, six years old at the beginning of the story, fourteen toward the end, and still older in the epilogue. The unusual name "Milbry" is apparently a childish pronunciation of "Mildred," the actual first name of the author (Mildred Prewett Bowen Ingram). A good part of the book is set in Nashville, Memphis, and Lebanon, but significant portions involve Gordonsville, the town in Smith County south of Carthage where Ingram lived at one time. Though described as a novel on the title page, the book reads more like an autobiographical memoir, detailing Milbry's relationships with her family, friends, teachers, and the African American community. Contempt for Appalachia voiced in other fiction certainly appears here, as Milbry's mother cautions her against picking up "the speech and manners and habits of hillbillies and loafers. . . . You must be on guard at all times against picking up slovenly errors of speech—grammar especially—so when you go back to the world of organized society you will take your place with the right sort of people."[15] Milbry is considerably less convinced than her mother about the cultural poverty of the area and delights in the fiddling and dancing that take place at the store in Gordonsville.

Another novel featuring a young girl as the central character is Anita Clay Kornfield's *In a Bluebird's Eye* (1975). Although the cover of the paperback edition claimed that the setting was the "Tennessee Smokies," it was actually Kornfield's native White County, a fact she disguised by using real place names only when they would be obscure to outsiders—Bon Air, Doe Creek Lake, and Rock Island. In other instances she substituted fictional names for the real ones: Sparta became "Olympia," and DeRossett "Du Casse"; "Margate" was apparently Ravenscroft. In part, the subject of the novel, a standard one in Appalachian fiction, is coal mining, its decline, and the consequences of that demise. The novel is set during the late Depression era of the 1930s, and hanging ominously over much of its action is an awareness that the coal company is about to close its operations in that part of the state.

The major focus, however, is on eleven-year-old Honor Jane Whitfield, daughter of the hard-drinking, adulterous school principal and friend of Lola, an African American woman released from the state penitentiary to be a maid for the doctor's wife in the little mining community. Like the family in Twain's *Gilded Age*, and the mother in *Milbry*, the Whitfields regard themselves as superior to others who live there.

In her novel *Wilder* (1990), Loletta Clouse drew on her childhood experience of growing up in a mining community in Fentress County. At one time, the Wilder community had a population of two thousand, though it has ceased to exist. There is a thematic similarity to the story Kornfield tells in *In a Bluebird's Eye*, the decline of coal mining in the Cumberland mountains in the 1930s. Central to the novel are sixteen-year-old Lacey Conners and the two men in love with her, John Trotter and Coy Wilson. Of almost equal importance is the conflict between the miners and the Fentress Coal and Coke Company, culminating in the shooting death of Union leader Barney Graham, an event detailed in the ballad discussed earlier. Historic events liven this plot, as when Myles Horton, director of the Highlander Folk School, shows up in Wilder and is arrested.[16]

Michael Lee West, formerly of Cookeville and now of Lebanon, has published two novels with Upper Cumberland settings: *Crazy Ladies* (1990) and *American Pie* (1996). West's parents owned the Ben Franklin Store on West Broad Street in downtown Cookeville from the 1960s to 1980s, and she was an English major at Tennessee Tech before turning to nursing and completing her degree at East Tennessee State.

The fictional town in *Crazy Ladies*, Crystal Falls, appears to be a composite of Cookeville and Lebanon. One of the characters attends Tennessee Tech, though his mother had hoped he would go to Harvard or Yale; his choice of Tech makes her ill. The Ben Franklin store appears in *Crazy Ladies,* though it is located on the Square rather than in the West Side Shopping Center. Details about downtown flooding in *Crazy Ladies* come from Lebanon rather than Cookeville.

For *American Pie,* West created another fictitious middle Tennessee college town. Tallulah is a name apparently borrowed from Georgia's Tallulah Falls and gorge. Again, readers may spot some resemblances to Cookeville and Lebanon, perhaps with a bit of Carthage thrown in, since the town is on the Cumberland River. The novel is peppered with names from the area: Center Hill Lake, the Caney Fork and Calfkiller rivers, and small towns such as Baxter. The "curvy, treacherous Highway 70" should be recognizable to anyone who has traveled between Cookeville and Carthage before the completion of I-40, though mention of "Highway 231" reflects Lebanon. The town's zip code is 38502, clearly Cookeville, and the "clock tower of the college" must be the one atop Tech's Derryberry Hall.[17]

Freddie McBroom Espy, returned from California because of her sister Jo-Nell's serious injuries from a collision involving her car and an L&N freight train, passes along Tallulah's Broad Street noting what are apparently the author's recollections of Cookeville's West Side: "I noticed that many of the old stores were gone—Grady's Dry Good, Bob's Shop for Men, Ensor's Stationary, Kuhn's 5 & 10. The whole downtown had been remodeled."[18] The square, the courthouse, the Princess Theater, even the National Guard armory are mentioned. West's novels show a marked departure from most earlier Upper Cumberland fiction in the use of profanity and obscenity, to say nothing of frequent sexual activity.

Another Tennessee woman, Lisa G. Brown, a teacher at Baxter's Upperman High School, has written a number of novels, most recently *Sleeping at the Magnolia* (1997), with its setting at the decaying resort community of Indian Springs, inspired by Red Boiling Springs in Macon County. Her Magnolia Hotel, one hundred years old, with its "big high-ceilinged parlor" and "fine, old-fashioned, down-home Southern cooking," was based on one of three surviving hotels, the Donoho, actually built in 1914. Brown's is a romance novel with a number of steamy scenes, especially between lovers Colley Rollins and Lainie Thorne. In fact, the dedication threatens Brown's daughters with dire punishment if they should ever "do what the girl in this book does."[19]

With the exception of Lela McDowell Blankenship, most who have written about the region have dealt with contemporary or fairly recent times; another who reached back into the nineteenth century was Michael Bohannan Jordan, a member of the law faculty at Pepperdine University in Malibu, California. His pseudo-historical novel *Crockett's Coin* (1997) takes place in what is now the Cookeville-Sparta area, between 1810 and 1818. It focuses on the experiences of Henderson Bohannan, eleven years old at the beginning, and the two girls in his life, Winnie Harp and Kate Gate. Kate is a budding abolitionist, furnished with all of the opinions that seem right today, and slavery is one of the novel's major concerns. One scene depicts a slave auction at Brotherton Stand on the Walton Road, northeast of Cookeville.

Since this was announced as the first in a series of novels based on Bohannan family history, Jordan's intention seems to be to make an interesting and exciting narrative out of family recollections and Tennessee history. Jordan may have been inspired by the success of one-time Cookevillian Cameron Judd, who in addition to many Western novels has published a series of novels based on Tennessee history, as well as books on Daniel Boone and Davy Crockett. Unfortunately, Jordan's novel contains a great many errors of spelling and grammar and a remarkable number of typos, as well as jarring anachronisms in the language of the characters and narrator.[20]

In addition to its appearances in fiction by local writers, the Upper Cumberland is showing up in an increasing number of novels by outsiders. In John Grisham's novel *The Firm* (1991), a character was told to stop at Cookeville and spend the night at the Holiday Inn. In Doris Betts's *Heading West* (1981), a character visited the Putnam County courthouse and the office of the *Dispatch*, a newspaper that for a time competed with the long-running *Putnam County Herald* or *Herald Citizen*. Before arriving at Cookeville, the character mistakenly stopped in the tiny Cumberland County community of Isoline, looking for the courthouse! Why anyone would think Isoline is a county seat is beyond me, and she is in the wrong county anyway. But such matters probably did not disturb readers in Betts's North Carolina, or even west or east Tennessee.

In *Tom Sawyer Abroad* (1894), one of two published sequels to *Adventures of Huckleberry Finn* (1885), Huck makes an observation I think is really Mark Twain's, that "there ain't anything that is so interesting to look at as a place that a book has talked about." That place may be London, Paris, New York, San Francisco, Concord, Massachusetts, Oxford, Mississippi, Hannibal, Missouri, or even . . . the Upper Cumberland of Tennessee.[21]

NOTES

1. Another version was edited by William Lynwood Montell, *Diary of Amanda McDowell* (Lexington: University Press of Kentucky, 1986)

2. Lela McDowell Blankenship, *Fiddles in the Cumberlands* (New York: Richard R. Smith, 1943): 45–46.

3. Lela McDowell Blankenship, *When Yesterday Was Today* (Nashville: Tennessee Book Co., 1966): 57–58.

4. Lela McDowell Blankenship, *The Uneven Yoke* (Nashville: Tennessee Book Co., 1962): 101.

5. Robert P. Hudson, *Southern Lyrics: A Series of Original Poems on Love, Home, and the Southland* (Nashville: Southern Lyrics Publishing Co., 1907): 47.

6. Clara Cox Epperson, *Scraps of Verse and Prose from Heartsease*, Lottie Farr, ed. (Cookeville: Tennessee Technological University English Department, 1973): 22.

7. The various songs and poems about Barney Graham were featured in *The Wilder-Davidson Story*, Homer Kemp and Steve Boots, eds. (Cookeville: WCTE-TV, 1986).

8. John Muir, *The Thousand Mile Walk to the Gulf* (Knoxville: University of Tennessee Press, 1989): 20.

9. Mark Twain and Charles Dudley Warner, *The Gilded Age: A Tale of Today* (Hartford, Conn.: American Publishing Co., 1873): 17.

10. Sherwood Bonner, *Dialect Tales* (New York: Harper & Bros., 1883): 104, 112.

11. Mary Noailles Murfree, "Drifting Down Lost Creek," in *In the Tennessee Mountains* (Boston: Houghton Mifflin, 1884), 62, 75.

12. Will Allen Dromgoole, *The Sunny Side of the Cumberland* (Phildelphia: Lippincott, 1886), 177.

13. Caroline Gordon, *Aleck Maury, Sportsman* (New York: Charles Scribner's and Sons, 1934), 279.

14. Caroline Gordon, *The Women on the Porch* (New York: Charles Scribner's and Sons, 1944), 4.

15. Bowen Ingram, *Milbry* (New York: Crown Publishers, 1972), 173.

16. Loletta Clouse, *Wilder* (Nashville: Rutledge Hill Press, 1990), 206, 222–23.

17. Michael Lee West, *American Pie* (New York: HarperCollins, 1996), 25, 113.

18. Ibid., 119.

19. Lisa G. Brown, *Sleeping at the Magnolia* (New York: Harper Paperbacks, 1997), 105.

20. Michael Jordan, *Crockett's Coin* (Edmonton, Alberta, Canada: Commonwealth Publications, 1997), 238–45.

21. The Upper Cumberland makes its appearances in nonfiction books as well. To cite one example, in William Least Heat Moon's *Blue Highways: A Journey into America* (1982), the author travels into Tennessee from Kentucky, spends the night on the courthouse square in Livingston, has breakfast in Gainesboro, engages in a lengthy conversation with Thurmond and Ginny Watts in the Jackson County community of Nameless (Defeated and Difficult are referred to, but Moon did not go there), and comes into Cookeville on a cold, rainy Easter morning. The city has already been mentioned; at Nameless, Thurmond Watts said that he had once attended a Tech football game at "Coevul" (Moon's version of one pronunciation of the city's name). "Do you like football?" Moon asks. "Don't know," says Watts. "I was so high up in that stadium I never opened my eyes" (35). Incidentally, "Nameless, Tennessee" is mentioned along with Ugly, Texas, and Peculiar, Missouri, in Elvis Costello's song "My Dark Life," included on his album *A Taste of Extreme Honey*.

Chapter 9

GOBBLE LIKE A TURKEY

Alvin C. York and American Popular Culture

M\ICHAEL E. B\IRDWELL

The image of Sergeant Alvin Cullum York etched into the collective consciousness of most people is not the famed Tennessee hero at all. They conjure up Gary Cooper's portrayal of York in the Warner Bros. film, *Sergeant York* (1941), gobbling like a turkey, licking the sights of his Enfield rifle, popping off Hollywood Germans.[1] Hollywood's York claimed Daniel Boone was his personal hero, and Walt Disney studios made a conscious link to Cooper's portrayal of York in *Davy Crockett: King of the Wild Frontier* (1955). Davy (Fess Parker) competed with frontier riflemen at a shooting match much like the one staged in *Sergeant York*. Just like Gary Cooper, who licked his thumb and wiped the sights of his rifle to reduce the glare and win the turkey shoot, Disney's Davy Crockett wet his sights before firing the winning shot. Audiences watching the Disney version of the American frontier in the 1950s made direct connections between Alvin York and Davy Crockett.

Even though York devoted himself to public education after World War I, and with the significant exception of World War II remained a pacifist his entire life, people continue to define York by what he did in the Argonne Forest on October 8, 1918. Ironically the warrior image continues to be the prevailing portrait of York in American popular culture. References to York appear in everything from literature and movies to comic strips and board games. Since the advent of cable television—with such networks as the History Channel and Turner Classic Movies—York should remain in the nation's memory for years to come. Nonetheless, the question remains: Why does York's image endure when other heroes fade?

Gary Cooper as Alvin C. York in the 1941 Warner Bros. film, *Sergeant York*. Courtesy of
the Sergeant York Patriotic Foundation.

Perhaps the only way to fully understand the York phenomenon is
to examine his background and the impact that World War I had on his
native region. When the United States declared war on April 6, 1917, it
seemed of little concern to the denizens of Pall Mall, Tennessee. The
Wolf River Valley was an isolated, rugged area virtually cut off from
the world. It had no macadamized roads before 1927; the Wolf River
was not navigable and no railway lines penetrated the valley connecting it to the outside world.[2] Lack of modern transportation and the
valley's remoteness hampered industrialization. Most people living there
were direct descendants of the original settlers of the area, all of whom
were of English, Scots-Irish, and German descent. Records show that
residents took as few as one trip a year to Jamestown thirteen miles
south, and that was to pay taxes, register deeds, or participate in elec-
tions.[3] The Civil War, which had temporarily opened the region to outsiders, created lasting ill will, for the war had taken place only a
generation before. For a person to go off to war in France was virtually
incomprehensible.[4]

Life in the valley was primitive by the standards of the day. Thirteen people shared cramped space in the two-room dogtrot log cabin
where York grew up. York's family and his neighbors eked out a living
through subsistence farming, blacksmithing, and cooperative carpentry, which were supplemented by hunting wild game, fishing, and the

production of moonshine. Poverty, isolation, and bitter memories of
the Civil War bred a quasi-independent and somewhat suspicious temperament. Denizens of the Wolf River Valley felt little kinship to people
within their own county, much less the rest of America.[5] Coupled with
the poverty, isolation, and suspicion was an almost superstitious Christianity based on the infallibility of the scriptures and a literal interpretation of the Bible. York's formal education consisted of only nine months,
spread over three years, in a subscription school after the crops had
been laid by. When York received his draft notice in June 1917, he was
twenty-nine years old and had never been more than fifty miles from
home. Yet the very primitive nature of York's prewar life experience
appeals to the romantic in people.

Corporal Alvin C. York fought with the Eighty-second Division, G
Company, 328th Infantry of the American Expeditionary Force (AEF).
The division fought in the St. Mihiel/Chatel-Chehery sector of the Meuse-
Argonne. G Company's objective on October 8, 1918, was to capture the
Decauville Railroad near Hill 223, which supplied Germans with food,
weapons, and reinforcements. York and seventeen other men, under the

Alvin York (in uniform) greeted in Washington, D.C. by Congressman Cordell Hull,
Hull's wife Frances, and admiring fans, 1919. Courtesy of the Sergeant York Patriotic
Foundation.

command of acting Sergeant Bernard Early, set out at 6:10 A.M. toward their objective.[6]

En route they stumbled on a few German soldiers eating breakfast. Surprised, the enemy dropped their plates and ran. Without firing, the seventeen Doughboys pursued the enemy and ran into the midst of a German squadron. In confusion, the "Boche" believed a larger American contingent supported York's band and hastily surrendered. As the Doughboys attended to the prisoners, machine-gun fire suddenly erupted from the ridge above them. A burst of bullets struck Sergeant Early, running diagonally across his chest and nearly cut him in two. Maxim gunners pinned down the American soldiers, who used their prisoners as cover to return fire. Two Americans lay wounded, while nine more, including York's best friend, Murray Savage, died in the attack. Meanwhile, York maneuvered around the flank of the hill and picked off the machine gunners one by one, eventually killing twenty-three.[7] He accomplished this armed only with an Enfield rifle and a .45 caliber service pistol. Before it was all over, six Germans charged York and he dispatched them with his pistol, shooting them in order from the back to the front. The tactic came from his days as a turkey hunter. If he had shot the soldiers front-to-back they would have scattered or taken cover.[8]

Amazingly, given the popularity he would gain, Alvin York's name does not appear in the field reports and operations memoranda from the Meuse-Argonne on October 8 or the days immediately following. The operations report merely says "Chatel-Chehery and Hills 223, 180 and 244 were occupied."[9] It continues, saying the Eighty-ninth Division was relieved by the Thirty-seventh and "the enemy also was pushed back 3 or 4 kilometers on the east of the Meuse and lost 3,000 prisoners and 18 210-mm mortars."[10] The deeds of G Company would have passed silently into obscurity had not *Saturday Evening Post* reporter George Patullo gotten wind of the story. It was Patullo who singled York out of the eight men involved and fashioned him into a hero.[11]

For Patullo, York's story sounded like something out of classical mythology. He symbolized a peculiarly American hero whose roots were firmly planted in the nineteenth century. Like his fellow countrymen who were leery of a standing army, York preferred not to fight; however, when his country needed him he went to war with little complaint. He represented the nostalgia for the frontier that Americans continue to harbor.[12] Literally born in a log cabin in the wilds of Tennessee, in a valley whose first explorer was Daniel Boone, and adhering to a rigid Protestant faith, York represented the American ideal of self-sufficiency. He eschewed Paris nightlife and the thrills it offered; he conducted impromptu prayer meetings on the troop ship back home.[13] The other seven survivors from G Company, by contrast, all came from northeastern, urban industrial centers (New York City, Philadelphia, New Haven, etc.); many were first-generation immigrants from Eastern and Central Europe. Religiously, the seven survivors were Catholic, Greek Orthodox, and Jewish in an era when America was experiencing its first Red Scare and was suspicious of anything foreign.

To a world disillusioned by the rapacious efficiency of modern and total warfare, York represented a simpler, more innocent time in America's history. He reminded Americans of Natty Bumppo, Daniel Boone, Davy Crockett, Abraham Lincoln, and even Dwight L. Moody—archetypal American heroes who sprang from humble origins to greatness without desire for personal aggrandizement. York's seeming innocence appealed to the nostalgia of Americans uncertain about the destruction unleashed on the world. He embodied the values of their nineteenth-century heroes. For a world devastated by a war of unimagined proportions, which killed traditional notions of progress, York represented a mythic past. His real importance rested in symbolism, not military prowess. Further, the way in which he was lionized exhibited contradictions inherent in the United States. Americans espoused a love of peace while clinging to their weapons; claimed to be Christian while practicing racism and hate; and avowed their love of nature while eagerly pursuing the hazardous fruits of each new technology.

York represented something else. Fentress County sided with the North in the Civil War, and though it played no important role in the war's outcome, its citizens suffered. Bushwhackers ripped the county apart using the war to settle personal scores. It is significant that York— a southerner and proud to be one—was singled out as the country's number one hero. There were other contenders for the title. General John J. Pershing favored regular Army Sergeant Samuel Woodfill of Ohio.[14] For many people, in the South especially, York was a symbol of healing the wounds from the Civil War. The South at long last had rejoined the Union.

George Patullo made the American public aware of the awkward red-headed mountaineer from Tennessee who seemingly did the impossible, but the public soon demanded more of him. Joseph Cummings Chase painted York's portrait and interviewed him for his book *Soldiers All,* which included other heroes of the war. Though York wanted initially only to return to Tennessee to marry his beloved Gracie Williams,

Joseph Cummings Chase's
portrait of Alvin York.
Courtesy of Edward M.
Coffman.

he was the toast of New York. Put up in rooms at the Waldorf Astoria, York saw Broadway shows, visited Wall Street, participated in a ticker-tape parade, and felt the first real rush of fame. Throngs of people longed to see him and have their picture taken with him—something that continued for the remainder of his life.

Initially, York attempted to avoid the limelight and return to the life he had known before the war. He said that he did not want to profit from his fame as a warrior, nor did he want to exploit his family's name. That proved impossible. For one thing, the "good-old life" in the Wolf River Valley was decidedly harder than life in the army. The military provided him with the best clothes he had ever owned, best shoes, and steady, nutritious meals. As he put it, "I began to fill out in the army."[15] After his return from Europe, Alvin York was determined never to go hungry again.

Prevailed on by friends, neighbors, and total strangers, York embarked on a campaign to use his fame to improve the homeland. For the rest of his life, York would be a booster for Fentress County, the Cumberland Plateau, and the state of Tennessee. As a result, he was never far from the glare of the media.[16] In 1920, York embarked on his first speaking tour, traveling the Southeast in an attempt to raise money for a school. Arthur Bushing, a New Yorker who had married a local girl, accompanied York on the tour acting as his speechwriter and secretary. Though it would take nearly a decade to make that dream a reality, York became a fixture in the popular culture. His image routinely appeared in newspapers and magazines and on posters across the country. As his mission to make the school a reality bogged down because of internecine fighting in his home county, York was also caricatured in political cartoons commenting on the struggle.[17]

His story appeared in *Ripley's Believe It or Not, Literary Digest, Liberty,* and in magazines geared toward children and religious literature. York's story inspired novelists and poets of various stripes. Characters based on York appear in two novels by Kentuckian Robert Penn Warren, *At Heaven's Gate* and *The Cave.*

Unfortunately, York's story was rarely in the hands of someone as gifted as Warren. More common was the doggerel of people such as Hazel Manley of Union City, whose poem "York of Tennessee" was published in the Memphis *Commercial Appeal* in 1940. It featured such scintillating lines as:

Waits for word of high command
Hears it, and with Enfield Gun
Metes out death to the Hun
York of Tennessee/ Gallant hero tried and true
Hands and hearts go out to you.

One anonymous poem among York's papers is the forgettable

After shooting Germans in the pants
Away over there in distant France,
He returned from across the ocean
To give his Gracie all his devotion.

York received hundreds of verses inspired by his heroics, few of them of literary merit. Many poems were printed, and a number of songs, including "The Ballad of Sergeant York," written by Reba Bacon of Cookeville and set to music by Tom Kirk, were actually recorded.[18]

By the late 1930s, York was returning to obscurity. Because of a number of political, financial, and physical setbacks, York was less in demand as a speaker or a celebrity. Though he continued to make public appearances through his agent, Bettye Smythe of Famous Speakers Agency in New York, Alvin York's fame was in eclipse. That changed forever with the release in 1941 of the film *Sergeant York*.

Initially intended to be a film about York's attempts to bring education to Tennessee's Upper Cumberland, the focus of the movie changed as the situation in Europe worsened. Producer Jesse Lasky and Harry Warner, president of Warner Bros., made York aware of the fact that Axis aggression threatened the United States. With his full cooperation, the focus of the movie changed from a plea for better education to an overt call for intervention in World War II. York the pacifist turned warrior who advocated preparedness, endorsed the peacetime draft, and became a spokesman for the Fight for Freedom Committee, an organization created to counter the isolationist rhetoric of the America First Committee and its chief spokesman, Charles Lindbergh.

When the film made its way into limited release in the summer of 1941, it was caught up in a whirlwind of controversy. Accused of warmongering propaganda, York defended the movie and his own belligerent stance. The film and York's reemergence on the public scene made the aging hero more popular than ever. Gary Cooper won a Best Actor Oscar for his taciturn portrayal of Alvin York, and the film earned another Academy Award for its use of sound. Though it was Warner Bros.' first movie to cost over $2 million, it went on to be one of the studio's most successful pictures.

The movie played regularly on American military bases. Prints were given to all of America's allies to promote the war effort. The film even inspired a calypso song, recorded by Prince Charming of Trinidad, which featured the snappy lyrics:

> Sergeant York the Big Strong Yank
> Didn't have a modern tank
> And he made the Germans a heap of junk
> Though dough he got for a heroic plot
> Bade him well for the Jerries he caught
> And furthermore, he got the Leslie girl
> Who's not a bad doll at all,
> A doll a doll a doll at all.[19]

Alvin York with Secretary of the Navy Henry Knox on a speaking tour during World War II. Courtesy of the Sergeant York Patriotic Foundation.

During World War II, Alvin York was constantly in the public eye. He was featured in magazines such as *Life* and *The Hollywood Reporter*, was mentioned in films such as *Guadalacanal Diary*, and was even included in a Porky Pig Looney Tunes cartoon as "Sergeant Pork." Acting as a civilian liaison to the Signal Corps, he toured training camps across the country and signed autographs for eager young GIs. He observed the war games during the Tennessee Maneuvers, raised money for Liberty Bonds and the Red Cross, and generously donated his time to the cause of war. Throughout the course of the conflict, York had his own weekly radio show, "Tennessee Americans," broadcast live by Knoxville's WNOX and nationally syndicated by the Mutual Broadcasting Company. The Sunday night show featured music, advice, discussions, and special guests such as Douglas MacArthur. Additionally, York allowed his name to be used on a weekly syndicated newspaper column "Sgt. York Says," though he did not write any of the short pieces. "Sgt. York Says" offered readers homespun humor, urged them to participate in rationing and to write letters to young men overseas who served their country.

After the war, York's health began to fail. He suffered from obesity, a series of strokes, and other ailments. Though he was less visible to the general public, he remained a person of interest. Visitors made the pilgri-mage to the York home to have their picture taken with the bedridden hero. Journalists sought his opinion on everything from the conflict in Korea to his reaction to nuclear weapons. York died on September 2, 1964, but he did not fade into oblivion.

Four years after York's death, legislators from Tennessee approached the noted sculptor Felix de Weldon—known for his mammoth sculpture celebrating the marines who raised the flag on Mount Surabachi after the battle of Iwo Jima—to create a tribute to Sergeant York. De Weldon created a maquette that met with approval of York's family and the state. The larger-than-life sculpture featuring York standing with his legs firmly planted, peering down the sights of a Springfield rifle, sits on the southeast lawn of the Tennessee state capitol grounds.

During the Vietnam era, however, York's memory receded into the background. His story did serve as inspiration for a television movie protesting America's involvement in Indochina. Though *No Drums, No Bugles* (1971) was set during the Civil War, it used York's story as an allegory against the war. Martin Sheen played a young man trying to come to grips with the realities of war, wrestling with his conscience in much the same way that the Hollywood York did over whether or not war is ever justified. Unlike York, however, Sheen's character has no happy ending. Interestingly, the film *Sergeant York* rarely appeared on television during the Vietnam War.

Few articles appeared about York in the 1970s and early 1980s, and those that did usually appeared in religious tracts. They focused on York's unwavering faith or his criticisms of fame and fortune. For a country struggling with double-digit inflation and staggering unem-

Statue of Sergeant York, designed by Felix de Weldon, on the grounds of the Tennessee state capitol in Nashville, Tennessee. Courtesy of the Sergeant York Patriotic Foundation.

ployment, a call for help from a higher power held renewed relevance. York's story helped buttress the faith of people reeling from the unhappy aftermath of Vietnam.

During the 1980s, by contrast, there was renewed interest in Sergeant York and his story. Perhaps the most famous case of the memory of York gone awry came on August 31, 1983, with the introduction of the "Sgt. York Division Air Defense Gun System" in Irvine, California. Built by Ford Aerospace and Communications Corporation, the primary mission for the Sgt. York Gun System was "to provide the U.S. Army's forward combat forces with a highly lethal, fire-on-the-move gun system for defense against tactical helicopters, high-performance fixed-wing aircraft, and ground targets."[20] The army rounded up all five of York's children, his widow Gracie, as well as actors June Lockhart, Joan Leslie, and Noah Beery Jr., for a demonstration of the new tank.[21] A gala reception featured dozens of larger-than-life plastic busts of Sergeant York painted gold. Secretary of Defense Caspar Weinberger officiated at the roll out, and a debacle ensued. A military equivalent of the Frankenstein monster, the DIVAD system was cobbled together from spare parts. Using the chassis of an Abrams M-48 tank, its main weapons were 40mm Bofors antiaircraft guns, artillery not usually placed on

U.S. Army DIVAD system, better known as the Sgt. York Tank. Courtesy of the Sergeant York Patriotic Foundation.

tanks. Designers added radar from F-16 fighter planes to complete the unusual mobile defense system. The tank was supposed to be deadly accurate and hit moving targets—ground based and airborne. Instead, the tank missed everything it shot at. The York family left California embarrassed, and Congress set up a special subcommittee to investigate what went wrong.[22] Despite the irony that the tank failed to match the legendary marksmanship of the sergeant, York probably would have been pleased that the tank ended up on the scrap heap. He wanted to be remembered for his humanitarian efforts after the war, rather than for his war record.

On a darker note, doctors discovered a new combat-related phenomenon in 1989 when working with Vietnam and Korean War veterans in V.A. hospitals. They dubbed it the "Sgt. York Syndrome." Trying to explain why Appalachia sent a disproportionate number of young men to war, Doctors Steven Giles and Charles Walter blamed the legacy of Sergeant York.[23]

During the Gulf War in 1991, *The Knoxville News-Sentinel* ran a front page story about a potential Sergeant York. The piece glorified a forty-nine-year-old Highway Department worker and National Guardsman, Rabon York of Livingston. Called to service in the Gulf War, the distant relative of Sergeant York announced, "It comes with the blood." This implied that anyone with the surname York is a rip-roaring rootin'-tootin' dead-eyed shot and a credit to any armed service. Throughout the brief conflagration, Tennessee newspapers, radio, and television media evoked the name of the sergeant as they pondered the significance of the Gulf War. Many hoped Tennessee would produce another hero who would be the envy of the nation.[24]

York returned to the nation's attention in multiple ways in 1995. A group of World War II veterans, politicians, reenactors, and businessmen launched a nonprofit organization—The Sergeant York Patriotic Foundation (SYPF)—to celebrate and promote Alvin York and keep his war record alive. Because of inaction and insufficient funding by the state of Tennessee, the Foundation stepped in to raise money and install interpretive signage and exhibits at the York Historic Area. Their efforts resulted in opening York's entire home to tourists, creation of an interpretive video narrated by Walter Cronkite, and a souvenir store. SYPF also began publishing a newsletter, *Sgt. York Says,* that reprinted York's columns from World War II along with other primary materials and features. The organization played a significant role, with the help of a serious York fan, Sandy Swanson of Rockville, Illinois, in persuading the U.S. Post Office to issue a stamp in York's honor. On May 3, 2000, the postal service issued four stamps celebrating American military heroes: York, Audie Murphy, General Joseph Hines, and General Omar Bradley.[25]

Sergeant York's name was invoked due to the intrepidity of an American fighter pilot on June 8, 1995. Because of the ongoing war in the Balkans, American troops served with NATO forces in concerted efforts to bring peace to the region. Captain Scott O'Grady was shot down over Bosnia on June 2. Using his wits and his training, O'Grady spent the next six days living off the land while trying to avoid capture. On June 8, the captain was rescued and the news media referred to him as a new embodiment of Sergeant York. Though their stories held virtually nothing in common, O'Grady was celebrated as a hero following in York's footsteps.

When Tennessee residents geared up for the state's bicentennial in 1996, most received a new telephone book with a mural depicting important Tennesseans. Sandwiched between the father of the Blues W. C. Handy, and war hero President Andrew Jackson in the pantheon of Tennessee's homespun heroes was an artist's rendering of Sergeant York.

In 1995, former Speaker of the House Newt Gingrich published a rather bizarre novel, *1945*. Based on the premise the United States had stayed out of World War II and Germany had defeated Britain, it began with the Nazi invasion of the United States. Nazis came to America intent on taking over Oak Ridge and stealing the atomic bomb. Sergeant York rescued the bomb and saved the day in Gingrich's imaginary history. Gingrich failed to do his homework, however, and his depiction of the hero bears little resemblance to the real man. In Gingrich's incarnation, York was the hard-drinking sheriff of Fentress County who saved the day because of his amazing abilities with a firearm.

In recent years, two very different groups have invoked the memory of Sergeant York and have claimed, speciously, to be heirs to his legacy. On the one hand are religious fundamentalists, alarmed at the changes in American society. Though they often have legitimate concerns—the general coarsening of American culture, lack of propriety, the media's fascination with prurient interests—they also generally want to create a society of strict conformity based on their beliefs. What this group fails to understand, or even wants to know, is that York became more inclusive in his faith as he became more educated. Rather than the exclusivist, judgmental fundamentalist Christian he was in 1917, by the late 1930s York espoused a religious philosophy that sought mutual respect of Christianity, Judaism, and Islam. One can assume, given his broader perspective, that he would also have found a spiritual common ground with Buddhists and perhaps other faiths as well. Radical, extremist, and mainstream fundamentalists all want to claim York as one of their own. He is the Christian Soldier who will purge the world as the embodiment of the wrath of God. York, no doubt, would find this troubling, for these groups tend to damn others rather than forgive.

The second, even more disturbing group that claims to be the heirs of York's legacy are right-wing militias. Always trumpeting York's skill with a firearm and the sanctity of the Second Amendment, militias argue that if York were living today he would have a bunker filled with all kinds of military hardware, ready to take on everybody. Their rhetoric is filled with a general paranoia toward federal and state governments, mixing the ideology of Ayn Rand with those of Adolf Hitler, Thomas Jefferson, Mikhail Bakunin (if they only knew), David Duke, and an odd assortment of misfits from the Aryan Nation's Wayne Metzger to the Unabomber. According to the various militia cells that yearn for a kinship with Alvin York, if he were alive today he would subscribe to *Soldier of Fortune*, read the *Turner Diaries* along with the Bible, and always pack heat.

Since 2000, York has been featured on the Arts and Entertainment Network's *Biography* series in the documentary "Sergeant York: A Reluctant Hero," as well as an episode of *Tales of the Gun*, entitled "Tales of Valor," and in a two-hour examination of the role of the noncommissioned officer in the U.S. Army, "Sarge." These shows have relied heavily on York's legendary military skills rather than his humanitarian efforts. Though they have offered a mild tonic to the romanticized view of York created by Gary Cooper and Warner Bros. studio, York remains primarily a super-soldier of mythic proportions.

Alvin C. York has been memorialized in a number of ways. There are bridges and roads named in his honor. The headquarters of the Eighty-second Division at Fort Bragg, North Carolina, contains the Sergeant York Theater. Likewise a movie theater named for the sergeant once stood in Red Boiling Springs, Tennessee.

Marketers have appropriated York's image, putting his face on T-shirts, knives, baseball caps, and assorted other merchandise. In California, there is even a hamburger called "The Sergeant York." A bluegrass band from Chicago calls itself "Sgt. York," taking pride in its renditions of southern mountain songs. For the past several years, competitive marksmen have held an annual "Sergeant York Memorial

Sergeant York commemorative stamp issued May 3, 2000, by the U.S. Postal Service.
Courtesy of the Sergeant York Patriotic Foundation.

Muzzle Loader Shoot" near York's home at Pall Mall. Serious sports-
men, tyros, and re-enactors descend on the Wolf River Valley every
March to display their prowess with heavy black powder weapons.
Using the movie *Sergeant York* as inspiration, men and women in overalls and Fedoras lie prone on the ground, taking aim at tiny targets
across the way. What York did out of necessity to put food on his
family's table, contemporary shooters do for recreation.

Why does York endure? Because his legacy is not one-dimensional.
Killing Germans never gave him any comfort, and York never took the
mantle of hero lightly. World War I changed him in profound ways. He
discovered a world he had never imagined existed and recognized his
own inadequacies in the process. Lesser men crumbled in the postwar
era, or joined the ranks of the lost generation, forever out of place and
time. York remained optimistic and spent the remainder of his life trying to drag his county and its people into the twentieth century at great
personal sacrifice. All the while, York possessed a splendid sense of
humor that never failed him. When he finally succeeded in building a
school to educate the children of his region, Fentress County officials
fought him every step of the way. They even refused to pay the teachers' salaries, so York mortgaged his own home and paid them out of his
pocket. In spite of the hardships placed on his family, he continued his

personal crusade for the betterment of his region. The private wars York fought domestically deserve and demand more attention. Those stories enrich and enlarge a complex and fascinating life.

NOTES

1. Gary Cooper looked nothing like York. Though both were six feet two inches tall, the resemblance stopped there. York weighed almost three hundred pounds when the film was made, had red hair, and wore a moustache his entire adult life. Contrary to the statue on the lawn of the Tennessee State Capitol in Nashville, York did not use a Springfield rifle. Like many other doughboys, York swapped his heavy, slow American weapon for a British Enfield.

2. There was an incline railway used by the Stearns Coal and Lumber Company to haul lumber out of the valley, but it was not for commuter traffic.

3. York Papers, Pall Mall, Tennessee.

4. During the Civil War, there was a Confederate cavalry encampment at Pall Mall, Camp McGinnis. York's paternal grandfather fought for the Union and settled in the valley after the war.

5. Animosity remains in Fentress County among the people who "live on the mountain," in Jamestown and Allardt, and the people of the valley.

6. Congressional Medal of Honor affidavits from York and the seven survivors. It should be noted that there are two different sets of affidavits. The first group, Colonel Edward Danforth's staff recorded October 9, 1918. The second group was recorded in 1920 and there are discrepancies between them.

7. Taylor V. Beattie with Norman Bowman, "In Search of York: Man, Myth & Legend," *Army History: The Professional Bulletin of Army History,* PB-20-00-3 (no. 50, summer-fall 2000): 1–14. Taylor Beattie's account of York's exploit is by far the best available. See Congressional Medal of Honor Affidavits; Tom Skeyhill, *Sergeant York: Last of the Long Hunters* (Reprint, Shelbyville, Tenn.: Bible and Literature Missionary Foundation, 1992): 1–13, 171–224 passim; David Lee's *Sergeant York: An American Hero* (Lexington: The University Press of Kentucky, 1985). Controversy surrounds the number of machineguns disabled by York. Some assert that York wiped out thirty-five while other American accounts say there were twenty-five. Germans argue that there were only four machine guns in the entire sector. See Sergeant F. W. Merton and W. C. Koenig, trans., "Die Entstchung von Kriegslegendon Feststellungen ueber die Angebliche Holdentat des Amerikanischen Sergeanten York an 8. 10. 18" (Washington, D.C.: National Archives, 1936). See also Timothy T. Lupfer, *Leavenworth Papers #4*, "The Dynamics of Doctrine: The Changes in German Tactical Doctrine during the First World War" (Fort Leavenworth, Kans.: Combat Studies Institute, July 1981).

8. Beattie with Bowen, 12–13.

9. *United States Army in World War I, 1917–1919* (Washington: U.S. Government Printing Office, 1938), 9: 235.

10. Ibid.

11. George Patullo, "The Second Elder Gives Battle," *Saturday Evening Post* (April 26, 1919): 3–4, 71–73.

12. The frontier closed in 1890 when York was only three years old. For many people, the Western frontier remained at the forefront of their memory.

13. Press releases from all over the country in 1919–1920 compared York to Boone, Crockett, and Lincoln, especially. York wrote a letter to Susie Williams in 1919 discussing the "prayer meetings" he held on the troop ship home.

14. Letter from George Patullo to Westbrook Pegler, January 17, 1958, pp. 2–3. Westbrook Pegler Papers, Box 142. Herbert Hoover Presidential Library, West Branch, Iowa.

15. Alvin C. York, "My Own Story" (Pall Mall, Tenn.: unpublished, hand-written manuscript, n.d.). Politically, he voted for the Democratic Party in a staunchly Republican region of Tennessee.

16. His first experience of the sour taste of fame came as early as 1920. York's mother, Mary, was contacted by the Chattanooga Medicine Company and asked for her endorsement for its patent medicine "Black Draught." Overjoyed by the attention, she gladly signed a testimonial. Mother York, however, was of little interest to the medicine makers; rather they wanted permission to use her son's image in advertising. York's photo, with his Medal of Honor prominently displayed on his chest, was used to hawk the cure for constipation. Embarrassed and incensed, York initiated the first of many lawsuits against a company for trying to exploit his name. See Chattanooga Medicine Files, York Papers.

17. By the late 1930s Alvin York wrote his own speeches. Though his first forays were largely the work of Bushing, his latter work improved greatly, and York became an accomplished speaker.

18. Reba Bacon later established the Benlee art show promoting the visual arts in the Upper Cumberland.

19. *Sergeant York Production Files* (Los Angeles: UCLA Warner Bros. Archives, Box A-52).

20. Roll Out Ceremony Public Relations packet, Gracie York's copy (Pall Mall, Tenn.: York papers).

21. York had ten children, of whom three still live. Mrs. Gracie died in 1984. Joan Leslie and June Lockhart are the last surviving members of the cast of *Sergeant York*.

22. Personal interviews with Andrew Jackson York, Helen York, George Edward Buxton York, Woodrow Wilson York, Betsy Ross Lowry, Gracie York, Colonel Gerald York. The Congressional Investigation was published in 1985 by the GPO. Oleh Borys Koropey wrote an unpublished investigation of the entire affair titled *It Seemed Like a Good Idea at the Time: The Story of the Sergeant York Air Defense Gun*.

See also, Bill Keller, "Pentagon Cancels Antiaircraft Gun," "Not Worth the Cost," and "Statement by Weinberger," *New York Times* (August 28, 1985): A1 & A18 ; George C. Wilson, "Weinberger Kills Antiaircraft Gun," *Washington Post* (August 28, 1985): A1 & A14 ; "After a Big Gun Comes up a Dud," *U.S. News and World Report* (September 9, 1985): 11 ; Michael A. Lerner and John Barry, "Sergeant York Musters Out," *Newsweek* (September 9,1985): 23 ; "Divad Was Intended to Protect U.S. Tanks," *Washington Post* (December 3,1985): A15.

23. "Appalachia Lost More in Vietnam due to 'York Syndrome,'" *Herald Citizen* (Cookeville, Tenn.: February 26, 1989):12.

24. *Knoxville News-Sentinel,* "A Sgt. York for a new age proud of patriotism, service" (November 6,1990): 1.

25. In 2000 SYPF was approached by the Hasbro Toy Company about the possibility of creating a Sergeant York GI Joe.

Chapter 10

GOOD TIMES

Vacationing at Red Boiling Springs

JEANETTE KEITH

Summer resorts were long patronized by southerners, who annually fled the heat of the cities for the relatively cooler air of mountain communities. During the late nineteenth century, resorts were so popular that the Nashville *Daily American* ran a special weekly column, "Amid Cool Breezes," which kept everyone up to date on "What Nashville Summer Wanderers Are Doing." There were columns from Tennessee resorts at Beersheba Springs, Lookout Mountain, Estill Springs, Tyree Springs, and such distant out-of-state spas as Manitou, Colorado.[1] The *Daily American*'s special correspondent recorded the names of those vacationing at Red Boiling Springs and described amusements found there. The newspapers kept the country informed of the doings of Vanderbilts at Newport—who attended what party, what entertainment was offered, and so on; the middle-class vacationers at Red Boiling Springs, faithful mimics, could enjoy knowing that the details of their vacations would appear in the Nashville *Daily American*, just like Mrs. Astor's.

By 1900, the Nashville *American* was running more Tennessee resort ads than it had in the early 1890s. There were ads for the springs at Tyree, Epson, Kingston, Fernvale, Nicholson, Capon, Estill, Easterbook, Beersheba Springs, and Castalian Springs, as well as ads for the "Lake Country" of Illinois, Michigan, and Minnesota. At the bottom of the page was an ad for Red Boiling Springs: "The Old Reliable." It mentioned the values of the waters and noted, "Hacks meet trains."[2]

At Red Boiling Springs in Macon County, about ninety miles northeast of Nashville, improvements in transportation, plus a prosperous national and regional economy in the 1920s, led to a boom in the resort business that lasted through the Depression. The town had approximately 800 residents in the winter; summer visitors could number in the thousands. Ironically, the end of the boom was caused primarily by improvements in transportation.

Taking the waters had long been seen as a therapeutic and sociable endeavor. European nobility had made annual pilgrimages to the great Continental spas, and White Sulphur Springs of Virginia had attracted the plantation elite of the antebellum South.[3] Red Boiling Springs' guests, by contrast, were mostly middle or upper-middle class: storekeepers, doctors, and lawyers from the small towns of middle Tennessee and southern Kentucky, or from Nashville, Louisville, and Chattanooga. They were the sort of people whose comings and goings were chronicled in the society pages of small-town newspapers. They could afford to take extended vacations or to send their wives and children off for two weeks or two months at Red Boiling Springs, while they visited on weekends. Red Boiling Springs offered them a change of scenery without any jarring change in lifestyle. There was nothing exotic about vacationing at Red Boiling Springs. The food and accommodations would not differ significantly from what they were used to at home. A hotel guest from Louisville might have found bathing with a pitcher and a basin in his room a nostalgic experience.

Red Boiling Springs historical marker, Macon County, Tennessee. Photo by the editors.

In addition to mineral waters and a restful atmosphere, Red Boiling Springs offered many varied forms of recreation: bridge, bowling, boating, horseback riding, swimming, and tennis. There were dances every night. Illicit pleasures such as moonshine liquor and high-stakes gambling also were available. Though Red Boiling Springs billed itself as "The South's Greatest Health Resort," and people did indeed come to the town to improve their health by drinking sulfur water, they also came to be amused. By the mid-1930s, the town had become an amusement center for the rural counties surrounding it, and hotel guests were joined on the crowded streets by local teenagers out for a lively Saturday night.

People had been coming to Red Boiling Springs since the 1840s, when a "red sulfur" spring bubbled up on Jessie Jones's farm. According to legend, the spring cured a local man's eye disease, and people began drinking the water or bathing in it for various ailments. In 1844 Jones sold the spring and twenty acres of land to Samuel E. Hare. With a partner, Hare put up a "house of entertainment" or inn in 1849 and initiated the resort industry in Red Boiling Springs.[4]

The resort remained small during the nineteenth century, probably because of the difficulty of getting to Red Boiling Springs. The town was in a valley of the Highland Rim, only seven miles from the Kentucky line. Macon County was totally landlocked, with no navigable rivers. In 1873, a Nashvillian who wanted to go to Red Boiling Springs could take the morning train to Gallatin, then catch the stage that ran through Carthage to Red Boiling Springs three days a week; or he could take a steamer to Carthage, then hire a hack for the twenty-five-mile overland trip to the town.

By 1876, there was at least one hotel in Red Boiling Springs, James Bennett's establishment. The *Hartsville Sentinel* commented: "The great virtues of the waters at Red Sulphur Springs seem to be obtaining daily a wider recognition. Were they better known the watering place would be more largely attended. Capt. James D. Bennett's merry twinkling eyes and infinite humor are enough to cheer the most despondent, and the solicitude he shows to find out what his visitors like best among edialbes [sic] and to make sure they have it in abundance would make a man build up anyhow."[5] Bennett's hotel consisted of a row of log cabins, with double beds and a large frame building with a dining room and "ball room" for dancing.

Access to the town was made easier when railroads reached Carthage and Hartsville, about twenty-five miles from Red Boiling Springs, in the late 1880s and the town began a period of slow and steady growth. By the mid-1890s there were at least two hotels, the Red Springs, run by physician J. E. Dedman (or Deadman), and the Cloyd, built by brothers Zack and Clay Cloyd. In 1905, the town rated a mention in *Richardson's Southern Guide*, a tourist guide to various attractions in the South. According to Richardson, Red Boiling Springs could be reached from either Carthage, which was on the Tennessee Central Railroad, or Hartsville, which was on the Louisville and Nashville: "The carriage fare to the springs from either place is $2.50, the hack running daily in summer. . . . The Red Boiling Springs Hotel is open the year round, rates $1, wk. $7. The 'red water' has undoubted curative properties for kidney and bladder troubles, while the 'black water' operates on the stomach and liver. There is very pretty scenery and the usual amusements, such as bowling, etc."[6]

Still, access to Red Boiling Springs remained difficult. The trip from railhead to the resort by horse-drawn hack took from dawn to sunset across unpaved roads, which rainy weather turned into what the *Macon County News* called "one big, long, deep, disgraceful mudhole."[7] Although the advent of automobiles shortened the trip into Red Boiling Springs from Carthage to two or three hours, the journey was still bone jolting. "Good roads" movements in Macon County could always find advocates in Red Boiling Springs. By 1916, a real estate advertisement could proclaim

> GOOD ROADS are being built into Red Boiling Springs from every direction. WORK IS NOW IN PROGRESS on the NEW ROAD from LAFAYETTE to RED BOILING SPRINGS, which connects it with HARTSVILLE, GALLATIN, and NASHVILLE. Where it formerly took a double team to pull a wagon, now the "Little Henry" goes up on high. Work is also in progress on the Carthage road up Peyton's Creek. The road from GAINESBORO is ALREADY FINISHED to above North Springs and will doubtless be completed into Red Boiling Spring, thereby connecting it with Gainesboro, Cookeville, Sparta, and all that section of the state.[8]

Red Boiling Springs had at least four hotels by 1916. First in importance was the Palace, which was advertised as a "brand-new 64-room structure with every convenience for the comfort of the summer guests."[9] Rooms started at $2. The Palace was owned by a corporation, which hired Henry Counts, a hotelier from Tompkinsville, Kentucky, as manager. Counts became a leader in town, and under his astute management the Palace dominated the resort business in Red Boiling Springs.

A rival to the Palace, the Donoho, was open for business in 1916 with a new building to replace the older hotel by the same name that had burned in December 1915. A two-story, white wooden structure with long verandas along the front and sides, the new Donoho had sixty rooms and electric lights. The hotel was owned and managed by B. W. and Tennie Chitwood.

In addition to the Palace, the Donoho, and the Cloyd, the "Central Hotel" had twenty-four rooms in the main building, and a row of cabins. The Central had electric lights, "waterworks," and a heater and bathtubs for giving hot sulfur and freestone baths.[10]

In 1919, the springs had their best season to date, with the crowds of more than seven hundred in town at times, and real estate speculation was booming. By 1924, there were six large hotels, the Cloyd, the Donoho, the Arlington, the Moss, the Red Boiling Springs, and the Palace. There were at least nine boarding houses, some of which really qualified as small hotels. In addition, many townspeople rented out spare bedrooms during the peak season.

The Palace was the town's largest hotel. With the original sixty-four-room building supplemented by two annexes to bring the number of rooms to 180, the Palace dominated the town's small business district. (One small hotel, the Farmers', was built next door to catch the Palace's overflow.) From the Palace on the northern end of town, up to the Cloyd, hotels lined the banks of Salt Lick Creek. Most were built on a similar plan; they were two-story, wooden, painted white, and featured long verandas both upstairs and downstairs.

Although the hotels looked much alike, they did tend to attract different clientele. The Palace was the favorite of the wealthy, the politicians, the "sports," the card players, and cigar smokers. Guests during the 1930s included Joseph W. Byrns, U.S. congressman from the Hermitage district, who was Speaker of the House of Representatives; U.S. District Judge John J. Gore; U.S. Senator Nathan L. Bachman; U.S. Congressman J. Will Taylor; Edd Bass, mayor of Chattanooga; L & N President J. B. Hill; W. N. Parrish, president of Keith Simmons Company; and assorted other lawyers and politicians, as well as many prominent small-town businessmen and their families.[11]

On the opposite, "upper" end of town, the Cloyd place entertained a more sedate crowd of health-seekers with ice cream suppers and after-dinner hymn sings around a piano in the lobby. The Cloyds, Presbyterians, also provided a church for their guests, a small frame building across the road from the hotel. Although the Cloyd family lost control of the hotel, which was sold to Joseph H. Peters of Nashville in 1916, it retained its name and reputation as one of the quieter, more restful hotels.[12]

The rest of the hotels, built along the road from the Cloyd to the Palace, were "all something alike," townspeople remember, but none was quite as grand as the Palace. In addition, guests whose budgets could not stretch to one of the hotels' rates could find accommodation at one of the boarding houses. Staying in Red Boiling Springs was relatively inexpensive. The Palace charged $2 a day in 1916—all meals included. By 1935, the rates increased to $2.50 and up.

In the 1920s, most visitors to Red Boiling Springs took the train to Carthage or Hartsville, where they were met by fleets of taxis. After chugging uphill to the resort, guests of the Palace were cleaned by white-clad porters plying feather dusters. On the veranda under the white columns, gentlemen in their white summer suits rested in wicker chairs, reading newspapers and smoking. Inside the hotel, a "private sitting room" or parlor was provided for the guests. Furnished in "Duncan Phyfe" style with chairs, settees, and overstuffed chairs, the sitting room included a piano and a record player for the guests' use.

The communal meeting places for guests were probably much used, since the guest rooms were somewhat spartan. They were furnished with iron bedsteads, straight chairs, and a washstand with bowl and pitcher. A curtained alcove served as a closet. Down the hall were large bathrooms for men and women. Rooms on the ground floor opened onto the veranda. There were three stories in the main building and two large annexes, connected to the main hotel by covered walkways.

Guests at the Palace were informed by manager Henry Counts on their arrival that H. C. Hesson, one of the town's two resident physicians, could advise them on which water to drink and how much. A visit to the doctor's little brick office beside his house cost $1. Dr. Hesson prescribed red sulfur water for kidney trouble, black for stomach problems, and baths for rheumatism and arthritis. He cautioned visitors not to drink excessively—one glass an hour before meals and one an hour after was enough.

The original red spring and a black spring were on the Palace grounds. (The color assigned to a spring is said to derive from the color of its precipitate; another theory is that the color derives from the color a silver coin will turn if placed in the water.) According to one of the

Pump that dispensed one of the varieties of mineral waters at the Donoho Hotel. Photo by the editors.

hotel's brochures, "The red is recommended for treatment of Bright's disease, diabetes, hemorrhages, cystitis, and rheumatism. The BLACK water is an alternative and laxative. It is a sulphur magnesia water of desired medicinal properties. The combination of magnesia with hydrogen sulphide present is recommended for treatment of gallstones, catarrhal conditions of the gall bladders, many forms of stomach trouble and constipation."[13]

At the Donoho, the "first course" at breakfast was black sulfur water, heated almost to boiling in the kitchen and carried out to the front porch, where guests gathered with their cups.

Guests could choose from four bathhouses. Dr. R. A. Leslie, a pioneer in the mineral business in the town, and Dr. W. A. Page both operated bathhouses. The bathhouse at the Cloyd used the "Double and Twist" waters, which were so full of dissolved minerals that it was not considered safe to drink. A brochure for the Palace bathhouse gives some indication of the services available:

BATHS: Mineral, Vapor, Sitz, Pine Needle, Steam, Immersion, Salt Glow.
BODY SHAMPOO: Sunbaths, Packs, Fomentations, Blanket Packs,

Enemas, Douches, Needle Showers, Colonic Irrigations
(internal baths)

MASSAGE: Complete Body (Swedish) Magnetic Tone Up; Relaxation
Nerve and Muscle; Circulation Tone, Joint Manipulation;
Scientific Reducing, Normalizing Build Up; Oil and Alcohol
Rubs. Electrotherapy; Electric Vibrating Circulation (machine
massage). Battle Creek Reducing (machine massage). Infra-Red
and Ultra-Violet.[14]

A guest at the Palace could stroll over to the bathhouse in his robe, submit to his choice of the rigors, and conclude with a shave and haircut at the Palace barbershop in the same building. Women could have their hair done in a beauty parlor. Then, fortified by the knowledge that they had done something to improve their health, they could look forward to a day at play.

The hotels provided various forms of recreation. Bowling was a favorite with the middle-aged, and all the hotels had five-pin alleys. Often, tournaments would be organized. Guests could hike through the surrounding hills or ride on horseback. The Palace had a tennis court, and during the 1930s both the Palace and the Cloyd had miniature golf courses. The Cloyd's eighteen-hole course was covered with green-painted cottonseed hulls; little bridges enabled golfers to cross back and forth over Salt Lick Creek.

For more sedentary guests, the hotels provided an ample supply of chairs in the shade. The Palace's private park was a pleasant place to spend the morning. Guests could stop at any of four sulfur wells, which were roofed over and surrounded by wooden benches. They would take their waters with a pinch of salt in small wooden containers, provided by the management. They could admire the canna beds or climb up to rustic benches on the hillside. At one point during the 1930s, the park included a lily pond and a concrete swimming pool, complete with boardwalk and brightly colored parasols. At the Palace shooting gallery on the park grounds, would-be marksmen could fire at mechanical ducks (three shots for a dime). Contract bridge players could always find fellow fanatics for a game at the Palace.

Some of the most popular entertainments were devised by the guests themselves. Many people came to Red Boiling Springs in family groups, or a number of young couples from some small town in middle Tennessee or southern Kentucky might make up a group and take their vacation together. In addition, the same people tended to come to the springs year after year. A vacation at Red Boiling Springs could take on the aspect of a house party as people, set free from their daily routines, filled the hours with contests and jokes. Some of these amusements were innocuous enough, but others retained frontier-style humor, which could be quite cruel.

A "tacky party" was an inverted costume ball. People would dress in old, mismatched clothes, and a prize would be given for the most tasteless effect. "Womanless weddings" were also popular. An elaborate mock wedding service would be held, but all the parts would be played by men, with the "brides" and "bridesmaids" decked out in women's dresses. Mock trials were also popular. One older Kentuckian, practically crippled with arthritis, was assisted to his baths by two "Spanish" women from Florida. His friends thought that was funny and arraigned him for running around with the two young women. A mock courtroom was set up in one of the boarding house lawns, complete with lawyers and judges.[15]

The "badger fight," a popular variant of the snipe hunt, was described by a former resident:

> People at the hotel they would find somebody that had never seen a badger fight. Back in those days they'd take them over to the dance hall. They had a room back in the back where they kept the musical instruments and piano and so on and it had doors to it where they could lock it up. So when they'd get everybody there they'd set it up . . . and they'd have three judges on who was going to win, the dog or the badger. And they'd always have someone that had never seen one to hold the rope the badger was tied to. And the badger would be inside this room where the piano stayed. . . . And they would line up the benches . . . in a small circle up there so the badger and the dog would have to stay in that. So when the time come this badger would be making a noise in the room and the dog would be outside, and the rope would be a shaking, and all of a sudden the doors would fly open, and out would come the badger whenever they pulled on the rope. And of course it was nothing in the world except a little tin chamber. A little flat one, you know, with a handle on it. . . . Made the doggonest racket you ever heard.[16]

The unsuspecting victim would be left holding a rope attached to a chamber pot.

Recreation was not limited to the hotel grounds. One of the most popular spots, both with hotel guests and with locals, was Simmons Lake, usually just called "the lake." In 1924, a Nashville man, M. A. Simmons, built a dam on the creek just above the Palace, flooding the valley. He added a swimming pool, a pavilion for dancing, skating, and bowling, and a small fleet of canoes for boating on the lake. The lake changed hands several times, but remained one of the town's strongest attractions. In the 1930s, according to a local man who was but a teen-ager at the time, "They had streetlights from town, all the way to the lake, so you could walk safely all the way. . . . And I can remember on occasion there would be so many people that was down there like on Sundays, Saturdays, that the parking area which was about a twenty-acre field up on one of those hills would be completely filled with cars . . . the cars would line up for a mile or two on the road and cars would be lined up all the way to town and people would park all round the square here and walk to the lake. . . ."[17]

Another curious attraction was Wooten's Park. In the midst of the Great Depression, T. S. Wooten, an elderly resident of the town, opened a small park on one of the hills overlooking the town. The park was decorated with wooden sculptures carved by Wooten: Popeye the sailor, Amos and Andy, Mutt and Jeff. Admittance was free, but most guests felt obligated to buy some of the apple cider that Mr. Wooten sold.

All of the hotels prided themselves on serving traditional south-ern-style food in ample portions. Three family-style meals per day were included in the cost of staying in a hotel. Breakfast might include ham

The Cloyd Hotel, currently known as the Thomas House. Photo by the editors.

or bacon, eggs, cooked cereal, biscuits, preserves of various kinds, and coffee. Other meals would include country ham or fried chicken, vegetables, and dessert. The Palace and the Cloyd had gardens and grew much of their own produce. The proprietor of the Cloyd kept hogs behind the hotel, fed them scraps and slop from the hotel, and cured his own hams. Local farmers sold fresh vegetables, extra eggs, and milk to the hotels and boarding houses. Local teenage girls worked as waitresses, making sure that the large bowls at each table were always full. At most of the hotels the regular kitchen staff was African American. Black cooks were considered to be both better at their jobs and better able to stand the heat of the hotel kitchens, where all the cooking was done on wood-burning ranges. The Palace had a special pastry cook to prepare desserts.

At the Palace, meals were announced by bells; the first bell was a signal to line up before the double doors to the dining room. The second bell signaled the staff to let the crowd in. Although the dining room accommodated 350 patrons, guests often had to eat in shifts during the height of the summer season. (Mr. Counts sometimes turned away as many as seventy-five people in one day when the hotel was full, but he always told them to come back for dinner. They could eat at the Palace even if they could not sleep there.) The Palace's resident band provided luncheon and dinner music. In the 1930s, Friday night suppers were served on the lawn under Japanese lanterns.

The evening meal was almost the start of another day, since the town kept late hours. After dinner, one could go dancing at the pavilions provided by the Donoho, the Arlington, and the Palace. The Palace was the only hotel, however, that kept a resident band. During the 1920s, the musicians were college boys who worked during the summer. By the mid-1930s, Roy Holmes's band from Glasgow, Kentucky, had become the Palace's house band. Francis Craig and his band came from the Hermitage Hotel in Nashville for special occasions. The band played popular music of the day, and the guests could perform the fox trot or waltz until late at night. Townspeople sometimes parked their cars across the street from the Palace and gathered to watch the guests as they strolled across the hotel's lawns to the Pavilion, dressed in formal wear: "Simmons Lake had its own particular attractions at night, as a town resident recalled. You could rent a boat, paddle off down through the water, and it wouldn't be very far until you could find a secluded spot where you could go many places, cause the lake had willow trees and trees hanging out over the water—it was no trouble to park the boat and be hidden. Romance."[18] The dance hall at the lake specialized in square dances with such luminaries as the WSM Fruit Jar Drinkers providing the music.

Night life in Red Boiling Springs could be fueled by alcohol. All during Prohibition and in the 1930s, liquor was readily available in the town. One former resident recalled, "All you had to do was whistle twice. You could get it coming in from any direction."[19] Bellboys in the hotels were especially good sources of information about bootleggers or "rum runners," as they were called locally. Since the town was not incorporated until 1953, law enforcement was left to the sheriff and one constable, whose forte was catching drunks, not bootleggers. The sheriff and a federal officer once caught a man and a pickup loaded with 170 gallons of moonshine. Another rum runner crashed his car through a roadblock. The officers fired at the car and hit a young man, killing him. Still, moonshine remained available. Much of it reportedly came from adjacent Jackson County, which was something of a center for the craft. Good "shine" was made from corn, grain, and sugar, and was distilled through copper tubing.

When Prohibition ended, roadhouses and "beer joints" sprang up. These places could serve beer, although liquor remained just as illegal—and as available—as it had during the Roaring Twenties. One of the more unusual of these establishments was the Cavern Dance Hall, which opened July 4, 1935. Referred to by its developers as a night club, it was located in the Leonard Cave, three and one-half miles from Red Boiling Springs. The entrance to the cave was 100 feet wide and 25 feet high, and always a cool 58° F inside. It accommodated a beer garden, a restaurant, and 1,200 square feet of wooden dance floor. The cave had two levels and many dark corners. People at the Cavern square danced to country string bands, got drunk, and fought. One Cookeville man was seriously injured in a fracas with a Clay County deputy over liquor at the cave.[20]

Simmons Lake had an unusual attraction: a gambling house. It was patronized mostly by visitors to the town (few of the locals had enough money to play). Gamblers could play poker and black jack, frequently for high stakes, without any great fear of the law, since the house was organized as a private club.

After a night on the town, hotel guests could make their way back to their rooms—or back to their cots in the hotel halls, especially during crowded seasons. During one such season, a boarding house proprietor rented one room to thirteen people, who used it as a dressing room and slept in their cars. During a particularly good summer—such as 1936—approximately 14,175 people stayed in hotels at Red Boiling Springs.

Religious revivals were as much a sign of the summer in Red Boiling Springs as they were in other small Tennessee towns. In the resort town, however, the audience was potentially much larger. A local resident remembers that evangelists from Holiness churches would set up a tent meeting, draw the crowds with "some real hot musicians," and then lambaste the wickedness of Red Boiling Springs. Other churches sponsored religious debates. But the biggest religious event—and possibly the biggest single tourist attraction even in the town—was a camp meeting held under the auspices of the local Church of Christ in August 1935.[21]

Brochures advertised the meeting, which featured evangelist Vernon M. Spivey of Chicago, a "fluent speaker," a "master of the Scriptures," and "the foremost evangelistic singer in this country." (The brochure also noted that he was a bachelor, and prominently featured a picture of the handsome preacher.) A description of the town itself was given, and prospective visitors were advised: "Plan your vacation so that you can attend the Great Camp Meeting throughout the month of August. You can secure camping ground just as thousands of others will do; or if you care for hotel accommodations, certainly you will find what you want at Red Boiling Springs."[22]

Advertising directors came to town just before the meeting to create additional publicity and attract visitors, who crowded into town on the Fourth to enjoy the usual entertainments. The *Macon County Times* noted that "candidates were present in large numbers, handing out their cards and wearing smiles nearly as large as a dish pan."[23] The Fourth of July, 1938, was also the occasion of the circus's annual visit. The "Mighty Haag Shows," a three-ring circus, toured the Upper Cumberland annually. They would parade into Red Boiling Springs—elephants, horses, and glittering performers stretched out along the town's streets for a mile—and set up their tent in a valley across the creek from the Palace.

Labor Day was a grand finale of the hotel season. In 1935, the *Red Boiling Springs News* listed events planned for the weekend: at the Palace, on Saturday evening there would be a poker game, a badger fight, and a dance. Roy Holmes's orchestra would give a concert on the veranda of the hotel on Sunday afternoon. At noon on Monday there would be a barbecue in the hotel's private park and a matinee dance from 4:00 to 6:00 P.M. in the Pavilion. Jimmy Gallagher's Orchestra would play at the dance on Monday night. At the lake, an "all-day affair" was planned with dancing to the music of Robert Lunn and his Night Hawks, boating, picnics, games, and a bowling contest. Leonard Cave would have a barbecue and a dance in the afternoon and evening.

The Depression seems to have had little impact on the resort business at Red Boiling Springs. In 1936, the town's newspaper attributed a successful season to the fact that Red Boiling Springs was a health resort. It continued to draw crowds while "other summer resorts," not blessed with these health-giving waters, "have been forced to close their doors for the lack of patronage."[24] The boom at Red Boiling Springs was even then in its last years, however, and by 1952 only two hotels were still open.

Townspeople give various reasons for the town's decline. Gas rationing during World War II discouraged long auto trips. Cheap labor, which had been so readily available during the 1920s and 1930s, became scarce during the war, as many people could find better jobs outside the county. Many hotel proprietors had taken profits out during the good years, rather than reinvesting money on maintenance and remodeling. All these factors undoubtedly played a part in the decline of the resort business. Yet one overriding factor is always cited—good roads.

Residents of Red Boiling Springs had been in favor of good roads, believing that all their resort needed to flourish was easier access. In 1924, a brochure advised would-be visitors that the roads were good; visitors could drive from Nashville via Gallatin and Hartsville, or from the north down through Bowling Green, Kentucky. By 1935 two hard-surfaced state highways, 52 and 56, ran through the town, and Consolidated Bus Lines' buses left town twice a day.

During the 1930s, the town attracted many people from surrounding counties who drove in for a day's or night's entertainment. In 1935, the town newspaper noted that two women from Glasgow, Kentucky, had been coming to Red Boiling Springs three times a week to take the mineral baths, and were also taking water home to drink. In 1936, a carload of couples from Gainesboro, twenty miles away, could drive over to attend the Palace's dance on a Saturday night. In that same year, a Shriners' motorcade left Nashville at 1:30 on Saturday, went to Carthage, which they left at 5:00 P.M., and reached Red Boiling Springs at 6:00 P.M.[25] The days were over when it took a week just to recover from the trip to Red Boiling Springs. People stopped spending their entire vacation in the town and began to come in for just one weekend;

then they might drive to one of the new state parks. The roads, which made it easy for the people of Nashville or Louisville to get to the town, also made it easy for the people of the Upper Cumberland to get out of the area entirely and vacation in the Great Smokies or on the Florida beaches.

No real effort was made to fight the erosion of the resort's business. The hotel proprietors who had built the resort in the 1920s were old by the 1940s, and their children were often not interested in continuing in the business. Wartime depletion of resources due to rationing, coupled with citizens moving to other cities to participate in war work or enlisting in the armed services took a toll as well. B. W. Chitwood closed the Donoho in the mid-1940s. Henry Counts, who had been the town's major booster, died in 1932. His wife and son held on at the Palace for a few years, then moved to a smaller hotel that they owned. After that, the owners employed various managers, but the hotel declined.

The Palace was torn down in 1958. Salvageable parts, such as doors, transoms, and the huge front columns, were sold. A rest home now stands on the site. The Farmers' Hotel and the Arlington burned in the early 1950s; the Colonial Hotel burned in the early 1970s. The Moss Hotel was torn down in 1973. The Red Boiling Springs Hotel (which had also been known as the Baker-Owens and the Lincoln), was first divided into apartments, and then torn down.

Three of the hotels have survived. After being closed by Mr. Chitwood in the mid-1940s, the Donoho stood empty until it was purchased by Ed Hagan, a former postmaster, in 1955. After extensive repairs and remodeling, Hagan reopened the Donoho and managed it until 1970. Its present owner, Mrs. Edith Walsh, a native of Chicago, bought the hotel in 1974. The Donoho underwent a number of renovations to make it habitable in the fall and winter, whereas it was previously open only in the summer. Its reputation for providing fine home-style dining after the peal of the dinner bell continues to draw visitors to the site.

The Cloyd has changed hands many times. In 1952, it was purchased by Dr. A. T. Hall of Lebanon. He added a new-style bowling alley, a golf course, and a swimming pool. It was managed by W. A. and Cornell (Cloyd) Moss for ten years in the 1950s and 1960s, and then went through another period of instability. By the year 2002, only three hotels remained standing. The Counts, renamed the Armour and run by Brenda Thomas, was one of the few where it was still possible to take the waters.

The Cloyd, currently called the Thomas House, suffered a fire in 2001 that destroyed a wing of the U-shaped building, along with historic

The Counts Hotel, currently known as the Armour Hotel. Courtesy of the Counts Hotel.

photographs and artifacts. The Thomas family rebuilt the structure in the traditional style with updated renovations. It gained a following during the 1990s when the Thomas family began hosting "Mystery Weekends," progressive dinners at Christmastime, and a variety of themed events.

Periodic attempts to revive the resort business have been made. Dr. Hall and Ed Hagan were leaders in such attempts in the 1950s. All boosterism was dealt a heart-breaking blow in June 1969, however, when a flood devastated the town. The damage was estimated at $2.2 million; the Red Cross spent $60,000 on relief in the town, which was declared a federal disaster area. After the flood, federal aid made it possible for the town to construct a thirty-unit low-rent housing project, obtain a new factory, extend the city limits and city water system, and build dams to avoid future floods. A small park was also constructed, with a tennis court, two covered bridges, a fountain and some playground equipment. During the 1980s and 1990s, several attempts were made to recapture the past excitement of Red Boiling Springs and the town began sponsoring an annual folk medicine show filled with questionable home remedies, presentations, entertainment, and storytelling. Deerwood Amphitheatre attracted musical talent from Nashville, introducing a number of new visitors to Macon County. The various hotels hosted beauty pageants and church groups throughout the 1990s.

Elderhostel programs at the Armour allowed visitors to come back to a place they remembered from childhood and relive the history of Red Boiling Springs. And in 2002 Perrier of France opened a factory to bottle water from the mineral springs there.

Some townspeople attribute Red Boiling Springs' decline simply to a change in fashion; it became the "in" thing to go somewhere else. But if fashions in vacationing change, so do fashions in health care. For the children of the middle-class people who crowded into Red Boiling Springs in the years between the wars, belief in the curative properties of mineral waters declined, much as did belief in the efficacy of the patent medicines that had been so heavily advertised during the Depression. It is more modern to take vitamins than Wine of Cardui, to calm a woman with tranquilizers rather than send her off for three months of rest at Red Boiling Springs, and to drive to Florida, the East Coast, or even across the country to Disneyland than to spend a vacation only a half-day's drive from home. Still, believers in mineral waters can be seen at the town, filling plastic jugs with red sulfur water; and the hotels entertain guests drawn to the town by its old-fashioned charm. It seems probable that the decline of the town's resort business was as much a result of the changing tastes of the area's middle classes as the availability of good roads. Any revival in the resort business will probably be due to the current fashion of nostalgia; the town may have been "out" long enough to be "in" again.

NOTES

This essay was originally published in a slightly different form in the *Tennessee Historical Quaterly* (42:3 [1983]: 223–42). Reprinted by permission of the Tennessee Historical Society and the author.

1. Nashville *Daily American* (August 4, 1890).
2. *Nashville American* (June 10, 1900).
3. Henry E. Sigerist, "American Spas in Historical Perspective," *Bulletin of the History of Medicine*, II (1942), 133–34.
4. Tourist brochure, "Red Boiling Springs" (c. 1925); *Macon County Times* (April 20, 1939).
5. *Hartsville Sentinel* (July 7, 1876).
6. Frank Herbert Richardson, *Richardson's Southern Guide, a Complete Handbook to the Beauty Spots, Historical Places, Noted Battlefields, Famous Resorts, Principal Industries and Chief Points of Interest in the South* (Chicago: Monarch Book Company, 1905): 82. For more about the importance of good roads to the area, see Jeanette Keith, *Country People in the New South:*

Tennessee's Upper Cumberland (Chapel Hill: University of North Carolina Press, 1995).

    7. *Macon County News* (January 1916).

    8. *Jackson County Sentinel* (September 22, 1916).

    9. Ibid.

    10. *Carthage Courier* (May 16, 1918).

    11. *Red Boiling Springs News*, various dates in 1935.

    12. "Red Boiling Springs, Tennessee," *Macon County Times* (August 2, 1979).

    13. Tourist Brochure, "Red Boiling Springs"(1925).

    14. Brochure for the Palace Hotel, 1930s.

    15. *Red Boiling Springs News* (August 3, 1935).

    16. Author's interview with Paul Wilson at Lafayette (December 19, 1981).

    17. Ibid.

    18. Author's interview with Comus Moss, Red Boiling Springs, December 22, 1981.

    19. Author's interview with Paul Wilson.

    20. Author's interview with Comus Moss; *Red Boiling Springs News* (July 1, 1935).

    21. *Red Boiling Springs News* (August and September 1935).

    22. Brochure in possession of Lois Denson, Red Boiling Springs.

    23. *Macon County Times* (July 7, 1938).

    24. *Red Boiling Springs News* (October 3, 1936).

    25. *Red Boiling Springs News* (July 1, 1935; October 12, 1935; October 19, 1935; August 2, 1936; June 27, 1936).

Chapter 11
_____

A BRAVE NEW DEAL WORLD

The Cumberland Homesteads

STUART PATTERSON

Unlike many utopian experiments, the Cumberland Homesteads cannot be judged according to a single, well-defined set of goals. Its original New Deal planners intended to create a "new pattern" of "dignified, wholesome, abundant living," to lead a select group of families from Tennessee's Cumberland Plateau out of the Depression, and thereby lay a path to an entirely "new type of civilization in America."[1] But these plans fit uneasily at times with the ideals and expectations of the colony's residents, who struggled to build for themselves a place they could simply call home. The pattern that ultimately defined the Cumberland Homesteads can thus be adequately conveyed only by a collection of stories told in many voices.[2]

For the plateau's mill workers and miners, the Depression meant a different kind of struggle. At the Harriman Hosiery Mill, the stink and dust of the spinning rooms, threats of summary firings, starvation wages for twelve-hour days, and management's refusal to bargain collectively led finally to a walkout in October 1933. It was the nation's first test of the National Recovery Administration's industrial codes. At Wilder, another strike for union recognition against the Fentress Coal and Coke Company had begun the previous summer. The action withstood marauding state troops and imported strikebreakers, but faltered when hired-gun thugs murdered union leader Barney Graham in April 1933. Many reluctantly returned to work or simply left, but a few held out.[3]

In November that year, a labor relations officer with the new Tennessee Valley Authority (TVA), Claire C. Killen, passed through Wilder and marveled at the patient dignity of the few remaining strikers. Fac-

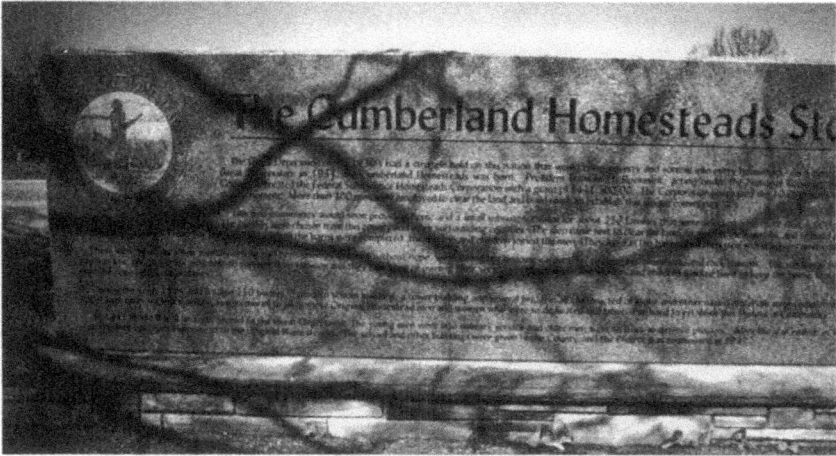

Sign commemorating the Cumberland Homesteads. Photo by the editors.

ing the winter in rags, pestilent housing, and with little to eat, they still refused "to accept conditions which are comparable to peonage." Killen was alarmed enough to warn of "impeding civil war" unless relief supplies and some steady, honest work were soon made available to the increasingly desperate miners. He found work for fifty young men with the Civilian Conservation Corps (CCC) digging drainage ditches, building bridges, and planting trees. Others were hired by TVA. Not long afterwards, in January 1934, another emissary of relief, Dagnall F. Folger, passed through Wilder, this time to screen whole families for inclusion in the plateau's biggest New Deal project, the Cumberland Homesteads.[4]

Cumberland Homesteads represented the nineteenth experimental resettlement colony built by the federal Division of Subsistence Homesteads. It marked one of four projects developed to resettle Appalachia's "stranded" coal miners such as those at Wilder, though it eventually included poor farmers, timber workers, a few professionals, and some of the Harriman strikers. In the words of an early public relations brochure entitled "A Homestead and Hope," they were to take part in "a program of social and economic salvage . . . designed to help families become self-supporting and to humanize living conditions."[5]

The intention of the plan was to provide destitute families with an opportunity to work on, and in time, purchase their own homestead, "a modern but inexpensive house and outbuildings, located on a plot of land upon which [they] may produce a considerable portion of the food required for home consumption." Subsistence farming, in concert with part-time wage work and cottage industries, would keep new "home-steaders" afloat in a cash economy. In the words of Milburn L. Wilson, an affable, pragmatic land economist with a philosophical bent who led the planning, the essential idea was to achieve "a balance between ur-ban and rural life—a balance which will offer the crowning advantages of both modes of life in a new structure of civilization."[6]

Wilson perceived the need to start small. Subsistence homestead colonies would be "demonstration models" of community with a tradi-tional village "cooperative spirit." To this end, Wilson meant to keep planning and operations as locally based as possible, using the Wash-ington office mainly to channel funding. He and his colleagues judged that the success of each colony would depend on the initiative and interest of those who best knew the lay of its land, and the characters and backgrounds of its intended residents.[7]

As of July 1933, Wilson's second in command, Clarence Pickett of the American Friends Service Committee, wrote Homer Morris of Fisk University suggesting a subsistence homesteads colony for Cumberland County. Morris signed on with the Division of Subsistence Homesteads as a field supervisor, and with the help of County Agent Bob Lyons began scouting locations for a colony near Crossville. Lyons proved in-strumental in gathering a group of local leaders to sponsor the project, and this group eventually formed the board for Cumberland Homesteads, Inc. With an initial loan of $431,000 approved by Harold Ickes and Wilson in Washington, they opened offices in Crossville on January 16, 1934.[8]

News of what the *Crossville Chronicle* called "this great develop-ment movement" spread quickly around and well beyond the plateau. The *Knoxville News-Sentinel* reported on February 4 that some four hundred men employed through the Civil Works Administration were clearing and grading a site the government had bought just south of Crossville—10,000 acres of woods and brush at less than $8 an acre. "Crossville finds itself transformed within a week from an easy-going county seat into a dizzily whirling cog in the machinery of the New Deal," as *The New York Times* reported that same day. "The county is in a festive mood, convinced that the Depression is gone and that a new day has dawned for the hills."[9]

The bustle of the project's first months was orchestrated by a trio transferred to Crossville from TVA—Francis O. Clark, William Macy Stanton, and D. F. Folger. Clark, formerly a Quaker missionary and dean of agriculture at Berea College in Kentucky, was first project manager.

Stanton, another Quaker who had designed homes for the model TVA town of Norris, joined as architect. He drew up fifteen different house plans for the Cumberland Homesteads, four of which were one of a kind, the others repeated with variations. At the outset, Stanton supervised construction of barns from boards milled on site to temporarily house homesteaders while they began construction of their own homes. The original plan called for 350 farms on tracts between four and thirty-five acres.[10]

Applications for farms poured into the offices at Crossville. More than two thousand were received in the first two months, and some six thousand inquiries flowed in before applications were cut off early the next year. The huge job of screening applicants went to D. F. Folger, an engineering student from Clemson University. As personnel director, Folger headed a staff of ten family selection workers, all deputized to canvas the plateau "investigating the character, ancestors and life environment of those who are applicants for farms."[11] Fliers published that winter warned all prospective homesteaders that:

Only families who have a reputation of being hard-working, honest, sober and good citizens will be chosen. Those selected must be willing to farm under the supervision of and in cooperation with the Agriculture Advisors. Only families willing to try new ways and who want to learn can succeed. It is absolutely necessary that each family is building a new community and a new way of living. Anyone not willing to work cooperatively for the good of the entire community should not apply.[12]

The impulse to provide relief for a few hundred stricken families became confounded with the imperative to shape them into citizens of a "new civilization." Folger's enthusiasm for "human engineering" was revealed in a 1935 article for *Mountain Life and Work*. "The people are mountain people," he wrote, "but they respond to new ideas and new ways of living about as readily as any of us. There are latent possibilities in the families we have, which we hope to see them develop."[13]

Folger's attitude was doubly ironic. Though he patronized the homesteaders as "mountain people," he was intimately acquainted with the diversity among those selected for the project. Though they had originally targeted miners and loggers, management quickly decided to cast a wider net, partly to meet overwhelming need and interest, but also with a view toward balancing the colony's variety of backgrounds and outlooks. Of the 228 selected heads of family who described their previous employment, 40 percent listed themselves as "unskilled laborers," mostly miners, textile workers or loggers. Another 20 percent described themselves as skilled or semiskilled, which could also mean mine or mill work, but often indicated some craft skill; homesteaders listed carpentry, plumbing, and blacksmithing as former occupations. The large majority of homesteaders had grown up on a farm, but a number had left the plateau, returning after losing "public work." About 30 percent described themselves as farmers or small businessmen. The remaining nine family heads had been "professionals," including the colony's doctor, nurse, and schoolteachers.[14]

The second and greater irony lies in the expectation that, though Folger and his family selection workers sought families with demonstrated initiative, ability, and character, they expected them to become pliant and dutiful once they arrived. Some project personnel did note some families' tendency to "distrust authority," especially those who came from Wilder and Harriman. As work progressed, a small but strident antimanagement group appeared, determined to keep the project's management aboveboard and honest in its dealings with homesteaders. In time, a majority of homesteaders supported this faction as Folger's paternalism began to rankle, and as the promise of "abundant living" faded.

At the outset, the collective optimism of the work seemed to warrant Folger's hopes for "building a spiritual community." A pattern emerged that fostered a feeling of common purpose. A selected family would move into temporary quarters, sharing a barn with one or two others until their own (or a large surplus army tent) was erected on their chosen plot. Though heated with oil drums and walled with tar paper, these shelters were, by many accounts, an improvement over the places they had left.[15]

Houses were the project's most important and lasting accomplishment. William Macy Stanton's achievement wedded vernacular, traditional, and modern Craftsmen styles into the most distinctive architectural statement of the entire "subsistence homesteads idea." Though they occasioned some grumbling at the time among envious neighbors, observers invariably marveled at their design and construction. Tennessee's own Senator Kenneth D. McKellar paid an unintended compliment when he groused about housing someone on relief in "a stone mansion very much handsomer than I ever lived in my life [sic]."[16]

Inspired by the back-to-the-land ideals of the subsistence home-

Homestead barn was originally used as a house while the home was being built. Photo by the editors.

steads program, Stanton designed houses to be built almost entirely with local materials. Native fieldstone provided the houses' main structure, lending them a dignified pride of place. Pine was cut and milled for shingling, interior framing and paneling, and some second-story structural framing, while oak was used for flooring. Local sand provided mortar. Most of the houses' cost, initially estimated at around $2,500, was for labor, mostly provided by homesteaders.

Employing homesteaders on house construction served to solidify their sense of common purpose and gave them a chance to learn new building trades. In under a year, a former miner could go "from laborer, mortar mixer to mason's helper, to mason," Macy Stanton later reflected. Others gained skills as carpenters, blacksmiths, plumbers, and even electricians; wiring was installed in anticipation of TVA power.[17] When "Moving-in Day" was celebrated the first of December 1934, ten homes had been completed and another forty were under construction with a hundred barns scattered around the site.[18]

F. O. Clark left the project in 1935, replaced by Stanton as project manager. Stanton stepped up house construction, and by July almost fifty houses were complete. A total of two hundred families were on site, all with houses in some phase of construction. While men built and farmed, women tended house and gardened. Day-long chores of cleaning, cooking, tending children, and washing were broken up by homemaking classes with Mary Ervin, the home demonstration agent. For completed houses, landscaping classes were conducted by a "special skills" agent from Washington.

Cumberland Homesteads' overall domestic style might be called "modern-day pioneer," a term frequently used to describe the homesteaders themselves. Middle-class respectability and rational convenience melded with stylized Appalachian rusticity. The latter—a theme then very much in vogue around the country—expressed simple, rugged endurance in the face of adversity. Indeed, the wives' homemaking programs went to the heart of Wilson's basic subsistence homesteads idea: Uniting urban and rural cultures was ultimately an affair of finding an appropriate domesticity for a troubled time.

Homesteaders worked hard, but they enjoyed themselves. They celebrated their first Christmas with a pageant, featuring a visit from Santa, carols, and stories. Milder weather brought ball games and cookouts. There were frequent round-robin community singings and plays staged in the colony's temporary schoolrooms. Washington approved funding for additional land on which to build a community center in June 1935.[19]

The colony received a steady stream of inspecting government officials, curious academics, and journalists. Eleanor Roosevelt, wife of the president and a great supporter of the subsistence homesteads program, came in July 1934 to commend Cumberland's small band of "modern-day pioneers" from the bed of a lumber truck.[20] A year after Mrs. Roosevelt spoke, Stanton entertained Rexford Guy Tugwell, who had recently taken over all the New Deal's colonization programs as head of the new Resettlement Administration. His visit marked an important new phase in the colony's life and its search for a lasting economic base.

Efforts to find outside employment for homesteaders suffered early setbacks. Congress disallowed directly employing them on government contracts. No reputable and sufficiently large private concerns proved willing to relocate to the remote highlands of the plateau during an ongoing Depression.[21] Tugwell and his legal advisers addressed the problem by forming the Cumberland Homesteaders Cooperative Association. A board of directors made up of homesteaders borrowed sufficient funds to establish and operate a manufactory. In January 1936, the Association received a loan of $550,000. Board members encouraged the trading post to expand operations, while the Association's profits were used to cover new, less profitable ventures such as a furniture factory. Dividends began to shrink and accusations of mismanagement led many of the cooperative's members to take their business to Crossville. In sum, the setup was a recipe for bad planning, mismanaged resources, and recriminations between residents and their government sponsors. Ironically, M. L. Wilson's original plans to base operations locally had led to more thorough control of the colony through Washington.[22]

The Association's problems were exacerbated by increasing friction between homesteaders and their on-site leaders. A happy choice as architect, Stanton proved less successful as a project manager. He seemed aloof and unsympathetic compared to the popular Clark. Under Stanton's direction, a series of controversies came to a head, prompting a *Chattanooga News* editorial to ask, in November 1936, "Do Homesteads Colonies Ever Succeed?"

One source of tension the editorial noted was an "attempt to force the people into a union church." In the beginning, homesteaders attended nondenominational community services, conducting worship and religious classes in temporary buildings because no churches could be built with federal funds. Folger and Stanton had actively supported the community church as a key aspect of the homesteaders' "spiritual community." But "the people began yearning to go back to their own churches," said Edna Gossage Blue. Baptists held a revival and, in 1936, began meeting in a brush arbor just outside the site. Methodist and Church of Christ congregations followed, meeting for a time in homesteader houses. The community church dissolved, and with it a good deal of Stanton's and Folger's credibility with the homesteaders.[23]

Homestead house belonging to Virgie Denton. Photo by the editors.

Just as tensions mounted over the church question, Stanton became embroiled in another public controversy, this time concerning an American Federation of Labor (AFL) union local joined by about a fourth of the homesteaders. In November, four union members were "checked out," or dismissed, they claimed, for their part in forming the union. They also charged Stanton with unfairly withholding part of their severance. For the time being, the Resettlement Administration's Regional Offices in Raleigh, North Carolina, settled the union dispute, but Stanton left under a cloud just a few months later.[24]

In September 1937, the Farm Security Administration (FSA) took over the Resettlement Administration in another New Deal bureaucratic shuffle. George L. Oliver replaced Stanton as manager of the Cumberland Homesteads. Known as "the Major" for his service stateside during World War I, he had more recently been a dairyman, extension agent, and cooperative manager. The Regional Office hoped the Major's expertise would prove valuable in getting the agricultural program and cooperative ventures on their feet as construction neared completion. A string of failed economic enterprises and the Major's militaristic management style made his tenure even more acrimonious than Stanton's had been.

Problems for the Major began with a large new sorghum plant the FSA built through the Association in early 1938. In less than two seasons, it succumbed due to a shortfall of cane, homesteaders' inexperience with the manufactory's machinery, and a new-fangled processing method that produced syrup that "tasted like a mixture of motor oil and glue."[25]

Meantime, the agricultural program provided little relief for homesteaders and more grief for management. Small plots, rocky soil, and serious erosion required more labor and produced less harvest. Despite these factors, many homesteaders tried farming, prompting the FSA to lend the Association $55,000 to build a cannery. Homesteaders failed to grow enough vegetables to keep the cannery's per-unit cost profitable. The homesteaders' union demanded that the cannery be a closed shop, and the Association and Regional Offices assented. This move cost the venture support from homesteaders who opposed the union, forcing the cannery to close in 1939 after two unprofitable seasons.

The campaign for a closed shop was symptomatic of divisions among homesteaders and management, leading the colony into bitter factional disputes and rampant politicking. The antimanagement faction that formed around the union sought to assert control over the Association and its labor policies, creating a schism among the homesteaders. The Major's regard for hierarchy exacerbated the divisions. Fierce loyalty to his FSA superiors alienated many homesteaders, leading them to suspect the government was trying to cheat them out of their wages. The Major's demands for loyalty led him to reward those who showed it, earning him the violent enmity of the growing antimanagement faction. Most homesteaders remained apart from the bitterest disputes, preferring to make their way quietly as long as food was on the table. Life on the project still beat the alternative, which was not too distant a memory.[26]

House construction ended in the spring of 1938. Though only half the proposed houses had been built, Cumberland Homesteads remained the largest of the subsistence homesteads colonies. In addition to 251 farms of between five and forty acres, the colony boasted a new community center, a handsome water tower, and a new school. To dedicate the school and mark the Homestead project's completion, two theater workers, Margaret Valliant and Sande Jaffray, were sent by the Federal Theatre Project to conduct an historical pageant. Entitled "New Ground," and scripted by Valliant, Jaffray, and Owen Metzger, a homesteader, the pageant recalled pioneer themes of the project's early years. It reads today like a somewhat tendentious exercise in FSA propaganda, climaxing in the advent of a "Homesteader" who arrives to lead the poor, rudderless, "Cumberland Family" into a brave New Deal world. Planning for the pageant met with indifference among many homesteaders, but it was an event for the whole plateau. It drew a huge crowd and was deemed a success by all. Its performance drew tears from many homesteaders, with its scenes of the devastating mining and mill work and of the hapless Cumberland Family. Some homesteaders appreciated the chance to enact a triumph, however symbolic.[27]

While the pageant briefly brought homesteaders together, they were destined for a final round of protracted struggles with their government sponsors. Even before the pageant ended, the union faction organized a widely supported rent strike. Steady work had not materialized, making it impossible to meet payments on now finished houses. In addition, payment accounts were not settled, making for confusing quotations on house prices. Finally, homesteaders simply wanted to be private homeowners, free from "community managers."

On May 25, 1939, FSA Director Will Alexander outlined these issues in a memo to FDR. The Major was replaced by Alva Taylor, a sociologist and Christian activist who proved much more sympathetic to

Water tower at Cumberland Homesteads village. Photo by the editors.

the homesteaders and their grievances. The reorganized Association continued to struggle. A new hosiery mill was completed in May 1939, but it operated at a bare profit because the machines proved unfit for the power supply. The war curtailed needed raw materials, and the transition from rayon to nylon accelerated the mill's demise in 1944. A furniture factory also limped along into the early 1940s, but by then homesteaders had found more lucrative work in northern cities and at the new Oak Ridge facility nearby.[28]

The lease-purchase contract dispute was resolved in 1941 at terms favorable to the homesteaders, who received the option to buy their homes and land in five years. The credit hour dispute was settled by a special act of Congress at terms favorable to homesteaders. In 1939, houses were appraised at an average of about $2,000. Most homesteaders who had found work elsewhere nonetheless chose not to purchase, and houses were sold by the late 1940s. In 1947, the buildings and land of the community center were transferred to Cumberland County, and the Cumberland Homesteads passed entirely out of federal control.[29]

Most of the New Deal's experimental resettlement colonies ended in the red, which might be accounted failures. A full balance sheet for Cumberland Homesteads, however, reflected the ideals, hopes, and expectations invested in the colony and their compounding return in the intervening decades. Conflicts between some homesteaders and its ever-shifting administration indicate the strength of these ideals and expectations but should not distort one's appreciation for what was achieved there. Like its sister colonies around the country, Cumberland Homesteads stands as a remarkable monument to its creative and daring New Deal planners and determined families who had seen the worst of times before they were given an opportunity to make something better.[30]

NOTES

1. Milburn L. Wilson, "The Place of Subsistence Homesteads in Our National Economy," *Journal of Farm Economics,* 16 (1934): 83; Russell Lord and Paul H. Johnstone, *A Place on Earth: A Critical Appraisal of Subsistence Homesteads,* U.S. Department of Agriculture, Bureau of Agricultural Economics (Washington, D.C.: U.S. Government Printing Office, 1942): 40.

2. For Fannie Burton, working the land on the plateau during the early 1930s was a struggle that is still difficult to convey. "Things were so hard then. We had seven dollars one year, and that went mostly for the doctor," she recalled decades later. "You just can't imagine it, 'cause you've never seen anything like it." Fannie and her husband Herman survived "one day at a time," scratching a living out of a few rocky acres on her father's land. Long days of hardscrabble farming turned into weeks and then months of hungry toil, but it was work that failed to lay any kind of lasting foundation. Author's interview with Fannie Lue and Herman Burton (November 16, 1997).

3. W. Calvin Dickinson and Patrick D. Reagan, "Business, Labor, and the Blue Eagle: The Harriman Hosiery Mills Strike, 1933–1934," *Tennessee Historical Quarterly* LV:3 (fall 1996): 240–56.

4. C. C. Killen, "Prevailing Conditions in the Wilder Coal Mining District," Memorandum to Dr. F. W. Reeves, November 3, 1933, National Archives Record

Group 142 (Records of the Tennessee Valley Authority), Atlanta, Georgia. (Southeast Branch). On the Harriman strike, see Mike Smathers, "The Search for the Garden," *Southern Exposure*, 8 (spring 1980), 57–63; Dickinson and Reagan. On the Wilder strike, see Tony Dunbar, *Against the Grain: Southern Railroads and Prophets, 1929–1959* (Charlottesville: University Press of Virginia, 1981).

5. U.S. Department of the Interior, Division of Subsistence Homesteads, *A Homestead and Hope* (Washington, D.C.: U.S. Government Printing Office, 1935): 10.

6. Wilson quoted in Smathers, 58.

7. Lord and Johnstone, 39–41.

8. Clarence E. Pickett to Dr. Homer L. Morris, July 5, 1933. Homer Morris Collection, Earlham College, Richmond, Indiana (copy of file in Archives of Cumberland County Playhouse, Crossville, Tennessee). Patricia B. Kirkeminde, *Cumberland Homesteads: As Viewed by the Newspapers* (Crossville, Tenn.: Brookhart Press, 1977).

9. "Cumberland Homesteads Incorporated Now at Work," *Crossville Chronicle* (January 18, 1934); Alan Forrest, "Homesteading Returns to Tennessee," *Knoxville News-Sentinel* (February 4, 1934); *New York Times* (February 4, 1934), quoted in Smathers, 58.

10. Liz Straw, "Cumberland Homesteads Historic District," National Register of Historic Places Nomination, Tennessee Historical Commission, Nashville, 1984.

11. Travis K. Hedrick, "Busy Tugwell Eludes Crowd at Crossville," *Chattanooga Daily Times* (July 22, 1935); "Must Have Character and Industry," *Crossville Chronicle* (January 25, 1934); Smathers, 58.

12. "Information Concerning Cumberland Homesteads," from Archives of Cumberland Country Playhouse.

13. Dunbar, 14; Dagnall F. Folger, "The History and Aims of the Cumberland Homesteads," *Mountain and Life Work,* 11 (July 1935): 7.

14. Lord and Johnstone, 84–85, and Avery H. Angus, ed., *Factual Data Compiled for Project #19 "Cumberland Homesteads" Near Crossville, Tennessee*, National Record Group 96 (Records of the Farmers Home Administration), College Park, Maryland (Main Branch). Malcolm "Tack" Denton of Moss and his wife Virgie of Alpine were the 169th family accepted at the Cumberland Homesteads on March 24, 1935. They received forty-eight acres at a cost of $2,800, which they eventually paid in full. Under the strictures of the time a woman's name was not recorded on the deed. Tack worked on the water tower during its construction. According to Virgie, "People in the area called the place 'Mrs. Roosevelt's New Ground.'" Interview with Virgie Denton at her home at Cumberland Homesteads, April 17, 2003.

15. Folger, 3.

16. Delos D. Hughes, "The Housing Ideal at Cumberland Homesteads," *Tennessee Historical Quarterly* (spring 2001), 44, 48. See Hughes and Straw for detailed discussions of the houses at Cumberland Homesteads.

17. William Macy Stanton, "Homes by Homesteaders," unpublished manuscript, National Archives Record Group 96, 3.

18. "Families Move in New Homes at Homesteads," *Chattanooga News* (December 3, 1934); Kirkeminde, 7; F. O. Clark, "Daily Reports of Cumberland

Homesteads Project" (February 21, 1934–December 29, 1934), Homer Morris Collection, Earlham College, Richmond, Indiana (copies in Archives of Cumberland County Playhouse).

19. Kirkeminde, 8–9; Emma Jean Pedigo Vaden and Doyle Vaden, *Looking Back. . . : Cumberland Homesteads Golden Anniversary Album* (Crossville, Tenn.: self-published, 1984): 42.

20. "Homes Project Inspected by Mrs. Roosevelt," *Chattanooga News* (July 7, 1934). There were so many visitors the first summer that Homer Morris complained to Washington that it was hard to get any work done. Homer Morris, "Report on Cumberland Homesteads," unpublished manuscript, Homer Morris Collection, Earlham College (copy in archives of the Cumberland County Playhouse).

21. Paul Conkin, *Tomorrow a New World: The New Deal Community Program* (Ithaca, N.Y.: Cornell University Press, 1959),116–17.

22. Lord and Johnstone, 87–90.

23. "Do Homesteads Colonies Ever Succeed?" *Chattanooga Times* (November 26, 1935); Edna Gossage Blue, *A People Dared, God Cared* (Crossville, Tenn.: self-published, 1984): 10; Vaden and Vaden, 22.

24. "Crossville Union Calls for Probe" *Chattanooga Times* (November 22, 1936). See also, "All Is Serene at RA Project" *Chattanooga Times* (November 24, 1936); and Lord and Johnstone, 86.

25. Smathers, 61; Lord and Johnstone, 89–90

26. This factional strife is outlined in Lord and Johnstone and noted in a memo from J. O. Walker to C. B. Baldwin of the FSA, dated December 12, 1939. See Howard N. Gordon to Dr. W .W. Alexander, "Meeting at Cumberland Homesteads" (May 29, 1939). Both documents are in Record Group 96, National Archives, College Park, Maryland.

27. Margaret Valliant, Sande Jaffray, and Owen Metzger, "New Ground," unpublished manuscript, in Valliant Collection, Mitchell Memorial Library, Mississippi State University; *Crossville Chronicle*, "Homesteads Pageant Gets Big Crowd" (August 4, 1938). See also, Leta Smith Colditz, "Cumberland Homesteads—the first years as I saw them," *Crossville Chronicle* (December 29, 1977).

28. Will W. Alexander to Franklin Roosevelt, May 25, 1939; The National Religion and Labor Foundation (multiple signers) to Mrs. Roosevelt, July 20, 1939; Mrs. Roy L. Gossage to Franklin Roosevelt, May 1939; see also, Gordon to Alexander (n. 26). All letters are in National Archives Record Group 96, College Park, Maryland. For general outlines of the project's difficulties in 1938–1940, see Lord and Johnstone, 90–94, and Smathers, 60–61.

29. Mouzon B. Peters, "A.W. Taylor Quilts Homesteads," *Chattanooga Times* (November 5, 1940). On Taylor and the Cumberland Homesteads, see also David Whisnant, *Modernizing the Mountaineer: People, Power and Planning in Appalachia* (Boone, N.C.: Appalachian Consortium Press, 1983); Lord and Johnstone, 94; Straw, section 8:8. The last community manager, Frank Foote, replaced Taylor when the latter grew frustrated with the FSA's bureaucracy.

30. For their invaluable insights into the life of the Cumberland Homesteads, then and now, I would like especially to thank Emma Jean Vaden, Fannie Lue and Herman Burton, Orion Miller Sr., Foress Kidwell, and Mike Smathers. James

Crabtree and his staff at the Cumberland County Playhouse were especially helpful in providing free access to a wonderful archive of material, as were those at the Cumberland Homesteads Tower Museum. Finally, I thank Alice and Gordon Patterson for their ongoing support.

Chapter 12

RADICAL HILLBILLIES

Socialism in Tennessee

W. CALVIN DICKINSON

Socialism has had negative connotations in America because of the propaganda directed toward the philosophy. So it may seem unusual that in the conservative state of Tennessee, and particularly the Upper Cumberland region of the state, numerous persons interested in socialism have launched several socialist experiments. In fact, one could contend that the Upper Cumberland region has been the center of socialist thought and activity in Tennessee.

Most socialist philosophy and experiments in the region, however, did not envision or advocate an absolute socialist economy. With the exception of the Socialist Party of America, in the early twentieth century, most socialist thinkers and actors in the state advocated "Christian Socialism." Like the Socialist Party, their main interest and goal was to better the lives of the laboring class; they proposed and organized "associations" or "cooperatives" rather than advocating government ownership of the means of production. Thomas Hughes in the nineteenth century, and Myles Horton, Kate Stockton, and Abram Nightingale in the early twentieth century, planned and worked toward the common welfare of labor.

The first experiment inspired by socialist philosophy was the English settlement of Rugby in Morgan County. Founded in 1880, Rugby was the dream of English judge Thomas Hughes, author of the popular novel *Tom Brown's School Days*. The book was a thinly disguised recounting of Hughes's experience as a student at Rugby School in England. Hughes studied under Dr. Thomas Arnold and was influenced by his egalitarian philosophy. At Lincoln's Inn in London, Hughes studied with Frederick Denison Maurice, a Christian socialist. In 1848, Maurice, Hughes, and two associates began a Christian socialist movement in England, and in 1850 Hughes was a member of the Society of Promoting Working Men's Associations, proclaiming these groups "the solution of the great labour question." He thought the society could "found an association or two in order to convert all England and usher in the millennium [for labor] at once."[1] Association workshops would be owned and managed by workers who would divide the profits among themselves. As a member of Parliament in the 1860s and 1870s, Hughes introduced a trades union bill to legalize labor

Thomas Hughes, founder of Rugby Colony, Morgan County, Tennessee. Courtesy of the Tennessee State Library and Archives.

unions. By 1878 he had become involved in another organization, the Guild of Co-operation, which also advocated workers' associations. The group met monthly, then quarterly, to promote their ideas.

With the considerable wealth acquired from the popularity of *Tom Brown's School Days*, Hughes and the London Board of Aid to Land Ownership joined the Boston Board of Aid to Land Ownership in purchasing 35,000 acres in Morgan County to establish a utopian colony. The site was chosen by Franklin Webster Smith of the Boston Board; Hughes joined the enterprise without visiting Tennessee.[2] This settlement was not created specifically for the labor class, but for the "Will Wimbles" of England, sons of affluent families graduating from English schools "who are entirely at a loose ends, not knowing what in the world to turn their hands to."[3] The colony was not to be limited to Englishmen and Will Wimbles, but was open to all.

Rugby colony, named for Hughes's alma mater, attracted about two hundred persons in 1880; only about 9 percent were single young men from England. The largest number of residents was approximately four hundred in 1884; half were English and half American. Hughes continued to work in England, never living in the colony, although his mother

Tabard Inn at Rugby. Courtesy of Historic Rugby.

and his niece resided at Rugby. He usually visited once a year until his
mother's death in 1887.

An agricultural village of approximately sixty-five buildings, Rugby
included two hotels, two general stores and a drugstore, a schoolhouse,
a beautiful Gothic Revival church, and a stylish library with 7,000 volumes of Victorian-era literature. Tourists were an early source of income for the colony, and *Harper's Weekly* featured Rugby in an 1880
issue. Rugby advertised itself as a health resort, and the Tabard Inn
provided stylish, comfortable accommodations for visitors. The inn,
owned by the colony, was leased to managers.

The *Rugby Handbook* advertised "Cheap Farming Lands" "in tracts
suitable to all purchasers at LOW FIGURES and with deferred payments."[4]
Some settlers did buy farmland, but the poor quality of the soil made
agricultural production difficult. One "association" idea that Hughes
advocated was the cooperative use of pastureland around Rugby for
raising livestock. Farmers could buy shares in this enterprise, and then
participate in joint use of the pasture with other shareholders. This
scheme was never initiated.

Attempting to market tomatoes, a stock company in which Hughes
invested built a structure to house $2,000 worth of canning equipment.
The cannery never operated because not enough tomatoes could be

grown. Another planned enterprise, the Rugby Pottery Company, prepared a prospectus; but the company never sold stock and never organized.

A commissary or general store offering stock certificates at $5 a share opened in 1880. "Our wish is to make this commissary a centre of supply, and that every settler . . . shall become a member and part owner of it. . . . In this way we shall have a common interest and common property." The commissary operated successfully for a time, offering "a large assortment of merchandise of nearly every description at lowest market prices."[5] Finally, the national rejection of socialism, and the settlers' sensitivity toward a socialist label, resulted in their selling the commissary to an individual.

Problems plagued Rugby from the beginning. Hughes's nonresidence created a vacuum in inspirational and practical leadership. The distance to the colony headquarters in London created misunderstandings and problems. In 1881, a typhoid epidemic, originating in a contaminated well at the inn, killed seven residents, and in 1884 the Tabard burned.

After 1887, Hughes never returned to the colony. He lost about $250,000 in the experiment. In 1899, Rugby Land Company, an American enterprise, bought the land, and the English connection was severed. The village continued to exist with limited economic opportunities and a steadily declining population.

Although Myles Horton referred to Rugby as a "Christian Socialist colony,"[6] it did not have a socialist economy. Land purchased from the Board of Aid was privately owned. Capitalistic enterprises financed by stock offerings were attempted. Hughes's Christian socialism held no sympathy for state-sponsored socialism or Marxist communism. Cooperative attempts at raising livestock and operating the commissary were continuations of Hughes's Christian socialist philosophy. Hughes formulated ideas for Rugby under the influence of his Christian socialist teachers in England. The nobility of labor and benefits for the laboring class were emphasized in socialist philosophy and Rugby's plan.

Another late-nineteenth-century thinker who introduced ideas of socialism into the Upper Cumberland region was Elmer Lincoln Wirt. Born in Minnesota in 1863, Wirt acquired only an elementary education; but he was an avid reader. One of the first members of the Populist Party, Wirt supported Populist candidate James B. Weaver for president in 1892. Later he supported William Jennings Bryan, a three-time Populist presidential candidate who ran on the Democratic ticket. Though

always a Populist, Wirt usually supported Democratic candidates because the Populist Party was a
minority in Minnesota and Tennessee. He espoused socialist ideas because they were congenial with the
Populist platform.

In 1894, Wirt brought his family to Tennessee, then to Cookeville
in the Upper Cumberland. In 1896,
he worked for the Putnam *Press*, and
in 1903 he founded the Putnam
County *Herald*. In his first issue, he
indicated that "politically the HERALD
will be democratic, with a little 'd'"[7];
and three years later he lauded the
benefits of socialism: "Socialism is
beyond doubt the only solution of
the science of popular government,
and socialist sentiment is rapidly

Elmer Wirt, editor of the Putnam County
Herald and political activist. Courtesy of
the *Herald-Citizen*.

increasing in all the civilized countries. In a nutshell, socialism is public ownership of public utilities and honesty in public affairs."[8]

This editorial indicated that Wirt did not accept the socialist
economy, but embraced only aspects of socialism that were in harmony
with his populist sentiments. Thus, his stance was compatible with those
of earlier and later Christian socialists in the Upper Cumberland.

Later, in 1920, Wirt lashed out at the developing "Red scare" en-
gulfing the United States: "The United States Government has forcibly
deported several hundred so-called Reds from the country and has cases
pending against many more. . . . When the Socialists elect a congressman or member of the legislature they are expelled and denounced as
traitors."[9]

Throughout his journalistic career, Wirt remained sympathetic with
socialist philosophy and the Socialist Party, although he always ran for
political office on the Democrat ticket. Wirt served as an alderman in
Cookeville and a representative in the Tennessee General Assembly, and
he ran unsuccessfully for the Democratic nomination for governor in 1920.

Another socialist leader in the Upper Cumberland, Myles Horton,
was born in Savannah, Tennessee. About 1925, he went to work for the
Presbyterian Church, conducting Bible schools in Cumberland County.

216   W. Calvin Dickinson

Myles Horton (on the left), founder of the Highlander Folk School, with Eleanor
Roosevelt. Courtesy of the Tennessee State Library and Archives.

He visited Rugby during this period, wanting to learn from this failed
utopian community. He also met Abram Nightingale in Crossville, who
urged him to further his education by attending Union Theological Seminary in New York.

In 1929, Horton enrolled at Union, where he was impressed by the
Christian socialist philosophy of professors Reinhold Niebuhr and Harry
Ward. Niebuhr headed the Fellowship of Socialist Churchmen. After
studying at Union for a year, Horton went to the University of Chicago
and traveled in Denmark. By 1932, he was ready to return to Tennessee
and establish a school for mountain people and labor leaders based on
the European Folk School model.

Joe Kelly Stockton and Kate Stockton of Fentress County helped
Myles Horton launch the school. Horton referred to the Stocktons as
"mountain socialists."[10] They owned a tract of land in Fentress County
that they offered to the Highlander Folk School. Eventually, the Highlander project abandoned the Fentress County site, and the school concentrated its efforts near Tracy City in Grundy County, just south of the
Upper Cumberland region. Joe Kelly and Kate Stockton often visited
the school in Grundy County and joined the lecture courses and other
activities.

Highlander Folk School opened with $1,300 in assets "to provide an adult-education center which would prepare rural and industrial [labor] leaders for a new social order." The Highlander staff "conducted study sessions on unionism, held classes on picket lines, . . . [and] wrote letters to secure relief for the strikers" during the Wilder coal strike of 1932-1933 in Fentress County.[11] Myles Horton persuaded Socialist Party leader Norman Thomas to come to Wilder and speak at a mass meeting of 700 strikers and their supporters on March 5, 1933.

Horton "emphasized that the school was not socialistic," although he admitted freely that he was a socialist: "The Socialist Party was a philosophical concept, and that was my philosophical bent."[12] He later responded to author Will Campbell, who asked him if he was a communist: "Don't be ridiculous! They were much too conservative for us. We were trying to teach democracy."[13]

Highlander Folk School was frequently labeled communist/socialist. Evangelist Billy Sunday, Nashville newspaper publisher James Stahlman, the Knoxville *Journal* and Chattanooga *Times*, and the American Legion sounded a chorus of denunciation of the school. In 1962, the state of Tennessee revoked Highlander's charter and confiscated its property.

During the three decades of the school's existence, Horton organized worker cooperatives in several locations. The first was at Summerfield in Grundy County in 1934. Members built a cooperative cannery and formed a sewing cooperative. The second attempt was at

Highlander Folk School. Courtesy of the Tennessee State Library and Archives.

Greenhaw in Franklin County. This group established a farmer cooperative to sell their crops and buy fertilizer at a discount. James Stahlman
of the Nashville *Banner* warned farmers against Horton's "communists"
from the "hotbed of radicalism at Highlander School.[14] Horton's greatest success with worker cooperatives was in Greene County in East Tennessee. Farmers in this area formed a dairy cooperative, enlisting five
hundred members.

Horton was encouraged by the Rugby colony to establish his social
experiment in the Upper Cumberland. Like Hughes, he was motivated
by Christian socialism in attempting to better the lot of the working
class in the region and the nation. Unlike Hughes, Horton was successful. He trained labor leaders; he worked with the unions; and he achieved
his greatest success in promoting equal rights for African Americans in
the United States.

Abram Nightingale encouraged and assisted both Kate Stockton and
Myles Horton in their Christian socialist activities. Reverend Nightingale came to the Upper Cumberland region in 1924 after serving ten
years as a minister on Fort Bertold Indian Reservation in North Dakota.
The First Congregational Church in Crossville offered him a pastorate.
Nightingale constructed his house with his own hands, living there
and serving as pastor of the church until 1956. In those three decades,
he introduced the church and community to new radical ideas.

Nightingale, a Christian socialist, had convinced Myles Horton to
adopt the philosophy and attend Union Theological Seminary. He suggested that Horton read *Our Economic Morality*, written by Union professor Harry Ward.[15] In 1930, Nightingale invited Norman Thomas,
Socialist Party candidate for president, to speak at Crossville, and in
1936 he supported Kate Stockton for governor of Tennessee. Suspicious
Tennesseans spread rumors that he used his shortwave radio to commu-
nicate with communists, that the blood bank sign on his car door was a
Nazi symbol, and that his church was actually a communist organization.

His generosity in the community became legendary. He opened his
home to travelers and to the needy. He opened his church to other religious groups. He worked as a volunteer in the local hospital. He promoted racial equality and cooperation before it was popular. He assisted
prisoners of war in the local POW camp during World War II. He encouraged and assisted persons seeking education. He promoted and assisted in the establishment of Cumberland Homesteads. Myles Horton
referred to "a kind of sainthood" he had.[16]

Cumberland Homesteads, a controversial program, was part of the

Subsistence Homesteads Program in Franklin Roosevelt's New Deal. Critics tagged the program socialist, along with TVA and other liberal New Deal programs. Negative images of Subsistence Homesteads derived in part from the reputation of the agency's first director, Rexford G. Tugwell. He wanted cooperation and collectivism in the American economy, and his critics called him a communist.

Of the one hundred subsistence homesteads communities planned by the program, only one was in Tennessee; it was in Cumberland County. Named Cumberland Homesteads, it was one of four "stranded" communities. They were to relocate and rejuvenate unemployed, or stranded, miners.

After a careful selection process, 228 families were selected for the Cumberland Homesteads community. Using cooperative methods, the settlers built their barns and houses on about ten acres of land. Although settlers believed from the beginning of the project that they would be able to purchase their land and buildings, continual bureaucratic delays in the transfer of property made them doubt they would ever own the farms. The dreaded label of "socialism" soon was applied to the community. After the Farm Security Administration took control of the project in 1937, the government finally agreed to negotiate purchase contracts with the homesteaders.

Since homesteaders were not expected to make their living on ten acres of land, cooperative industrial enterprises were planned. Cumberland Homesteads, like other subsistence homesteads programs, organized cooperatives in the form of industrial enterprises and consumer outlets. During its first year, Cumberland organized five cooperatives: a general store, a cannery, a medical association, a community church, and women's clubs. In the medical association, each family paid $1.50 per month for complete medical care. The women's clubs taught home management, child care, health, nutrition, and crafts. The Trading Post, a general store, was financed by contributions from resident members and paid consumer dividends, and the cannery was operated cooperatively by resident members to preserve and provide garden produce for the members.

In 1936, the Co-operative Association at Cumberland negotiated a $550,000 federal loan to finance a sorghum plant and a coal mine. The next year, another loan financed a hosiery mill. The cooperatives provided jobs for the homesteads' residents, and each resident had a vote in operating the cooperative projects; in this they were reminiscent of Thomas Hughes's associations. Eventually all the cooperatives were economic failures.

Cumberland Homesteads represented the completion of a circle of socialism in the region. In both Rugby and Cumberland Homesteads the ideas of socialist philosophy formed the foundation. Cumberland Homesteads, like Rugby, attempted to provide a better life for neglected groups. Both communities used socialist cooperative techniques to achieve their goals.

The Christian socialist philosophy began in the nineteenth century, but socialism as a political party was a twentieth-century phenomenon in America. In 1898, Eugene Debs and his followers organized the Social Democratic Party, and in 1900 this party supported Debs for president of the United States. The next year, they selected Socialist Party of America as their new name, a name that became permanent. In 1900, the national party addressed an eight-page pamphlet to the citizens of Tennessee, *The Socialist Democratic Party's Address to the Voters of Tennessee.* Proclaiming in its opening statement, "ALL THE WORLD'S WEALTH IS PRODUCED BY THOSE WHO LABOR," the document suggested that "the government—that is, the people—shall own the railroads, telegraphs, telephones, trusts, etc., AND OPERATE THEM AT COST FOR THE BENEFIT OF THE WHOLE PEOPLE." The people should "SHARE EQUALLY IN THE PRODUCT." In addition to this national platform, the Social Democratic Party of Tennessee, "in Convention assembled," demanded for their state

1. Abolition of the poll tax.
2. Free and compulsory education for all under 16 years.
3. Public ownership of private turnpikes.
4. State employment of all unemployed laborers.
5. Laws to prevent destruction of timber.
6. Discharge of the public debt.
7. Abolition of penal lease system.
8. Local public ownership of public utilities.

The party candidate for governor in 1900 was C. H. Stockwell. Tennessee electors for presidential candidate Eugene Debs were W. G. Pennington, John Ray, T. J. Rowland, W. G. Markland, E. D. Morgan, H. Kleiser, J. T. Hines, J. E. Voss, R. N. Morris, L. H. Gibson, W. M. McCaul, and H. Martin.[17]

Membership numbers for the Socialist Party in Tennessee are not available, but the group operated out of headquarters in Nashville to support the national party and to issue demands on behalf of the laboring class. The 1912 *State Platform of the Socialist Party of Tennessee* declared "the party of the working class, able and competent to represent the interests of the producers."

The 1912 party platform included

1. Equal suffrage for men and women.
2. The initiative and referendum and right of recall.
. . . . .
4. Orphan and delinquent homes maintained by the state.
. . . . .
6. Minimum wage for women workers.
7. Collective ownership of land.
. . . . .
11. Right to strike, boycott, and picket.
. . . . .
19. Free medical service "to the destitute."
20. Free medical service for all school children.
. . . . .
24. Abolition of capital punishment.

The document invited "all progressive people who are in sympathy with the just cause of labor," as well as "the negro workers, and those of other races," to support the Socialist Party to "hasten the day of man's emancipation from all forms of ignorance and slavery."[18] The Socialist Party candidate for governor that year was C. G. Harold.

Interest in the Socialist Party in Tennessee was evidenced by attendance figures from a lecture series the party sponsored in Memphis in 1915. A total of 685 persons attended four lectures, with an average attendance of about 170. The report also indicated that a total of eighty-five persons joined the party during the lecture series.[19]

The Socialist Party in Tennessee consisted of only a few hundred members by 1936. The poor areas of the state had voted in large numbers for Eugene Debs in the early part of the twentieth century, but support had diminished under Norman Thomas's leadership. Thomas, the presidential candidate, received only 187,342 votes in 1936, mostly from New York; in 1932, he had polled 884,781 votes. Eugene Debs had drawn a higher percentage of votes in 1900 than Thomas did in 1936. The party never recovered from this debacle. Norman Thomas noted the reason for failure: "It was Roosevelt in a word."[20] FDR's greatest victory was the 1936 election. He had co-opted the better ideas of other parties, including the Socialist, and he stole their voters and their votes.[21]

In 1936, the Socialist Party of
Tennessee, meeting in Nashville,
nominated Kate Stockton as its candidate for governor.[22] Stockton's gubernatorial candidacy was part of a
national effort by the Socialist Party
to place a candidate on the ballot in
every state. Kate Stockton was the
descendent of a distinguished family of radical thinkers, and she was
the product of the Upper Cumberland radical tradition. Kate was born
in Stockton, California, in 1880. Her
grandfather, Arthur Bullus Bradford,
had been a Presbyterian minister in
Pennsylvania.

Kate's father, Arthur, was an
entrepreneur. He moved with his
wife to California in 1879 to assist
family members in running a sheep

Kate Bradford Stockton, Socialist Party
candidate for governor, 1936. Courtesy
of the Tennessee State Library and Archives.

ranch. When this proved unprofitable, he returned to Pennsylvania,
accompanied by his wife and two daughters born in California. Friends
advised the Bradfords of an opportunity with the railroad in Tennessee,
so Arthur moved again in 1884, settling at Clarkrange in Fentress County.

The Bradford property joined the Stockton property at right angles.
In the back fields of both farms, Joe Kelly Stockton and Kate Bradford
courted. The couple married in their mid-twenties. Joe Kelly Stockton
was a justice of the peace (1912–1914) and a Fentress County trustee
(1919). Registered as a Democrat, he voted for Socialist candidate Eugene Debs in 1920. During the Depression, he continued to support the
Socialist Party, voting for Norman Thomas.

Neighbors and friends remember Kate's early interest in politics.
One county resident recalled long political discussions in her father's
house, when Kate Stockton argued her point of view with the men.
These views, radical in 1930, are accepted today as the viewpoint of a
woman ahead of her time. Joe Kelly defended his wife's unusual behavior whenever anyone criticized her lifestyle or her teaching.

An article in the Knoxville *News Sentinel*[23] credited Henry George's
Progress and Poverty, and studies in economics, as the factors leading
Kate Stockton to socialism. Henry George, an American social reformer,

proposed that land is a free gift of nature; all men have an equal right to use the land; and it is unfair for a few to acquire great wealth by holding land that increases value. He proposed the "single tax" on landholdings to equalize wealth.

Kate Stockton ran for governor in 1936, largely because there was no other willing candidate. Though she had served as a state committee chairperson, she had no previous political experience. The *Crossville Chronicle* carried an announcement on April 2: "At a meeting of the Socialist Party in Nashville, Mrs. Kate Bradford Stockton was chosen as the gubernatorial candidate for Tennessee. The home of Mrs. Stockton is at Allardt, Fentress County. She enjoys the distinction of being the first woman to ever be nominated for governor of the Volunteer State by any political party." The Chattanooga *Free Press* noted that "Mrs. Stockton hasn't the slightest appearance of a radical, until she begins talking."[24]

Socialist Party headquarters in Nashville issued regular bulletins to keep party members informed about the campaign. Two mimeographs for printing state and local issues were used. One was located at campaign headquarters in Nashville, and the other belonged to Hugo Gernt of Allardt.

Expenses of the campaign included support of Herbert Harris, national party organizer, "to keep his sound truck moving over the State, to pay traveling expenses for State and National Candidates, to print thousands of leaflets and other Socialist literature, . . . [and] to cover state highways with Socialist signs." Harris was in the state for the entire campaign with his red sound truck, directing a "modern campaign" with a "planned itinerary." He planned a schedule wherein Stockton would do active campaign work on alternate weeks after July 1.[25]

The sound truck was used extensively during the campaign. In Memphis the sheriff gave the party a permit to use the truck, but he warned that someone "might throw a ripe tomato or something" if she went too far in denouncing Gordon Browning, the Democratic Party candidate. Later, in Knoxville, Kate Stockton felt she could speak freely. She "branded Browning as a tool of merchants and manufacturers," and warned he would never be a friend to labor.[26]

The campaign was expected to cost "at least $200 monthly." The party made an appeal for "ONE DOLLAR A MONTH from each employed comrade." One bulletin noted that "$746.25, or almost 3/4 of the campaign quota for the entire state was pledged" shortly after the campaign began. Local chapters of the party in Knoxville, Nashville, Memphis,

Chattanooga, Allardt, and Crossville were each assigned fund quotas, but campaign contributions were small. Kate Stockton and her husband "were able to contribute only five dollars from their slender cash income."[27]

The Socialist national campaign also experienced financial problems. George A. Nelson, candidate for vice president, could not attend the National Socialist convention because he was "not fixed financially."[28] After his nomination, he was able to join Norman Thomas to support local candidates. Kate Stockton, U.S. Senate candidate Howard Kester, Herbert Harris, and William Hollister appeared with Norman Thomas and George Nelson at a campaign rally in Knoxville in July. The party encouraged its members to listen to Norman Thomas's radio broadcasts and phone their friends whenever a broadcast was scheduled. "The future is full of hope if the workers will only understand they can bring these things about by uniting. I'm working to unite them," exclaimed Mrs. Stockton.[29]

Stockton's campaign was delayed in July when Kate took time to harvest her garden. Freezers and electricity were unknown in most rural counties. "Forced to forego a campaign speech" in Cookeville because she was "busy with her summer canning," she was replaced for the rally by William Hollister and George Lambert, National Socialist Party organizers. They "addressed everyone . . . within hearing distance of their sound truck."[30]

Kate Stockton knew her chances of winning were improbable if not impossible. The Associated Press agreed: "Mrs. Kate Bradford Stockton is a Socialist Candidate in Tennessee and, barring upset, the Union will have no woman in any governorship for at least two years."[31] Majority party candidates in the state continued to denounce each other and ignore the socialist platform and candidate.

Stockton lost the election by a large margin. Gordon Browning, Democrat, received 332,522 votes; Republican P. H. Thach received 78,292; and Kate Stockton received 3,786 votes. No mention was made of Stockton's defeat in the national or state press. The largest number of votes cast for Kate Stockton were in Knox County (512), Davidson County (231), and Washington County (219). Shelby County, the home of the political boss Ed Crump, gave her 118 votes. In Fentress County she received 89 votes, less than 3 percent of the total.[32]

Kate had attempted the impossible. She was a woman running for the office of governor, and she ran on the Socialist Party ticket. But she was the most obvious example of the presence of socialism as a political and economic philosophy in the Upper Cumberland region.

Although socialists held idealistic and worthwhile goals in the state and the nation, they never exerted a strong influence on the economy or on politics. Socialism had a very short life in the region and the state. Myles Horton was the only Tennessee socialist whose ideas and actions brought about significant changes. With the exception of the Socialist Party of Tennessee, the socialist philosophy expressed in the Upper Cumberland was most often Christian socialism; it was concerned with promoting a better life for the laboring class. It was not state socialism and was never Marxism. Socialism was usually expressed and practiced by individuals rather than parties or movements, individuals who were either outsiders or natives influenced by outsiders. These individuals were usually idealists, utopians, or dreamers. They did not use the violent methods of socialists in other countries. Socialism was set in rural rather than urban areas in Tennessee, whereas socialism in the rest of America and in Europe was usually active in urban industrial settings. Socialism was not well financed in Tennessee, and individual socialists never sought personal gain from their practice of the philosophy.[33]

Notes

1. Edward C. Mack and W. H. G. Armytage, *Thomas Hughes* (London: Ernest Benn, 1952): 61.

2. For a detailed discussion of Smith's part in the Rugby experiment, see Bonita J. Howell: "Rugby, Tennessee's Master Planner: Franklin Webster Smith of Boston," *Journal of East Tennessee History* 73 (2001): 23–38.

3. Thomas Hughes, *Rugby, Tennessee: Being Some Account of the Settlement Founded on the Cumberland Plateau* (London: Macmillan, 1881): 3.

4. *The Rugby Handbook*, 2nd ed. (Rugby, Tenn.: Historic Rugby Press, Facsimile Reprint, 1996): 34.

5. Hughes, 36.

6. Myles Horton with Judith and Herbert Kohl, *The Long Haul: An Autobiography* (New York: Teachers College Press, 1988): 21.

7. George Wayne Watters, "Elmer Lincoln Wirt, Editor and Politician: A Study of Grassroots Populism and Progressivism in Tennessee, 1903–1920" (Cookeville: Master's Thesis, Tennessee Technological University, 1973): 23.

8. Ibid., 33.

9. Ibid., 96.

10. Horton, 65.

11. John Glen, *Highlander: No Ordinary School* (Knoxville: University of Tennessee Press, 1996): 364.

12. Horton, 35–36.

13. Interview with Will D. Campbell (Cookeville, Tenn.: December 2, 2000).

14. Glen, 131.

15. Horton, 31–32.

16. Ibid., 21.

17. Papers of the Socialist Party, "Socialist Party of Tennessee" (Durham, N.C.: Duke University Special Collections, Microfilm Reel 111). Capital letters were used in the original text.

18. Ibid.

19. Ibid.

20. David A. Shannon, *The Socialist Party of America* (Chicago: Quadrangle Books, 1967): 248.

21. Ibid. In June of 1934, the party's state convention convened at Highlander Folk School in Monteagle. In addition to resolutions concerning the miners' strike at Wilder, the convention elected the following state executive committee: Kate Bradford Stockton of Allardt, chair; Howard Kester of Nashville; Hugo Gernt of Allardt; Myles Horton of Monteagle; Lynn Hall of Knoxville; W. B. Hiord of Chattanooga; Joe Kelly Stockton of Allardt; N. P. Watson of Memphis; and John Dillingham of Nashville. Dillingham was an African American and Kate Stockton was a woman.

22. The author has quoted verbatim lengthy amounts of material concerning Kate Stockton from an essay that he co-authored with Rebecca Vial of Lincoln Memorial University, "Kate Bradford Stockton," *Tennessee Historical Quarterly* LXIX (fall 1990): 152–60.

23. April 9, 1936.

24. July 26, 1936.

25. Papers of the Socialist Party, Reel 111.

26. Knoxville *Journal* (October 15, 1936).

27. Ibid.

28. Knoxville *News-Sentinel* (May 26, 1936).

29. Ibid. (April 9, 1936).

30. Nashville *Tennessean* (July 26, 1936).

31. Ibid. (November 1, 1936).

32. In 1944, the Socialist Party made another attempt to rally support in Tennessee. Alfred D. Moore was state party chairman and Joan Livingston was state secretary. State campaign director Constance Rumbough announced a convention for July 11 in Nashville. Thirteen party members and one Democrat attended. Presidential electors selected at the convention were James Best, Ruth Moore, William Legant, Joan Livingston, J. B. Campbell, Hugo Gernt, W. H. Kirkpatrick, Mrs. W. R. Dotson, Raymond Hammond, Daniel C. Gibson, and John T. Melton. During the campaign, the party distributed about seven hundred leaflets, and held one public meeting for candidate Norman Thomas, with about fifty attendees. The party collected $66.54 and spent $52.03 on the campaign; the biggest individual donation was $10 from Hugo Gernt. In the election, Thomas received five hundred votes statewide. Socialism in America and in Tennessee was dead thanks to the programs of the New Deal and Americans' negative opinions about the philosophy.

33. The author thanks Dr. James B. Jones Jr., of the Tennessee Historical Commission, for the valuable information concerning the Socialist Party of Tennessee that he provided.

Chapter 13

SOMEWHERE IN TENNESSEE

The Cumberland in Wartime, 1940–1947

G. Frank Burns, Kelly Sergio, and Rex Bennett

Late in the summer of 1938, listeners to Cookeville's WHUB radio station became more aware of events in Europe. The crisis over Czechoslovakia brought Adolf Hitler's voice into Upper Cumberland living rooms. That July, Sergeant Alvin C. York of Pall Mall wrote a lengthy telegram to the New York *Journal-American* calling for strengthened defenses and compulsory military training in all Civilian Conservation Corps (CCC) facilities. By the fall of 1939, county newspapers were publishing columns about European affairs. Dr. Gus Dyer of Vanderbilt spoke to the Cookeville Rotary Club, warning them to prepare for war.[1]

Congress passed the Selective Service Act in September 1940. It called reserve officers into active duty in October and initiated America's first peacetime draft. That same year, Tennessee Governor Prentice Cooper organized a special committee on war preparedness, cochaired by Major Rutledge Smith of Cookeville and Sergeant York. That same year, York squared off against Colonel Charles Lindbergh, a spokesman for the America First Committee, in a series of heated speeches calling for American intervention.[2]

General George C. Marshall sent Army and National Guard personnel in search of sites suitable for training soldiers. Camp Forrest became one of the largest training camps built for the duration. Located just east of Tullahoma, a tiny town of 4,500, the camp started as a 1,040-acre National Guard training site. Originally called Camp Peay, in honor of Tennessee Governor Austin Peay, the site had been used by the local National Guard since 1926. After the introduction of the peacetime draft, Camp Peay and the Tennessee National Guard were federalized. Renamed

227

Camp Forrest, Tullahoma, Tennessee. Courtesy of the Tennessee State Library and Archives.

Camp Forrest, after Confederate General Nathan Bedford Forrest, the base was expanded to a whopping 85,000 people.[3]

Construction began in 1940. When troops arrived for the first cycle of basic training in March 1941, just over 19,000 people were already employed, building barracks, mess halls, warehouses, hospitals, chapels, theaters, and administrative offices.[4] Persons from Knoxville, Huntsville, and Chattanooga, hired by the federal government, commuted daily from those cities or had to find lodging in local homes and businesses. Soldiers who first arrived at the facility found their biggest enemy to be "General Mud." This created mass confusion in Tullahoma. Luther Bennett said that simply commuting to the post was an ordeal. Near the end of the construction, a bulldozer was placed at the front gate to literally push cars out of the way to allow workers and military personnel into the post.[5]

The attack on Pearl Harbor increased the importance of Camp Forrest. Thousands of eager young men hastily enlisted in the armed services after hearing the news, and thousands more would be added to the ranks through an expansion of the draft. The volunteer tradition was so strong in some Upper Cumberland counties that no man was drafted in 1942.

The Illinois National Guard—later the Thirty-third Infantry Division—was the first large contingent to arrive at Camp Forrest after the United States declared war. They were soon joined by such reactivated

Guard units as the Seventy-fifth Field Artillery Brigade and the 109th Cavalry (converted to the 181st Field Artillery) from the Upper Cumberland. Before the war ended, Camp Forrest was home base for the Eightieth, Thirty-third, Ninth, and Seventy-ninth Infantry divisions, the Seventeenth Airborne division, and various units in Tennessee, for field maneuvers from 1941 to 1944.[6]

Preparing for war in Europe required a staging area that simulated the climate and terrain. Finding a location for the field exercises fell on Major General George Smith Patton Jr. Familiar with the Cumberland River Basin because his grandmother had lived at Watertown in Wilson County, and he had spent some time in the region over the years, Patton and his staff chose middle Tennessee as the prime location to prepare servicemen for the invasion of Europe. The Tennessee Maneuver Area, which operated from 1941 to 1945, included a twenty-one-county area stretching from Cumberland County in the east to Humphreys County in the west. The main arteries of troop movement were U.S. Highway 70N west to east and State Highway 10 north to south. Between May 1941 and May 1945, twenty infantry divisions, eight armored divisions, four airborne divisions, and five cavalry regiments (mechanized) traversed the region. Two infantry divisions (the Thirtieth and the Eightieth) took part in three separate maneuver phases, and the 101st Airborne participated twice. This amounted to a total of more than half a million combat soldiers and at least another 100,000 support troops operating in Middle Tennessee. Or, to put it another way, 800,000 young men invaded middle Tennessee to prepare for invading Europe.[7] Called "war games" in peacetime, maneuvers were far from contemporary video games. They involved sweat, toil, tears, and, in a few instances, blood. The Tennessee Maneuvers simulated actual field conditions, usually without live ammunition, bringing to the Upper Cumberland, the Cumberland Valley, the Highland Rim, and Duck River Valley the verisimilitude of war.[8]

The Tennessee Maneuvers made three major contributions to victory in Europe. They proved that armor could be used swiftly and decisively with powerful precision. They demonstrated how airborne troops could be moved in division strength over a considerable distance. And they showed that the Cumberland River, a river as wide and swift as the Rhine, could be crossed even under adverse weather conditions.[9]

Other than this, the principal function of maneuvers was to train field-grade officers in the command and deployment of large military units. Regimental and division commanders demanded training condi-

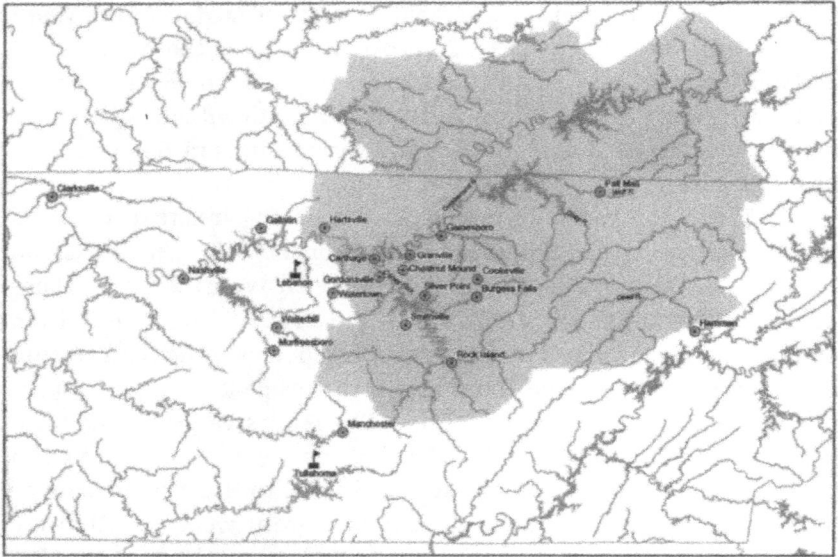

Map 4. Tennessee Maneuvers training area.

tions close to actual field situations. These things could not be learned from textbooks, so the War Department was determined to hold large-scale war games in the area around Camp Forrest and similar installations in Louisiana.

Included in this first phase of maneuvers were troops of the Thirty-third and Eightieth Infantry divisions, based at Camp Forrest, and the Fifth, Twenty-seventh, Twenty-ninth, and Thirtieth, originally National Guard divisions. The Twenty-ninth, guardsmen from Maryland, Virginia, and the District of Columbia, later won fame at Omaha Beach under the command of a Tennessee native, General Charles Hunter Gerhardt.[10] The star of the show, during the first phase of the maneuvers, was the flamboyant Major General Patton, whose Second Armored "Hell on Wheels" Division showed skeptics their effectiveness. Patton left Fort Benning for the Cumberland Plateau in the summer of 1941, leading two columns, each sixty miles long, into the heart of the Upper Cumberland. The demonstration began at Cookeville and concluded southeast of Murfreesboro, both technically outside the official maneuver area.[11]

On June 17, 1941, Patton and his Second Armored troopers gave civilians a taste of what blitzkrieg was like as he whipped down Highway 70N from Chestnut Mound to flank an "enemy" infantry division southeast of Murfreesboro. Shortly after midnight, the tank column, with Patton in the lead tank enthusiastically waving his pistol, reached the intersection with Highway 10 and whipped into a ninety-degree turn leaving rubber on the pavement. Then came armored combat cars equipped with machine guns and radio, light tanks burning dim blue "blackout" lights, 37mm cannon protruding from buttoned-up turrets. For hour after hour, the Second Armored—11,000 soldiers and 2,300 vehicles—roared down Highway 70N and Murfreesboro Pike, crossing Stone's River at Walter Hill before veering off to the east to catch its unwary prey.[12]

Jeeps, six-by-six personnel carriers, ambulances, and supply trucks followed the tanks. Supporting engineer units carried pontoon bridges, water purification equipment, earth augers, and signal units. Patton led an entire armored division on the road, a small sample of what would cross northern France in 1944 under his command as the Third Army. With the objective in sight, Patton's Second Armored Division pounced on the Old Hickory Division. The hapless Thirtieth became the victim of Patton's first triumph in World War II. His victory marked the first time in the annals of American military history that a full armored division had engaged in maneuvers and had an opportunity to test itself in combat.[13]

In the spring of 1942, the War Department resumed field training maneuvers in middle Tennessee, enlarging the Tennessee Maneuver Area from fifteen to twenty-one counties after carrying out exercises in Louisiana and California. Although many would later take credit, someone realized that the Cumberland River and the hilly country along its south bank from Wilson to Trousdale, Smith, Putnam, and Jackson counties was remarkably similar to Western Europe.[14]

Soon men in uniform, military equipment, and journalists were ubiquitous throughout the Upper Cumberland. Counties included were Cumberland, Putnam, Jackson, Smith, Wilson, Trousdale, DeKalb, Cannon, White, Warren, Sumner, Rutherford, Maury, Moore, Coffee, Perry, Williamson, Hickman, Lawrence, Humphreys, and Wayne. Camp Forrest acted as the barracks and hospital. The maneuvers created confusion throughout Upper Cumberland, for General Patton ordered tanks and troops to avoid the use of roads, where in actual combat conditions they would be sitting ducks. As a result, armies simply cut through farmers' fields and fences.

Stories abound about frightened cattle, ruined fences, and pilfered crops commandeered by the Red or Blue armies. Farmers found bridges constructed across the Caney Fork, the Collins, the Cumberland and Duck rivers, which they happily used, only to find them blown up later. The infusion of military hardware—trucks, jeeps, mobile offices, telephone wires, and all manner of "disposable material," made one soldier remark that if the maneuvers had continued another year or so the "South would have got back from the Yankees all that was lost during the War of Rebellion, including old family silver."[15] Citizens simply had to work around the military's maneuvering for the duration.[16]

Soldiers and civilians had a great deal to contend with, from inclement weather and K rations to torn up flowerbeds and irritated animals. Combat engineering units, trying to string wires for field communications, found their task daunting. Difficulty negotiating the rugged terrain of the maneuver area, with its bluffs, sinkholes, and rolling hills, was exacerbated by curious farm creatures. Goats found the insulation on army field telephone wire particularly tasty.[17] Soldiers unfamiliar with farm life often found themselves being chased around area barn lots by angry bulls, hogs, chickens, or dogs. Some soldiers fell into area wells and sinkholes only to be hauled out by amused citizens. Property damage in the maneuver area exceeded $4.5 million by the time the war games ended.[18]

Lieutenant Colonel William Hubert Crawford of Cookeville, pro-

Soldiers work on a bridge near Granville, Tennessee. Courtesy of the Granville History Museum.

vost marshal for General Benjamin Lear's Second Army, used his personal influence to bring Maneuver Director Headquarters to Lebanon, where space was available at Cumberland College and Castle Heights Military Academy. Lebanon, situated at the crossroads of U.S. 70N and Highway 10, was on the Tennessee Central Railroad, whose main line ran from Clarksville to Harriman. Lebanon also boasted an airport capable of accommodating C-47 transport planes, used to carry parachute troops as well as cargo.[19]

In August 1942, the first troops to arrive in the area were engineer battalions of the Fifth "Red Diamond" Infantry Division from Camp Crowder, Missouri, followed by a Signal Pigeon company and a Signal Photo company. The Ninety-third Signal Battalion, composed of Indiana Bell Telephone personnel in the Army for the duration, came in before the first field problem.

Second Army delegated actual operational control of the maneuvers to I Corps. On September 14, the first problem of I Corps maneuvers began. Divisions involved were the Sixth Infantry, Eighth (Mechanized) Infantry, and Eightieth Infantry and the Fourth Armored Division. The pattern was much the same for all the operation. There were six major "phases," from September 1942 to January 1945. Each phase contained eight problems, one each week.

The first problem focused on movement of troops north from Manchester, in Coffee County, to the Gallatin area. Second was a simulated parachute drop at the Harsh Bridge over the Cumberland River at Hunter's Point between Wilson and Sumner counties. This had to be simulated because no airborne troops were ready for this stage of training.

Next came the first crossing of the Cumberland River at Rome in Smith County. This inaugurated the first mass presence of troops in the Upper Cumberland, but it would not be the last. Armored forces went into action in the fourth week, followed by an attack by "Blue" army composed of infantry and armor toward a railhead at Hartsville, defended by "Red" army, made up of one infantry division and two tank battalions.

In the sixth week, the Blue force worked on an axis moving eastward from Donelson into the hill country of Smith and DeKalb counties, illustrating the strength that high ground gave to defending forces. Then for the next problem, the tables were turned and the Red force, numerically superior, took the offensive, moving from Chestnut Mound toward Donelson.

Pontoon bridge across the Cumberland River. Courtesy of the Granville History Museum.

The last problem involved the defense of Murfreesboro and a ranger raid by Blue tactical forces. Rangers performed in Phase II of the 1943 Second Army maneuvers, climbing the cliffs at Carthage and at Hunter's Point on the Cumberland River.[20]

Dignitaries arrived for the maneuvers in October1942, including seven southern governors who were treated by General Lear to a camouflage demonstration that both amazed and amused them. It was said, but never confirmed, that President Roosevelt came to Tennessee secretly to meet with a Chinese major general who represented Chiang Kai-Shek. Other visitors included soldiers and diplomats from Great Britain, Free France, Norway, Yugoslavia, Iran, Czechoslovakia, Sweden, and the Soviet Union.[21]

Troops participating in the 1942 maneuvers left in mid-November. Weather delayed the implementation of the second phase of war games. Heavy rains pounded the area and the Cumberland River, swollen beyond its capacity, went to flood stage in January 1943. Because of the deluge, preparations for a much larger operation were implemented. Rain soon turned to snow. On February 28, in the midst of a heavy snowstorm, signal and engineer companies arrived in the maneuver area and bivouacked along the Tennessee Central Railroad. Other troops began to roll in by truck and by train. The Second Army made preparations to begin Phase I maneuvers, as the training exercise was to be officially called. It was the advent of the largest number of troops in the area during the entire maneuver period.

That March, distressed representatives from the area's chambers of commerce went to Washington, begging the powerful Office of Price Administration (OPA) for increased allocations of commodities and food to the twenty-one counties affected by the thousands of troops and dependents in the maneuver area. The government granted some relief in equal shares to Wilson, Rutherford, Smith, Trousdale, DeKalb, Putnam, and Jackson counties.[22]

On April 11, as troops began to move to staging positions, a third weather event, more violent than flood or snow, wracked the region. An early morning tornado swept across the airport at Lebanon, demolishing fourteen army planes and the mess hall, killing one soldier, and injuring eleven other troops and several civilians.[23]

By Easter Sunday, the Eighty-first Infantry Division was in bivouac near McMinnville and the NBC Army Hour broadcast Easter services from "Somewhere in Tennessee" to the nation. On April 24, beneath sunny spring skies in a grove west of Carthage, officers and correspondents gathered to see a special demonstration of ground-air support coordination. Phase I was ready to begin. Three infantry divisions (Seventy-ninth, Eighty-first, and Thirtieth), two armored divisions (Fifth and Sixth), the 101st Airborne, and two regiments of mechanized cavalry (Sixth and Sixteenth) participated, nearly 90,000 men for this single phase. Support troops included nearly 40,000 soldiers in signal, engineer, military police, quartermaster, medical, field artillery, and motor maintenance, ordnance units, a company of WAGS (war rescue dogs) attached to an airborne glider regiment, and the 10,000 headquarters troops camped in tents around Maneuver Director Headquarters. For this part of the Tennessee Maneuvers, there were at least 140,000 troops in the area, camped from Lawrence and Wayne counties in the south to southern Kentucky in the north.

The 1943 maneuvers began on April 26, with one infantry division between Murfreesboro and Manchester, another between McMinnville and Smithville, and a third between Murfreesboro and Lebanon. The movement in this problem was southwest to northeast, with 30,000 infantry and an armored division with mechanized cavalry on the roads going cross-country against another 27,000 riflemen and 12,000 defensive tankers.

In May, ranger training was introduced. In Putnam County, farm-

War games between Red and Blue armies. Courtesy of the Granville History Museum.

ers around Burgess Falls were startled in the predawn hours by rangers in soot-faced camouflage crawling through their backyards. Highway 42 to Sparta formed the eastern edge of the active area, and night traffic moved with only the blue blackout lights visible. At Carthage, barrage balloons appeared on the Cordell Hull Bridge from Highway 70N to the town. Used extensively in the maneuvers, barrage balloons made in Paris, Tennessee, proved crucial to the success of the D-day invasion in 1944.

Umpires observed maneuvers from the air in Piper Cubs, flying out of Sewart Air Base at Smyrna. C-47s carried paratroopers over the Upper Cumberland, who practiced landing in "hot zones" under heavy enemy fire. Observers on the ground, known as Ground Air Support Command (GASC), issued orders and information to pilots by means of radio transmitters.[24] GASC spotters provided the main line of communication between pilots, informing them about targets, ground action, and locations of troops on either side.

As other pilots trained in B-25 Mitchell bombers, problems soon arose. Flying empty planes in no way simulated combat conditions, nor did it allow pilots to acclimate themselves to the different ways in which fully loaded planes handled. To alleviate this problem, local gristmills soon found all of their surpluses requisitioned for the maneuvers. Flour and corn meal were placed into large sacks, some weighing as much as 500 pounds. Loaded sacks filled the bomb bays of the B-25s, approximating the weight of bombs they would later carry. Grain sacks accomplished two purposes. Young pilots, training to fly wing-to-wing with heavy payloads, learned how much runway and how much speed was necessary to get their planes off the ground. Additionally, debris left by the large white and yellow explosions of the grain bombs left tangible evidence of the success or failure of pilots in hitting their prescribed targets.

Mistakes happened. During one problem, bombers headed from the Great Falls Dam at Rock Island State Park en route to the Cumberland River at Gainesboro. Pilots received orders to drop their bombs on the defenses of the Red Infantry south of the Cumberland River. Sirens sounded, warning civilians to take cover. GASC radiomen soon learned the difficulty of directing planes in a precision bomb run. Gainesboro became the only American town to be bombed during World War II, when a Mitchell B-25 dropped a simulated but loud bomb filled with flour on the public square just east of the Jackson County Courthouse by mistake.[25]

On June 16, in the Carthage-Hartsville area, a spectacular operation occurred. Paratroopers staged the first division-size airborne drop

Soldiers wade through one of the tributaries of the Cumberland River in search of enemy activity. Courtesy of the Granville History Museum.

of glider and parachute troops from the 101st "Screaming Eagles." Nearly two years later, those troops did the same thing in Normandy.

On June 22, troops began to move out as new divisions came in, not quite as many this time. There were the Eighty-third, the Seventy-sixth, the Eightieth Infantry for the third time, the 101st Airborne again, the Tenth Armored, and the Forth Cavalry (mechanized) Regiment, about 20,000 fewer combat troops. A significant new unit was to be brought up from Camp Forrest in July, however, the Second Ranger Battalion, hand-picked by ranger commander Lieutenant Colonel James Earl Rudder, which would be trained to scale the heights of Pointe du Hoc's ninety-foot bluffs above Omaha Beach at Normandy. The first action in the July problem occurred at Silver Point in Putnam County. The mission was observation and then sabotage.

After the maneuvers ended in 1944, Major General Lloyd Fredendall, commander of Second Army and maneuver director, called the Eighty-third and, later, the 100th "the most efficient infantry divisions to take part."[26] In Europe, the Eighty-third had two unique distinctions: near St. Nazaire in June 1944, the division captured an entire German Army Corps, 20,000 men, the largest number of prisoners taken in a single instance in the European Theater. In December, moving to rescue the beleaguered Bastogne force, the Eighty-third lost 1,600 men killed in a single day, the greatest number an Allied division suffered in one day's fighting.

The winter of 1943–1944 was hard. Homesick soldiers were relieved at Christmas by a party given at Watertown for black troops. Christmas dances took place at Sparta and Cookeville, and a ham supper at Readyville. Carthage, Gordonsville, Cookeville, Lebanon, Gallatin, Donelson, and Hartsville high school gymnasiums were opened for Christmas Eve and Christmas Day 1943. Cookeville had wrapped presents for every soldier who attended its party.[27]

In 1943, Christmas came on a Saturday, and because it was a holiday the United Service Organization (USO) at Cookeville was nearly overwhelmed. The canteen opened early Christmas morning "to serve coffee and doughnuts to men and their wives who were here for overnight passes as well as visitors here to be with their cadet students." Because all restaurants in town had closed for the day, the USO was the only source of food for the troops.[28] The Putnam County Herald praised the USO women for their efforts and documented their task: "2,400 cups of coffee, 74 home baked cakes, 100 pounds of homemade candy, 5 bushels apples, 6 orange crates, 300 packages of cigarettes, 576 Hershey bars were given to service men during the afternoon and night. In addition some 1,500 presents donated by the citizens were handed to the boys Christmas night. One thousand articles were checked and 50 telephone calls completed for the men."[29]

The maneuvers infused considerable money into the Upper Cumberland economy. The army distributed two payrolls, and many army wives came to the area to be with their husbands, renting rooms and apartments in county towns. Retail stores did increased business.

The sound of a siren blaring from a Piper Cub flying over the maneuver area signaled the end of a problem and the beginning of the weekend. Streets of every town filled with soldiers on weekend furlough. Drugstore fountains, movie theaters, and USO recreation houses were packed, as were hospitality centers sponsored by churches. Dances were held in high school gymnasiums and at state parks. Maneuver Recreation Centers, organized at the suggestion of the American Legion posts, provided bathrooms and recreation areas. The Tennessee Department of Health worked to control venereal diseases.[30]

Cookeville, designated an "R and R" station for soldiers on weekends, both welcomed and feared the servicemen who filled the town's streets. The City Commission wanted to keep them occupied. They suspended a number of local Blue Laws, bending the rules in a spirit of both patriotism and self-preservation. Cookeville's two movie theaters, the Princess and the Palace, opened their doors on Sundays, but only after 2:00 P.M. Only people in uniform and their guests could attend movies on the Lord's Day. A closed-door session of the Cookeville City Commission recommended the sale of alcohol for the duration of the maneuvers, but establishments serving those libations had to be located within walking distance of the Cookeville depot where the troops gathered. Beer gardens opened and establishments such as Poppy's Billiards and Fox Cafe on the West Side advertised: "Cold Beer, 5 Cents." According to the rules, only men in uniform could purchase alcohol, and soon a black market emerged with soldiers "renting their uniforms to locals."[31] In spite of the availability of legal alcohol, bootleggers plied their trade in Cookeville and the surrounding communities.

A larger concern focused on the good girls of Cookeville. There was a general fear that, with the sea of servicemen washing onto Cookeville's shores each weekend, the town's single women would, in the parlance of the day, "go Khaki-Wacky." Their honor had to be protected.[32]

The Cookeville USO opened in an old shoe factory, providing showers, refreshments, food, music, and dancing for the soldiers. It gave them

Cookeville's Fox Café advertises beer on the West End during the Tennessee Maneuvers. Courtesy of Cookeville History Museum.

something to do and someone to talk with when away from the drudgery of training.[33] Local residents helped organize, staff, and chaperone the USO to keep it "safe for the rest of the community."[34] To ensure the safety of the local girls who came to the USO, a series of Service Center Rules was established: "Girls had to secure membership cards to visit the USO facility and membership was limited to those over sixteen and a half. Any girl whose card was taken away because of misconduct was barred from further attendance. No girl could leave the club and be re-admitted during that evening. Any girl under the age limit might attend when she received a membership card, and if she was chaperoned by her mother. The committee invited those girls who had membership cards to visit the club when soldiers were in town."[35] Despite the USO's hard work, the Putnam County *Herald* reported "hundreds of soldiers [were] roaming our streets and lying around in front yards with no where to go."[36]

Prostitutes were common features of the Tennessee Maneuvers. Camp Forrest was the first army base in the nation to fall under the May Act, which made soliciting for prostitution a federal offense.[37] Two health stations were established for the express purpose of checking servicemen for venereal disease. One was located at the maneuvers' headquarters in Lebanon; the other one was in Cookeville. In time, rumors circulated of a brothel on Cedar Street in Cookeville. According to some sources, the notorious closed-door session of the Cookeville City Commission resulted in the decision to bring "pros here to entertain the boys."

One Cookeville resident, Zane Steele, recalled his parents telling him about the infamous Cedar Street brothel.[38] Christine Jones "knew a girl who had been a prostitute in Cookeville during the maneuvers training. There were five girls in all that worked together, some of them were from Jackson County and some from Putnam County. They were recruited by a woman from Jackson County who promised they would make a lot of money with this job." When asked if the girl was a member of the brothel on Cedar Street, Jones replied, "No, they worked out of their car. Soldiers always knew where to find them, and they would go into the woods to conduct their business. Eventually the girl's sister grew worried for her safety and called the police to have the girls stopped. The police were called and they were all arrested."[39]

There was a general fear that Cookeville's streets "would be filled with a bunch of little bastards once the war was over. This is a Christian town, but even the best of us fall prey to temptation. And let me tell you, in those days, due to the excitement of the war and all, there was a lot of sex to be had in this town. Believe me when I tell you, this place played its role in the Baby Boom."[40]

Another chapter of the region's direct participation in World War II was the location of a prisoner of war camp in Cumberland County, Tennessee. The state housed four of the 155 main POW camps located in the United States—at Nathan Bedford Forrest Camp near Tullahoma, at Fort Campbell near Clarksville, at a Mississippi River loading station near Memphis, and in Cumberland County near Crossville. Camp Crossville was the earliest of the four Tennessee camps, and it was one of the first such facilities in the nation. It opened in November 1942 to house German and Italian officers captured in North Africa. There were several Italian generals in the camp, including the highest ranking officer in the Italian army. A lieutenant colonel in the Panzer Korps was the highest ranking German officer. The camp housed about a thousand officers and four hundred enlisted men, of whom about one-third were German. American guards considered the Italians docile and relatively contented, while the Germans were considered belligerent.

Enlisted men labored in the camp or on nearby farms, but officers worked only if they volunteered. Prisoners received pay for their work in the form of coupons, which they could trade for items at the camp canteen—cigarettes, Cokes, ice cream, clothing, candy, and beer. If they had cash they could order from the Sears catalog—clothing, curtains, luggage, sports equipment, lingerie. Sports activities were popular at the camp, and prisoners took classes in various academic subjects and music. An orchestra of prisoner musicians performed at concerts and dances. Only one prisoner escaped the camp, and only one was killed during the three years of the facility's existence.

Although World War II was fought thousands of miles from the Upper Cumberland region, the area experienced significant activities closely related to the conflict. In addition to the daily reminders of food and gasoline rationing, periodic war bond sales, patriotic speeches, and soldiers in uniform on the streets of the small towns, the region was part of the main war effort as a stage for the war games of 1942–1943, and as the site of one of the major prisoner of war camps operated in this country.

No soldier was supposed to die during the war games, yet 268 deaths occurred. The highest ranking officer killed was a major whose jeep was struck by a train on a rainy night at a blind crossing. Sixteen other officers, ninety-three noncommissioned officers, and 158 privates and privates first class died in accidents. The death total included four homicides resulting in Army courts martial and two death sentences. Nine civilians died in traffic accidents. A monument to their memory was placed at Maneuver Director Headquarters on the Cumberland University campus by the Tennessee Commission to Commemorate the Tennessee Maneuvers.[41]

The maneuvers left an imprint on Tennessee and Upper Cumberland society. They opened the world up to the rural folk of the region who encountered hordes of young men from all over America. For many people, the maneuvers acted as their first window on a wider world. Young men from far-flung places such as New York City found their true loves in the hills of the Cumberland region, returning after the war to marry. The average folk in the area encountered large crowds for the first time and battled with issues of society and morality that tested their resolve. In the end, all who participated, whether soldier or civilian, believed that they were participating in an important cause. Regardless of the hardships the troops endured or wartime shortages the citizenry coped with, the two groups came together in mutual participation and admiration in the Upper Cumberland of Tennessee. They were intent to win a war against Nazism and Japanese imperialism, using the Upper Cumberland as the first stage of the global drama in which they participated.

NOTES

1. Michael E. Birdwell, *Celluloid Soldiers: Warner Bros. Campaign Against Nazism* (New York: New York University Press, 1999): 133–34.
2. Ibid., 131–53.
3. Michael Bradley, "Camp Forrest" (Tullahoma, Tenn.: unpublished conference paper, 1995): 1, 4; Frank Burns, *A Newspaper for Its Community* (Lebanon, Tenn.: n.p., 1998): 57. Jess Lewis, "Coffee County Enters the Space Age," www.cafes.net/jlewis/AEDC.htm (September 15, 2001). Camp Forrest lay just south of the Upper Cumberland region. Many other sites mentioned in this essay, such as the Maneuvers Headquarters in Lebanon, were located just beyond the Upper Cumberland.
4. Bradley, 6–7.
5. Rex Bennett, personal interview with Luther Bennett (Cookeville, Tenn.: 5 November 2001); Bradley, 7.
6. Ibid.
7. Eugene Sloan, *With the Second Army Somewhere in Tennessee* (Clarksville, Tenn.: World War II Commission, 1956): 8.
8. Ibid.,3.
9. *Commemoration Newsletter* (1994):1.
10. Thomas G. Webb, *Tennessee County History Series: Dekalb County*, vol. 21 (Memphis: Memphis State University Press, 1986): 95.
11. Carlo D'Este, *Patton: A Genius for War* (New York: HarperCollins, 1995): 394.
12. The Thirtieth "Old Hickory" Division gained fame in World War I when it broke through the Hindenburg Line in September 1918.
13. Each tank carried a crew of four—driver, assistant driver, gunner, and the radio operator. Besides cannon, tanks were armed with .30 and .50 caliber machine guns. Patton's convoy moved at sixty miles an hour.
14. *A Newspaper for Its Community*, 16. The maneuvers in Louisiana and California occurred in the fall of 1941. The bombing of Pearl Harbor and the U.S. declaration of war against Japan and Germany necessitated the resumption of field maneuvers in Tennessee to prepare for the allied invasion of Europe.
15. Sloan, 6.
16. D'Este, 394; Luther Bennett interview.
17. Sloan, 20.
18. Ibid., 6.
19. Ibid., iii; Sam Bone, "Annual Report of the University Business Manager" (Lebanon, Tenn.: Stockton Archives, Cumberland University, 1943).
20. Sloan, 55.
21. Sloan, 3, 7–8.

22. Frank Burns, *Wilson County, Tennessee County History Series*, vol. 95 (Memphis: Memphis State University Press, 1983): 89–90.

23. Sloan, 42–43.

24. Action in Sicily proved the impracticality of the system, and GASC was abandoned in the European Theatre of Operations (ETO) and was never used in the Pacific.

25. This incident was censored at the time. The reference is from a letter to G. Frank Burns from Judge Willis Spear of Celina, Tennessee.

26. Sloan, 3.

27. Ibid., 58.

28. William and Marilyn Brinker, "Not Exactly the Hollywood Canteen" (Cookeville, Tenn.: unpublished conference paper, 1998): 11.

29. Putnam County *Herald* (December 30, 1943).

30. Sloan, iii.

31. Kelly Sergio, interview with Mark Harris (Cookeville, Tenn.: August 20, 2001).

32. Kelly Sergio, interview with Christine Jones (Cookeville, Tenn.: August 23, 2001). Weekly records of the USO at Cookeville show that, for the period of August 22–29, 1943, approximately 5,000 men visited; 3,000 took showers, 2,000 went swimming, 700 attended dances, 500 went on picnics, 250 attended church services, 800 attended sports events, 350 visited the homes of local citizens, and 75 found overnight accommodations. See Brinker, 5.

33. Kelly Sergio, interview with Sterling McCanless (Cookeville, Tenn.: August 24, 2001).

34. Ibid.

35. Kelly Sergio, interview with Dr. William Brinker (Cookeville, Tenn.: August 26, 2001).

36. Putnam County *Herald* (September 26, 1943): 1.

37. Bradley, 12.

38. Kelly Sergio, interview with Zane Steele (Cookeville, Tenn.: August 27, 2001). Steele said that his "grandfather and grandmother had been in Cookeville because [his] grandmother had to go to the hospital. While she was there [his] grandfather got arrested for soliciting a prostitute on Cedar Street." This unfortunately could not be confirmed because the arrest records were destroyed in the courthouse fire in the early 1960s.

39. Kelly Sergio, interview with Christine Jones (Cookeville, Tenn.: August 23, 2001).

40. Personal interview, name withheld by request (Cookeville, Tenn.: February 9, 2002).

41. In September and October 1944, after D-Day and as Patton's Third Army tanks rolled toward the Rhine, it was decided that the Twentieth Armored Division at Camp Campbell would be needed for the final push. There were field exercises from September 27 to October 15, 1944, with the Thirty-third Cavalry Reconnaissance Squadron acting as the simulated opposition. This unit also hailed from Camp Campbell and was assigned to join the Twentieth in European Theatre service, and then the Twentieth joined Fifteenth Army in

France, February 17, 1945, after a three-day live fire event at Fort Campbell December 14–16.

Entering Germany with the Seventh Army on April 3, 1945, the division liberated Dachau Concentration Camp near Munich and was at Salzburg on V-E Day; it discovered the German gold reserves hidden in a salt mine near that city, truly one of the most remarkable experiences any Tennessee-trained division had and one for which it could not forecast.

On March 11, 1944, the 276th Combat Engineers left camp Gruber, Oklahoma, to participate in Phase V of the Tennessee Maneuvers. The miles-long convoy of trucks, jeeps, half-tracks, dump trucks, road graders, and other heavy vehicles was followed by army wives, hangers on, and well-wishers. "The motor convoy made good time with only a minimum of vehicles having breakdowns near conveniently located beer joints." [Allen L. Ryan and Clayton A. Rust, *Rough and Ready: Unit History, 276 Combat Engineer Battalion* (Fort Belvoir, Va.: Book Department of the Engineer School, 1946): 16.] Traveling at the congressionally mandated speed of thirty-five miles an hour, the convoy arrived in Tennessee on March 16, joining soldiers from all over the United States. Thanks, in part, to the realistic conditions of the maneuvers, the 276th would later earn distinction as the engineering battalion that secured the last bridge over the Rhine at Remagen in 1945 [ibid., pp. 75-93].

Chapter 14

MADE ON THE MOUNTAIN

Upper Cumberland Arts and Crafts

W. Calvin Dickinson and Michael E. Birdwell

In Tennessee and Kentucky, crafts played a larger role than the fine arts in the history of culture. Craftsmen produced notable work in wood, clay, and fibers. During the period before contact with Europeans, Native Americans engaged in the creation of utilitarian crafts and ceremonial art objects. Perhaps the best known objects still found throughout the Upper Cumberland are the myriad flint arrow and spear points. Clovis points of varying description have been found in rock shelters, recently plowed fields, and along streams and river banks. Numerous mounds dot the landscape of the Upper Cumberland from the Woodland and Mississippian periods and have revealed pottery, weavings, various stone tools, and ceremonial art. Effigies of animals carved in stone and in stylized drawings represent some of the earliest art from the area. Indian artifacts also exist in a number of caves in the Upper Cumberland, ranging from pictographs to petroglyphs. Though the use of some objects remains unknown, Native Americans in the region exhibited significant skill and ingenuity in creating art objects for ceremonial and personal use.

Anglo settlers moved into the Upper Cumberland just before 1800. Generally, high culture does not accompany the first settlers in a region, and fine art showed little presence in the Upper Cumberland until a more urban climate developed. Handcrafted objects, however, were a necessary part of everyday life. Settlers used chairs and tables daily. Tools, baskets, pottery, musical instruments, and quilts—also constructed at home—were in constant use. Many craftsmen, such as potters J. A. Roberts and Jefferson Spears, sought to put their own identifiable mark on a product, distinguishing it from the work of others. Solomon Allred of Overton County made wooden bowls and plates on a treadle lathe from felled trees on his property around 1830.[1]

Production of several crafts divided along gender lines whereas others, such as chair making, often involved both sexes—men made the frames while women caned or wove the seats. Some individuals eventually specialized in a specific craft, producing surplus products that others purchased from them. These specialists became professional craftsmen who taught others—usually family members—their skills. As the necessity for those skills diminished with the availability of mass-produced items, schools such as Berea in Kentucky organized to keep those dying crafts alive. Nostalgia and recognition of the inherent aesthetic beauty of those objects elevated crafts to the level of art in the twentieth century.

Weaving, one of the oldest crafts considered "woman's work," was absolutely necessary on the frontier. People raised goats or sheep and planted small stands of flax because cotton grew poorly in the thin soil of the Upper Cumberland. Most farmsteads contained a flax wheel, which women and their daughters used to spin a combination of linen and wool commonly referred to as linsey-woolsey. Clever women improvised buttons from goose quills, wood, and other found objects. Women fashioned basic clothing from what the farm provided, weaving and dying their own cloth. The main dyes used were walnuts, maple bark, madder, copperas, and stone dye.[2]

The necessity of storage vessels of varying types played a significant role in the production of one of the most enduring crafts of the Upper Cumberland. Although earthenware was produced all over the country, White, DeKalb, and Putnam counties in Tennessee earned a reputation for producing some of the area's finest crockery.[3] The stoneware industry in the Upper Cumberland lasted from roughly 1824 to 1938. Andrew Lafever, the regional patriarch of the craft, brought his skills with him from Wayne County, Kentucky, earning a reputation as an expert potter who created exceptional pieces. Lafever taught the craft to his sons, who passed their knowledge on to other families in the region. As a result, many families earned a reputation for making fine stoneware, including the Dunn, Elmore, Elrod, Hedgcough (who changed their name from Hitchcock), Lacy, Rainey, and Roberts families. In fact, there were so many potteries and people involved in the industry that the southwestern edge of White County was commonly referred to as "Jugtown."[4] J. E. Killebrew quipped about the cottage industry: "So great has been the number of wagons engaged in the 'crock trade,' that some persons in other counties have jocularly remarked that there can be nothing left of White County but a hole in the ground."[5] Eli Lafever, the last of the family to practice the craft, closed his operation in 1938.

Potters dug clay from the banks of the Caney Fork River, loaded it on wagons, and hauled it to sheds near the kiln to dry. Once dry, the clay was ground and mixed in the mill with red, white, and sometimes blue clays to produce the consistency needed to throw vessels. Seasoned hands formed familiar shapes on a homemade kick wheel, usually made from improvised materials. On

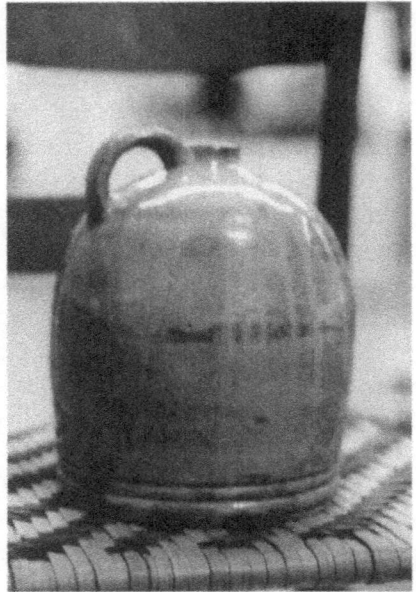

Typical Upper Cumberland pottery. Courtesy of Appalachian Center for Crafts.

average, it took from two weeks to seventeen days for a skilled potter to produce enough unfired green vessels to fill a kiln. The process required three days and nights of firing and upwards of five cords of wood to reach the proper temperature. Salt glazing finished the process, giving the curing crocks their sheen and increasing their durability. It took an additional three days for the kiln to cool sufficiently. During the procedure the potter expected to lose about 10 percent of his product to breakage.[6]

Crocks came in a variety of shapes and sizes and had myriad uses. Small vessels and plates were used as dinnerware. Larger vessels were used in salting meat, making hominy, and churning butter. Jugs, pitchers, bottles, pipes, grease lamps, candle holders, and novelties such as birdhouses emerged from the kilns of the Lafever family and other area potters. Some of the most unusual products created by Upper Cumberland potters came from the kiln of William C. Hedgcough, who fashioned earthenware headstones for area cemeteries.[7] Potters peddled their wares all over middle Tennessee and southeastern Kentucky, spreading their reputation for well-made, reliable products.

Quilting, an old craft tradition that came to America from Europe, was largely associated with women. The necessity for frugality and invention on the frontier allowed women to express their creative urges with scraps of cloth painstakingly sewn into a host of different patterns. Frontier men and women were loath to throw anything away, for it could be put to some use in the future; therefore, old clothes and scraps of cloth were put away until a woman had enough to make a quilt. During the antebellum period, women primarily quilted alone, a tedious task that entailed days of hard work. After the Civil War, however, quilting bees became popular, and women worked together to produce quilts. Quilting became a social event as well as a means for creating bed covers. Art critic Robert Hughes said of quilting, "This is a particularly, if not uniquely American form, an art based on modular arrangements, intricate geometry, luscious colors—and salvage, not wasting, 'making do' . . . and from them created America's first abstract art."[8]

Made for daily use and special occasions, quilts came in a variety of patterns, including the Double Wedding Ring, Grandmother's Flower Garden, Log Cabin, Double Irish Chain, Grandmother's Fan, Overall Boy, Sunbonnet Baby, Star, Sunburst, Friendship, Drunkard's Path, and Crazy quilts. Providing warmth on cold winter nights, utilitarian quilts added a splash of color to any household. Their intricate interconnecting patterns of often dazzling colors livened up drab, spare cabins in the frontier period when people could hardly afford fancy appointments for their home. With industrial society and the ready availability of manufactured cloth, quilts became more ornamental and less functional. Brought out for special occasions such as weddings and holidays, family quilts were lovingly placed in storage, hung on walls, and passed down to succeeding generations. The names of the women who manufactured quilts in the Upper Cumberland would almost certainly have to include all those who lived and toiled in the preindustrial era and well into the twentieth century. Young girls learned to quilt at the feet of their mothers, piecing patterns and quilt tops. Nancy Page of Crossville was a quilter of some renown during the early 1940s. Later, Inez Wrenn of Crossville earned a reputation as one of the finest quilters on the plateau. Etta Cummins of White County continued the tradition of African American quilters, incorporating asymmetrical designs, slightly off balance, with bold, clashing colors. Some women, including Willie Catherine Davis of Sparta, Tennessee, could recognize the maker of a quilt by the quality of the stitching. Minnie Pearl Phillips, who was raised in Wilson County before she moved to Cookeville, quilted until the age of ninety.

Resourceful women used ordinary found objects, transforming them into something useful and aesthetically pleasing. At Cumberland Homesteads, Mrs. Homer Roy made corn shuck hats that were sold at the craft shop. A Mrs. Ridenour of Cumberland County created sturdy and attractive corn shuck hats for daily use and special occasions. Her reputation as a milliner created a demand for her hats outside of the Upper Cumberland, allowing her to buy luxury devices such as a pressure cooker, which she acquired in 1939.[9]

Women also made dolls to amuse children and help teach girls their intended gender roles. Using materials on hand—corn shucks, dried apples, scrap pieces of wood, and cloth—some women gained notoriety for their skill and creativity. Corn shuck dolls represented the oldest and most plentiful toy, because everyone grew corn for their own dinner tables and for their livestock. Simple forms without articulated limbs, corn shuck dolls were usually intended to be temporary playthings, good for a season and thrown out with the spring when children could go back outdoors. Most corn shuck dolls represent grown women or young girls in floor-length skirts. Some people added hair made from corn silks, paper bonnets, and faces drawn on the finished product. Others were plain, simple suggestions of the female form. Many people created more permanent dolls with wooden bodies and articulated arms or legs. Securing a dried apple atop the wooden trunk, they fashioned a simple head. Two brads driven into the apple approximated eyes and a small mouth was cut into the dried flesh, creating the illusion of an old woman. Cloth dresses, hair made of thread or yarn, and a bonnet completed a simple doll made from readily available items. Polly Page of Pleasant Hill carved more elaborate dolls, not meant for play but for aesthetic pleasure. She carved a number of Uncle Pink and Aunt Jenny dolls from native wood.

Chair making has a long tradition in the Upper Cumberland. Men such as Preacher Tinch would harvest and season timber, carefully selecting the proper wood to make a sturdy chair that would last for generations. The Frank Tabor family from eastern Cumberland County made ladder-back chairs from oak, selling them at the Lowe shop in Rockwood and Bilbrey's store in Crossville. Using traditional hand implements—axe, adz, maul, drawknife, and plane—the Tabors produced chairs for more than thirty years. Frank Tabor learned the craft from his grandfather, who primarily made wagons. The patriarch made chairs on the side, which he hauled from Westel to McMinnville and points in between, trading them for salt, coffee, and sugar.

Frank Tabor of Cumberland County, Tennessee, fashions a chair with hand tools. Courtesy of the Tennessee State Library and Archives.

To make a chair, Tabor first hewed out a log with an axe. Sections of log were split and further shaped on a shaving horse, and the spokes were dressed down with a drawknife and carving knife. Wood chisels expertly tapped with a hand maul hewed the legs. The slats for the chair back were split and shaped on the shaving horse with a drawknife and plane. Pieces of the chair were driven together with mallets, without nails, screws, or glue. The finished structure was then bottomed with white oak splints. Simple, functional, and strong, the chairs were held together by the tension created as the wood continued to cure, made sturdier by the tight split oak bottoms. Tabor chairs proved so sturdy that a popular saying in the region was, "Always club your enemy with a Tabor chair 'cause it won't shatter when you flail him."[10] Frank Tabor made chairs until his death in 1968.

Willie and Rob Doss of Fentress County made chairs in the same tradition. Willie Doss learned the craft from his great grandfather Billy Doss and passed his knowledge on to his son. Willie preferred to make his posts from maple or cherry and bottom his chairs with oak. He specialized in ladder-back and rocking chairs. One of the Doss family chairs traveled with a group of Upper Cumberland craftsmen and musicians to a folk life festival at the Smithsonian in Washington, D.C., in the mid-1980s, and became a part of the permanent collection.

In the Upper Cumberland, men and women often worked together to make chairs. Men dressed the wood and put the frames together while women wove the bottoms of white oak splints, cane, or even bailing twine. Likewise, men and women both earned reputations as excellent basket makers. Just as crockery was needed for a number of daily uses from tableware to food storage to grease lamps, so, too, were baskets common on the average farmstead. Baskets in a variety of shapes and sizes were used as hampers and to carry laundry, coal, eggs, and even small infants. Like many basket makers, Laura Blaylock of Ravenscroft learned the craft from both her parents, who made baskets and sold them for pin money. Made of white oak splints, the baskets were lightweight and so sturdy that a person could stand on larger ones without breaking them. Blaylock's baskets were traded widely in the mining community in exchange for farm produce, canned vegetables, and other items. The mother of eleven children, Blaylock helped support her family by peddling wares. Basketry has long been tied to the history of the Upper Cumberland, especially in Cannon and Warren counties.

The craft history of the Upper Cumberland grew more public and contentious in the 1930s and 1960s. With the advent of Franklin Roosevelt's New Deal and Lyndon B. Johnson's "War on Poverty," craft in the Upper Cumberland was politicized. Traditional folk crafts were regarded as a source of economic salvation for one of the poorest areas of the country. Professional artists and critics sent representatives to the region to promote and cultivate Appalachian folk arts.

Established in 1935 under Federal One of the Works Progress Administration (WPA), the Federal Arts Project (FAP) represented the first time in American history that the government subsidized visual arts. An expert on American folk art, Holger Cahill spearheaded a massive program that employed more than 6,000 artists all across the nation for a period of eight years. FAP artists and bureaucrats promoted art education and established community art centers and galleries, while generating an enormous amount of original artwork. Employing a variety of artists from painters, sculptors, and muralists to handicraft artisans and folk artists, the FAP popularized American folk art and celebrated the nation's frontier heritage.

In Appalachia, traditional crafts such as split-oak baskets and patchwork quilts were rediscovered and elevated from the realm of the necessary to *objets d'art*. Seeking out traditional artisans in Appalachia, the FAP sent younger craftsmen to catalog Appalachian folk art for the Index of American Design (IAD) and document the region's material culture. Additionally, the federal government employed folk artists in Appalachia, paying them a wage of $23.50 per week for their output. Upper Cumberland artists were also employed to teach their art or craft at community centers and workshops in an attempt to keep traditional crafts and music alive. The FAP played a crucial role in promoting folk art, showcasing the work in public exhibits in the region and throughout the country.

Basketry. Courtesy of Appalachian Center for Crafts.

New Deal agencies and Christian missionaries traveled to the Upper Cumberland to improve the plight of the poor people eking out an existence. At Alpine in Overton County and Pleasant Hill in Cumberland County, missionaries established institutions of vocational education.

Pleasant Hill featured a number of skilled artisans who passed their knowledge on to struggling young people in the 1930s and 1940s. It sponsored a number of crafts workshops and instruction in a variety of "practical arts." The woodworking shop featured motorized lathes, state-of-the-art tools, and ample work benches. Winifred Rankhore learned wood carving, specializing in the depiction of animals. Such ornamental craft items were sold at the Pleasant Hill community center to northern visitors who traveled to the town.

The Presbyterian Church established Alpine Academy to help the "poor mountain folk."[11] Ollie McDonald taught weaving to a number of young women from Overton County, including the spouse of Reverend S. A. D. Robbins, and to wives and daughters of coal miners from Wilder-Davidson. Among the women who learned the craft were Arizona Sells and Erma Neely. Alpine Academy featured a number of large looms. Pottery classes were conducted by Jean Baker, who taught teenagers and adults how to fashion graceful objects that were sold throughout the region.[12]

Christ Church at Alpine, a neo-Gothic structure made of native stone quarried on site, was built with help from the WPA and a number of talented craftsmen. Designed by professional architects Walter L. Rapp and Standish Meacham of Cincinnati, the church's cornerstone was laid in 1934. Ed Copeland supervised construction. Local laborers felled native chestnut for the joists and wainscoting of the sanctuary. Elmer Carlock quarried and fashioned the stone, creating a rugged and beautiful Celtic cross that sat at the peak of the church's front gable. Walter Norris, a stone mason, fashioned an outdoor pulpit above which was a recessed Greek cross. Carpenters fashioned a Latin cross of oak to adorn the entryway porch. One of the most unusual aspects of the building was a stained glass rose window depicting the risen Christ, a strange inclusion in the normally staid sanctuary of a Presbyterian church.[13]

Harry Caudill's famous book *Night Comes to the Cumberlands* vividly portrayed the crushing poverty throughout the region, while depicting the people as hard-working, proud, and resourceful. Caudill's book caught the attention of the Kennedy administration, leading in part to the creation of the Appalachian Regional Commission under President Johnson. The plight of the Appalachian people gained national attention through such media reports as Charles Kuralt's CBS White Paper "Christmas in Appalachia," which aired in 1964.[14]

During President Johnson's War on Poverty, grants allowed traditional artisans to pursue their craft while gaining a market for their products. Craft fairs displayed works that were advertised as pieces of Americana, direct links to the past, rather than utilitarian objects. The counterculture, which sought a break from the so-called Establishment and a purer simpler lifestyle, embraced the arts and crafts movement in the 1960s, and many moved to areas such as Whitleyville, in Jackson County, to produce handmade crafts. During that decade, new artisans emerged, such as Zeke Reddick who specialized in pottery; others pursued chair making, quilting, caning, broom making, and other crafts. Craft fairs began to flourish in places such as Gatlinburg, Tennessee, which opened a number of sales outlets for tourists visiting the Smokies. By the 1970s, the academic community embraced crafts as a worthy contemporary art form, leading to numerous shows and permanent acquisitions by galleries and museums throughout the country. Traditional folk crafts received greater attention with the creation of the National Endowment for the Arts, and the advent of the Smithsonian's folk life exhibits elevated craft to the realm of high art.[15]

Folk art buyers descended on the area in the 1970s and 1980s, buying quilts that had been family heirlooms for exorbitant prices in the neighborhood of $300. Demand for quilts soared. Women at senior citizens centers and churches were encouraged to essentially mass produce them. They pieced the patterns by hand and then had the quilt assembled on a sewing machine. These hybrid quilts were sold at even higher prices than authentic, handmade quilts. The high demand and increasing appreciation of quilts led to a number of events, including the Kentucky Quilt Project and the Algood Quilt Show. Both celebrated the craft of quilting, and the Algood Quilt Show grew from a one-day event into an annual weekend celebration of the art/craft form.[16]

Overton County native John Maxwell acted as a broker for Upper Cumberland craftsmen. He opened a showroom, the Upper Cumberland Craft Center, on the north side of Cookeville, beside his home. Maxwell cultivated the talents of a number of people who worked primarily in wood, such as Earl Pennington of Berea, Kentucky, and carver Dow Pugh of Monterey. He encouraged his workers to sign and date their creations, signifying not only the creator of the product but its importance as a work of art. A craftsman himself, Maxwell specialized in making dulcimers. In 1973, Maxwell received a commission to carve

the seal of the United States for President Richard Nixon and the seal of
the state of Tennessee for Governor Winfield Dunn. He demonstrated
his talents at the Smithsonian's Arts and Industry Building in the late
1970s.[17]

Maxwell and other craft outlets such as Polly Page's Craft Shop cultivated a number of folk artists, giving them a wider audience. Birds
and animals were a particular favorite theme. Charles and Jo Morgan of
Baxter worked together to produce a menagerie carved from buckeye.
Bonnie Lawson of Pleasant Hill and Carl Ford of Mayland preferred to
carve groups of native birds against natural backgrounds made of drift-
wood, lichen, and pine cones. Tony Selby of Crossville specialized in
owls.

Adam Turtle of Gum Spring Mountain in White County carved
massive chainsaw sculptures all over the Upper Cumberland. Living
with his parents in Tokyo during the American occupation after World
War II, Turtle learned to appreciate intricate wooden sculptures associated with Shinto shrines and Buddhist temples. His creations included
large stylized figures reminiscent of the work of Henry Moore, abstract
constructions, and portrait pieces. Included among his portrait chainsaw
sculptures were likenesses of Mark Twain, Alvin C. York, and idealized
depictions of Native Americans.

University of Chicago graduate Helen Bullard of Ozone in Cumberland County created wood sculptures of "sophisticated primitive forms
. . . with a minimum of chisel and gouge cuts and no sanding or pretti-
fying," which were inspired by the work of Constantin Brancusi and
Alexander Archipenko. Using dead chestnut timber from the woods on
her property, Bullard created lean, angular, spare renditions of mountain people. Her sculptures capture the pride, simplicity, and grit of the
people of the Upper Cumberland.[18]

Pleasant Hill native Tom Brown created highly refined, polished,
lacquered, and waxed wooden sculptures, primarily nudes. Margaret
Campbell at Pleasant Hill Academy taught Brown to carve, recognizing
his talent and convincing him to study art at the Chicago Art Institute.
After graduation, Brown returned home to pursue his art. His Cumberland County alma mater commissioned him to create a portrait of Reverend Benjamin Dodge, the member of the American Missionary
Association who founded Pleasant Hill. The portrait sculpture, made
from cherry, is one of the few extant pieces in the region, for most of
Brown's work was sold outside the South.

Jean Horner of Westel constructed his first fiddle at the age of six-

Two chainsaw sculptures at the Forbus store in Fentress County, Tennessee. Photo by the authors.

teen. Time in the navy made him aware of his gift for woodworking. He returned from a hitch in the navy in 1954, setting up a cabinet shop in a log crib on his father's farm. After ordering a pattern from *Popular Mechanics,* Horner set to work to build his second violin. More elaborate than his first, it included designs of wooden inlay. By 1958, he could produce about five violins per year, each more decorative and with a richer sound. Throughout the 1960s, his custom musical instrument business grew steadily, and Horner added mandolins, banjos, and guitars to his repertoire. Handmade to his exacting specifications, Horner's instruments soon became the envy of country music performers and regular fixtures on the Grand Ole Opry.[19]

Since the 1970s, craftsmen dedicated to the creation of handmade objects for exhibition have coexisted with traditional artisans. Tinkering, enlarging, abstracting, and diverging from folk arts, studio craftsmen produce wares for galleries, museums, and special exhibits. Though some may retain a utilitarian function, the forms are created as a celebration of a specific craft and are not intended for daily use. Lewis Snyder of the craft division of the Tennessee Arts Commission (TAC) established guidelines for a residential facility to train students in studio crafts, conduct workshops, display objects, and market the wares produced. Snyder and members of his staff contacted U.S. Congressman Joe L. Evins of Smithville, who championed the project in the federal Congress. Evins secured $5 million to create a craft center near Center Hill Lake, and ground was broken on October 18, 1976. The finished facility was named the Joe L. Evins Appalachian Center for Crafts. Tennessee Technological University (TTU) President Arliss Roaden strongly supported the project, and TTU soon played a key role in the administration of the facility.[20]

By 1981, the craft center had a number of BFA degree programs in place, allowing students to specialize in clay, fibers, glass, metal, and wood. Situated in the woods on a promontory overlooking Center Hill Lake, the craft center includes 50,000 square feet of studio space and living quarters on site. The clay studio provides a variety of wheels and kilns for salt firing, wood firing, and primitive firing. The fibers studio supports a number of looms, a dye kitchen, and a darkroom. The glass studio includes materials for blowing, slumping and casting, mold making, and cold working facilities for craftsmen. The metals studio houses a bench room, a raising and workroom, a buffing room, a chemical room, and a blacksmithing shop. The wood studio contains a huge machine room with a full range of stationary equipment, including a reequipped turning studio, industrial spray room, and separate bench room for work with hand tools. As it evolved, the Appalachian Center for Crafts earned a reputation as the finest facility in the country available to undergraduate students, who worked side by side with skilled professional artisans such as metalsmith Robert Coogan, who has been at the facility from the beginning.[21]

The center hosted eighteen renowned ceramic artists from thirteen countries in August 1985 at the International Ceramic Symposium, which led to a series of twenty traveling clay exhibitions entitled "Clay Confluence." In 1999, the craft center hosted the Furniture Society's third annual conference, bringing artisans from all over the world to the Upper Cumberland.[22] The featured exhibition, "The Circle Unbroken: Continuity and Innovation in Studio Furniture," displayed thirty creations from craftsmen with international reputations out of three hundred entries.

Tim Hintz of Smithville graduated from the craft center, earning a reputation for making exquisite ladder-back chairs with split oak bottoms in the tradition of Frank Tabor and Willie Doss. Operating a studio in Smithville called "Fresh Chairs," Hintz produces chairs with traditional tools, adding contemporary twists in their design. In 2001, one of Hintz's chairs was chosen for the permanent collection of the Tennessee State Museum.

Vince Pitelka's works have been elevated to the realm of high art. His ceramic pieces run the gamut from beautiful, intricate dinnerware to whimsical objects such as his miniature Volkswagen beetle that looks as if it were made from tiny red bricks. Merritt Kardatzke creates raku pottery and both representational and abstract clay sculptures.[23]

In addition to traditional folk and studio crafts, there are a number of people throughout the Upper Cumberland who express themselves creatively by unconventional means. A man in Overton County turned a derelict motorcycle into a mailbox stand. The sheer variety of improvised mailboxes in the region—from old milk jugs to boxes that look like tractors—is worthy of a study itself. One of the most unusual creative expressions is the Savage house in Allons, Tennessee. Millard Savage built a home made from Coke bottles held together with Portland cement. The "Bottle House," as it is commonly called, exhibits not only creativity but the willingness to improvise and "make do."[24] Herman Whiteaker indulges in the creation of "whirligigs," simple wooden weathervanes with propellers that spin in the wind. His home in Putnam County's Dry Valley community is festooned with dozens of brightly

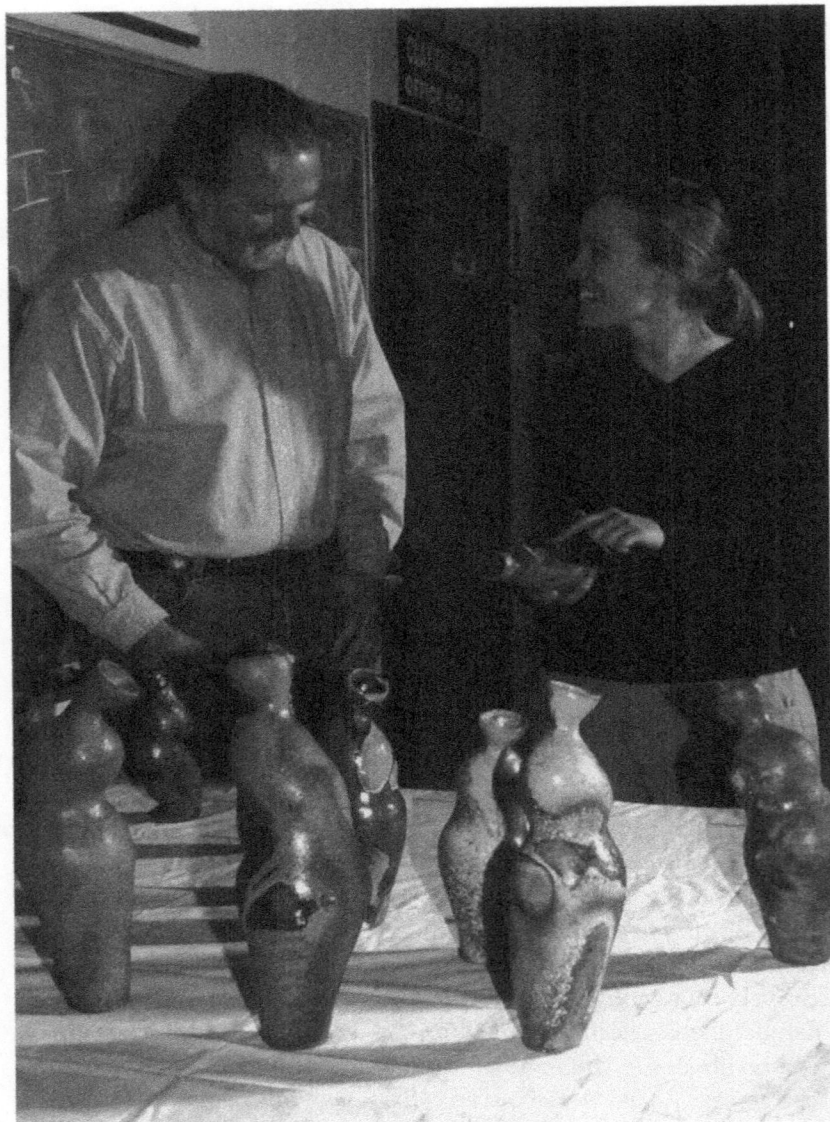

Vince Pitelka discusses clay with a student at the Appalachian Center for Crafts.

painted whimsies. Ben Sisco fashioned primitive clay roosters and humorous objects. Raymond Stamps of Monterey made pink flamingoes from gourds, which he situated about his yard. William Buck of Jackson County created a self-portrait in concrete. He painted the figure

Detail of the Bottle House in Overton County, Tennessee. Photo by the authors

and included his favorite pair of sunglasses. When he died, it was placed over his grave in the Pleasant Hill cemetery. Evan Decker of Wayne County, Kentucky carved and painted a life-sized horse as a conversation piece. For awhile during the late 1980s, a number of people painted landscapes and portraits on crosscut saw blades; they have recently been supplanted by persons painting on worn-out circular saw blades. These kitschy expressions of creativity both confound and amuse, but they display a longing in people to make something they feel to be objects of beauty.

Painting was the last of the arts to develop in the Upper Cumberland because it was unnecessary for everyday life. Perhaps the first person to produce artistic renderings about the region was a Frenchman, Charles A. LeSueur. A zoologist and illustrator, LeSueur passed through the Upper Cumberland in 1831. With pen and ink he drew seventy-three sketches of the area between Nashville and Kingston, along the Great Stage Road and Old Walton Road. Scenes he recorded included the village of Liberty, Burgess Falls, Window Cliffs Falls, Kemmer Stand, Crab Orchard Inn, and Ozone Falls. Though his illustrations were hastily drawn, LeSueur was a "skilled scientific illustrator by profession"; his more detailed drawings exhibit the talent of a gifted landscape artist.[25]

John Wood
Dodge's *The
Posthumous
Likeness of Felix
Grundy Eakin*,
(1846). From the
Collection of
Cheekwood
Museum of Art,
Nashville,
Tennessee.

The earliest notable artist who lived in the Upper Cumberland was John Wood Dodge, who, like most other artists later living in the area, emigrated there. Born in New York City in 1807, Dodge exhibited at the National Academy of Design in 1830 and for several years after; in 1832 he was elected an associate member of the Academy. Dodge specialized in highly detailed miniature portraits, paintings only a few inches in size. His usual technique involved painting on pieces of ivory with watercolor, an unusual and distinct medium in which Dodge excelled.

Dodge and his family moved in 1840 to Nashville, where he lived for two decades. In 1842, he painted seventy-five-year-old Andrew Jackson in watercolor on a six-inch square piece of ivory; the next year he completed a portrait of Henry Clay, also on ivory.

In 1845, the Dodge family bought 5,000 acres in Cumberland County. Dodge constructed a log house and planted thousands of apple trees, naming his estate Pomona Fruit Ranch. (This is still called "Pomona.") He continued to paint, completing, in 1847, four large works covering two hundred square feet of canvas. One was a scene of New York, another was the interior of St. Peter's in Rome, and the other two were fantasy scenes. Charging admission in several cities to view the dioramas, Dodge made one or two thousand dollars. Those large murals marked a drastic departure from his miniatures; they were a commercial venture to provide capital for his agrarian pursuits.

Dodge, like many other representational artists, initially felt threatened by the appearance of cameras. In the 1850s, however, he recognized the artistic possibilities of photography. Dodge bought a camera and hired an assistant to take photographs, which he colored. In this way, he took advantage of the perceived threat and embraced what he had once considered his competition.

At the beginning of the Civil War, Dodge feared for his family's safety because they were Union sympathizers, despite the fact that most Cumberland countians also favored the Union. He returned to New York, where he established a studio, devoting most of his time to photography. In 1889, the Dodge family returned to Cumberland County and built several houses in Victorian styles. Dodge continued to paint portraits, landscapes, and miniatures. He died in 1893, and he was buried on his estate in Pomona.[26]

The Upper Cumberland's second famous representational artist, Gilbert Gaul, also emigrated into the region from the north. Born in Jersey City in 1855, Gaul trained at the National Academy of Design. He became an associate of the Academy in 1879. In 1881, Gaul moved to Van Buren County to claim a farm he had inherited from his uncle. The will stipulated that Gaul must live on the farm at least four years to claim it. Gaul brought his wife and her parents to the Cumberland region, built a log house and studio in what is now Fall Creek Falls State Park, and lived there the four required years.

During the early 1880s Gaul painted imaginary scenes from the Civil War in a realistic style. In 1882, he won a gold medal from the American Art Association for "Holding the Line at all Hazards." Known primarily as a military artist, Gaul also painted landscapes of the Cumberland area and Western scenes with Indian motifs. His work was reminiscent of his more famous contemporaries, Winslow Homer and George Bellows.

Returning to New York in 1885, Gaul spent another four-year period in Tennessee, from 1891 to 1895. His art during this period won bronze medals at the 1893 World's Columbian Exposition in Chicago. Returning to Tennessee for a third time after 1900, Gaul taught art in McMinnville and Nashville. He continued painting Civil War scenes and contemporary World War I actions. In 1919, Gaul died in New Jersey of tuberculosis.[27]

A few private colleges, which were actually secondary schools,

Gilbert Gaul, *A Scene on the Caney Fork River* (1913–1914). *Tennessee Historical Quarterly.*

opened in the Upper Cumberland during the nineteenth century. Burritt College in Van Buren County may have been the first to employ an art instructor. Fanny Kuykendall taught there around 1900, then moved to the new Dixie College in Cookeville, teaching art until it closed in 1916. Afterward she taught art at Cookeville City School and Cookeville Central High School until the 1947–1948 academic year.

The daughter of Church of Christ preacher William Young Kuykendall, Fanny was born in 1871 in the family's two-story log house north of Cookeville, in the Smyrna community. When she died a spinster in 1949, Fanny was buried in Smyrna Cemetery.

Miss Kuydendall was not a prolific painter, although some of her creations still decorate the walls of houses in the region. She had to be encouraged to paint, according to one of her former students, and "she did not promote her own paintings." Her usual subjects were landscapes, still lifes, and portraits.

In her classes Kuykendall taught oils, watercolors, pastels, and china painting. Reproductions of other paintings, postcards, and photographs provided models for her students. A photograph of her studio shows paintings on the walls that students copied. An annual art exhibit in the studio completed the academic year for her students.

Fanny Kuykendall painting of a
young woman playing guitar.
Courtesy of Claudine Smith.

A former student described her as a "Victorian lady." It was said
that she never spoke an angry word. If her students could not pay for
art lessons, she accepted payment in kind, sometimes in food or in living accommodations. If a student's work did not meet her high standards, she improved the imperfections with her own brush. One former
student commented, "I never would have recognized it [as my art work]
when she got through with it."[28]

Reba Bacon inherited the teaching mantle of Fannie Kuykendall.
She joined the faculty of Tennessee Polytechnic Institute (TPI) in 1949
after earning the MA at George Peabody College in Nashville. She had
also studied fine arts at Watkins Institute in Nashville for five years.
During her long career at TPI—1949 to 1972—she became well known
throughout the Upper Cumberland as a teacher and promoter of art. In
1961, she organized the Cookeville Arts Society, which recruited a large
membership throughout the Upper Cumberland region and changed its
name to the Cumberland Art Society. In 1961, she initiated the BenLee
Art Show and sale on her farm north of Cookeville; it provided a venue
for local and regional artists to display and sell their works. This project
continued until 1988. In 1978, she initiated The Reba Bacon High School
Art Competition, which invited young artists in Upper Cumberland
high schools to submit artwork for judging and awards. A project al-

Reba Bacon, *Still Life*.
Courtesy of Sam Bacon.

most completely supported by Reba and her husband Sam, this art pro-
motion was still active in 2002. Though not a prominent artist herself,
she did exhibit at Watkins Institute and at the Parthenon in Nashville;
her major contribution was promoting awareness and appreciation of
art in the region.[29]

During the Great Depression of the 1930s, the FAP employed thousands of artists and sculptors who painted murals and sculpted pieces
to decorate public buildings. Many of examples of this artwork still
exist, thirty of which are in Tennessee. In the Upper Cumberland, two
post offices house WPA murals and one boasts a bas-relief sculpture. In
Livingston, the west wall of the New Deal post office supports a mural
of New York artist Margaret Covey Chisholm. "The Newcomers," painted
in 1940, depicted a group of residents raising a house for new settlers in
the county. In Cumberland County, a New Deal post office built of Crab
Orchard stone had a mural by WPA artist Marion Greenwood. "The
Partnership of Man and Nature" shows a farm family with barn and silo
juxtaposed against a TVA dam. The obvious message was that modern
technology improved the traditional lifestyle. This mural was later moved
to the new post office in Crossville. In Rockwood, a ceramic bas-relief
created by New York artist Christian Heinrich in 1939 decorates the
post office lobby. Entitled "Wild Life," the terra cotta piece depicts a
family of deer at rest.[30]

O. D. Abston, *John's Vision of the Eternal City*. Courtesy of Alvin C. York Patriotic Foundation.

O. D. Abston, a self-taught artist, was born in the England Cove community of White County in 1905. An orphan, he suffered through a terrible childhood. Shunted from place to place, he took solace in doodling. As a young adult he moved to Fentress County, where his creative talents came to the attention of Sergeant Alvin C. York. Abston lived for a while with the York family, who encouraged him to take his talent more seriously. Inspired, Abston turned from pencil to paint and created a number of fascinating paintings for the Yorks and other people in Fentress County. Most of the images depicted biblical scenes—Daniel in the lion's den, John's vision of paradise, Jesus—but he also painted landscapes of Pall Mall and its environs and a stunning pen and ink portrait of York that captured the intensity and humanity of the hero. During a grim personal period in Abston's life, in the 1930s, he spent nearly a week in the dark of York Cave. Struggling with his personal demons, he reaffirmed his faith and etched a haunting rendering of Christ on a wall in the cave. York persuaded Abston to create the large stone letters in front of York Institute, which endure as a reminder of his vast talents.

During the 1940s, Abston moved to Knoxville where he continued to paint and create a variety of canvases. He landed a job as a sign painter for Kern's bakery and later became "Cas Walker's favorite sign painter."[31] He painted pictures of Cas Walker's hunting dogs and even a stylized depiction of a fanciful graveyard where they were all buried. Returning frequently to the Upper Cumberland, Abston presented a number of people, like Doyle Jones, with paintings in appreciation of their support over the years.[32]

One of the most interesting and controversial self-trained painters from the Upper Cumberland was Billy Dean Anderson of Pall Mall, Tennessee. Known to some as the "Outlaw Painter," Anderson was born in 1934 and attended the Rotten Fork Elementary School as a child. He liked to draw more than doing his lessons, and he filled notebooks with sketches and designs. Anderson displayed a prodigious talent, and under different circumstances might have been able to devote his life to his art. He grew up poor, however, and his formal schooling ended with the seventh grade. He worked a number of jobs and earned a reputation as a kind-hearted, religious young man. Teaching Sunday school and occasionally preaching, Anderson used his art to reflect his notions of Christianity. His preaching career abruptly ended when he became embroiled in a series of events that led to numerous incarcerations, partial paralysis due to gunshot wounds, and his eventual execution-style slaying at the hands of the FBI.

Billy Dean Anderson turned his doodles and sketches into approximately three hundred full-fledged paintings, some life-sized, in prison. Most of his paintings are idealized renderings of Jesus. Displaying his inherent talent, the paintings depict a muscular, self-aware Christ. His Jesus is not the Lamb of God, but more like the angered Messiah who drove the money changers from the temple. In a painting owned by Mitch and Linda Hurst, the risen Christ is shown with his wounds in vivid red, looking directly at the viewer. The painting is particularly emotionally evocative. A more curious painting is Catholic in its iconography, depicting Jesus with a sacred heart. Anderson grew up in the Protestant tradition, and it is assumed that he became aware of Catholic imagery during his time in Indiana. Over the course of his pursuit of art, Billy Dean Anderson produced hundreds of paintings of various sizes, primarily between 1967 and 1971.[33] In addition to the paintings, Anderson produced a number of wood carvings, including interlocking chains, bas-relief plaques, and crucifixes. Made from three pieces of chestnut, the crucifixes were minutely detailed, and were adorned with red paint where the nails enter the stylized flesh of Christ.

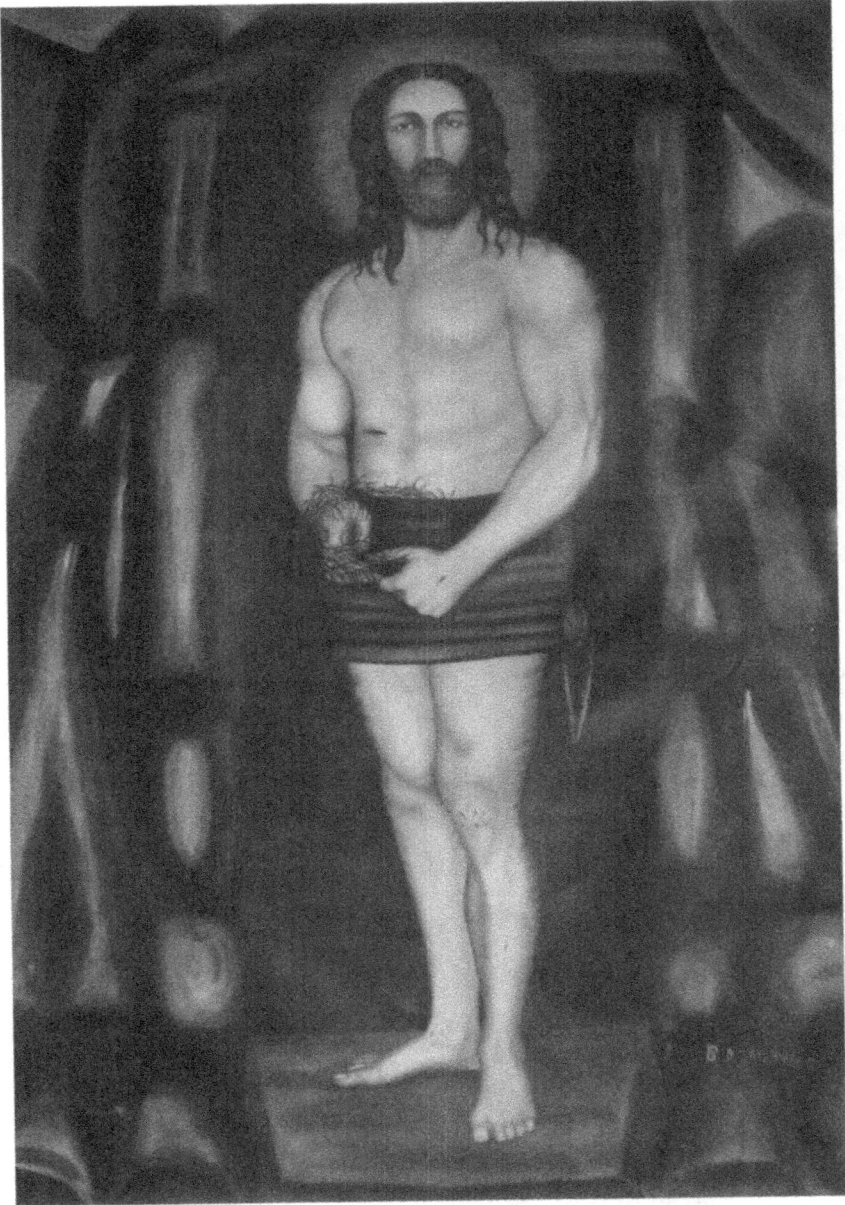

Billy Dean Anderson, *Muscular Jesus*. Courtesy of Mitch and Linda Hurst.

Joan Derryberry, Upper
Cumberland Landscape.
Courtesy of Calvin Dickinson.

Joan Derryberry came to the Upper Cumberland in 1940 with her husband, Everett, the new president of Tennessee Polytechnic Institute. Born and educated in England, she attended Bideford Art School in Devon, winning certification in The English National Society of Art Masters. At TPI she taught music, but art was her avid avocation. "[Painting] opened up a totally new world; . . . [painting] is part of me; it's no effort." Trained in England in watercolor, she successfully moved to oils; she "loved the feel of oils on canvas."[34] Derryberry was a charter member of the Cumberland Art Society in 1961, and in 1964 she resumed her art work.

Employing an impressionistic style in painting landscapes, her subjects were usually Devon, England, or the Upper Cumberland. Joan had particular expertise in depicting sky and sea. "If you want to improve your painting, paint a sky a day. . . . You would be surprised how agonizing it is to paint a sky." As with many great artists, light was of particular importance to her. "The thing that interests me most in painting is the way light reacts on things."[35]

She exhibited locally, had several solo shows, and won several competitions. In 1985, one of her pieces was chosen for an exhibition of landscape and genre painting in Tennessee, organized by the Tennessee State Museum. Her large atmospheric canvases are displayed in many prominent homes and offices in the Upper Cumberland. By 1990, Derryberry had painted more than 1,300 pieces.

Art and crafts have played an important part in the history and culture of the Upper Cumberland region. Artists and craftsmen have operated in the shadows of everyday life and events, but they have been devoted to their interests, and they have produced notable products. Names of leading artists and craftsmen are well known in the region, though few are nationally recognized. Products made to assist in the chores of everyday life became prized *objets d'art* as they were perfected after generations of production and use. The functional became beautiful as it weathered time, gaining character and distinction. Upper Cumberland craftsmen lived in a symbiotic relationship with their work, bringing out the natural characteristics of their preferred medium while leaving a piece of their own personality in the finished work. Upper Cumberland artists found a refuge where they could work in relative isolation, producing art that reflected their muse. Many men and women are imbued with a desire to create and leave their stamp on the world. The people of the Upper Cumberland have found many interesting and lasting means, from kitsch objects like macrame and clothespin toy soldiers to the studio work of serious artists, to leave a legacy of their existence.[36]

NOTES

1. Livingston Academy Senior Class, comp., "Echoes from the Foothills" (Livingston, Tenn.: Overton County Heritage Museum, 1952): 13.

2. May Cravath Wharton, *Doctor Woman of the Cumberlands* (Pleasant Hill, Tenn.: Uplands, 1953): 67; Helen Bullard, *Crafts and Craftsmen of the Tennessee Mountains* (Falls Church, Va.: Summit Press, 1976): 51.

3. There were six potteries in DeKalb County, nineteen in Putnam County, and twenty-two in White County.

4. Samuel D. Smith and Stephen T. Rogers, *A Survey of Historic Pottery Making in Tennessee,* research series no. 3 (Nashville: Division of Archaeology, 1979): 94.

5. Joseph B. Killebrew, *Natural Resources of Tennessee* (Nashville: Tavel, Eastman & Howell, 1874): 988.

6. Smith and Rogers, 23–24.

7. One of the crockery gravestones is on display at the Tennessee State Museum.

8. Robert Hughes, *American Visions: The Epic History of Art in America* (New York: Alfred A. Knopf, 1997): 43.

9. Arts, Crafts and Folk Life Collection (Nashville: TSLA, 1939): RG 82, Box 7, File 104.

10. Quoted in Bullard, 109.

11. Interview with Claudine Bilbrey (Livingston, Tenn.: March 29, 2003).

12. The Overton County Heritage Museum features the wheel that Jean Baker used to teach students and examples of the pottery created.

13. "Alpine," Scrapbook compiled by the Overton County Archives, n.d.

14. Julia S. Ardery, *The Temptation: Edgar Tolson and the Genesis of Twentieth Century Folk Art* (Chapel Hill: University of North Carolina Press, 1998): 49–51.

15. Ibid., 101–73. The Kentucky Arts Commission was one of the first established in the United States. In the mid-1980s, Bob Fulcher of the Tennessee Department of Environment and Conservation gathered together a number of Upper Cumberland craftsmen and musicians, including Willie Doss, Bud Garrett, Dee and Delta Hicks, and Frazier Moss. They built a roley hole marble court on the mall with clay imported from Overton County, while Bud Garrett played his guitar and made marbles from flint. Frazier Moss played his fiddle, even going so far as to climb on stage and join a group of Japanese Koto drummers as they performed. Willie Doss fashioned chairs from raw logs using the tools that had been in his family for generations. Interview with Bob Fulcher (November 17, 2002). See Burkhard Bilger, "The Roley Holers," in *Noodling for Flatheads* (New York: Scribner, 2000): 205–48.

16. Barbara Tolleson organized the first Algood Quilt Festival in 1988.

17. At the time, Maxwell's shop was the largest of its kind in Tennessee.

18. Bullard, 135–36. Bullard exhibited her work at the Appalachian Corridors II Art Biennial and had a one-woman show at the Tennessee State Museum in 1972.

19. Ibid., 113–14; interview with Robert Cogswell (April 2, 2003).

20. Interview with Ward Doubet, former director of the Appalachian Center for Crafts (April 2, 2003). The first director of the center was TTU's associate vice president for research Don Caplenor, who served as interim until the hiring of Barry Geise, a professional potter with an MFA, who shepherded the facility through its earliest incarnation. Once the hope of an MFA program was lost, Geise resigned to be replaced by Margaret Perry in an interim position, and then painter Sally Crain, who served as director until 1984. She was followed by metal craftsman Alf Ward, who served as director until 1989. Ilene Qualls served as the interim director for the next academic year. Ward Doubet headed the craft center from 1990 to 2002, when Scot Davisson succeeded him.

21. The BFA programs earned accreditation from the National Association of Schools of Art and Design (NASAD).

22. The first two conferences were held in New York and San Francisco.

23. Merritt was primarily a print maker before she turned to clay and fibers as her principal medium.

24. Interview with Ronald Dishman (Livingston, Tenn.: April 3, 2003).

25. Bob Fulcher, "Tennessee in 1831: The Sketches of Charles A. LeSueur." *Tennessee Conservationist* (March/April 2001): 7–11.

26. James C. Kelly, "John Wood Dodge, Miniature Painter," *American Art Review* VI: 4 (1994): 98–103.

27. James A. Hoobler, *Gilbert Gaul, American Realist* (Nashville: Tennessee State Museum Foundation, 1992).

28. Sally Crain, "Handmade in Tennessee: Arts and Crafts in the Upper Cumberland," in *Lend an Ear: Heritage of the Tennessee Upper Cumberland* (Lanham, Md.: University Press of America, 1983). Interview with Christine Jones (TTU Library, May 30, 2002); interview with Maurine Patton and Dr. Eleanor Mitchell (June 8, 2002).

29. Cookeville *Herald-Citizen* (April 21, 2002)

30. Barbara Melosh, *Engendering Culture: Manhood and Womanhood in the New Deal Public Art and Theater* (Washington, D.C.: Smithsonian Institution Press, 1991); Carroll Van West, *Tennessee's New Deal Landscape* (Knoxville: University of Tennessee Press, 2001).

31. Interview with O. D. Abston (Norris, Tenn.: July 24, 1998).

32. There are a number of Abston's paintings at the Museum of Appalachia at Norris.

33. Interview with Mitch Hurst (March 6, 2003).

34. "A Loving Eye: The Painting of Joan Derryberry," interview with Charles Denning (Cookeville, Tenn.: WCTE, October 1983).

35. Ibid.

36. During the last quarter of the twentieth century a number of artists worked in the Upper Cumberland. Presbyterian minister G. David Campbell pursued watercolor and pen and ink drawings when not attending to his pastoral duties. His subjects were primarily architectural and landscape. Evelyn Sissom of Cookeville created highly detailed canvases in vivid colors of bucolic scenes of the Upper Cumberland's native beauty. Award-winning artist Butch Hodgkins of Fentress County painted large watercolors depicting scenes of bygone eras, rural mountain folk, and derelict buildings. Marc Burnett of Cookeville employed a neoprimitive style to depict scenes of African American life. Wayne Hogan created whimsical graphic art pieces. Sally Crain-Jager originally worked in oils, producing lively abstract and muted representational pieces. While working on her MFA, she began using encaustics, which have become her primary medium. Chris Koczwara was known for her large neo-Impressionistic canvases, which often employed patriotic themes. A number of people such as Cella Neapolitan and Jesse Kaufman turned to photography as a means of expression, especially with the advent of software that made the manipulation of images easier. Brad Sells of Cookeville is a renowned wood carver and sculptor who has showcased his art nationally, including at the Smithsonian.

Chapter 15

"OLD CUMBERLAND LAND"

The Musical Legacy of the Upper Cumberland

CHARLES K. WOLFE

In December 1882, a twenty-five-year-old black railroad section hand named Willis Mayberry married a local girl named Amanda Galbraith in the village of Kingston, Tennessee. Willis had a reputation as a mean, violent man, and before the marriage was many months old, rumors began to reach the Galbraith family that Amanda was being mistreated. One of her brothers, Tom Galbraith, accosted Willis and words were exchanged; pulling a knife, Tom "cut" Willis. The wound was not serious, but Willis vowed to remember it. A few weeks later, he loaded an old musket with iron scrap and nails and set out for the home of Galbraith's brother in Old Oakdale. He saw Tom coming up the road, pointed the gun at him, and shouted, "By God, Mr. Tommy, I was fast enough for you today." He pulled the trigger and walked away. Friends rushed out to help the wounded man into the house; witnesses recall him saying, "I'm a dead man Willis Mayberry has shot." He died shortly thereafter.[1]

Willis stood trial for murder, but he denied the accusation, saying that he and Tom were "good friends" and fellow workers for the Cincinnati, New Orleans and Texas Pacific Railway Company. For some reason—a hung jury, a mistrial, an escape—Willis was not convicted, and began to wander around the country: Bluff City, Tennessee; Baltimore; Nebraska. Finally, after twenty-five years, he returned to Roane County, the scene of the murder. Before long, he landed in jail again on a minor charge, this time in Knoxville; officers from Roane County heard about his arrest and notified the Knoxville sheriff that Willis Mayberry was still wanted there to stand trial for a murder that had occurred twenty-five years before. Mayberry was extradited, tried, and sentenced to life in prison for the old crime. In November 1909, he began a term at the Tennessee State Penitentiary in Nashville.

While in the Kingston jail, Willis composed a song. Known as a good vocalist, Willis had led singing schools in the area. He taught his song to a fellow inmate, Booger Gilbreath. This man—apparently no relation to Willis's wife—was an itinerant minstrel who sang and played guitar on the streets of Rockwood. Gilbreath began singing the song during his travels; Willis, meanwhile, was transferred to the Nashville prison and continued to develop his own version. Before long a number of printed copies were circulating. Some people learned the song from printed copies, while others picked it up from various singers. Though the song was about a black man, white singers performed it as much as blacks. Gradually the song became known throughout the Upper Cumberland, and though several variations have been found in the region, the basic text usually goes something like this:

In the beautiful hills, in the midst of Roane County,
There's where I have roamed for many long years.
There's where my heart's been tending most ever,
There's where my first steps of misfortune I made.

I was thirty years old when I courted and married,
Amanda Gilbreath was then called my wife,
Her brother stabbed me for some unknown reason.
Just three months later I'd taken Tom's life.

For twentyfive years this old world I rambled,
I went to old England, old France, and old Spain.
I thought of my home way back in Roane County,
I boarded a steamer and came back again.

I was captured and tried in the village of Kingston.
Not a man in that county would speak one kind word,
When the jury came in with the verdict next morning,
A lifetime in prison were the words that I heard.

The train it pulled out, poor Mother stood weeping,
And sister, she sat all alone with a sigh.
The last words I heard were: Willie, God bless you,
Willie, God bless you; God bless you, goodbye.

The train left the shed about eleven thirty,
The chains they did rattle, the handcuffs were tight.
When Sonny Gibson took hold of the throttle,
The engine one thirty was soon out of sight.

In the scorching hot sun and sand I've been toiling,
Just working and worrying my sweet life away.
You can measure my grave on the banks of Old Cumberland,
After I've finished the rest of my days.

No matter what happens to me in Roane County,
No matter how long my sentence may be,
I love my old home way back in Roane County,
Way back in the hills of East Tennessee.

Titles associated with the ballad were usually "Willis Mayberry," "Roane County Prison," or "In the Hills of Roane County." Some versions present Spencer as the place of the trial, but most correctly say Kingston. By the late 1920s, as the song continued to circulate in oral tradition, it began to enter repertoires of professional entertainers. The first attempt to record the ballad was made on May 2, 1929, when Warren Caplinger and Andy Patterson recorded a song listed as "Willis Mabry" for the Gennett Record Company in Richmond, Indiana. For some reason, the recording was not released, however, and the team re-recorded it on June 9, 1930, this time listing the title as "Willie Maberry (Hills of Rowan [sic] County)." This recording, too, was not released, but in 1934 the two singers included the song in their custom-printed songbook sold from West Virginia radio stations. This apparently marks the first appearance in print of the ballad entitled "Roane County Prison Song":

In the beautiful hills, in the mid'st of Roane County,
There's where I have roamed, for many long years,
There's where my heart's been tending most ever,
That's where the first step of misfortune I made.

I was about thirty years, when I courted and married,
Amanda Gilbreath was then called my wife,
Her three brothers stabbed me for some unknown reason,
Just three months later I had taken Tom's life.

For twenty-five years this old world I rambled,
I went to old England, to France and to Spain,
I thought of my home, way back in Roane County,
I boarded a steamer and I come back again.

I was captured and tried, in the village of Kingston,
Not a man in the county would speak one kind word,
When the jury come in with the verdict next morning,
A life time in prison were the words that I heard.

When the train she pulled out, poor mother stood weeping,
And sister she sat, alone with a sigh,
The last words I heard, was Willis, God bless you,
Was Willis God bless you, God bless you, good bye.

When the train left the shed, about eleven thirty,
The chains they did rattle, and the handcuffs were tight,
And when Denny Gleason taken hold of the throttle,
The engine one thirty was soon out of sight.

Some went to the mines, in the hills of Big Brushey,
Some went to their graves, I'm sorry to say,
But I came to this prison, here stationed at Nashville,
To labor and worry, the rest of my days.

In the scorching hot sands of the foundry I'm toiling,
Yes toiling and worrying, my life all away,
They'll measure my grave, on the banks of old Cumberland,
Just as soon as I've finished the rest of my days.

No matter what happens to me in Roane County,
No matter how long my sentence may be,
I love my old home, away back in Roane County,
Because it's away up in East Tennessee.

Le Polar was great, but Borah was better,
There's worse and there's better, all over you see,
Boys when you write home, from this prison in Nashville,
Place one of my songs in your letter for me.

The reference to "Big Brushey"—Brushy Mountain Prison—is curious; Willis Mayberry was never incarcerated there, but singer Andy Patterson worked there as a guard in the early 1920s, and several of his colleagues believed that he learned the song while working there.[2]

In 1940, the ballad was finally recorded by the Blue Sky Boys, a duo composed of Bill and Earl Bolick. Perhaps the most popular duet of the day, their recording assured the song wider regional exposure. After World War II, when soldiers carried country songs even further afield, the Willis Mayberry song was recorded several times by early bluegrass singers. In 1957, Bill Monroe, the father of bluegrass music, recorded the tune, and his version's popularity confirmed its status as a country music standard. He learned the song from Tommy Magness, an old-time fiddler who had played with Monroe's band in the early 1940s. Magness had learned it earlier when he had worked in Knoxville.

Willis Mayberry's song moved from the dark confines of a black man's prison cell in 1909 to the brightly lit stage of the world-famous Grand Ole Opry in 1957. It is probably the most famous single song to emerge from the rich folk tradition of the Cumberland region. Its long winding trail in and out of mass media, in and out of print, from amateur to professional singer, is in many ways typical of the songs of the area. The song proved profitable for different people over the years, but Willis Mayberry saw none of it, or ever knew how popular his song became; he died on the poor farm in Knoxville in 1925.

"Willis Mayberry," the story and the song, form but one short chapter in the story of music in the Upper Cumberland. Few regions in the South are as rich in traditional musical culture as this region. Yet, for a variety of reasons, the area has been one of the least studied in Tennessee. Whereas folk-song hunters traveled to eastern Tennessee as early as World War I, and mass media in Nashville and Memphis assured attention for the music of these areas by the mid-1920s, the Upper Cumberland remained a neglected backwater. It lacked the romance and glamour of the Smokies, or the excitement of Nashville and Memphis. The few attempts to document folk music of the Upper Cumberland were not widely known or disseminated. Partly because of this, and because the area included some of the poorest counties in the state, with the worst roads and services, many old songs and old performing styles have been preserved better than in other places. Only in the last few years have any serious attempts been made to study the area's folk music in a modern, systematic form. Though the region has given the country many of its finest and most influential folk performers, from

Mandolin player at the Granville
Heritage Day celebration, 2003.
Photo by Michael Birdwell.

balladeer Dee Hicks to bluegrass pioneer Lester Flatt, the general public remains unaware of the importance of the Cumberland's musical traditions.[3]

Like most settlers of the Upland South, people moving into the Upper
Cumberland country at the dawn of the nineteenth century brought
with them a rich trove of songs from England, Scotland, and Ireland.
Some had been sung for generations in the old country; others were
new and topical, concerning the day the immigrants set sail for the new
world. Old-timers called (and still call) some of them "love songs," but
those tunes bore little resemblance to a Frank Sinatra standard or a
Barry Manilow lyric; they were long, dealing in great detail with el-
emental themes of love, death, murder, betrayal, and guilt. Most were
sung unaccompanied, and were carefully passed on from family to family, generation to generation. Other songs called by one area native
"dang-dabble" or "dang-devil" songs were funny, occasionally bawdy
songs full of nonsense words about cheating wives and philandering
husbands. These, too, came from England, and had pedigrees at least as
long as their serious counterparts. That any of these old songs survived

into the twentieth century is a minor miracle; they had to endure challenges by American popular songs brought into the region as early as the 1870s by minstrel shows, piano music, and mail-order catalogs. Many details in the songs became increasingly irrelevant to people's lives. Who were these lords and ladies, these milk-white steeds, and these kings and princes? But survive they did, though in some areas stronger than in others. By the mid-1930s some places yielded relatively few old English ballads to folk-song hunters, and most of those were found in isolated pockets. Yet as recently as the mid-1970s, collectors were in Pickett and Fentress counties. Perhaps the most popular of these old songs collected in Tennessee, and, indeed, the nation was "Barbara Allen."[4]

Beside these old British songs grew up an equally interesting tradition of native American balladry; singers moved from an English to an American song with ease and without self-consciousness. Many of the same songs that were favorites across the South were favorites in the Upper Cumberland. They included "Pearl Bryan," a song about a couple of Kentucky medical students who killed a girlfriend; "The Knoxville Girl," another murder song adapted from an older British model; "Charles Guiteau," a song of criminal confession about the man who assassinated President James Garfield; disaster songs about the great Mississippi Flood, the wreck of the Old 97, or the killing of President William McKinley. Although these songs marked the area's richness, they did not distinguish it from the rest of the country.

Some songs, though, were unique to the area; they originated there, were about events in the region, and gained their early popularity in the Upper Cumberland, such as "Willis Mayberry." But a lesser-known song paints an even more particular picture of the area; this remarkable ballad is known variously as "Old Cumberland Land," "The Cumberland," or "The Indian Tribes of Tennessee." An epistolary ballad in the form of a letter written by a woman who came from the East coast to settle with her family on the Cumberland Plateau, it told about the hardships they had to endure and the natural beauty they witnessed:[5]

The Cumberland

The day that I parted away from you
In sorrow, grief, and trouble too,
You gave to me your parting hand,
And wished me safe on the Cumberland.

Then on our journey we did steer,
O'er hills and valleys and rivers clear,
Through a desert place in a barren land,
We steered our course for the Cumberland.

When we got there, there was ice and snow;
It rained and hailed and the wind did blow,
Which caused us all to weep and cry,
Staying here with cold we all must die.

But thank the Lord our health we found;
We landed here both safe and sound,
In the happy land, Oh the fertile soil:
Here's milk, here's wine, both corn and oil.

We saw ten thousand human graves,
All walled in with mason's sign,
Which made me think in the days of old,
Some human race had passed this place.

I've nothing more to write to you,
Since preaching's scarce, and religion's low,
We're here in love, peace, and hope to be,
With the Indian Tribes in Tennessee.

My love to you I can't unfold,
It's like some lovely ring of gold,
It's round, it's pure, Oh: it has no end,
So is my love to you my friend.

This particular version of the song was collected in 1935 from L. P. Carlock of Alpine, in Overton County; it had been handed down from father to son in his family. Other versions of the song have been found in southeastern Kentucky, in Fentress County, and in Crossville. Some omit the stanza about "ten thousand human graves" walled in with "the mason's sign," which possibly referred to Indian graveyards. Indian symbols would seem strange to settlers in the way a secret Masonic sign would seem strange. But few songs give as gripping a picture of the cruel winters that faced settlers in the wild new land on the Cumberland Plateau.[6]

A third song unique to the region and rather well known there is a long murder ballad entitled "The Braswell Boys." In 1875, Teek and Jo Braswell apparently murdered two men named Russell and John Allison, relatives of J. B. Allison, then sheriff of Putnam County. The Braswells were convicted and hanged on Billy Goat Hill in Cookeville in 1878. There was nothing especially unusual or spectacular about the crime, its victims, or its perpetrators, and the hanging, though widely attended, would probably have not been especially remembered in folk history. Someone at the time, however, wrote and published a long ballad about the event, and the song caught on. The ballad in its original form ran to at least twenty-nine stanzas. It presented, in journalistic detail, not only the exact dates, but the name of the sheriff who presided at the hanging, the name of the minister who read the Braswell boys their final prayers, and even the chapter of the Scripture (Romans 3) that was read to them. Such details are common in American murder or tragedy ballads, and mark one important difference between native American ballads and their British counterparts. Also typical of American balladry is the conclusion of "The Braswell Boys"; the listener is urged to "take warning" from the song, and to see the fate of the Braswells as a lesson in temperance and avarice.[7]

Such topical ballads may seem to be a thing of the past, but some still live today. In the 1980s, Linnie Johnson of Sparta could still sing a ballad about her family running rafts down the Caney Fork River:

> Oh you poor people do not know,
> What we poor raftsmen undergo,
> Although we came to take a ride,
> Most every time there comes a tide.

Other songs continue to be circulated by records, cassette tapes, eight tracks, and compact discs instead of the newspaper, the "ballet card" (sold by wandering minstrels, little postcards with a song lyric printed on them), or oral tradition. One recent example is a locally produced recording, "Smithville Jail," that deals with the trials and tribulations of a "good ole boy" from Cannon County arrested for drag racing near Center Hill Lake.

The earliest extensive folk-song collection compiled in the region by Lillian Gladys Crabtree included songs on a variety of topics. A graduate student at Peabody College in Nashville, Crabtree traveled throughout Overton County by auto and on horseback looking for old songs. A native of the area, she collected songs from her own family as well as many others. Using the guidelines of her Peabody professors—very conservative parameters that demeaned any song touched by the mass media—she did not include any songs found in newspaper or magazine articles or advertisements. Even by omitting those, she came up with a total of 323 song texts, dividing them into the following categories:

Family life	10%
(including songs about mother)	
War songs	3%
Crime and Bandit songs	11%
Religious songs	5%
Death and Sentimental songs	10%
Western and Cowboy songs	5%
Humor	7%
Blues	4%
Love songs	27%
Miscellaneous	3%

Obviously, people preferred to sing about love, but included in this category were many older ballads such as "Pretty Polly" and "The Knoxville Girl" that deal with love mainly in terms of a jealous sweetheart and/or murder. They were not love songs of the spoon moon June sort. If the two categories of sentimental songs—the family life category and the death and sentimental category—were combined, a very high percentage of the songs in the collection would fit that category. Songs such as "The Little Old Log Cabin in the Lane," though seldom heard today, were vastly popular in an age of sentimentality.

Though many people in the rural Cumberland could sing these old songs—it was one of the few forms of entertainment available to a rural household—some people became so adept at it that they acquired reputations in the community as singers, or as repositories of old songs. Some were men, some women; there seems to have been little sexual discrimination. Some, like blind singer Dick Burnett, who wandered through Pickett and Fentress counties performing on street corners and selling his ballet cards, became semiprofessional singers, the ancestors of modern country music entertainers. But most singers were accustomed to performing in less formal, more domestic settings: the kitchen, the hearth, the front porch.

In 1936, the Special Skills division of the Resettlement Administration sent Sidney Robertson (later to become the wife of composer Henry Cowell) into the Upper Cumberland with a portable recording machine to make the first audio recordings in the area. In a few days, she recorded more than sixty selections. In Crossville, Robertson recorded fifteen songs performed by the family of Henry Garrett, and nine more unaccompanied ballads from Ruby and Oliver Hughes. Moving on to Smithville, Robertson discovered a remarkable balladeer, L. L. (Flora) McDowell, who recorded twenty-nine songs, one-fourth of which were old English ballads. McDowell was later recorded by the venerable Alan Lomax (1942), and she was probably the most noted ballad singer from the area during this time. She and her husband were members of the Tennessee Folklore Society, and they later collected and published several songbooks. Also in 1936, Rebecca and Penelope Tarwater, from Rockwood, were invited to perform at a folk festival in Washington. While there, the Tarwaters recorded several of their haunting vocal numbers for the Library of Congress.

Sometimes entire families were known as singers, and in many cases singing had been in the family for several generations. Such was the case of Dee and Delta Hicks, from the Tinchtown Community near Jamestown. Dee, born in rural Fentress County in 1905, learned literally hundreds of songs from his father, Daniel Hicks, who had a reputation for being, in Dee's words, "a mighty singer." Most of Dee's relatives

Dee and Delta Hicks. Courtesy of Bob Fulcher.

could also sing, and when he married Delta, he married another singer. Dee was one of the few people left in the Upper Cumberland—or, indeed, the whole country—who could get through long, complicated ballads without any recourse whatsoever to written texts or notes. His repertoire included more than three hundred old songs, many learned from his father; one, "Jimmy and Nancy," with over fifty verses, took more than twenty minutes to sing. The songs ranged from marathon British ballads such as "The Young Sea Captain" to local ditties Dee's father or brother made up about a neighbor's fight. Some are funny and bawdy; others, like "The Vulture," a rare ballad about a baby carried into the frozen Alps by a giant vulture, brought tears to Dee's eye when he sang it.

In the late 1970s, Dee and Delta began recording songs for the Library of Congress, and both were asked to perform at the fiftieth anniversary of the Archive of American Folksong in Washington in 1978—two of only three traditional artists so honored. Some folklorists argued that Dee Hicks was the largest living repository of traditional ballads in the country. In later years, Dee saw two recordings of his songs released, and he appeared in two television documentaries, *Chase the Devil* and *Mouth Music*. Dee died in 1983, and for a time his second cousin Johnny Ray Hicks carried on his ballad singing tradition before his own death in 2000. Delta died in 1996.[8] One of the most intriguing problems in traditional culture is the question of why and how these old songs have been so well and carefully preserved for so long. In the case of Dee and Delta Hicks, the answer was bound up in their whole way of living and looking at life. For more than forty years, Dee labored over a sandy ten-acre farm, clearing and working it by hand. He and Delta raised their family there and seldom left their isolated home. Songs were the primary entertainment for the poor, rural household; the Hicks family sang in the fields and at night to relax. "When I would come in from work at night," recalled Dee, "I liked to have my hair combed, over and through, and my daughters would do this, and I would sing to them as they combed my hair. They'd ask me for one song or another that they liked." Dee also felt that the songs—many of which came from his father—represented a sort of heritage, and that in singing and sharing them with others, he kept the memory of his father alive. Dee and Delta both took the old songs seriously; to them, the characters in the songs were real, and had real problems. They saw them in much the same way other old people see soap opera characters, and it is not surprising to learn that Dee liked watching soap operas on television. Dee tended to sing the older, statelier British ballads, while Delta preferred more sentimental, nineteenth-century songs. Yet, when they sang, each became totally absorbed in the story of the song, and in the trials and tribulations of the lords and ladies of centuries before. It was only in the last seven years of his life that Dee learned his songs were important to people outside Fentress County.[9]

Old ballads, interesting as they may be, were not the only type of vocal folk music found in the Upper Cumberland. For many people, singing is synonymous with religious music. In the nineteenth century, many church songs of the frontier were codified in books such as M. L. Swan's *Harp of Columbia,* published in Knoxville in 1848. Books like this were extremely popular in northern and eastern Tennessee, and were published in a format in which the shape of the song notes, not the position on the scale, determined the pitch. *Southern Harmony,* an 1838 collection by "Singing Billy" Walker, made its way into the Caney Fork Valley well before the Civil War, and in 1936, when Lucius McDowell was collecting religious folk songs for his pioneering work, *Songs of the Old Camp Ground,* he found a number of older Cumberland natives who could sing songs in *Southern Harmony* from memory. The collection, like many others, had become a source for the oral tradition of the singers.

People did not sing just in church, though. By the end of the 1800s, some song leaders conducted singing schools throughout the area. In these schools—usually lasting from one to three weeks—pupils learned the rudiments of music: how to sight-read shaped notes, how to pitch songs without using a piano or organ (few churches had them), and how to mark time (usually by slapping the desk). "Singing conventions" were popular, and especially active ones were found in Bedford and Cannon counties. Nondenominational associations of the best singers from churches in the county, singing conventions gathered once a month to sing either older songs or new ones from paperback songbooks introduced to the region by the turn of the century. "Convention songbooks," published by people such as James D. Vaughan in Lawrenceburg, Tennessee, or R. E. Winsett in Chattanooga, were also printed in shaped notes. They contained more optimistic, lively, and modern—sounding songs. To popularize their new songbooks, many companies hired semiprofessional quartets to tour the countryside, performing songs from their latest books at churches, social gatherings, and singing conventions. These quartets eventually became a force in their own right, though, and by the 1920s many amateur singers performed as quartets. The original quartets sponsored by the songbook companies started going out on their own, thus forming the foundation for modern gospel music.

One group from the Upper Cumberland that achieved national popularity was the LeFevre family. They hailed from DeKalb County, and as early as 1921 brothers Urias and Alphus, along with their sister Maude, were traveling as a family trio. After graduating from a Bible Training School in Cleveland, the two brothers created a quartet and began touring for the James D. Vaughan Company. After two years, they struck out on their own and soon had a radio show sponsored by NuGrape soda. By the mid-1930s they were causing a good deal of excitement and some controversy—with their fast, up-tempo versions of such warhorses as "Keep on the Firing Line," which featured dazzling, complex vocal parts accompanied by a pumping ragtime piano. They continued to prosper and remained intact, through several personnel changes and through several generations of LeFevres, until 1977. Historians today regard them as pioneers in the gospel music industry.

Almost as popular and influential in later years was the Looper family of Monterey. About 1963, brothers Oral and Coleman Looper (originally farmers from Overton County) joined Oral's daughter Brenda to form the Looper Trio. For the next decade, they cut a series of custom records and traveled extensively, bringing their high, hard mountain harmony to a rich variety of songs. They were credited with introducing and popularizing standards such as "The Other Side of Jordan" and "Walk Around Me Jesus," and had especially strong followings in Ohio, West Virginia, and southwest Virginia. In later years, as other family members and in-laws joined the group, they became known simply as The Loopers, and they laid the cornerstone for a complex dynasty that continues to this day. Coleman Looper founded The Grand Ole Gospel Barn near Crossville, for many years a major venue on the plateau for southern gospel. Though Oral died in 2001 at age seventy-one, Coleman continued a "singing ministry," playing as many as two hundred dates a year. Coleman's son Justin traveled widely with his wife, Terry, and continued the Looper song writing tradition.

Like vocalists, fiddlers on the plateau plied their trade at square dances, barn raisings, auction sales, political rallies, house parties, and fiddling contests throughout the nineteenth and twentieth centuries. Tunes heard in the area were probably not all that different from those heard elsewhere in the upland South, and included such favorites as "Forky Deer," "Tramp the Devil's Eyes Out," "Jennie Blow the Fire

Strong," "Hole in the Kettle," "Turkey Buzzard," "Sally Ann," and "Sleepy Lou." Fiddling was respected enough that in 1886 the two main candidates running for Tennessee governor, brothers Alf and Bob Taylor, actually fiddled against each other during their stump speeches. In later years, figures such as Smith County's Albert Gore Sr., pulled out a fiddle and played a few courses of "Soldier's Joy" as he ran for the Senate. Indeed, according to Joe Wilson, when Gore first went to Congress in 1938, some of his fiddling was recorded by the National Folk Festival Association just before he took the oath of office.

At country dances in the nineteenth century, the fiddler would hold forth by himself, a one-man band who generated the music, the occasional singing, and much of the rhythm. The string band, in which the fiddle is backed by banjo, guitar, or mandolin, did not become common in the Upper Cumberland until after the turn of the century. Many old-timers can remember when they first saw a guitar and recall the time when the string band consisted of a fiddle and banjo, or even just a fiddle.

No one, of course, could tape-record an old-time country frolic back in the 1800s, but several written descriptions of such affairs exist. One of the most engaging accounts appears in Will Allen Dromgoole's 1886 travel book *The Sunny Side of the Cumberland;* the narrator, a young woman from Nashville, attended a square dance in Wild Cat Cove on the Calf Killer River in southern White County. The dance started at 4:00 P.M. and concluded the next morning at 9:00. As the partygoers neared the cabin, they could hear the clatter of shuffling feet in the distance; upon arrival they were told, "Light and look at your saddle," a customary greeting. The narrator described the scene:

> As we are not interested in the saddle regulations, we leave our
> driver to look to the team, and take our way timidly into the
> ballroom. The house is a little, one roomed hut, with the custom-
> ary shedroom in the rear. We stand a moment in the porch
> looking in on the scene open before us: the low, square room is
> crowded with old men, old women, boys and girls; the bench set
> round the wall for lookers-on is full; the standing room is taken
> to the last foot. The fiddler wedges his way in and out among the
> whirligig figures, dexterously avoiding protruding elbows and
> reckless heels, playing for dear life, he cracked fiddle fairly
> groaning with the terrors of the "Rolling River," or screaming the
> wonderful acts of "Cottoneye Joe."

While we stand looking on, an old man hobbles to the door and invites us in. The music stops in the very height of the time, and fiddler and dancers stop to stare at us; but only a moment: we are no sooner crowded into a corner than a stout little man with a paper and pencil calls out

"Three minits yit." And the music begins again, and the dancers fairly fly, determined to crowd as much as possible into the precious three minutes.

"Time up," cries the same man, and instantly the set is at an end.

This man proves to be the bookkeeper, and holds the high position of deputy sheriff of the county. The dancers are allotted special sets of twenty minutes each. Every one knows the number of his set before the bookkeeper calls it. This, however, applies to the gentlemen only; the girls are chosen, and the same one can dance all night if she is asked.

When the next set is called we notice our young driver has taken a place upon the floor, and our interest centers almost entirely in him.

Some one calls for "Crippled Chicken." Our little friend objects. "Give us a lively one, C'lumbus; one with some git up to it. Give us 'Sally Gal.'"

And away goes the fiddle, and away go the dancers, and away goes our comical little driver. He dances; dances for dear life, dances as if the future of the government depends on the rapidity with which he lifts his lithe young legs. And the fiddler, too, grows jubilant; every moment the tune quickens in the glories of "Sally Gal"; the fiddler himself is dancing in the excitement, and with every motion of the bow our little driver grows more limber, more merry, more determined. The tail of his tiny coat, that seems to be all tail, flies like the pennant of a war vessel or the black flag of a pirate ship. Fiddle, Fiddler, coat and dancer have all gone mad, mad with tile mirth, and mad with the thrilling wonders of "Sally Gal."

In the years since this square dance took place, fiddling continued to play an important role in the traditional music of the Upper Cumberland. Square dances offered a forum for fiddling and fiddling styles, and by the 1920s local fiddling championships were being held that stimulated new interest in this complex art. In the twentieth century, a

The Grand Ole Opry's first major star, Uncle Jimmy Thompson. Courtesy of the Country Music Hall of Fame.

number of fiddlers began to win regional and even national fame as they took their skills into the recording studios and radio stations.

Though he called Laguardo, Tennessee, his home when he became one of the Grand Ole Opry's first stars, legendary fiddler Uncle Jimmy Thompson was born near Baxter in Putnam County in 1848. His niece, Eva Thompson Jones of Cookeville, often accompanied him when he performed. Thompson traveled about middle Tennessee with his second wife, Ella Manners, competing in fiddling championships or putting on impromptu shows from the bed of his truck. As high spirited and as fond of white lightning as her husband, Ella buck danced while Uncle Jimmy entertained with his distinctive style. George D. Hay invited the seventy-seven-year-old Uncle Jimmy to perform on WSM in November 1925; he became a regular performer on *The Barn Dance*, as the Opry was originally known. He traveled to Atlanta in 1926 to cut records for the Columbia label, including "High Born Lady," "Karo," and "Billy Wilson." Uncle Jimmy's radio career ended that same year because of his failing health, his unpredictable behavior when drinking, and the advent of a more structured format on *The Barn Dance*.[10]

Uncle Jimmy McCarroll, born in 1892 in Wheat in Anderson County, released twelve influential records on the same label in 1928 and 1929. McCarroll incorporated into his sharp, driving fiddling some licks and turns he had learned from his grandmother, who was part Cherokee. These "Indian pieces" helped give McCarroll's recordings a wild, skirling, "hollering" sound. His most famous record was his train piece, "Southern 111," a prototype of the dozens of later fiddle tunes built around train imitations. (The actual Train No. 111 ran from Knoxville to Danville, Kentucky.) Other McCarroll specialties included his "Home Town Blues," the archaic "Green River March," and ferocious break-downs like "Johnson City Rag" and "Roane County Rag." As late as the 1970s, McCarroll continued to play square dances in the area, and in 1971 most of his classic recordings were reissued by Country Records. By the 1990s, some of his records, made seventy years before, made it onto compact discs, and even onto Internet Web sites.

The most commercially successful of the area's modern fiddlers was Sparta native Benny Martin (1928–2001). He grew up in the large fam-ily of George and Polly Martin, and spent his youth traveling with the family band. He learned to play a bewildering number of instruments from the guitar to the dulcimer, but his main love was the fiddle. At the age of eleven, he ran away from home to play on the Knoxville radio

Fiddler Benny Martin at work. Courtesy of the Country Music Hall of Fame.

show *Mid-Day-Merry-Go-Round*, and by the time he was thirteen he had made his way to Tennessee's capital city. The Nashville music scene was just getting into its role as a center for country radio and recordings, and Martin found a spot with one of the more popular bands, Big Jeff and His Radio Playboys, on station WLAC. In fact, he was informally adopted by the leader, Jeff Bess, and his wife Tootsie, and quickly learned the techniques of the new commercial country music.

Starting in the late 1940s, Martin worked with many Grand Ole Opry stars, including Curly Fox, Milton Estes, Bill Monroe, Roy Acuff, and Flatt and Scruggs. He soon developed a unique fiddling style derived from the new bluegrass music—a fast, angular style full of odd timings and complex harmonies. With his rugged good looks and songwriting skills, Martin was soon groomed as a headline country singer. He signed with a number of major labels, and actually had some hit singles including "Me and My Fiddle" and "Ice Cold Love." He also wrote songs for major stars such as Kitty Wells, and for a time was even managed by Colonel Tom Parker. In later years, however, Martin devoted himself to fiddling, and by his death in 2001 was hailed as probably the single most influential bluegrass fiddler. Along with fellow bluegrass legends Lester Flatt, Bill Monroe, and banjoist Blake Williams, Benny Martin helped put Sparta on the map as a wellspring of bluegrass music.

Other influential fiddlers, however, preferred not to seek outside fame and remained in the Upper Cumberland to ply their trade in less conspicuous ways. One of the very best of these—a fiddler some regarded as the finest Cumberland traditional fiddler—was John Sharp (1894–1964), who spent much of his life at Sharp Place, northeast of Jamestown. Born in one of the oldest log structures along the Kentucky-Tennessee border, Sharp learned a battery of odd, old tunes such as "Fourteen Wildcat Scalps" from his father. After a short emigration to Iowa, Sharp returned and spent much of his life as a logger and farmer. With a neighbor, banjoist Virgil Anderson, he formed a band called The Kentucky Wildcats, which toured coal camps during the Depression and later played for political rallies, reunions, and dances at Pickett State Park.

Sharp never made commercial records and was missed by Library of Congress teams that occasionally came through the area. Fortunately, in 1949 Sharp's old friend Alvin C. York invited him to cut some records on a new disc-cutting machine he had bought, and Sharp was able to preserve some of his signature tunes. One was his favorite square dance tune, "Five Miles Out of Town"; another was the difficult and complex "Three Way Hornpipe," which Sharp composed. His relatives preserved some of these old discs, which were finally released to the public in 1983 on the LP *Traditional Music from the Cumberland Plateau* (County Records). Some of Sharp's music has been carried on by his two sons, a daughter, and Mike DeFosche. Another influential dance fiddler from the area was Clarence Ferrill (1908–1977) from Alpine, who for many years played pieces such as "New Five Cents" at dances in Standing Stone State Park near Livingston.

During the last three decades of the twentieth century, the fiddler most associated with the Upper Cumberland was Cookeville resident Frazier Moss (1910–1998). Born in the Sugar Creek community in Jackson County, Moss first became interested in fiddling when listening to old-timers bring their fretless banjos and fiddles to the little one-room schoolhouse he attended. Determined to get his own fiddle, he sold garden seeds throughout his community to win a "prize"—a fiddle. What he received was a little tin fiddle—"a toy." Starting anew, Moss earned enough money to buy a real fiddle from a neighbor, and by the time he was eight he was playing at house dances like those described by Will Allen Dromgoole. During one of his first fiddling contests, at Lafayette, he competed against eighty-year-old Uncle Jimmy Thompson, the legend who started the Grand Ole Opry. After the contest, Uncle Jimmy sat young Frazier down on the curb and showed him how to play "Grey Eagle." He also gave the youngster advice: never fiddle a religious tune, especially at a contest. It leaves a bad impression.

Through the late 1920s, Moss was playing professionally, traveling with a series of vaudeville and medicine shows that barnstormed the small towns of the region. He learned to play pop and jazz tunes such as "Darktown Strutters Ball," and was exposed to the blues. Moss recalled of one particular show, "We had a lot of black people who traveled with us." The Depression, though, brought an end to the salad days for such shows, and to support his growing family, Moss turned to construction work. Here, too, he traveled widely over the South, playing fiddle and picking up new tunes. Around 1970, he retired from construction and began to play music more seriously. Though he had offers to play with country and bluegrass stars, he preferred to explore the burgeoning fiddling-contest circuit. Often working with guitarist John Henry Demps, he started winning contests regularly, playing signature pieces such as "Grey Eagle," "St. Anne's Reel," and "Black Hawk Waltz." When the Smithville Fiddlers' Jamboree started in 1972, Frazier Moss

Portrait of Frazier Moss. Courtesy of Jim Heard.

quickly established himself as the "senior fiddler" to beat. He made several recordings and was featured in a television documentary, *Showdown at the Hoedown*.

In later years, Moss traveled even farther afield, representing Tennessee at the Smithsonian Festival of American Folklife and the National Old Time Fiddlers' Contest in Wieser, Idaho. He often appeared at school programs and concerts, introducing old-time music to new generations. He was one of the first modern fiddlers to introduce the complex "long bow" technique to the middle Tennessee area. Young fiddlers began learning from him, as did veteran professionals such as John Hartford, Ramona Jones, and Mark Howard. Generous, effusive, and preferring the company of young people, Moss fostered emerging talent, such as the Cookeville bluegrass group The Cluster Pluckers. "He almost had the largest band in Middle Tennessee," said his friend John Hartford in his eulogy "because everybody played with him and everybody loved to play with him."

Mass media had a significant impact on the region's traditional music, although the impact was not as dramatic or as sudden as in other areas. For one thing, no radio station existed in the Upper Cumberland until 1940, when Luke Medley established WHUB at Cookeville. Until then, people listened to WSM in Nashville (though daytime reception was only fair), or to distant stations in Chicago, New Orleans, and Cincinnati. After WHUB took to the air, the station wisely tapped into the rich music of the region by airing the *WHUB Jamboree*, broadcast live from the Cookeville courthouse every Saturday night. This show allowed just about any amateur performer or group to step up to the microphone and perform.

Mass media provided the prime vehicle for the most famous modern performer to come from the Upper Cumberland—Lester Flatt. Before his death in 1979, Lester Flatt's distinctive mellow voice was known to millions of television viewers across the country who watched *The Beverly Hillbillies* or listened to *The Grand Ole Opry*, and his famous "G run" on the guitar had become a cliché known to every would-be country guitar picker. Born in 1914 in Overton County, one of nine children of a tenant farmer, Lester grew up near Sparta in White County. Music ran in his family, and both parents played the five-string banjo in the old drop-thumb "clawhammer" style; his father also played fiddle. Flatt's whole family would sing hymns together after a hard day in the fields. As a teenager, Lester worked in a silk mill in Sparta, and married a local girl, Gladys Stacey. In the midst of the Depression, the young

Earl Scruggs and Lester Flatt perform at the Grand Ole Opry. Courtesy of the Country Music Hall of Fame.

couple moved to Virginia to find work; while there Lester began to play in a string band with some of his pals from Tennessee. By 1939, he had the first in a series of radio jobs, and soon he and Gladys were playing music full time. In 1944 he joined Earl Scruggs, who was busy revolutionizing banjo picking into the new bluegrass style. From the stage of the *Grand Ole Opry*, in 1946–1947, Flatt and Scruggs helped Bill Monroe forge his bluegrass music into a genre that was to become internationally known. Soon Flatt and Scruggs set out on their own, and in the next twenty years the duo wrote the second chapter of bluegrass history. When they broke up in 1969—partly because of Lester's stubborn adherence to older, traditional forms of music—Flatt continued to perform with his own group, The Nashville Grass. Though many of his songs were now as much country as traditional, Lester Flatt to the end reflected his basic training in White County. Through songs such as "Why Did I Wander," a tribute to his Cumberland home, and singing styles including the "catch" at the end of a line that characterizes many of the singers of the Upper Cumberland, Flatt's music helped popularize the musical tradition of an often ignored region of Tennessee.[11]

Proud of the Upper Cumberland's musical tradition, Congressman Joe L. Evins of DeKalb County used his influence to start an annual competition in Smithville in 1972. With the aid of Evins's longtime friend

Berry Williams, the county secured a grant from the federal government's Model City Program to stage the event. The annual Smithville Fiddlers' Jamboree started as an attempt to stimulate tourism in the Upper Cumberland while preserving Appalachian music and culture. From the outset, the competition has taken place over the Fourth of July holiday. The first year's outing drew roughly 8,000 spectators and 714 musicians from 16 states who competed on stage, while inspiring unknown thousands who got together and jammed informally. The second and third year sealed the success of the event, with more than 50,000 people in attendance and over 1,000 competitors from 36 states and 16 foreign countries.

The Smithville Fiddlers' Jamboree continues to grow, keeping the Cumberland musical tradition alive. The event has been covered by nearly 500 newspapers and magazines from across the country and has been broadcast over 595 television and radio stations, including the BBC, TBS, and documentary films about old-time mountain music. Since 1988, Cookeville's PBS station WCTE earned the role of recording the event for posterity, filming all the events on the main stage and sending its camera crews to record noncompetitors, vendors, and the Jamboree's faithful audience.

Perhaps the most important person in making the event flourish is the fiddler James G. "Bobo" Driver. While serving in the Civilian Conservation Corps in 1936, Bobo formed his first band, Jimmy Driver and the Tennessee Playboys, playing covers of Bill Monroe and Bob Wills tunes. Branching out, writing his own compositions, and playing with a host of musicians, Bobo Driver became a frequent guest on the Grand Ole Opry. Invited to help organize the very first Smithville Fiddlers' Jamboree in 1972, Driver invited professional musicians to attend or assist in the event, and he was a driving force in its success for more than twenty years. Driver convinced the sponsors to include aspiring children who wanted to play music, allowing them to interact with like-minded peers and adults willing to share their experience. The Children's Competition has since become one of the Jamboree's favorite events.

Generally black musicians found it harder to gain access to an audience than their white counterparts, and their music is thus much more spottily documented. What exists is a handful of rare recordings, a few remembered songs, and a host of memories by those who heard them or were influenced by them. They included people such as Uncle Dave Woods, a fiddler, singer, and composer from the Bradyville community in Warren County. In the 1880s and 1890s, Uncle Dave was routinely called on by both white and black folks to play for local dances. At least one of his songs—or a fragment of it—survives, "The Monroe Bynum Song," about an 1887 murder that contained the well-known refrain, "I'm as free a little birdie as I can be." Farther up the road, near Campaign and Rock Island, emerged a string band headed by fiddler John Lusk and banjoist Murphy Gribble. Murphy began playing in his unique "stroking" style as early as 1914, and throughout the 1920s, 1930s, and 1940s this band was a fixture in the area.

By a stroke of luck, a Library of Congress recording team stumbled onto the Lusk band in the late 1940s and preserved some of its music on disc. In fact, the recording session turned into a local celebration, with most of the community turning out for the event. Some fiddle tunes played by the band were archaic favorites such as "Crippled Chicken," "Cincinnati," and "Rolling River"—tunes that have been traced back over one hundred years in White and DeKalb counties. Still another set of influential black string band musicians was the Bertram family, from Pall Mall in Fentress County. Coodge Bertram was remembered by fiddlers in the northern Cumberland as being second only to Kentuckian Leonard Rutherford for smoothness and bowing style. Brothers Andy (on guitar) and Cooney (on banjo) accompanied Coodge when he performed. Cooney played banjo in what one witness described as a "chord style," picking but fingering chords in a manner possibly learned from old minstrel shows. Coodge spent his later years in Indianapolis, only mildly aware of his reputation and influence.

Many people today associate black folk music exclusively with blues or gospel music; yet increasing evidence suggests that there once existed a rich, complex pre-blues tradition of singing and string band music among rural blacks across the South. Many musicians in the Upper Cumberland played what DeFord Bailey described as "black hillbilly music," which included banjo and fiddle pieces, square dance tunes, ballads, and sentimental songs.

Possibly the most famous black musician to come from the Cumberland was DeFord Bailey, a native of Carthage who achieved nationwide fame as the harmonica soloist on WSM's *Grand Ole Opry*. DeFord's grandfather was a state champion fiddler and his uncle was, in DeFord's words, "the best banjo player I ever knew." DeFord survived a bruising bout with infantile paralysis when he was only three, but the disease left him weak and permanently disabled. While recovering, he turned to music. He learned to play banjo and guitar well, but he excelled with the harmonica. In 1925, while working as an elevator operator in Nash-

DeFord Bailey, the legendary Harmonica Wizard. Courtesy of the Country Music Hall of Fame.

ville, DeFord attracted the attention of George D. Hay, program director for the *Grand Ole Opry*, and soon found himself playing harmonica on the program every Saturday night. For about fifteen to twenty years, he was one of the Opry's most popular performers—and the show's only black artist. He often toured with Uncle Dave Macon, who told suspicious hotel clerks that DeFord was his "valet" so DeFord could get a room in the pre–civil rights-era South. Though *Opry* managers and patrons insisted that he play his famous "imitation" pieces on the harmonica—numbers such as "Fox Chase" and train imitations such as "Pan American Blues"—DeFord knew and preserved countless examples of "black hillbilly music" on the harmonica, banjo, and guitar. Sadly, he was not allowed to record them at his few commercial recording sessions, and DeFord seldom performed them in public. It was only in later years that he allowed a few trusted friends to tape his full repertoire, and in 1999, some seventeen years after his death, his family consented to their release on a CD issued by the Tennessee Folklore Society.[12]

One of the few classic blues players to come from the area was guitarist and singer Bud Garrett. Widely hailed as the unofficial mayor of Free Hill, one of the last surviving black communities dating from before the Civil War, Garrett was known for his handmade flint marbles used in the regional game of "Roley Hole." In the 1960s, Bud had tried his luck as a professional blues singer in Nashville. Accompanied by his electric guitar and a small blues band, he covered versions of older favorites including "Who Threw the Whiskey in the Well?," "Cordele Blues," and original songs such as one about his home, "Free Hill." Rediscovered by folklorists in the 1970s, Garrett began performing at folk festivals and dances, recording his music on a number of LPs. With his zany sense of humor and high spirits, he became a favorite of white and black audiences alike.

The "backwater" image of the area has been both a blessing and a curse as far as music is concerned, for it has prevented extensive commercialization and contamination of this musical tradition, but it also has prevented the kind of documentation needed to really understand the area. In spite of that, the music remains rich, complex, rewarding, and reflective of a history and a culture that is both proud and distinctive.

NOTES

1. The Galbraith family spelled their surname in a variety of ways. Testimony from court transcript, July 7, 1909. Roane County lies due east of the Cumberland Plateau, just outside the region.

2. The history of the "Willis Mayberry" song came from Patricia Kirkeminde, "The Confession of Willis Mayberry," *Tennessee Folklore Society Bulletin* XXX (March 1964): 7–21, with additional data from the author's files.

3. Beginning in the 1970s, the Tennessee State Parks Folklife Project sent a number of folklorists and musicologists to interview people and collect songs in Putnam, Overton, White, Smith, DeKalb, Clay, Pickett, Jackson, Fentress,

Cumberland, Warren, Macon, Van Buren, Scott, and Roane counties. Among those who conducted this important research were Bob Fulcher, Elizabeth Peterson, Tom Rankin, Ray Alan, Betty Belanus, Drew Beisswenger, Lisa Moody, Brent Cantrell, and Elaine Lawless. Their work led to the Old Timers' Day Festival at Pickett State Park, the Mountaineer Folk Festival at Fall Creek Falls, the National Roley Hole Marbles Championship, and the Foothills Music and Crafts Festival at Frozen Head State Park.

4. The songs collected in Fentress and Pickett counties are a part of the Tennessee Folk Life Collection housed at the Tennessee State Library and Archives in Nashville. Bob Fulcher played a key role in collecting and cataloging the music found. He was also instrumental in starting the annual music festival at Pickett State Park.

5. Some scholars argue that the song refers to the Cumberland settlements in middle Tennessee, so the song is still open to interpretation.

6. The text of "Old Cumberland Land" appeared in Lillian Crabtree's "Folk Songs of Overton County, Tennessee" (master's thesis, Peabody College: 1935).

7. Ibid., with additional material from the research of the late Jesse Huddleston.

8. Based on research conducted by Bob Fulcher of the Tennessee Department of Environment and Conservation.

9. Information on Dee and Delta Hicks is drawn from author's interviews, as well as the research of Bob Fulcher. The quotation about singing in Cannon County comes from Robert Mason's "Life of People of Cannon County Tennessee" (Ph.d. diss., Peabody College: 1946).

10. Charles Wolfe, *A Good Natured Riot: The Birth of the Grand Ole Opry* (Nashville: Vanderbilt University Press, 1999):

11. Data on Lester Flatt from essay by Neil V. Rosenberg, in Judith McCulloh and Bill Malone, eds., *Stars of Country Music* (Urbana: University of Illinois, 1976). All other data are from author's own research.

12. Material on black musicians from author's own interviews and research, with additional material on Coodge Bertram from Bob Fulcher. Data are available on Uncle Dave Macon from author's own files, and from his essay on Macon in McCulloh and Malone.

Chapter 16

LIGHTS, CAMERA, ACTION!

The Upper Cumberland in Theater and Film

MICHAEL E. BIRDWELL

The Upper Cumberland debuted on film during the silent era. Because of early-twentieth-century fascination with the Hatfield-McCoy feud, stories of mountain romance and violence piqued the curiosity of movie-goers. A garish stereotype emerged, featuring hard-drinking, violent, isolated, and ignorant people. Unaware of the fruits of industrialization, these latter-day Luddites were clannish, unkempt, homegrown exotics. These hillbillies prided themselves in their prowess with weapons and their ability to produce and consume moonshine. As a result, a number of films were set in the Upper Cumberland region of Kentucky and Tennessee.[1]

Perhaps the first film set in the region was produced and directed by Kentucky native David Wark (D. W.) Griffith. Fascinated by the Civil War and the myth of the Lost Cause, Griffith made a number of movies about the conflict, with *Birth of a Nation* (1915) being his most famous and controversial. One of Griffith's lesser known examinations of the subject, *The Fugitive* (1910), took place in the border region of the Upper Cumberland. The film, though fictional, graphically portrayed how divided the region truly was. The principal characters, good neighbors at the film's inception, became bitter enemies as the war progressed—one choosing the Union and the other the Confederacy.

The Civil War served as the inspiration for other films, including *The Guerrilla Menace* (1913, Bison). It featured a young man joining the Confederacy, leaving his sweetheart at the mercy of a malicious tavern owner. The barkeeper encourages Union guerrillas to harass southern sympathizers along the Kentucky-Tennessee border. Guerrillas menace the girl, threatening to rape her. The young Rebel discovers what is happening and returns home. He chokes the sadistic tavern owner to death, restoring order to his community while preserving the chastity of his girlfriend.

Several films focused on the relationship between indigenous people of the Cumberland and outsiders. *Moonshine and Love* (1910, Powers Picture Plays), *A Mountain Maid* (1910, Edison), and *The Grip of Love* (1917, Universal) featured northern interlopers who came into the region. In *Moonshine and Love,* a new teacher moves to the area. He accidentally stumbles on an illicit moonshine still and is held hostage by menacing mountain rustics. A moonshiner's daughter falls in love with the captive and helps him flee. *The Grip of Love* featured another schoolteacher-moonshiner encounter. This time the teacher was a female intent on educating the public about the evils of moonshine. She represented all that was good and virtuous, while the mountain moonshiner represented all that was evil and vile. In *A Mountain Maid*, a traveling theater troupe visits the region to observe local color for a play it is rehearsing. The two lead actors go separately into the hills and unwittingly act out the plot of the play they are preparing.

The feud motif recurred in a number of films in the silent era, merging the Hatfield-McCoy conflict with other sources of inspiration. *A Tennessee Love Story* (1911, Selig) flagrantly plagiarized William Shakespeare's *Romeo and Juliet,* using the moonshine and family feuds as glue to hold the plot together. An accidental killing is blamed on Romeo, who marries Juliet in spite of the danger. She gives birth to a child in the final reel, and the feuding families agree to put their muzzle loaders away and end the feud.

Blatantly capitalizing on the Hatfield-McCoy story, *The Feud at Beaver Creek* (1914, Kay-Bee) featured the Hatfields at war with the Coles. The film was set along the Kentucky-Tennessee border, with plenty of violence and caricatured mountaineers.

Moonshine featured prominently in these early films in a number of guises. In *Madge of the Mountains* (1911), the bored son of a rich New Yorker decides to "go slumming" in the Cumberland Mountains with a team of revenuers. He enjoys destroying stills of poor mountaineers and jeers at their plight, regarding them as unworthy. During one raid, the New Yorker kills Madge's father and is wounded in the gun battle. Madge, the Christian daughter, puts her animosity aside and nurses the New Yorker back to health. Impressed with her resolve and her ability to forgive, the New Yorker asks for Madge's hand in marriage. At the film's end, she is living happily in a mansion in New York with the man who killed her father. In *The City Feller* (1913, Majestic), a New York hustler comes to the timber country of the Upper Cumberland and stumbles into a nest of moonshiners. Falling in love with a moonshiner's daughter, he is determined to "save her" from her fate. The girl is "lusted after by an uncouth and unscrupulous mountain man" with no education, no marketable skills, and no ambition. True to his desire, the New Yorker saves the moonshiner's daughter, taking her away from the decadence of the hills to the decorum of New York City life.[2]

A variation on the story occurred in the movie *In Old Tennessee* (1912, IMP), featuring Nell Gwinn as a government agent under cover in the Cumberland Mountains. She bribes a poor mountain man to betray his neighbors, but he has a change of heart and rats her out to the moonshiners. They get the drop on Nell and are about to kill her when the man she bribed steps in to save her life. The film ends with Nell and the poor mountaineer headed to the marriage altar. Another variation of that story occurred in *Tennessee* (1914, Kay-Bee), in which a revenuer with a heart of gold falls in love with a moonshiner's daughter.

Some films tried to demonstrate the disruption of industrialization. The coming of coal mines, steel mills, and large lumber operations significantly transformed the lives of the generation before World War I. One film that tried to depict the difficulties of the transition from an agrarian to an industrial economy was *In the Tennessee Hills* (1914, Kay-Bee). The story featured an industrial worker living in company housing who lost his job. Needing desperately to find work because his mother is bedridden, the situation worsens. The company landlord evicts them and the hero's mother dies as a result. The young man kills the landlord in a fit of righteous rage. The company forms a posse to hunt him down. The serious nature of the film's subject is undermined by the way in which the conflict is resolved. The hero's lover emerges in the nick of time, saving him from a lynching. In spite of its *deus-ex-machina* denouement, the film depicted serious issues facing people who lived in company towns. It pointed out problems concerning social class and the difficulty inherent in making the transformation to a market economy.

The work of Kentucky author Charles Neville Buck inspired producers at Paramount to film *The Call of the Cumberlands* (1916). An antidote to the rash of mountain films featuring inbred, moonshine-guzzling hillbillies, *The Call of the Cumberlands* argued that city life was dehumanizing and stifling. Celebrating the natural beauty of the

Cumberland region and the invigorating qualities of working outdoors, the movie attempted to change the prevailing stereotype of mountain people. They were depicted as honest, loyal, friendly, God-fearing, and patriotic. Similarly, *At Piney Ridge* (1916), adapted from Gilson Willet's stage play, depicted mountain people as hardworking and honest. Adding to the film's significance was the fact that portions of it were shot on location in Tennessee.

Another film about the Upper Cumberland was *Judith of the Cumberlands* (1916), which used a local writer's work for inspiration. Loosely based on an eponymous short story by Emma Bell Miles, the Hollywood version significantly changed the emphasis of her work. When prohibition became the law of the land, the film was reissued in 1921 with the new title, *The Moonshine Menace*. An allegorical film merging the story of Judith and Holofernes with the Hatfield-McCoy feud, the movie, with its painted backdrops and melodramatic staging, presented the Upper Cumberland as a land of violence and intrigue. Changing the location of events from Tug River Valley along the Kentucky-West Virginia border to the Tennessee-Kentucky border, *Judith of the Cumberlands,* a tortured love story, featured rival clans trying to corner the illicit alcohol trade. Judith Barrier (Helen Holmes) fell in love with Pony Card (William Brunton), a ne'er-do-well moonshiner in competition with her father on the Cumberland Plateau.

Moviegoers' first glimpse of real people in the Upper Cumberland came in the form of silent newsreels. Perhaps the first was *Through the Cumberland Mountains, Tennessee* (1913, Essanay), an early "Scenic." The film featured a glimpse of the Upper Cumberland from on board a train traveling through the region. Paramount released a documentary, *Our Southern Mountaineers* (1918), which featured common people at work and play; a portion of the movie was shot on the Cumberland Plateau.

Newsreel cameramen covered the return of Sergeant Alvin C. York to Tennessee in 1919. Greeted at the docks in Hoboken, New Jersey, by Upper Cumberland Congressman Cordell Hull, Eugene Tumulty, and members of the Tennessee Society of New York, a sheepish York grinned and waved at the throng. Newsreel cameramen followed his ticker-tape parade down Fifth Avenue, his visit to the Stock Market, and other events in New York. When he turned his back on fame and fortune to return to Pall Mall, Tennessee, cameras recorded York's journey as well. Footage was shot of the hero's humble log home, his proud mother, and the friends and family who gathered to meet him in Fentress County.

These herky-jerky flickering images, which are now part of the permanent film collection at the National Archives, represent the country's
initial impression of Tennessee's Upper Cumberland. The newsreels depicted sturdy, proud people eking out an existence. They were, for the
most part, rail thin, wiry men and women in plain clothes, uncomfortable in the glare of the spotlight. Images of York's triumphal return
were essentially lost to public memory until the Arts and Entertainment Network (A&E) reintroduced them for a segment of its *Biography*
series, *Sergeant York: A Reluctant Hero* (2000). The footage offered a
glimpse into the past, graphically depicting the region before the introduction of good roads and industrialization. What is significant about
the images is the contrast they provide for later depictions of the Upper
Cumberland.

With the return of Alvin York and the renewed focus on the Appalachian region, some filmmakers created more sympathetic portrayals
of mountain folk. In an attempt to clean up the image of the mountains
and capitalize on it in the process, Realart Pictures released *A Cumberland Romance.* Loosely based on John Fox Jr.'s *A Mountain Europa,* the
movie version examined the clash between mountaineers and outsiders
and industry versus agriculture. The filmmakers attempted to show both
sides of the conflict and not paint the culture clash in simple black and
white. The land itself became a character in the drama as the two sides
aired their differing opinions on how it should be used. The conflict
was mediated by a mild-mannered mountain preacher.

Moonshine again served as inspiration for filmmakers in post-World
War I America as the Volstead Act went into effect. *The Moonshine Trail*
(1920, Pathe), essentially a propaganda film, extolled the virtues of prohibition. Using exterior footage shot on location in Tennessee—probably Fentress County when newsreel cameras followed Alvin York
home—the film denounced alcohol production and consumption. It
argued that moonshine was responsible for ignorance, domestic abuse,
violence, insanity, and greed. Moonshine was the culprit that caused
mountaineers to be backward, superstitious, and ominous.

The newsreels from 1919 showed the nation a community of people
who endured a hardscrabble existence with dignity, but that picture
was reversed in 1925 by those earlier images that continued to be the
dominant stereotype. In 1925, John W. Butler of Macon County introduced the infamous Butler Bill. Outlawing the teaching of evolution in
Tennessee's public schools, it was passed by the legislature and reluctantly signed into law by Governor Austin Peay.[3] Butler's bill repre-

sented an attempt of local communities to maintain control over the education of their children and a resistance to centralized authority.[4] The bill created a national furor, leading to the first so-called trial of the century, and sparked a debate about the theory of evolution that continues to this day. Reaction to the Butler Bill also played a key role in resurrecting the nation's negative perception of the people of the Upper Cumberland and Tennessee. It granted a new lease to the stereotype of mountain Tennesseans as ignorant hillbillies who revel in their roles as the nation's Philistines.

Several factors collided during the summer of 1925 to cause newsreel cameramen and the national press to descend on Dayton, Tennessee. Flamboyant evangelist Billy Sunday started a religious rally at Memphis, denouncing the blasphemy of "EVIL-lution." The nascent American Civil Liberties Union (ACLU) offered free counsel in its first important test case. The nation's most famous trial lawyer, Clarence Darrow, imposed himself on the ACLU, offering his services in the only pro-bono case of his career.[5] Three-time presidential candidate and former Secretary of State William Jennings Bryan weighed in, announcing that he would defend the state's antievolution bill. The heady mixture of Billy Sunday, William Jennings Bryan, and Clarence Darrow demanded the nation's attention, inspiring "The Sage of Baltimore," H. L. Mencken—arguably the most influential journalist and cultural critic of the day—to travel to Dayton. Following close behind were newsreel cameramen from Hollywood and radio technicians from WGN, Chicago. As news of the titanic battle spread, people from the Upper Cumberland descended the plateau into Dayton, just south and east of the region.

Mencken rightly predicted that "Dayton, when it put the infidel Scopes on trial, bit off far more than it is able to chew. . . . When people recall it hereafter . . . it will be a joke town at best and infamous at worst."[6] The Scopes Trial created an image of the denizens of the Upper Cumberland and the Upland South that endures. When newsreel cameramen wandered about the streets of Dayton and its environs, they made a conscious choice in the images they filmed. Rather than focusing their cameras on men of intelligence and integrity such as Attorney General Tom Stewart, Dudley Field Malone, or Arthur Garfield Hays, they went out of their way to find filthy, ignorant grotesques worthy of a Federico Fellini film. The Scopes Trial and the images generated there laid the foundation for stereotypes of Upland southerners as clannish, inbred, incestuous, violent, ignorant, Bible-thumping pariahs.

Spencer Tracy and Fredric March in *Inherit the Wind,* which was based on the Scopes Trial.

The Scopes Trial, and the infamy it generated, led to the creation of a stage play by Jerome Lawrence and Robert E. Lee, *Inherit the Wind.* Drawing from the trial's transcripts, the play enlarged on the spectacle, making the Darrow character, Henry Drummond, a crusader out to save the South from itself. Though compelling drama, the play distorts history and makes the Scopes Trial a showdown between Bryan and Darrow. For most people, *Inherit the Wind* is historic truth rather than drama, and the majority of Americans remain blissfully ignorant of the fact that neither Bryan nor Darrow was chief counsel for the prosecution or the defense. The play has been filmed four times; the best production was Stanley Kramer's version in 1960 starring Fredric March as Matthew Harrison Brady and Spencer Tracy as Henry Drummond. Gene Kelly played E. K. Hornbeck, the acerbic character based on H. L. Mencken. In 1965, the play was filmed for television, starring Ed Begley as Brady and Melvyn Douglas as Drummond. In 1998 and 1999, two very interesting and well-made versions were also produced for television. The 1998 installment, inspired by renewed debates over the theory of evolution, captured the circus atmosphere of the trial and featured two fine performances. Kirk Douglas played Matthew Harrison Brady with more compassion and intelligence than Fredric March (who was made up to look exactly like Bryan), squaring off against a hard-bitten, world-weary Jason Robards as Drummond; Darren McGavin portrayed a more believable Hornbeck. The 1999 version, also quite watchable, starred George C. Scott as a fiery, dogmatic Brady doing battle with a more sensitive, less strident Drummond, played by Jack Lemmon.

Newsreel footage reemerged in 2002 with the broadcast of *Monkey Trial*, a documentary in PBS's *American Experience* series. The archival footage graphically demonstrated the cameramen's delight in photographing a gallery of mountain weirdos and Judge John T. Raulston's love of attention. While the film attempted to strike a balance and provide a broader context for the events that unfolded in Dayton in 1925, it continued the focus on Bryan and Darrow, omitting the importance of attorneys Tom Stewart, Dudley Field Malone, Arthur Garfield Hays, Herbert Hicks, and his brother Sue Hicks.[7]

Filmmakers generally avoided the Upper Cumberland during the Great Depression, but the seeds of lasting community theater were sown during that period. Though there had been a tradition of informal public entertainment in earlier times—tall tales from the frontier era, womanless weddings, medicine shows, and even vaudeville at the turn of the century—formal theater was rare. Franklin Delano Roosevelt's New Deal made theater available to the common man for the first time. In 1935, under Federal One of the Works Progress Administration (WPA), the Federal Theatre Project (FTP) was established. Under the direction of Hallie Flanagan, its mission was to make theater available to the masses while promoting a distinctly American culture. The FTP encouraged creation of local theaters, staged "Living Newspapers," and sent traveling theater companies to the hinterlands. One "Living Newspaper," *Power*, by Arthur Arent, extolled the virtues of the Tennessee Valley Authority (TVA) and was performed on numerous occasions throughout the region.

In 1938, at the behest of Undersecretary of Agriculture Rexford Tugwell, Hallie Flanagan dispatched members of her staff to the Cumberland Homestead Project near Crossville.[8] Former Memphis opera singer Margaret Valliant and her assistant, Sandy Jeffers, arrived at Homesteads with a mission—to restore order to the beleaguered project. After spending time in Pleasant Hill, the Homesteads, and other villages in the vicinity, Valliant began work on a play meant to unify the factions tearing the planned community apart. Conducting interviews with project families and local residents, Valliant collaborated with Oren Metzger. They wrote a play with musical interludes, *New Ground*, which celebrated the frontier heritage of the Cumberland Plateau and the promise of Cumberland Homesteads. Members of the Homesteads community built the stage and sets for the open-air amphitheater. Likewise, Homesteaders performed in the play. Edna Gossage Blue, who later became a potent force in Cumberland County, made her stage debut in *New Ground*.[9]

In 1940 Jesse Lasky, former executive at Paramount, ventured to Pall Mall to persuade Alvin C. York to allow him to make a film based on his life. After months of negotiations, York relented in March of 1941. Originally, the film was to be about York's struggles to bring education to Tennessee after his return from World War I, rather than his exploits on the battlefield. That changed drastically as world events grew more dire. Starring Gary Cooper as Alvin York, the film *Sergeant York* (1941) became an urgent call for American preparedness. The film featured York as a resolute, religious man, firm in his convictions. He had to be convinced that war is sometimes necessary, a message intended to convert the audience from pacifism to belligerence.[10]

Though *Sergeant York* (1941) is most remembered for Gary Cooper's

Gary Cooper in his Oscar-winning role as Sergeant Alvin C. York. Courtesy of the Sergeant York Patriotic Foundation.

Academy Award–winning performance, it also perpetuated stereotypes created at the Scopes Trial. Backward mountain rustics represented quaint anomalies in an industrialized world. Denizens of cinematic Pall Mall harkened back to the images of mountaineers seen in Scopes Trial newsreels. They talked funny, dressed funny, and acted peculiar, but were not threatening. York, the Daniel Boone of the machine age, was a fish out of water when removed from his native environment and thrust into training at Camp Gordon, Georgia, or on the battlefield at Chatel-Chehery, France. Soldiers initially poked fun at him, but ultimately looked to him to save them. Cooper spoke in stilted language far different from the polished speech of the real Sergeant York, who was a gifted orator. True salvation for the movie character York came in two significant forms. First, audiences witnessed a drunken York struck by a lightning bolt that demolished his muzzle loader, convincing him to change his ways and accept Fundamentalist Christianity. More important, York's second conversion came from outlanders who forced him out of his native Tennessee into a larger, more cosmopolitan world. Major George Buxton acted as York's avatar, awakening him to the broader world and its myriad possibilities, leading him away from the superstition of the hills toward a new promised land. *Sergeant York* treated the folk of the Upper Cumberland as interesting curiosities out of step with the rest of the nation, in total awe of such things as subways, telephones, and indoor plumbing.[11]

Though the Warner Bros. biopic of Alvin York proved extremely popular, creating a lasting public perception of the mythic hero, his exploit served as inspiration for two other films. Joseph P. Kennedy produced a curious film, *The Judgement of the Hills* (1927), for R-C pictures. Directed by Leo Meehan, the film centers on two brothers from the Upper Cumberland, Tad and Brant. A wastrel and public nuisance, Brant receives his draft notice and reports reluctantly to go fight in World War I. Chafing under the restrictions of the military life, Brant shines on the battlefield. A natural warrior, Brant returns home a national hero. Unlike Sergeant York, however, Brant returns to his life as a hellion, leading a life of dissipation. The film reinforced the cultural stereotype of mountaineer as no-account, condemning alcohol as the source of the region's myriad woes. The theme of alcohol as social ill is odd since Kennedy made his considerable fortune in the illicit booze trade.

During the Vietnam War, York's story was trotted out yet again, with another twist. *No Drums, No Bugles* (1971), though set during the

Civil War, consciously evoked York's own struggle over whether war is ever justified. Martin Sheen played the mountaineer trying to come to grips with the moral ramifications of war. A thinly veiled polemic against the war in Southeast Asia, Sheen's character undergoes a different conversion than York, to far different results.

During the 1960s, a raft of films and television shows emerged, capitalizing on the stereotype of the mountaineer. Movies such as *Li'l Abner* and television shows such as *The Andy Griffith Show* and *The Beverly Hillbillies* toyed with the prevailing image. Capitalizing on the national fascination with mountain culture, MGM released *Kissin' Cousins* in 1964. Starring Elvis Presley in two roles—a good mountain boy and his evil doppelganger—the film showcased Elvis's musical ability. Supposedly set in the Cumberland Mountains, the thinly plotted film's title suggested mountain incest while buttressing negative cultural images of the region.

In 1963, Hollywood and Broadway came to the Upper Cumberland in a new and influential way. Paul Crabtree, whose wife, Mary, had relatives in Cumberland County, moved temporarily to Crossville that year.[12] The Crabtrees left Hollywood for the Cumberland Plateau because it was more affordable than California and more conducive to writing. A veteran of stage, screen, and television, Crabtree came to Tennessee to complete a book. The publication, *Doby Creek*, was a loosely veiled fictitious memoir of his childhood in Virginia.[13]

While working on his novel, Crabtree was approached by Cumberland County School Superintendent O. C. Stewart, who asked him to do theater with the Crossville school children.[14] After some consideration of the rather vague request, Crabtree decided to stage a play that he had co-written with Sister Thomas Gertrude, entitled *The Perils of Pinocchio*.

Cumberland County Playhouse. Photo by the editors.

First produced at the Rosarian Academy in Palm Beach, the play proved to be an excellent choice for his first theatrical event in Cumberland County. According to Crabtree's son Jim, "Pinocchio set the town on its ear. They wanted to know how to keep it going."[15] A corporation was formed with the intention of perpetuating theater on the plateau. The organization, with the full cooperation of Crabtree, embarked on building a permanent theater facility, the Cumberland County Playhouse.[16]

Crabtree used local actors, musicians, and artisans from the region, staging well-known plays and original works. One of his most enduring productions was the musical *Tennessee, USA*, which opened at the Playhouse in July 1965. Actors and technicians rehearsed while the building was completed, running up and down gravel aisles amid the din of rattling hammers and buzzing saws, and hundreds of community volunteers pitched in to lend a hand. *Tennessee, USA* sent the fictional Willoughby family backward in time to witness key events in Tennessee history. Led by the Daniel Boone-like Johnny Timberlake, the Willoughbys learn the importance of history, regional identity, and Tennessee's place in the nation. Johnny Timberlake was the first professional role for Bob Gunton, who first portrayed the frontier guide. A frequent guest at the Playhouse, Gunton went on to a solid career in films such as *Glory, Born on the Fourth of July, Matewan, The Shawshank Redemption, Elvis Meets Nixon,* and *Patch Adams.*

After *Tennessee, USA*, Crabtree wrote *An Evening with Paul Crabtree* (based on his novel *Doby Creek*) and *Step to the Music.* The first large-scale musical after *Tennessee, USA, Step to the Music* was a story about growing up and making one's life successful. Paul Crabtree wrote, directed, and produced shows for the first six years of the Cumberland County Playhouse's existence. He then moved on to be the first creative director of Opryland, where he wrote, directed, and produced all of the shows at the theme park for

Paul Crabtree. Courtesy of Amy Woods.

its first three years. His work at
Opryland continues to influence live
entertainment at theme parks across
the United States.

Creative direction and management of Cumberland County Playhouse fell under the auspices of
Crabtree's wife, Mary. After Mary's
several years at the helm of the theater, her son Jim joined her to operate the facility and its programming.[17]
The Playhouse continues to be a vital force in the region, making it
possible for people to work on or
offstage with professional actors and
technicians. Jim has continued his
father's legacy of promoting local
history, writing and staging an on-

Mary Crabtree. Courtesy of Amy Woods.

going series of plays. His first venture, in 1984, was *Homestead Album*,
which dramatized the story of the Cumberland Homesteads. That was
followed by *Second Sons*, about the Victorian utopian village of Rugby.
Tennessee Strings celebrated regional music and its influence on the nationally popular country, bluegrass, and rock and roll genres. *Good
Neighbors* staged the life of the Pickett County native who served the
longest term as secretary of state, Cordell Hull. *Wings over Appalachia*
once again paid tribute to the musical legacy of the Cumberlands; it was
based on the songs of Billy Ed Wheeler. *The Cumberland Trail* resur-
rected *Tennessee, USA's* Willoughby family, sending them on a new historic journey, once again guided by Johnny Timberlake. In the future,
Jim Crabtree intends to stage plays about Emma Bell Miles (entitled
Spirit of the Mountains), Dr. May Cravath Wharton, and Sergeant Alvin
C. York.

Out of humble beginnings, the Cumberland County Playhouse has
flourished. It inspired local theater throughout the region and continues to introduce children to the magic of live drama. For many children
and adults in the region, the Playhouse was their first introduction to
live theater. The Playhouse fosters and cultivates area talent and provides an invaluable service to the community economically and culturally. By 2001, the Playhouse accounted for 1 percent of the jobs in
Cumberland County and was the largest, most active, and most influen-

tial theater organization in Tennessee. It has touring companies in Memphis, Nashville, and Knoxville, and ongoing relationships with the Ryman Auditorium in Nashville and the Bijou Theatre in Knoxville.

In 1970, the Upper Cumberland became, for the first time since the Scopes Trial, the site of film production. Veteran filmmaker John Frankenheimer, the director of such classic films as *Birdman of Alcatraz, The Manchurian Candidate,* and *Seven Days in May,* set up headquarters at Cookeville's new Holiday Inn for the production of *I Walk the Line.* Using the eponymous novel by Madison Jones as source material, Frankenheimer told reporters for the Nashville *Tennessean* and Cookeville's *Herald-Citizen* that the film would feature local inhabitants and locations to create a sense of verisimilitude. The film boasted a first-rate cast, including Gregory Peck, Tuesday Weld, Estelle Parsons, Ralph Meeker, and Charles Durning. The cast would interact with locals so they could accurately imitate the regional patois on film. Though people of the Upper Cumberland rolled out the red carpet for Hollywood, they turned resentful upon the film's release, for the movie not only dredged up negative images worthy of Scopes Trial newsreels, it expanded on them, making a mockery of the area and its inhabitants.

The plot revolved around moonshiner Carl McCain (Ralph Meeker), who was willing to prostitute his daughter Alma (Tuesday Weld) to the local sheriff (Gregory Peck) to protect his illegal whiskey operation. Peck, no longer the matinee idol of his youth, played against type in the picture as a flawed middle-aged man who succumbs to his baser desires. Tuesday Weld, trying to expand beyond her television persona on the *Dobie Gillis Show,* played a bad girl with a heart of coal. Contrasts between the life of Sheriff Tawes and the McCains were graphically manifested in the houses, vehicles, and dress of the characters. Tawes lived in a comfortable, well-appointed home, upset only by the persistent whining of his wife, Ellen (Estelle Parsons). The McCains lived in the former mining community of Davidson (a near ghost town) in a rundown hovel lit by kerosene lamps and heated by a decrepit wood stove.[18] They drove a beat-up 1950 Chevrolet pickup truck while the Tawes family rode in newer vehicles of relative luxury. The McCains were profane, filthy, and backward. Cookeville teenager Freddy McCloud played Tuesday Weld's illiterate little brother who violates the law with impunity, driving without a license and getting drunk on his dad's product.

Filmed entirely on location in Smith, Overton, Fentress, Jackson, White, and Putnam counties, the film featured the Jackson County Court-

house and Center Hill Lake as key locations. Director Frankenheimer
went out of his way to find the absolute worst the region could offer, in
contrast with the Upper Cumberland's natural beauty. The movie contains images of rusted cars on blocks sitting derelict on people's lawns.
Gratuitous images of tumble-down homes on Gum Spring Mountain,
south of Sparta, featured pigs frolicking in front yards among rusting
washing machines and other refuse.

I Walk the Line could have been an intriguing film about class bias,
marginalization of the underclass, sexual predators, and criminalization
of a long-time cultural product; but it is lurid melodrama instead. Gregory Peck's Sheriff Tawes is Humbert Humbert in uniform to Tuesday
Weld's mountain Lolita. Frankenheimer's approach to the movie is predi-
cated on assumptions that pedophilia, moonshining, and incest are the
family values that keep kith and kin together in the Upper Cumberland. Carl McCain not only uses his daughter Alma to seduce and black-
mail Sheriff Tawes, but he proves that "Daddy loves her best," as he is
an incestuous pederast who uses his daughter for his own pleasure.
When, at the film's climax, Alma must choose between Tawes and
McCain, she violently chooses her father. Sinking a hay hook in Sheriff
Tawes's shoulder, Alma jumps into the crowded pickup with her family. The defeated sheriff stands in the middle of the gravel road, watching as the mountain nymph and her family drive off into the wilderness.
Justice is a mockery and the wild mountaineers are untamable, Darwin-
ian throwbacks, just a step above savagery. Johnny Cash's song *I Walk
the Line* was the movie's ironic theme song. Steven W. Gwilt, after watching the film, commented that if Sheriff Tawes had kept a closer watch
on his crotch, he might not have gotten into the mess that ensued.[19]

After the production and release of *I Walk the Line,* people of the
Upper Cumberland grew wary of filmmakers who ventured into the
region. In 1983, Governor Lamar Alexander took a cue from the state of
North Carolina and established the Tennessee Film, Tape and Music
Commission (now the Tennessee Film, Entertainment and Music Commission). Its purpose was to encourage location shooting in Tennessee
and generate additional revenue for the state. Because Tennessee uses
an open-shop labor policy, films could be produced at a fraction of the
costs in California, and for a time, filmmaking flourished in the Volunteer State. During the Alexander administration, a number of films were
shot in Tennessee, some of them in the Upper Cumberland.

Director John Guillermin chose Fall Creek Falls State Park in Van
Buren County for the production of the ironic feature *King Kong Lives*

(1986). The filmmaker wanted to take advantage of the natural beauty of the park. A temporary swinging bridge was erected between two of the park's bluffs, with the falls visible in the background. Crucial to a few action sequences in the film, stunt men tossed dummies to the ground below. Rangers and naturalists intervened during the middle of the shooting and eventually evicted the cast and crew from the state natural area. The heavy equipment—cranes, semi-trucks, electrical generators, and trailers for the cast—created havoc in the park and threatened rare flora. Ranger Stuart Carroll alerted the Tennessee Department of Environment and Conservation that the crew intended to plant a series of explosives along the cavern floor. This led to the cessation of filming, and the production had to be completed elsewhere.

Cookeville once again found itself in thrall to Hollywood in the summer of 1994, when the Holiday Inn acted as the home to not one, but two film crews. In both instances, Tennessee's Upper Cumberland was used as an exotic film location, representing the jungles of Colombia and India. Sylvester Stallone, James Woods, and Sharon Stone starred in the action film *The Specialist,* directed by Luis Llosa. Though the bulk of the movie takes place in Miami, initial sequences of the film that provide the context for the story's conflict were shot in White and Warren counties at Rock Island State Park. Palm trees and other vegetation were brought in by set dressers to make the location look like the Colombian jungle. One sequence, filmed on the Collins River Dam, featured an explosion rigged to kill henchmen of a Colombian warlord. Detonation of the bomb caused a Land Rover to careen off the dam and into the water below. A fight scene between Stallone and Woods was also filmed at Rock Island. The co-stars battled it out on the rocks beneath the dam where the explosion occurred.

The other film, which had a longer shooting schedule and created more interaction with the local populace, was the live-action version of Rudyard Kipling's *The Jungle Book,* directed by Stephen Sommers. Filming took place at a number of locations, including Lost Creek Cave in White County and Fall Creek Falls, and included the use of exotic animals. It starred an impressive cast—Jason Scott Lee, Cary Elwes, Sam Neill, and John Cleese—who made themselves at home in Cookeville and its surroundings. Cary Elwes visited local nightspots and watering holes, while ex-Monty Python trouper John Cleese spent untold hours away from the set in Wal-Mart, fascinated by the ongoing spectacle. For filming of *The Jungle Book,* large tropical plants were air-craned into Fall Creek Falls State Park, and Lost Creek Cave acted as a key location throughout the shooting. Director Sommers cultivated friendly relations with local inhabitants and allowed citizens to visit the set during production. He employed members of TTU's Sigma Alpha Epsilon fraternity as crewmen.

In 1999, two film crews came to the Upper Cumberland. Joe Johnson directed *October Sky,* the film version of Homer Hickam Jr.'s, memoir *Rocket Boys.* Coalfield, in Morgan County, acted as the central location, but filming also occurred in Cumberland, Roane, Scott, and Anderson counties. Frank Darabont chose a few Upper Cumberland locations for Stephen King's *The Green Mile,* which was filmed primarily at the old state penitentiary in Nashville. The chase sequence, in which John Coffey (Michael Clarke Duncan) is apprehended, took place in DeKalb County on the Caney Fork River. Likewise, country sequences were filmed near Chestnut Mound, Temperance Hall, and other locations in DeKalb and Smith counties. Local folk were used as extras and small speaking parts.

Positive images of people of the Cumberland have emerged on documentary television. A&E produced *Dear Home* (1999), featuring correspondence of doughboys from World War I. A Cookeville native, Albert Perrine Smith, whose father, Rutledge Smith, was in charge of the draft for the entire southeastern region of the United States, was prominently featured throughout the program. Albert Smith's poignant letters to his family provided excellent insight into the war and his home region.[20]

The Kentucky and Tennessee regions of the Upper Cumberland were also featured in a compelling two-hour documentary for PBS, *People Like Us* (2001). Produced by Louis Alvarez and New American Media, the program examined social class in America. The segment "Gettin' above Your Raisin'," featured Kentuckians and Tennesseans, focusing on the story of Dana Felty. The segment examined class tensions existing in the Upper Cumberland and what one generation expects of the next. It explored the importance of place in defining people and their values. The film examined cultural stereotypes in a sensitive, yet humorous way, comparing people of the Cumberland with folks from the Hamptons, New York City, and other parts of the United States.

Over the years, Hollywood movies and television have provided opportunities for talented people from the Upper Cumberland. Sparta native and Grand Ole Opry star Lester Flatt and his partner Earl Scruggs turned to television to expand their popularity. On September 26, 1962, a new situation comedy aired on CBS. It featured a song with lyrics by Paul Henning, the show's producer, sung by Lester Flatt, as well as an ending theme also performed by Flatt and Scruggs. The "Ballad of Jed

Clampett" became one of the most recognizable themes in television history, and was heard weekly from 1962 to 1971 on *The Beverly Hillbillies*. Flatt and Scruggs made annual cameo appearances, playing themselves over the span of the show's prime-time existence. Lester did most of the speaking, while Earl generally remained mute.

In addition to Lester Flatt, the Upper Cumberland had another connection with *The Beverly Hillbillies*. The Clampetts originally hailed from Bugtussle, a real community in Macon County. The connection with *The Beverly Hillbillies* led to Flatt and Scruggs providing the theme music for *Petticoat Junction*. Flatt and Scruggs made an indelible mark on the cultural landscape, in addition to television, when they agreed to provide music for Arthur Penn's watershed film *Bonnie and Clyde* (1967). Flatt and Scruggs' rendition of "Foggy Mountain Breakdown" underscored key action sequences and became the film's unofficial theme song. Of the thirteen songs on the *Bonnie and Clyde* soundtrack, Flatt and Scruggs performed six.

Though the Upper Cumberland has generally been depicted in a better light in the media since the mid-1980s, events in 1998 cast another dark shadow and put the region back in the public eye. Popular state senator Tommy Burks was running for reelection against a peculiar candidate. His opponent, Byron Looper, the tax assessor for Putnam County, had visions of grandeur and legally changed his middle name

Flatt & Scruggs. Courtesy of Roni Christian.

to "Low Tax." Most people did not take Looper seriously, and the campaign he ran bordered on the ridiculous. Weeks prior to the election, Looper in desperation murdered the incumbent. Once again the media descended on the Upper Cumberland, and just as the newsreel cameramen had done at the Scopes Trial, journalists from CNN and the national networks sought out people who fit their preconceived notions. Rather than interviewing intelligent, thoughtful people, the media chose rustics who were an embarrassment to the community. As the Looper case dragged on, images of snaggletoothed, incest-ridden, gun-toting, Bible thumpers reemerged and calcified once again. By 2002, most people believed that the Looper debacle had faded into the distance. It had not. In an installment of A&E's popular true crime series *The Justice Files*, host Bill Kurtis revived the Burks murder, showing footage from the crime scene that had not been previously witnessed by the public at large. Curtis provided Looper a forum, where he continued to plead his innocence while asserting that the Upper Cumberland was filled with nincompoops and incompetents, and that he alone was wise. Looper emerged from the show a rather pathetic narcissist, but the filmmakers upheld his assertion that the region is one filled with *Homo Neanderthalensis*.[21]

The diversity of the Upper Cumberland, its people, and its landscape will no doubt continue to attract and inspire dramatists. The region's storytelling tradition and its rich history offer a trove of untapped resources rife with possibility. Stereotypes will continue to be perpetuated, but new paradigms are waiting in the wings.

NOTES

1. J. W. Williamson, *Hillbillyland: What the Movies Did to the Mountains and the Mountains Did to the Movies* (Chapel Hill: University of North Carolina Press, 1995): 1–20. See also, Altina Waller, *Feud: Hatfields, McCoys, and Social Change in Appalachia, 1860–1900* (Chapel Hill: University of North Carolina Press, 1988).

2. Quoted in the description of the film in the filmography compiled by Jerry Williamson at the Appalachian State University Web site: appstate/apcoll/filmography.html

3. Butler offered the bill in response to the governor's General Education Bill, which called for the expansion of public education and more oversight from the Tennessee Department of Education.

4. Jeanette Keith, *Country People in the New South: Tennessee's Upper Cumberland* (Chapel Hill: University of North Carolina Press, 1995): 184–85, 203, 205–9.

5. Edward J. Larson, *Summer for the Gods: The Scopes Trial and America's Continuing Debate over Science and Religion* (Cambridge, Mass.: Harvard University Press, 1997): 28, 44, 47, 54–55, 65, 73, 100–102.

6. H. L. Mencken, "Tennessee in the Frying Pan," *The Baltimore Evening Sun* (July 20, 1925): 1. Though largely forgotten, most of Mencken's comments about Dayton and the Cumberland region were complimentary. His barbs were saved for publicity seekers, hypocrites, religious fanatics, cranks, and the Tennessee legislature. Mencken attacked the ignorant, who wandered off the Cumberland Plateau to get a glimpse of William Jennings Bryan or to participate in the pandemonium created by the circus-like atmosphere of the trial. The "yokels from the hills," or "rustics," were drawn to Dayton because their faith was on trial, and their pastors sent them to defend it against infidels from the outside [H. L. Mencken, "Mencken Likens Trial to a Religious Orgy, with Defendant a Beelzebub," *The Baltimore Evening Sun* (July 11, 1925): 1]. It was not until July 14 that Mencken called those curious people "Hill billies,"[sic]—a term of derision that has stuck ever since. The next day Mencken coined another phrase that became part of the national consciousness, referring to Tennessee as the "buckle of the Bible Belt" [H. L. Mencken, "Darrow's Eloquent Appeal Wasted on Ears that Heed Only Bryan, Says Mencken," *The Baltimore Evening Sun* (July 14, 1925): 1; "Law and Freedom, Mencken Discovers, Yield Place to Holy Writ in Rhea County," *The Baltimore Evening Sun* (July 15,1925):1].

One of the worst malefactors was former Cookevillian and presiding judge in the Scopes Trial—John T. Raulston. An incompetent who should have recused himself from the trial because of his open bias for Bryan, Raulston played a key role in the creation of the negative stereotype of southern mountaineers. Raulston, like Judge Ito in the infamous O. J. Simpson case, ruled that having radio and newsreel cameras in the courtroom would not in any way compromise the trial. He craved publicity and loved being the center of attention, offering to pose for photographs or give interviews, reveling in the spotlight. Over the objections of the defense, he opened each day's proceedings with prayer and made a number of juridical errors with apparent glee [Larson, 109, 142]. Mencken found Raulston a repellent "bucolic ass" and consistently referred to him as "Dogberry," an unctuous character from William Shakespeare's *Much Ado about Nothing*.

7. Sue Hicks was the inspiration for Johnny Cash's song "A Boy Named Sue."

8. Tugwell was an original member of Roosevelt's "Brain Trust" and a former professor of economics at Columbia University.

9. Interview with Jim Crabtree (Crossville, Tenn.: Cumberland County Playhouse, May 29, 2002).

10. Michael Birdwell, *Celluloid Soldiers: Warner Bros. Campaign Against Nazism* (New York: New York University Press, 1999): 107–30.

11. For more about the film *Sergeant York*, see the essay "Gobble Like a Turkey," chapter 9 in this volume.

12. Mary Crabtree's mother, Eula Ducy, was from Crossville; Mary grew up in Pittsburgh, Pennsylvania, but spent her summers in Crossville as a child.

Mary's grandparents were Seward C. [S. C.] and Eva Bishop. S. C. Bishop founded the *Crossville Chronicle* and acted as its first editor. Paul Crabtree was from Pulaski, Virginia.

13. Interview with Amy Crabtree Woods (Cookeville, Tenn.: August 18, 2002)

14. Stewart had been approached by Ethel Metcalfe and the owner of Hotel Taylor, Joe Ed Hodges, persuading him to ask Crabtree if he would do something theatrical with the children. The Hodges had been friends with the Crabtrees for a time, and knew them when the Crabtrees lived in New York.

15. Interview with Jim Crabtree (Crossville, Tenn.: Cumberland County Playhouse, May 29, 2002).

16. The first board of directors included Margaret Harrison, C. C. Simonton, Carroll Davenport, Moses E. Dorton, and Bettey Evans.

17. Mary Crabtree actually operated the theater for a longer period than her husband. The Playhouse has been an important family venture, for many of the children have acted, sung, directed, designed, and painted sets for the theater, including Amy Crabtree Woods and her husband, Rick Woods, and Abigail Crabtree.

18. The Upper Cumberland Institute and Cookeville's PBS station WCTE produced a four-part history of the Wilder-Davidson coal mining region under the direction of Dr. Homer Kemp and Steve Boots in 1985. The series, *The Wilder-Davidson Story*, incorporated interviews with former miners, union and anti-union sympathizers, National Guardsmen, and residents, and proved quite popular in the region.

19. Steven W. Gwilt, Elderhostel at the Armor Hotel, Red Boiling Springs, Tennessee (November 9, 1999).

20. Albert Smith's son, Albert Smith Jr., of Lexington, Kentucky, has been a prominent journalist, served as the head of the Appalachian Regional Commission, and the moderator of the KET program *Comment on Kentucky*.

21. Cookeville native Lucy Jane Webb left the Upper Cumberland to pursue an acting career. She began as a stand-up comedian in Los Angeles and went on to be a cast member of the television series *Private Benjamin*. When that series was canceled, Webb joined the cast of HBO's sketch comedy *Not Necessarily the News* in 1983. She married actor Kevin Pollack and has acted in *National Lampoons' The Don's Analyst* (1997), *Outside Ozona* (1998), and *The Story of Us* (1999). Another Cookevillian, Sidney Lunn, worked on a number of Hollywood films as a set dresser. Though she worked on *The Green Mile* and *The Last Castle* at the former state penitentiary, much of her craft has been done in conjunction with films made by the Coen Brothers, Ethan and Joel. Lunn worked on *Fargo* and *The Big Lebowski,* among others. Unable to assist them when making *O Brother, Where Art Thou* (because she was working on *The Last Castle*), the Coen Brothers included a reference to Sidney Lunn and the Upper Cumberland in their script, when a character mentions that he is from Cookeville.

Chapter 17

"BRING YOUR OWN TOWEL"

Nudism, Federal Courts, and the Timberline Lodge

ALLISON BARRELL

Nudity, as typically viewed by American society, is usually regarded as a taboo topic, often equated with pornography and prostitution. The problem with nudism in American society is one of perception, and nudists tend to be condemned as perverts. There are more than three hundred nudist camps in forty-one states in the United States today, where some 300,000 Americans claim membership.[1] There are over one million practicing nudists worldwide.[2] This means that there could be a nudist in line at the local grocery store, or maybe playing the organ at the Baptist Church on Sunday. Practicing nudists can be found teaching in public schools, in the halls of the U.S. Congress, and throughout American society.

Nudism has deep historic roots, and the idea of being nude for recreational purposes is not a new or trendy phenomenon. The philosophy is thousands of years old, going back to ancient cultures as diverse as the Japanese, Romans, Hawaiians, and Greeks. These people did not view nudity as gross or vulgar, for it was the Greeks above all who set the standards for beauty and proportion. The Greeks commonly practiced nonsexual, social nudism.[3]

Exposing skin has always been a topic of great discussion in this country, and despite that, some citizens simply prefer to practice their right to be nude. This is the case in Cumberland County, Tennessee, specifically at the Timberline Lodge Resort. Established in the mid-1960s, the Timberline Lodge is nestled in the heart of the Cumberland Plateau. One resident complained, "There's a bunch of crazy people running around naked outside Crossville. They take part in orgies and who knows what all. I've heard that they swap wives and just do all sorts of disgusting stuff."[4] The reference to the nudists in the woods is in regard to Timberline Lodge, Tennessee's oldest clothing optional facility. It may strike one as unusual that a nudist camp exists on the Cumberland Plateau in the buckle of the Bible Belt, but Timberline's history is interesting and significant.

Though early pioneers called the plateau "the Barrens," and it developed late industrially and commercially, it was the remoteness of the plateau that made it appealing. It is a place of rugged beauty on a par with the Great Smoky Mountains, but without the traffic and overcrowding. After the construction of Interstate 40, which allowed for greater travel and easier access, Cumberland County flourished, encouraging tourism and the creation of retirement communities. Its average elevation is 1,980 feet, and its average temperature is a mild 54° F. It is the perfect location for a relaxing vacation, which includes the "Timberline experience" for a number of enthusiasts.

A nudist movement of sorts existed in Cumberland County as early as the late 1800s, long before open nudity was even an option in America. A well-educated group from Indiana came to the area to grow apples, calling their settlement Pomona. A woman from this group, who was particularly interested in health and well-being, encouraged the ladies of Pomona to join her, rising early in the morning to dance nude in the apple orchards, hoping that the dance would assist the apple-growing process. Prurient interests encouraged males to take the train from Monterey to Pomona, where they might espy the naked lasses bouncing around. Other Peeping Toms, Dicks, and Harrys hid in the woods to watch the ladies dance.[5] A painting in the Timberline Lodge office is named "The Ladies of the Fields of Pomona." It depicts barely clothed women dancing in an apple orchard. Despite apples and nude dancing, Pomona failed to thrive, though remnants of the establishment remain. There is a road named Pomona, and prints of the picture of the dancing women can be found in many stores throughout Cumberland County.[6]

Though they do not grow apples, members and visitors of Timberline Lodge and Resort share a common bond with Pomona. At Timberline, women, men, and children are all welcomed and encouraged to be free from clothing. The original owners who established the lodge consisted of a group of twelve to fifteen people from Nashville, Knoxville, and Oak Ridge, Tennessee. Participants in this founding group were highly educated professionals engaged in stressful jobs. Among the founders were employees from Oak Ridge National Laboratory with

Billboard advertising Timberline Resort on Peavine Road in Cumberland County, Tennessee. Photo by the author.

PhDs—engineers, scientists, and teachers. They sought a place where they could enjoy outdoor activities, from camping to skinny-dipping. Originally, they investigated some property in east Tennessee, in Union County, informing the owner that they intended to create a clothing-optional retreat. They were turned away, in spite of their academic and working credentials. Bea Terry recalled sarcastic newspaper articles published in Knoxville-area newspapers about people who practiced nudism. Founders of Timberline were accused of everything from atheistic hedonism to behavior just short of child molestation.[7]

The question remains: How does a facility like Timberline function within the law? Public nudity clearly violates the law. One cannot go to Wal-Mart and romp naked up and down the aisles. Nor can a person go to a restaurant and sit unclothed on a chair. Public nudity is seen as a potential threat to the health of the nation, especially at restaurants or sporting events. Topless bars and all-nude bars cater to a specific clientele with the intention of eroticizing nudity, which is clearly not the mission of Timberline. Families visit Timberline, not lap dancers. Timberline fought for its existence against formidable odds.

Opposition failed to deter Timberline's founders from meeting for one year in an area east of Knoxville; but the most serious challenge to the nudist camp came in a federal court case on January 12, 1966. The case, *Tennessee Outdoor Club, Inc., and the American Sunbathing Association, Inc.* vs. *Frank G. Clement, Individually and as the Governor of the State of Tennessee, George F. McCanless, Individually and as the Attorney General of the State of Tennessee, and Archie Weaver, Individually and as the Sheriff of Knox County*, was argued before three judges of the District Court in Knoxville.

The plaintiffs argued that Tennessee's law against nudist practices was unconstitutional. Chapter 176 of the *Public Acts of 1965* made it "unlawful for any person, firm or corporation to operate or carry on, or engage in the operation of a nudist colony." The plaintiffs complained that the act was vague and indefinite; that it violated their rights of expression and association; that it deprived them of property rights and rights of privacy; and that it infringed on their individual liberties.[8] The plaintiffs argued that not only were their First Amendment rights trampled on, but their Fourth, Ninth, and Fourteenth Amendment constitutional guarantees as well. Criminalizing nudity precipitated a sharp decline in visitation to Timberline because members, who were professionals in the main, feared having their reputations sullied. Tennessee's antinudism law caused an immediate decrease in the number of members to the Tennessee Outdoor Club and led to a decrease in membership fees in the American Sunbathing Association in the Volunteer State.[9]

After hearing arguments in the case, the three judges agreed with the plaintiffs against the defendants—Governor Frank Clement, Attorney General George McCanless, and Knox County Sheriff Archie Weaver. They found the Tennessee law poorly written and vague to the point that "if literally construed, would prevent nudism . . . in the home." Likewise, the statute failed to define the parameters of a nudist colony or how many people it required.[10] Judge Darr argued that "the operators of nudist colonies and persons engaged in nudist practices are constitutionally entitled to the right of privacy, which is [a] liberty protected by the Due Process Clause of the Fourteenth Amendment, rendering this statute invalid. . . . It is quite clear that nudists have the constitutional freedom to engage in association for the advancement of beliefs and ideas. . . . I can come to no other conclusion but that nudists have a constitutional right to practice their belief in the manner heretofore indicated."[11] Darr closed his concurring opinion with this addendum:

> Lest I be heralded as the patron saint of nudism, let me add this hasty remark. It seems in fact something of a mystery why those

who engage in its strange practices are willing to suffer both the stings of public outraged public opinion and voracious, ravenous insects in order to pursue their illusory rewards. To my personal way of thinking the theories of nudism are not only foolish but down right [sic] distasteful and indelicate. . . . [I]t is the particular duty of the judiciary to protect individuals and minorities in their constitutional rights even though their beliefs and activities may be heretical or unpopular.[12]

In short, the court recognized that privacy, constitutionally protected and guaranteed by the Fourth Amendment, was a right no less important than any other. Indecent exposure or lewdness must occur in a public place to be a criminal offense. Timberline Lodge failed to fit the criterion of a public place. Its bylaws made it clear that the camp condemned prostitution and did not act as a place for sexual procurement. This court decision made nudist colonies on privately owned property legal in the state of Tennessee. It also served as a precedent in future cases. The *Timberline Case* made it possible for clothing-optional facilities to flourish throughout the entire United States, marking the first time a federal court sanctioned nude recreational facilities.

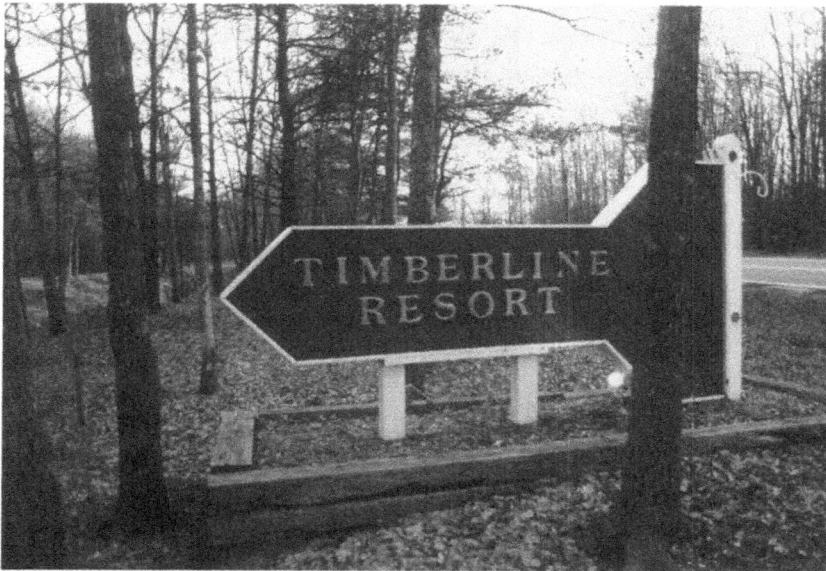

Entrance to the Timberline Resort, Cumberland County, Tennessee. Photo by the author.

Due in part to the publicity generated by the lawsuit, the membership of Timberline looked for a new home outside Knox County. The
BRB Corporation bought land from the Deck family west of Crossville
and named the new resort Timberline Lodge.[13] BRB leased the land to
the Tennessee Outdoor Club, and Timberline was chartered as a cooperative. The benefits—and limitations—of the club being a co-op meant
that everyone helped to take care of the land and shared in the basic
maintenance of Timberline.

In its early stages, Timberline was a rustic camp with minimal resources. There were few electric connections for trailer hookups and no
permanent lodging, though there were a clubhouse and bathrooms.
Basically, it had the appearance of a campground. To make it easier for
interested people to find Timberline Lodge, a round ball hung from a
tree indicating the dirt road entrance. Today the ball has been replaced
with a sign, and the lodge and grounds have been almost completely
transformed. The complex now contains a public diner, a lodge, a swimming pool, permanent and temporary housing, landscaping, and other
amenities.[14]

Two former elementary school teachers from Knoxville, Bea and
Glen Terry, bought Timberline and spearheaded the transformation from
rusticity to modern conveniences. In 1987, they abandoned public education, devoting their full attention to the clothing-optional facility.
Before purchasing Timberline, the Terrys conducted research, visiting
a well-known nudist resort in Florida, whose owner they considered an
authority on the subject. After the purchase, the Terrys continued to
live in Knoxville, coming to Timberline on the weekends. That soon
became impractical. They moved to Crossville in the early 1990s, after
many improvements were made.[15]

The Terrys injected new life into Timberline. One of the first things
they added was the pool, soon followed by a hot tub and a deck. Adjacent to the pool is the Tiki Bar, which was built by the members one
March during their annual work party. It was literally built in one day
with professional carpenters and volunteers.

When the Terrys bought Timberline they added more land. Total-
ing about two hundred acres, the camp provided complete privacy surrounded with lush forest.[16] Within four years of buying it, the Terrys
built the resort's first guesthouses. Before the rooms were constructed,
members slept in tents or recreational vehicles. Guesthouses were built
after a massive hailstorm that occurred in the early 1990s. This hailstorm caused so much damage to the plateau and its surroundings that

the state and federal governments declared it a disaster area. Low-interest small business loans were made available by the federal government to stimulate the local economy and to replace what was destroyed. The Terrys applied for and received a disaster-relief loan. Instead of replacing old RVs that had been pummeled by the hailstorm, Timberline took this opportunity to make sweeping changes, including the construction of the guesthouses and a visitor's lodge. There are currently fifteen hotel-like guestrooms, several one-bedroom log cabins with lofts and ceiling fans, and an RV park.

Perhaps the most comforting thing about Timberline is that there are no room keys. It is one the safest places for single women and single mothers because of the strict rules in the camp. If rules were violated, one could not ever enter another camp registered with the American Association of Nude Recreation (AANR). Violator's names are placed on a nationally circulated caution list. Leaving jewelry or valuables around the camp was not cause for alarm or worry. Several years ago, a security gate, which required a coded key, was installed to give visitors and members an extra sense of security and privacy. Members and visitors come from locations including Europe, Australia, Canada, and of course, the United States.[17]

Timberline is affiliated with the AANR, the Naturist Society, and the Eastern Sunbathing Association (one of AANR's seven regions).[18] AANR is the oldest and largest organization of nudists in North America, with more than 50,000 members, including enthusiastic groups of Christian Nudists.[19] The AANR recognizes five classifications of nudist camps, from rustic to luxury. In 2000, AANR celebrated its 25th Annual Nude Recreation Week from July 10 through July 16. This created an opportunity for families from every class and race to visit the more than 238 clothing-optional camps in the United States.[20]

The Naturist Society has encouraged body acceptance through recreation for more than fifteen years. Doctors who share the positive benefits of nude recreation support them. Dr. Alayne Yates, MD, Professor of Psychiatry at the University of Arizona, has argued that in cultures where nudity is common, children mature healthier, tending to be less critical of the human body in general. Dr. Marilyn Story, Professor of Family Studies at the University of Northern Iowa, who has conducted a great amount of longitudinal research concerning nudist families, says "Social Nudity takes on an increased societal, as well as personal importance when it is viewed as a significant factor in determining body self-concept." Moreover, the famous anthropologist Margaret Mead said that acceptance of nudity "would ultimately lead to a decrease in neurosis and certain types of crime." The members at Timberline wholeheartedly agree with these assessments.[21]

Timberline has a positive relationship with the local population. It is surrounded by a Mennonite community. Despite their belief in modesty, the Mennonites have a comfortable relationship with the owners and guests of the Timberline. Troyer's Store, run by Mennonites and located a mile from Timberline, warmly welcomes the resort's visitors because they are very good customers and good neighbors. In fact, when the Terrys host a luncheon at Timberline, Troyer's often caters it.[22]

Bea Terry recalled only one instance in which the residents of Timberline Lodge clashed with Cumberland County's denizens. At a Christian bookstore in Cumberland County, a window sign read, "PRAY FOR RAIN ON SEPTEMBER 15TH AND 16TH." It was an attack on Timberline, because a music festival was slated for that weekend at the camp. The event, which had been heavily advertised, provoked the bookstore's reaction. God refused to listen to those prayers, and it did not rain a drop. Other than the conflict with the Christian bookstore, Timberline continued to receive support from the community.

Former state representative from Crossville, Shirley Duer, supported Timberline during her tenure. She regularly auctioned, for Nashville charity, an honorary membership to Timberline. The Tennessee Tourist Bureau considers Timberline Lodge an asset that brings tourist dollars into the area. As a member of the Chamber of Commerce, Timberline has hosted business after-hours meetings for the chamber at the resort. These meetings have attracted record numbers of attendees.[23]

The Terrys do not go out of their way to market the resort in Cumberland County. They generally advertise in *Travel and Resort Guide* and other publications outside the Upper Cumberland to attract a clientele. Advertising their resort as clothing optional, they attracted a wide group of people, from ages twenty to sixty.[24] Steady growth at the resort continued throughout the 1990s and the Terrys connected with other nudist resorts. Timberline was the first nudist camp in the United States to have an 800 number. Belonging to a network of nudist camps, it provides the names and numbers of nudist camps all over the country as one of its services.

Between two hundred and three hundred people attend functions at Timberline on an average weekend, even more on holiday weekends. The Fourth of July 2000 weekend drew crowds of about five hundred people; buses were lined up, and about twenty-seven large tents were erected around the camp to accommodate the overflow. Halloween, a perennial favorite holiday, was celebrated over the course of two weekends. People designed ingenious costumes that allowed for both creativity and nudity. A national holiday isn't needed to have a celebration at Timberline; there is some kind of party every weekend.[25]

Weekend activities at Timberline include dancing, pool parties, theme parties, and lounging in the Sun Bun Bar. Located in the clubhouse is a disco dance floor, used every Saturday night, equipped with a disc jockey (DJ), strobe lights, and a gigantic mirror ball. Every Friday during the summer months, a pool party is emceed by a guest DJ followed by a bonfire. A favorite feature of the party is volleyball in the pool.

Timberline residents and guests also celebrated a weekly theme party. Past themes include a Toga Party minus the toga, Pioneer Days, and Fifties Night. A favorite recent retro theme was "going to the prom." Men wore cuffs and a bow tie while the females displayed an assortment of jewelry and wrist corsages. Limos picked up prom dates, escorting them to the Sun Bun Bar, where a magical evening awaited them.[26]

When not involved in planned activities, the Sun Bun Bar is available for poolside adult liquid refreshments. Attached to the Sun Bun Bar is a gift shop that sells interesting lingerie, souvenir T-shirts, and a

The lodge at Timberline. Photo by the author.

variety of tanning lotions. The camp provides a wide assortment of activities, appealing to a broad range of tastes. More than seven miles of hiking trails range through the woods surrounding Timberline Lodge. Additionally, there are badminton courts, canoes and paddle-boats, shuffleboard, and a game room. A horseshoe pit remains a favorite among the older guests. The lake, which is stocked regularly, provides leisurely fishing for young and old alike, though it may strike some people as odd to see someone with waders and a hat and nothing else, dangling their pole in the lake's cool waters.

Another project the Terrys launched was the building of a small chapel in the woods. Named the Cross Ties Chapel, it is a special place for reflection and meditation, and is visited by church musicians and ministers of all denominations. The chapel has only one scheduled service, the Easter Sunrise Service.[27] One couple's wedding in the chapel attracted national attention. GTE filmed a commercial about a couple from Alaska having a nude wedding at Timberline Lodge. As the cameras panned the top of the mountain, the voice-over said, "We install phones everywhere . . . even in nudist camps."[28]

Timberline has hosted several meetings over the years. Many times they have welcomed the regional meeting for the Eastern Sunbathing Association Board of Trustees' annual midwinter conference. In the mid-1990s, Tennessee Wildlife Resources Agency (TWRA) held a conference there. Carl Cude, a White County agent, put together an entire seminar that dealt specifically with the nudist experience outdoors, and how park employees should treat them. Cude's model has helped workers at TWRA develop a proper attitude toward nude recreation, and has taught them the proper skills necessary to deal with unfamiliar situations with nudists.[29]

Timberline's history has played a key role in nude recreation in America. Today, clothing-optional facilities can be found throughout the United States. This was made possible when a few people in the Upper Cumberland chose to fight for their rights to be naked in the woods. Their fight led to a federal appeals decision upholding the nudist rights under the First, Fourth, and Fourteenth amendments. Timberline provides a place to experience this "trend" that millions practice, but there is one cardinal rule—bring your own towel!

NOTES

1. Naturist@naturist.com
2. Ibid.

3. Kenneth Clark, *The Nude: A Study in Ideal Form* (Princeton: Princeton University Press, 1990): 3–29.

4. Name withheld by request. Notes from a discussion with a woman at a convenience mart just off I-40 in Cumberland County, Tennessee (July 7, 1999).

5. Personal interview with Bea Terry (Crossville, Tenn., Timberline Lodge: July 18, 1999).

6. Ibid.

7. Ibid.

8. The author thanks John Nisbett III for information concerning this case. The Terrys repeatedly referred to a "Supreme Court case" making Timberline legal. No such state supreme court case could be found. Nisbet discovered that the case was tried in a federal appellate court. United District Court, E.D. Tennessee, Northern Division, *Henry Roberts, John Roberts, Tennessee Outdoor Club, Inc., and the American Sunbathing Association, Inc., vs. Frank G. Clement, Individually and as the Governor of the State of Tennessee, George F. McCanless, Individually and as the Attorney General of the State of Tennessee, and Archie Weaver, Individually and as Sheriff of Knox County, Tennessee* (Civ. A. No. 5410, January 12, 1966: 252 F. Supp. 835): 1, 3. Hereafter *Timberline Case*. The membership of Timberline also argued that "the practice of nudism produces healthier children, fewer delinquents, and fewer divorces."

9. Ibid., 13.

10. Ibid., 11.

11. Ibid., 17.

12. Ibid., 20.

13. Personal interview with a woman who requested that her name be withheld at the Mayland Senior Citizens Center (Mayland, Tenn.: July 26, 1999). BRB got its name from the first letters of the names of three of the group's founders.

14. Personal interview with Glen and Bea Terry (Crossville, Tenn.: Timberline Lodge: July 18, 1999).

15. Personal Interview with Glen and Bea Terry (Crossville, Tenn.: Timberline Lodge, July 22, 2000).

16. Ibid.

17. Ibid.

18. Trynude@anrr.com

19. NudistsforChrist.com, *Fig Leaf Forum*, and NudeNotRude.Com.

20. Ibid.

21. Naturist@naturist.com

22. Personal interview with Glen and Bea Terry (July 18, 1999).

23. Ibid.

24. Ibid.

25. Ibid.

26. Ibid.

27. Ibid.

28. Ibid.

29. Ibid.

BIBLIOGRAPHY

AFRICAN AMERICANS

DuBois, W.E.B. *Autobiography of W. E. B. DuBois*. New York: International Publishers, 1968.

Franklin, John Hope and Loren Schweninger. *Runaway Slaves: Rebels on the Plantation*. New York: Oxford University Press, 1999.

Harrison, Lowell H. "Memories of Slavery Days." *The Filson Club Historical Quarterly,* 47:3 (July 1973).

Inscoe, John C. *Appalachians and Race: The Mountain South, from Slavery to Segregation*. Lexington: The University Press of Kentucky, 2001.

Kharif, Wali R. "School Desegregation in Clinton and Cookeville, Tennessee." In *Tennessee, State of the Nation*. 2nd edition, W. Calvin Dickinson, and Larry H. Whiteaker, eds. New York: American Heritage, 1995, 233–42.

Lucas, Marion Brunson. *A History of Blacks in Kentucky*. Frankfort: Kentucky Historical Society, 1992.

NAACP. *Thirty Years of Lynchings*. Washington, D.C., 1919.

Negro Population in the United States, 1790–1915. New York: Arno Press, 1968.

Peterson, Ellen, and Tom Rankin. "Free Hill: An Introduction," *Tennessee Folklore Society Bulletin* L:1 (1985): 5, 6, fn 9–10.

Romaine, Ann. "In Memoriam: Robert 'Bud' Garrett (1916–1987)," *Tennessee Folklore Society Bulletin* LIII:1 (1988): 27–28.

Schmitzer, Jeanne Cannella. "The Black Experience at Mammoth Cave, Edmonson County, Kentucky, 1838–1942." Master's Thesis, University of Central Florida, unpublished, 1996.

Southern Education Reporting Service. *A Statistical Summary, State by State, of Segregation-Desegregation Activity Affecting Southern Schools from 1954 to Present, Together with Pertinent Data Enrollment, Teachers, Colleges, Litigation and Legislation*. 6 volumes. Nashville: n.p., 1957–1964.

Tennessee State Department of Education. Equal Education Opportunities Program. "Desegregation Report on Tennessee's Public Elementary and Secondary Schools, Fall 1966."

Turner, William H., and Edward J. Cabell, eds. *Blacks in Appalachia*. Lexington: The University Press of Kentucky, 1985.

ARCHITECTURE

Carpenter, John. *Tennessee Courthouses: A Celebration of 200 Years of County Courthouses*. n.p., 1996.

Dickinson, W. Calvin. "Smith County Historical Homes." *Tennessee Anthropologist*, XVII (spring 1992).
———. "Log Houses in Overton County, Tennessee." *Tennessee Anthropologist*, XV (spring 1990).
Dickinson, W. Calvin, Michael E. Birdwell, Homer Kemp. *Upper Cumberland Historic Architecture*. Franklin, Tenn.: Hillsboro Press, 2002.
Montell, William Lynwood, and Michael L. Morse. *Kentucky Folk Architecture*. Lexington: The University Press of Kentucky, 1976.
West, Carroll Van. *Tennessee's New Deal Landscape*. Knoxville: University of Tennessee Press, 2001.

ARTS AND CRAFTS

Ardery, Julia S. *The Temptation: Edgar Tolson and the Genesis of Twentieth Century Folk Art*. Chapel Hill: University of North Carolina Press, 1998.
Beardsley, John. *Gardens of Revelations: Environments by Visionary Artists*. New York: Abbeville Press, 1995.
Beckham, Sue Bridwell. *Depression Post Office Murals and Southern Culture: A Gentle Reconstruction*. Baton Rouge: Louisiana State University Press, 1989.
Bilger, Burkhard. *Noodling for Flatheads*. New York: Scribner, 2000.
Bullard, Helen. *Crafts and Craftsmen of the Tennessee Mountains*. Falls Church, Va.: Summit Press, 1976.
Dodge, Emma Florence. *Souvenir History of Pleasant Hill Academy, 1884–1924*. n.p., 1924.
Eaton, Allen. "The Mountain Handicrafts: Their Importance to the Country and the People in the Mountain Homes." *Mountain Life and Work* 6 (July 1930): 22–30.
Fulcher, Bob. "Tennessee in 1831: The Sketches of Charles A. LeSueur." *Tennessee Conservationist* (March/April 2001): 7–11.
Hoobler, James A. *Gilbert Gaul: American Realist*. Nashville: Tennessee State Museum Foundation, 1992.
Hughes, Robert. *American Visions: The Epic History of Art in America*. New York: Alfred A. Knopf, 1997.
Jones, James B., Jr. *Tennessee's First State Parks*. Nashville: Tennessee Historical Commission, 1985.
———. *The WPA and CCC in Tennessee*. Nashville: Department of Conservation, 1983.
Kelley, James C. "John Wood Dodge: Miniature Painter." *American Art Review* 6:4 (1994): 98–103.
———. "Landscape and Genre Painting in Tennessee, 1810–1985." *Tennessee Historical Quarterly* XLIV:2 (summer 1995): 7–152.
———. "Portrait Painting in Tennessee." *Tennessee Historical Quarterly* XLVI:4 (winter 1987): 195–276.

Lampell, Ramona and Millard. *O, Appalachia: Artists of the Southern Mountains*. New York: Stewart Tabor & Chang, 1990.

Melosh, Barbara. *Engendering Culture: Manhood and Womanhood in the New Deal Public Art and Theater*. Washington, D.C.: Smithsonian Institution Press, 1991.

Ramsey, Bets, and Merikay Waldvogel. *The Quilts of Tennessee: Images of Domestic Life Prior to 1930*. Nashville: Rutledge Hill Press, 1986.

Rogers, Stephen. "Family Potters: Tennessee's Forgotten Craftsmen." *The Courier* 18:2 (February 1980): 4–5.

Russell, Judith. "From the Hills of Appalachia to Heaven: Billy Dean Anderson the Folk Hero and Folk Artist." Master's thesis, Middle Tennessee University, 1995.

Smith, Samuel D., and Stephen T. Rogers. *A Survey of Historic Pottery Making in Tennessee*. Research Series, no. 3. Nashville: Division of Archaeology, 1979.

Wharton, May Cravath. *Doctor Woman of the Cumberlands*. Pleasant Hill, Tenn.: Uplands, 1953.

BURIAL PRACTICES

Aries, Philippe, *The Hour of Our Death*. New York: Oxford University Press, 1991.

Cantrell, Brent. "Traditional Grave Structures on the Eastern Highland Rim." *Tennessee Folklore Society Bulletin* LXVII:3 (October 1981): 93–103.

Little, M. R. *Sticks and Stones: Three Centuries of North Carolina Gravemarkers*. Chapel Hill: University of North Carolina Press, 1988.

Myer, R. E., ed. *Ethnicity and the American Cemetery: Cemeteries in American History*. Bowling Green, Ohio: Popular Press, 1993.

Sloane, D. C. *The Last Great Necessity: Cemeteries in American History*. Baltimore: Johns Hopkins University Press, 1991.

CAVES

Bailey, Thomas L. "Report on the Caves of the Eastern Highland Rim and Cumberland Mountains." *The Resources of Tennessee*. Nashville: State Geological Survey, April 1918, 86–138.

Barr, Thomas C. "Caves of Tennessee." *Tennessee Division of Geology, Bulletin* 64, 1961.

Douglas, Joseph C. "Miners and Moonshiners: Historical Industrial Uses of Tennessee Caves." *Midcontinental Journal of Archaeology* 26:2 (2000):251–67.

Matthews, Larry E. "Saltpeter: The Forgotten Industry." *Tennessee Conservationist* (July/August 1996), 11–14.

Miller, Wilbur R. *Revenuers and Moonshiners: Enforcing Federal Liquor Law in the Mountain South, 1865–1900*. Chapel Hill: University of North Carolina Press, 1991.

Simek, Jan F. "The Sacred Darkness: Prehistoric Cave Art in Tennessee." *Tennessee Conservationist* (March/April 1997), 27–32.

Smith, Marion O. "In Quest of a Supply of Saltpeter and Gunpowder in Early Civil War Tennessee." *Tennessee Historical Quarterly* 61:2 (2002): 96–111.

———. *Saltpeter Mining in East Tennessee*. Maryville, Tenn.: Byron's Graphic Arts, 1990.

CIVIL WAR

Blankenship, Lela McDowell. *Fiddles in the Cumberlands*. New York: Richard R. Smith, 1943.

Brents, Major John A. *The Patriots and Guerillas of East Tennessee and Kentucky: The Sufferings of Patriots, Also the Experiences of the Author as an Officer in the Union Army, Including Sketches of Noted Guerillas and Distinguished Patriots*. New York: Henry Dexter Publishers, 1863.

Confederate Collection. Diary of William E. Sloan, mfm 154. Nashville: Tennessee State Library and Archives, March 9, 1863.

Confederate Collection. Letters—Lacy, Andrew Jackson, 1862–1863, box C-28, folder 17. Nashville: Tennessee State Library and Archives.

Connelly, Thomas Lawrence. *Army of the Heartland: The Army of Tennessee, 1861–1862*. Baton Rouge: Louisiana State University Press, 1967.

DeLozier, Mary Jean. "The Civil War and Its Aftermath in Putnam County." *Tennessee Historical Quarterly* 36:2 (1977): 237–38.

———. "Civil War in Putnam County." *Tennessee Historical Quarterly* 38 (1979): 452.

Dudney, Betty Jane. "Civil War in White County, Tennessee, 1861–1865." Master's Thesis, Tennessee Technological University, 1985.

Duke, Basil W. *History of Morgan's Cavalry*. Cincinnati: Miami Printing and Publishing Company, 1867.

Dyer, Frederick H. *Compendium of the War of the Rebellion*. 1908, rept. New York: Sagamore Press, 1959. Vol. 2.

Fisher, Noel C. *War at Every Door: Partisan and Guerrilla Violence in East Tennessee, 1860–1869*. Chapel Hill: University of North Carolina Press, 1997.

Hill, Amanda Meredith. "My First 85 Years: The Memoirs of Amanda Meredith Hill, Sparta, Tennessee." Sparta, Ten.: Partial typescript, n.p., 1941.

Mays, Thomas D. *The Saltville Massacre*. Abilene, Tex.: McWhiney Foundation Press, 1998.

McFarland, Jerry; William Newkirk; and David Gilbert, eds. *The Battle of Mill Springs, KY, January 19, 1862*. Somerset, Ky.: Mill Springs Battlefield Association, 1999.

Montell, William Lynwood. *Diary of Amanda McDowell*. Lexington: University Press of Kentucky, 1986.

Official Records of the Union and Confederate Armies of the War of the Rebellion. Washington, D.C.: U.S. Government Printing Office, 1880–1901.

Report of the Adjutant General of the State of Tennessee of the Military Forces of the State, from 1861–1866. Nashville: 1866.

Sensing, Thurman. *Champ Ferguson: Confederate Guerrilla.* Nashville: Vanderbilt University Press, 1942.

Talley, Spencer Bowen. "Memoirs of Spencer Bowen Talley, First Lieutenant of the Tennessean Twenty-eighth Regiment Company F." Lebanon, Tenn., typescript in the possession of Jerry McFarland, n.p., n.d.

Tarrant, Sergeant E. *The Wild Riders of the First Kentucky Cavalry: A History of the Regiment in the Great War of the Rebellion, 1861–1865.* Reprint. Lexington, Ky.: Henry Clay Press, 1969.

Tennessee Civil War Centennial Commission. *Tennesseans in the Civil War,* 2 vols. Nashville: Tennessee Historical Commission, 1964.

Williams, Samuel Cole. *General John T. Wilder, Commander of the Lightning Brigade.* Bloomington: Indiana University Press, 1934.

Cumberland Homesteads

Blue, Edna Gossage. *A People Dared, God Cared.* Crossville, Tenn.: self-published, 1984.

Bullard, Helen, and Joseph Marshall Krechniak. *Cumberland County's First Hundred Years.* Crossville, Tenn.: Centennial Committee, 1956.

Casteel, Britt A. "Homesteading on the Cumberland Plateau." *The Courier* 17:3 (June 1980): 4–5.

Conkin, Paul. *Tomorrow a New World: The New Deal Community Program.* Ithaca, N.Y.: Cornell University Press, 1959.

Folger, Dagnall F. "The History and Aims of the Cumberland Homesteads." *Mountain Life and Work,* 11 (July 1935): 5–8.

Hughes, Delos D. "The Housing Ideal at Cumberland Homesteads." *Tennessee Historical Quarterly* (spring 2001), 38–53.

Kirkeminde, Patricia B. *Cumberland Homesteads: As Viewed by the Newspapers.* Crossville, Tenn.: Brookhart Press, 1977.

Lord, Russell, and Paul H. Johnstone. *A Place on Earth: A Critical Appraisal of Subsistence Homesteads.* U.S. Department of Agriculture, Bureau of Agricultural Economics. Washington, D.C.: U.S. Government Printing Office, 1942.

Malanka, Anne. "The Homesteader Experience at Cumberland Homesteads, Tennessee." MS. Nashville: Department of Conservation and Environment, 1992.

Moore, James Collins. "An Analysis of the New Deal Subsistence Homesteads Program in Cumberland County, Tennessee." Master's thesis. Tennessee Technological University, 1967.

Vaden, Emma Jean Pedigo, and Doyle Vaden. *Looking Back . . . : Cumberland Homesteads Golden Anniversary Album.* Crossville, Tenn.: self-published, 1984.

Wilson, Milburn L. "The Place of Subsistence Homesteads in Our National Economy." *Journal of Farm Economics,* 16 (1934): 80–85.

Film and Theater

Birdwell, Michael E. *Celluloid Soldiers: Warner Bros. Campaign Against Nazism.* New York: New York University Press, 1999.

Kemp, Homer D., and Stephen Boots. *The Wilder-Davidson Story: The End of an Era.* Four-part documentary. WCTE Public Television Station, 1987.

Klein, Sue Ellen. "The Cumberland County Playhouse: Storyteller of the Legend and Lore of the Upper Cumberland." Master's thesis, Tennessee Technological University, 1995.

Larson, Edward J. *Summer for the Gods: The Scopes Trial and America's Continuing Debate over Science and Religion.* Cambridge, Mass.: Harvard University Press, 1997.

Tretter, Evelyn K. "Doctor Woman." *Tennessee Conservationist* 54 (November-December 1988): 18–22.

Williamson, J. W. *Hillbillyland: What the Movies Did to the Mountains and the Mountains Did to the Movies.* Chapel Hill: University of North Carolina Press, 1995.

Folklore and Folkways

Arnow, Harriet Simpson. *Flowering of the Cumberland.* New York: Macmillan, 1963.

———. *Seedtime on the Cumberland.* New York: Macmillan, 1960.

Carter, Frances D. *From Then to Now.* Gainesboro, Tenn.: n.p., 1989.

Caudill, Harry M. *Night Comes to the Cumberland.* Boston: Little, Brown, 1962.

Doran, Paul E. "The Legend and History of a Man Who Was Feared and Hated: Champ Ferguson—The Civil War Guerrilla of the Highlands." *The Kentucky Explorer* (October 2002): 48–50.

Harris, Edith. *Thomas Sharpe Spencer: Big Foot of the Cumberland County.* Gallatin, Tenn.: Quality Printing, 1976.

Harvey, Stella Mowbray. *Tales of the Civil War Era.* Crossville, Tenn.: Brookhart Press, 1977.

Hayes, Marjorie. *Life on the Caney Fork.* Smithville, Tenn.: Caney Fork Historical Association, Inc., 1986.

———. *Temperance Hall Remembers: A Brief History of Temperance Hall, Tennessee.* 2 vols. Temperance Hall, Tenn.: Temperance Hall Community Club, 1986 and 1990.

Hendricks, John. *Once upon a Lynching: The Jerome Boyett Story.* Waynesboro: Southern Tennessee Publishing Company, 1985.

Howell, Benita. "The Saga of Jerome Boyett: A Mirror of Attitudes toward Law and Lawlessness." *Tennessee Anthropologist* 8:1 (1983): 1–19.

———. *Survey of Folklife along the Big South Fork of the Cumberland River.* Knoxville: University of Tennessee Press, 1981.

Hull, Cordell. *The Memoirs of Cordell Hull.* 2 vols. New York: Macmillan, 1948.

Johnson, Jane. *Tales of the Hebbertsburg and Cumberland Folklore.* Crab Orchard, Tenn.: The Center, 1986.

McNeil, W. K., ed. *Appalachian Images in Folk and Popular Culture.* 2nd edition. Knoxville: University of Tennessee Press, 1995.

Melton, Callie. *'Pon My Honor: Folk Tales From the Upper Cumberland.* n.p., 1979.

Montell, William Lynwood. *Don't Go Up Kettle Creek: A Verbal Legacy of the Upper Cumberland.* Knoxville: University of Tennessee Press, 1983.

———. *Upper Cumberland Country.* Jackson: University of Mississippi Press, 1993.

Montell, William Lynwood, and Nancy Keim Comley, eds. *Those Were the Days: Bob Dudney's Recollections of Yesterday in Free State and Tennessee's Upper Cumberland.* Gainesboro, Tenn.: Jackson County Historical Society, 1996.

Spurlock, Donald E. *The Braswell Hangings of Putnam County, Tennessee.* Cookeville, Tenn.: Southland Printing Co., 1981.

White, Linda C. "Champ Ferguson: A Legacy of Blood." *Tennessee Folklore Society Bulletin* 44:2 (1978): 66–70.

LITERATURE

Bell, Ed. *Fish on the Steeple.* New York: Farrar and Rinehart, 1935.

Bierce, Ambrose. "Three and One are One," *Cosmopolitan* (October 1908), 550–552.

Blankenship, Lela McDowell. *The Uneven Yoke.* Nashville: Tennessee Book Co., 1962.

———. *When Yesterday Was Today.* Nashville: Tennessee Book Co., 1966.

Bonner, Sherwood. *Dialect Tales.* New York: Harper & Bros., 1883.

Brown, Lisa G. *Sleeping at the Magnolia.* New York: Harper Paperbacks, 1997.

Clark, Jim. *Dancing on Canaan's Ruins.* Memphis, Ars Gratis, 1983; reprinted Wilson, N.C.: Eternal Delight Productions, 1997.

———. *Handiwork: Poems.* Laurinburg, N.C.: St. Andrew's College Press, 1998.

Clouse, Loletta. *Wilder.* Nashville: Rutledge Hill Press, 1990.

Dromgoole, Will Allen. *A Moonshiner's Son.* Philadelphia: Penn Publishing Co., 1898.

———. *The Sunny Side of the Cumberland.* Philadelphia: Lippincott, 1886.

Epperson, Clara Cox. *Scraps of Verse and Prose from Heartsease,* Lottie Farr, ed. Cookeville: Dept. of English, Tennessee Technological University, 1973.

Grisham, John. *The Firm.* New York: Doubleday, 1991.

Hudson, Robert Paine. *Southern Lyrics: A Series of Original Poems on Love, Home, and the Southland.* Nashville: Southern Lyrics Publishing Co., 1907.

Ingram, Bowen. *Light as Morning.* Boston: Houghton Mifflin, 1954.

———. *Milbry.* New York: Crown Publishers, 1972.

Jordan, Michael Bohannon. *Crockett's Coin.* Edmonton, Alberta, Canada: Commonwealth Publications, 1997.

Kornfield, Anita Clay. *In a Bluebird's Eye.* New York: Avon Books, 1975.

Moon, William Least Heat. *Blue Highways: A Journey into America*. Boston: Little, Brown, 1982.

Moore, Frank, ed. *Anecdotes, Poetry, and Incidents of the War: North and South, 1860–1865*. New York: Bible House, 1867.

Muir, John. *The Thousand-Mile Walk to the Gulf.* William Frederic Bade, ed. Boston: Houghton Mifflin, 1916.

Murfree, Mary Noailles. *In the Tennessee Mountains.* Boston: Houghton Mifflin, 1884.

Twain, Mark, and Charles Dudley Warner. *The Gilded Age: A Tale of To-day.* Hartford, Conn.: American Publishing Co., 1873.

West, Michael Lee. *American Pie.* New York: HarperCollins, 1996.

———. *Crazy Ladies.* Atlanta: Longstreet Press, 1990.

Music

Watson, Kurt. "The Smithville Fiddlers' Jamboree." Cookeville: Tennessee Technological University Library, 1999.

Wolfe, Charles. *A Good Natured Riot: The Birth of the Grand Ole Opry.* Nashville: Vanderbilt University Press, 1999.

———. *Stars of Country Music: Uncle Dave Macon to Johnny Rodriguez.* Urbana: University of Illinois Press, 1975.

———. *Tennessee Strings: The Story of Country Music in Tennessee.* Knoxville: University of Tennessee Press, 1994.

Wolfe, Charles, and James Akenson, eds. *Country Music Annual 2000.* Lexington: The University Press of Kentucky, 2000.

———. *Country Music Annual 2001.* Lexington: The University Press of Kentucky, 2001.

———. *Country Music Annual 2002.* Lexington: The University Press of Kentucky, 2002.

———. *Country Music Goes to War.* Lexington: The University Press of Kentucky, 2004.

———. *The Women of Country Music: A Reader.* Lexington: The University Press of Kentucky, 2003.

Red Boiling Springs

Blankenship, Harold. *History of Macon County, Tennessee.* Tompkinsville, Ky.: Monroe County Press, 1995.

Denning, Jeanette Keith. "A History of the Resort Business in Red Boiling Springs, Tennessee." Master's Thesis, Tennessee Technological University, 1982.

Roddy, Vernon. *Thousands to Cure: On the Early History of Red Boiling Springs, Tennessee with Selected Supporting Materials.* Hartsville, Tenn.: Upper Country People Probe, 1991.

Thorne, Charles B. "The Watering Spas of Middle Tennessee." *Tennessee Historical Quarterly* XXIX (winter 1970–1971): 321–59.

Weiss, Harry B., and Howard R. Kemble. *The Great American Water Cure Craze: A History of Hydropathy in the United States.* Trenton, N.J.: Past Times Press, 1967.

Wilson, John M., and John Michael Kernodle. "The Black Shale and Double and Twist: A Study of the Physical Setting of Red Boiling Springs." *Tennessee Conservationist* XXXVI (February 1970): 7–9.

RELIGION

Ahlstrom, Sydney E. *A Religious History of the American People.* New Haven, Conn. and London: Yale University Press, 1972.

Burnett, J. J. *Sketches of Tennessee's Pioneer Baptist Preachers.* Nashville: Marshall & Bruce, 1919.

Cantrell, Gerry R., ed. *History of White County Churches.* n.p., 1980.

Cartwright, Peter. *Autobiography of Peter Cartwright, Backwoods Preacher.* W. P. Strickland, ed. Cincinnati: Cranston and Curtis, n.d.

Conkin, Paul K. *Cane Ridge: America's Pentecost.* Madison: University of Wisconsin Press, 1989.

Cullen, Carter. *Methodism in the Wilderness, 1786–1836.* Nashville: Parthenon Press, 1960.

DeLozier, Mary Jean. *Putnam County, Tennessee, 1850–1970.* Nashville: McQuiddy Publishing, 1979.

Dickson, Bruce D., Jr. *And They All Sang Hallelujah: Plain Folk Camp-Meeting Religion, 1800–1845.* Knoxville: University of Tennessee Press, 1974.

Dillon, Sheila Tompkins. *Fellowship United Baptist Church, 1857–1992.* Jamestown, Tenn.: Fentress Courier, 1993.

Finger, John R. "Witness to Expansion: Bishop Francis Asbury on the Trans-Appalachian Frontier." *Register of the Kentucky Historical Society* 82:4 (1984): 334–47.

George, Gilbert Jasper. *A History of the First Baptist Church of Carthage, Tennessee: Centennial Edition, 1881–1981.* Carthage, Tenn.: The First Baptist Church, 1981.

Grime, John Harvey. *History of Middle Tennessee Baptists.* Nashville: Baptist and Reflector, 1902.

Halsell, Orpha. *History of Bethlehem Church and Early Settlers, 1776–1976: With Some Updating to 1978.* n.p., 1978.

Hughes, Richard. *Reviving the Ancient Faith: The Story of Churches of Christ in America.* Grand Rapids, Mich.: William B. Eerdman's Publishing Co., 1997.

Maggart, Sue. "Mt. Zion Methodist Church." *Smith County Historical and Genealogical Society Newsletter* 4:2 (spring 1992): 79–81.

———. "New Middleton Free Church." *Smith County Historical and Genealogical Society Newsletter* 6:1 (winter 1994): 29–30.

Mansfield, Stephen, and George Grant. *Faithful Volunteers: The History of Religion in Tennessee.* Nashville: Cumberland House, 1997.

Marriott, Victor E. *The First Hundred Years of the Pleasant Hill Community Church: United Methodist Church of Christ Pleasant Hill, Tennessee, 1885– 1985*. Pleasant Hill: The United Methodist Church of Christ, 1985.

Nixon, W. H. *History of Indian Creek Baptist Church & Related Events*. Dowelltown, Tenn.: n.p., 1965.

Norton, Herman A. *Religion in Tennessee, 1777–1945*. Knoxville: University of Tennessee Press, 1981.

Robinson, Robert, ed. *Salem Baptist Church, 1809–1994*. Liberty, Tenn.: Salem Baptist Church, 1994.

Rogers, John. *The Biography of Elder Barton Warren Stone*. Joplin, Mo.: College Press, 1986.

Rudolph, L. C. *Francis Asbury*. Nashville: Abingdon Press, 1966.

Toomey, Glenn A. *Silver Anniversary History of the Cumberland Plateau Baptist Association, 1953–1978, Crossville, Tennessee*. Morristown, Tenn.: Toomey, 1979.

Wright, F. A., ed. *Autobiography of A. B. Wright, of the Holston Conference M.E. Church*. Cincinnati: Cranston and Curtis, 1896.

Socialism

Brookheart, Ms. George F. *First One Hundred Years of the First Congregational Church*. Crossville, Tenn.: Chronicle Publishing Company, 1987.

Dickinson, W. Calvin. "Whose Sons Settled Rugby? A Study of the Population at Rugby, Tennessee, in the 1880s." *Tennessee Historical Quarterly* LII (fall 1993): 192–98.

Egerton, John. *Visions of Utopia: Nashoba, Rugby, Ruskin, and the "New Communities" in Tennessee's Past*. Knoxville: University of Tennessee Press, 1977.

Horton, Myles, with Judith and Herbert Kohl, *The Long Haul: An Autobiography*. New York: Teacher's College Press, 1998.

Hughes, Thomas. *Rugby, Tennessee: Being Some Account of the Settlement Founded on the Cumberland Plateau*. London: Macmillan, 1881.

Mack, Edward C., and W. H. G. Armytage. *Thomas Hughes*. London: Ernest Benn, 1952.

The Rugby Handbook. 2nd edition. Facsimile Reprint Edition. Rugby: Historic Rugby Press, 1996.

Shannon, David A. *The Socialist Party of America*. Chicago: Quadrangle Books, 1967.

Socialist Party of America, Papers of the. Microfilm. Durham: Duke University Archives. [Papers of the Socialist Party of Tennessee are on Reel 111.]

Stagg, Brian L. *The Distant Eden: Tennessee's Rugby Colony: A History of the English Colony at Rugby, Tennessee with a Guide to the Remaining Original Buildings*. Rugby, Tenn.: Paylor Publications, 1973.

Vial, Rebecca, and W. Calvin Dickinson. "Kate Bradford Stockton." *Tennessee Historical Quarterly* XLIX (fall 1990): 152–60.

Watters, George Wayne. "Elmer Lincoln Wirt, Editor and Politician: A Study of Grassroots Populism and Progressivism in Tennessee, 1903–1920." Master's Thesis, Tennessee Technological University, 1973.

TENNESSEE MANEUVERS

Bradley, Michael R. *Reveille to Taps: Camp Forrest, Tennessee, 1940–1946.* Nashville: Southern Library Bindery and United States Air Force Legacy Program, 2000.

Brinker, William J. "Cookeville's 109th Cavalry Troop." *Tennessee Historical Quarterly* 53:4 (winter 1994): 228–45.

Burns, Frank. *Wilson County.* Memphis: Memphis State University Press, 1983.

———. *A Newspaper for Its Community.* Lebanon, Tenn.: n.p., 1998.

Cornwell, Ilene J. "Albert R. Hogue: A Centenarian Reflects." *The Courier* 14:2 (January 1976): 6.

D'Este, Carlo. *Patton: A Genius for War.* New York: HarperCollins, 1995.

Dickinson, W. Calvin. "Camp Crossville, 1942–1945." *The Journal of East Tennessee History* 68 (1996): 31–40.

Simon, McCall. "An Overview of the U.S. Army Maneuvers in Tennessee, 1941–1945." Cookeville: Tennessee Technological University, 2002.

Sloan, Eugene. *With Second Army Somewhere in Tennessee.* Clarksville, Tenn.: World War II Commission, 1956.

TIMBERLINE

Clark, Kenneth. *The Nude: A Study in Ideal Form.* Princeton: Princeton University Press, 1990.

Dickinson, W. Calvin. *Cumberland County Tennessee.* Cookeville: Tennessee Technological University, 1992.

ALVIN C. YORK

"After a Big Gun Comes up a Dud," *U.S. News and World Report*, September 9, 1985: 11.

Allen, Bert, ed. *Now and Then:* "Special Issue on Veterans of the Appalachia." Center for Appalachian Studies and Services/Institute for Appalachian Affairs, 1987.

"Appalachia Lost More in Vietnam due to 'York Syndrome,'" *Herald Citizen* (Cookeville, Tenn.), February 26, 1989, 12.

Beattie, Taylor V., with Norman Bowman. "In Search of York: Man, Myth & Legend." *Army History: The Professional Bulletin of Army History,* PB-20-00-3, no. 50 (summer-fall 2000): 1–14.

Birdwell, Michael E. "A Change of Heart: Alvin York and the Movie Sergeant York." *Film and History* 27:1–4 (1997): 22–33.

———. "'The Devil's Tool': Alvin York and Sergeant York." In *Hollywood's World War I: Motion Picture Images.* Peter C. Rollins and John E. O'Connor, eds. Bowling Green, Ohio: Bowling Green State University Press, 1997.

Bowers, John. "The Mythical Morning of Sergeant York." *MHQ: The Quarterly of Military History* 8:2 (winter 1996): 38–47.

Cowan, Sam K. *Sergeant York and His People*. New York: Funk and Wagnalls, 1922 and 1941.

"DIVAD Was Intended to Protect U.S. Tanks," *Washington Post*. December 3, 1985: A15.

Holloway, Elma, ed. *Unsung Heroes*. New York: Macmillan, 1938.

Hoobler, James A. "Sergeant York Historic Area." *Tennessee Historical Quarterly* 38:1 (1979): 3–8.

Humble, R. G. *Sergeant Alvin C. York: A Christian Patriot*. Circleville, Ohio: The Churches of Christ in Christian Union, 1966.

Koropey, Oleh Borys. *It Seemed Like a Good Idea at the Time: The Story of the Sergeant York Air Defense Gun*. Washington, D.C.: National Archives, n.d.

Lee, David. *Sergeant York: An American Hero*. Lexington: The University Press of Kentucky, 1985.

Patullo, George. "The Second Elder Gives Battle." *Saturday Evening Post* (April 26, 1919): 3–4, 71–73.

"A Sgt. York for a New Age Proud of Patriotism, Service." *Knoxville News-Sentinel* (November 6, 1990): 1.

Shanks, Maudean W. *History of Alvin C. York Agricultural Institute, Jamestown, Tennessee, 1926–1992*. Allardt, Tenn.: the author, 1994.

Skeyhill, Tom. *Sergeant York: Last of the Long Hunters*. Reprint. Shelbyville, Tenn.: Bible and Literature Missionary Foundation, 1992.

York, Alvin C. "The Diary of Sergeant York: A Famous Hero's Own Story of His Great Adventure." *Liberty* (July 14, 1928): 7–10; (July 21, 1928): 14–19, (July 28, 1928): 26–29; (August 4, 1928): 41–46.

MISCELLANEOUS SOURCES

Allardt: A History. Jamestown, Tenn.: Fentress Courier, 1986.

Ansley, Fran, and Brenda Bell. "Strikes in the Coal Camps: Davidson-Wilder, 1932." *Southern Exposure* 1 (winter 1974): 113–36.

Bandy, Anna Grace. *Field Trips into White County History*. Sparta, Tenn.: White County Retired Teachers Association, 1986.

———. *It Happened in White County, Tennessee*. Sparta, Tenn.: White County Retired Teachers Association, 1986.

Barlow, Timothy Joe. *The Life and Writings of Moses Fisk*. Collegedale, Tenn.: College Press, 1980.

Boyd, Dr. Willis Baxter. *The March of Progress in the Upper Cumberland of Tennessee*. n.p., n.d.

Bryant, Betty Huff. *Building Neighborhoods: Jackson County, Tennessee Prior to 1820*. n.p., 1992.

Crabtree, Font F. "The Wilder Coal Strike of 1932–33." Master's thesis, Peabody College, 1937.

Crouch, Arthur Weir. *The Caney Fork of the Cumberland: The Story of a River, Its History, Features, Moods, People, and Places, with Particular Reference to Rock Island and the Area above Great Falls*. n.p., 1973.

Crutchfield, James A. *Tennesseans at War: Volunteers and Patriots in Defense of Liberty*. Nashville: Rutledge Hill Press, 1987.

Dickinson, W. Calvin, Leo McGee, Larry Whiteaker, and Homer Kemp, eds. *Lend an Ear: Heritage of the Tennessee Upper Cumberland*. Lanham, Md.: University Press of America, 1983.

Douglas, Byrd. *Steamboating on the Cumberland*. Nashville: Tennessee Book Co., 1961.

Elridge, Robert L., and Mary Elridge. *Bicentennial Echoes of the History of Overton County, Tennessee, 1776–1976*. Livingston, Tenn.: Enterprise Printing Co., 1976.

Graves, Susan B. *Evins of Tennessee: Twenty-Five Years in Congress*. New York: Popular Library, 1971.

Hale, Will T. *History of DeKalb County*. McMinnville, Tenn.: The Ben Lemond Press, 1969.

History of Overton County, Tennessee. Dallas: Curtis Media Corporation, 1992.

The History of Smith County. Carthage, Tenn.: Smith County Homecoming '86 Heritage Committee, 1987.

Hogue, Albert R. *History of Fentress County, Tennessee*. Reprint. Baltimore: Regional Publishing Co., 1975.

Johnson, Rena J. *History of Sparta-White County, Tennessee*. n.p., 1982.

Jones, Christine Spivey. *Gleanings from Jackson County, Tennessee*. Cookeville: Tennessee Technological University, 1987.

———. *Jackson County, Tennessee: History from Many Sources*. 2 vols. Cookeville: Tennessee Technological University, 1983–1984.

———, comp. *Nuggets of Putnam County History*, n.p., 1985.

Keith, Jeanette. *Country People in the New South: Tennessee's Upper Cumberland*. Chapel Hill: University of North Carolina Press, 1985.

Knight, George Allen: *Our Wonderful Overton County Heritage*. Knoxville: Southeastern Composition Services, Inc., 1975.

Leonard, Charles. *A Pictorial History of Sparta-White County Tennessee*. Cookeville, Tenn.: Anderson Performance Printing, 1984.

Marchbanks, Nell, and Wally Gillian, comp. *A Pictorial History of White County, Tennessee*. Sparta, Tenn.: The Expositor, 1994.

McNeil, W. K. *Appalachian Images in Folk and Popular Culture*. Knoxville: University of Tennessee Press, 1995.

Parsons, Barbara Buchman. *Facts, Folks, and Photos of Cumberland County, Tennessee*. Crossville: Cumberland County Historical Society, 1988.

Perry, Samuel D. *South Fork Country*. Detroit: Harlo Press, 1983.

Perry, Vernon F. "The Labor Struggle at Wilder, Tennessee." Ph.D. Dissertation, Vanderbilt University, 1990.

Phillips, William James Henry. *Pioneers of White County, Tennessee*. Whitesburg, Ga.: Wide Services, 1991.

Ragland, Hobert D. *Historical Clippings of Smith County, Tennessee, 1985*. Colorado Springs: n.p., 1985.
Remembering Oak Hill's Past. Livingston, Tenn.: Hibbs Printing Company, 1986.
Rich, Jesse W. *Cutting, Rafting, and Running Logs Down the Obey River, 1880–1920*. n.p., 1972.
Rogers, Eliza G. *Memorable Historical Accounts of White County and Area*. Collegedale, Tenn.: College Press, 1972.
Seals, Monroe. *History of White County Tennessee*. Reprint. Spartanburg, S.C., n.p., 1974.
Stanley, Bryan. *The Way It Was: Crossville, Cumberland County*. Nashville: Parthenon Press, 1983.
Stratton, Lora S., and Nettie M. Stratton. *And This Is Grassy Cove*. Crossville, Tenn.: Chronicle, 1938.
Sutton, Nina, and Sue Maggart, eds. *The History of Smith County, Tennessee*. Dallas: Curtis Media, 1987.
Taylor, Amy Beth, and Lynda Sue Mann, eds. *Pictorial History of Putnam County, Tennessee*. Cookeville, Tenn: First American Bank, 1988.
Tayse, Moldon Jenkins. *Jackson County, Tennessee*. Whitleyville, Tenn.: n.p., 1989.
Tichy, Charles R. *Dixon Springs, Tennessee: A Pictorial History*. Norris: Tennessee Valley Authority, 1985.
Toplovich, Ann, and Susan Gordon. "Town Life: Commercial Development in the Rural Counties of the Upper Cumberland, 1875–1950." Nashville: Study Unit prepared for the Tennessee Historical Commission, August 31, 1994.
Webb, Thomas G. *A Bicentennial History of DeKalb County Tennessee*. Smithville, Tenn.: Bradley Print Co., 1995.
———. *Tennessee County History Series: DeKalb County*. Memphis: Memphis State University Press, 1986.
Wheeler, Hazel. *The History of Wilder, Davidson, Highland Junction, Sandy and the Hollow*. n.p., 1994.
———. *Jamestown: Back Then . . . & Now. Containing 194 Photographs of the Past & The Progress in Recent Years*. n.p., 1990.
White County Heritage Book Committee. *Heritage of White County, 1806–1999*. Waynesville, N.C.: Walsworth Publishing Co., 1999.
Williams, Samuel Cole. *Early Travels in Tennessee*. Johnson City, Tenn.: Watauga Press, 1928.
Young, Kim. *History of Jackson County: Sketches from Yesterday, Towns, Communities, People*. n.p., 1994.

Contributors

ALLISON BARRELL. Barrell graduated cum laude from Tennessee Technological University in 2001. "Bring Your Own Towel" was a paper she wrote in a Tennessee history class. Since graduation, Allison has moved to Nashville, married Jason Strickland, and taken a position with the Department of Veterans Affairs.

MICHAEL E. BIRDWELL. "Birdie" graduated from Tennessee Technological University in 1985, completed his master's degree there in 1990, and earned his doctorate in history at the University of Tennessee in 1996. He taught at both Tennessee Tech and the University of Tennessee as a student, and accepted a tenure-track position at Tech after earning his doctorate. He is the author of a monograph about World War I and of innumerable essays on war and popular culture.

G. FRANK BURNS. A retired English professor at Tennessee Technological University, Burns earned his doctorate at Vanderbilt University. Before joining the professorial ranks, he worked with the *Lebanon Democrat* newspaper. He has authored histories of Davidson County, Wilson County, and Cumberland University. Burns now lives in Texas. (Kelly Sergio and Rex Bennett were students at Tech.)

W. CALVIN DICKINSON. Dickinson earned two degrees at Baylor University and his doctorate at the University of North Carolina. He taught at Tennessee Technological University for thirty years and then retired in 2000. Calvin has written or coauthored fifteen books, mostly about the history of Tennessee. History of architecture is his hobby.

JOSEPH C. DOUGLAS. Having earned his doctorate at the University of Texas, Douglas is a member of the history department at Volunteer State Community College. His dissertation concerned the historic use of caves, and spelunking has been his longtime hobby. He has published numerous articles about caves and their role in history.

ALLISON ENSOR. A Tennessee native, Ensor earned his doctorate in English at the University of Tennessee. He has been a long-time faculty member of the English department at that university. Allison has authored a number of essays concerning the history of literature in Tennessee. He is a specialist on Mark Twain.

RICHARD C. FINCH. Finch earned his PhD at the University of Texas, joining the geology department at Tennessee Tech University in 1975. Serving as chair of the department for a number of years, he retired in 2000. He has conducted a number of geological studies and has led several historical/geological tours of South American countries.

JAMES B. JONES JR. Having earned his doctorate at Middle Tennessee State University, Jones is a public historian with the Tennessee Historical Commission. He is author of *Every Day in Tennessee History*, and he has compiled a complete documentary sourcebook concerning the Civil War in Tennessee. He maintains a website that offers e-publication in Southern history—www.SouthernHistory.net.

JEANETTE KEITH. Keith's childhood home was on the Jackson County–Macon County line. She graduated with honors from Tennessee Technological University and earned her PhD at Vanderbilt University. Keith is chair of the honors program at Bloomsburg University in Pennsylvania. She is the author of *Country People in the New South: Tennessee's Upper Cumberland*.

WALI R. KHARIF. Kharif earned all of his degrees at Florida State University. The doctorate was awarded in 1983. He has taught at South Georgia College and Tennessee Technological University. He is working with Lynwood Montell on a manuscript concerning African Americans in the Upper Cumberland.

WILLIAM LYNWOOD MONTELL. Montell was the longtime director of the Center for Intercultural and Folk Studies at Western Kentucky University. Now retired, he has authored a number of books concerning history and folklore in Kentucky and Tennessee, including *Kentucky Folk Architecture, Upper Cumberland Country, Saga of Coe Ridge, Don't Go Up Kettle Creek,* and *Killings: Folk Justice in the Upper South*.

STUART PATTERSON. Patterson is completing his doctoral work at Emory University. He dissertation concerns the history of two New Deal subsistence homestead communities. He lives in Washington, DC.

LARRY WHITEAKER. Whiteaker earned his bachelor's degree at Tennessee Technological University and his PhD at Princeton University. He has been a member of the history department at Tennessee Tech since 1973. He is the author of a number of book reviews and essays and has also authored or coauthored a number of books.

CHARLES K. WOLFE. Well known as a dean of country music history, Wolfe has authored more than a dozen books on the subject, including *Tennessee Strings, A Good-Natured Riot*, and *The Devil's Box*. He is a professor in the Department of English at Middle Tennessee State University.

INDEX

www.ingramcontent.com/pod-product-compliance
Lightning Source LLC
Chambersburg PA
CBHW030636270326
41929CB00007B/93